POVERTY ERADICATION
WHERE STANDS AFRICA ?

Published by Economica Ltd,
9 Wimpole Street
London W1M 8LB

© Economica Ltd, 2000

First published 2000

Printed in France

UNDP

Poverty Eradication
Where Stands Africa ?

ISBN 1-902282-08-6

UNITED NATIONS DEVELOPMENT PROGRAMME

POVERTY ERADICATION
WHERE STANDS AFRICA ?

Mbaya KANKWENDA
Luc-Joël GREGOIRE
Hugues LEGROS
Harouna OUÉDRAOGO

ECONOMICA
London • Paris • Genève

The authors

Mbaya Kankwenda is the United Nations Resident Coordinator on Operational Activities for Development and UNDP Resident Representative in NIGERIA. His previous appointments were Director of UNDP's Regional Programme and Policy Analysis Division and Senior Economist at UNDP Africa. He was formerly a member of the Zairean government and professor of economics at Kinshasa University and the Institute of Information Technology (Institut des Sciences et Techniques de l'Information) in Kinshasa. He has published several studies on African development issues.

Luc-Joël Grégoire is Senior Economist at UNDP. He was previously in charge of the Africa region at the Country Risk Division of the Bank Société Générale and Director of the French Association for International Trade Promotion (Association française de Promotion des Echanges internationaux). He has also worked as a Senior lecturer at the Center for Banking Studies (Centre d'Etudes Supérieures de la Banque) and the High Institute of Insurance (Institut Supérieur des Assurances de Paris) in France. He has written several books and articles on the world economy and international finance.

Hugues Legros is a program officer and economist at the UNDP country office in Burkina Faso and associate researcher at the Center for Social and Cultural Anthropology at Brussels Free University. He has previously worked as a researcher at the Belgian National Scientific Research Foundation (Fonds National Belge de la Recherche Scientifique) and a senior lecturer at Brussels University. He has written several books and articles on contemporary history and social change in Africa.

Harouna Ouédraogo is Assistant Resident Representative/Economist at the UNDP country office in Burkina Faso. He has many years' experience as a consultant to the public sector in Burkina Faso. He has also worked as a lecturer at the Faculty of Economic Science and Management at Ouagadougou University. He is a member of the research group on competition at the Center for Social and Economic Research (Centre d'Etudes, de Documentation, de Recherche Economique Sociale/CEDRES) in Burkina Faso and has written several studies on economics and transport.

Foreword

Since the early 1990s, the focus on poverty reduction has intensified, both in terms of international awareness and national development strategies and programs. However, this renewed interest has encountered major obstacles. The information and research tools on living standards available in many countries are often obsolete or deficient, so that poverty assessment has been neither systematic nor useful for policy-making.

Moreover, cross-cutting approaches to assessing poverty and developing operational responses are often at variance with conventional adjustment plans, sectoral development policies and the conditionalities attached to external assistance.

The time has come for Africa to step up the fight against poverty with more accurate research, a balance sheet of the impact of national and international projects and strategies, and redoubled efforts to raise internal and external human and financial resources.

Alleviating poverty requires defining the concept of poverty, identifying the underling causes and designing multidimensional operational poverty reduction strategies.

World conferences and summit meetings have stressed the urgency of eradicating poverty. The World Summit for Social Development held in Copenhagen in March 1995 — and attended by representatives of 185 countries and an unprecedented 117 heads of State and government — sharpened this focus. Countries at the summit made a clear commitment to the goal of poverty eradication, as an « ethical, social, political and economic imperative of humankind », and recognized people-centered developments as the key to achieving it.

At the same time, the eradication of poverty has become an overarching goal of international action and the work of the United Nations, which declared 1997-2006 the first « Decade for the Eradication of Poverty ». The United Nations Development Programme (UNDP) has made poverty eradication its essential priority in the pursuit of « sustainable human development ». One of UNDP's main missions is to assist countries, particularly the least developed countries (LDCs), in designing and implementing focused poverty reduction strategies and programs.

In Africa, UNDP promotes operational poverty reduction strategies through policy dialogue from a sustainable human development perspective, coordination of aid and the implementation of multidimensional poverty alleviation programs and projects encompassing economic, social, environmental and institutional issues.

UNDP also works as a partner and ally with African governments and civil society in designing innovative sustainable human development strategies. In this capacity, it acts as a focal point for knowledge and experience. As an example of this, I hail the work accomplished by UNDP's country office in Burkina Faso in preparing this report. This initiative opens new horizons for our knowledge and understanding of the multidimensional phenomenon of poverty in Africa. The report analyzes poverty reduction policies and strategies and outlines an innovative methodological approach to the process of designing national poverty reduction strategies in Africa. It also endeavors to define the roles of the various national stakeholders and external partners, such as UNDP.

This report is primarily intended as a tool for development stakeholders, particularly governments, in partnership with the national civil society and the private sector. It should also foster reflection and consultation among all of Africa's external partners.

Although prepared and published under the auspices of the United Nationas Development Programme (UNDP), this report offers an independent analysis by four eminent experts from the United Nations system, to whom I express my appreciation and gratitude.

Thelma Awori
Assistant Administrator and
Director, UNDP Africa

Acknowledgements

The idea for this publication developed from a contribution from UNDP's country office in Burkina Faso to a study on progress against poverty in Africa initiated by the Policy Unit at UNDP's Regional Bureau for Africa. From the outset, we realized the potential of that exercise and decided to scale it up to a comprehensive publication on poverty reduction in Sub-Saharan Africa.

The preparation of this report would not have been possible without the support and valuable contributions of a large number of individuals and national and international organizations, particularly the United Nations system, to whom we express our deep gratitude.

Several international institutions generously shared their experience, research material and data with the authors. The report drew from the databases and material of the African Development Bank (ADB), World Bank (WB), International Labour Organization (ILO), United Nations Economic Commission for Africa (ECA), United Nations Food and Agriculture Organization (FAO), International Fund for Agricultural Development (IFAD), International Monetary Fund (IMF), Office of the United Nations High Commissioner for Refugees (UNHCR), Organisation for Economic Co-operation and Development (OECD), Joint United Nations Programme on HIV/AIDS, Population and Statistical Divisions of the United Nations Department of Economic and Social Information and Policy Analysis, Stockholm International Peace Research Institute, United Nations Centre for Social Development and Humanitarian Affairs, United Nations Children's Fund (UNICEF), United Nations Development Fund for Women (UNIFEM), United Nations Capital Development Fund (UNCDF), United Nations Educational, Scientific and Cultural Organization (UNESCO), United Nations Population Fund (UNFPA), United

Nations Research Institute for Social Development, World Health Organization (WHO), World Food Programme (WFP) and, of course, the United Nations Development Programme (UNDP).

The preparation of this report also benefited from the analysis, comments and special contributions of Rosine Coulibaly, Robert Da, Diene Keita, Henriette Keijzers, Eric Lacasse, Mette Ravn and Amidou Ouédraogo. Special thanks go to Mbolatiana Rambonilaza and François Museruka for their contributions to the public spending reviews and local development activities, particularly through the Africa 2000 Network.

Jacqueline Ditoumba, Mariam Drabo, Nur El Dine, Régina Sènou-Dandjinou and Amy Tapsoba contributed to background research and layout.

The report also benefited greatly from the advice and guidance of numerous individuals. The authors wish to thank Gilbert Aho, Christian Béré, Patrice Blaque-Bellair, Bonoudaba Dabiré, Frédéric Grahmel, Jean Le Nay, Christine Loquai, Frédéric Martin, Jaquie Nachtigal and Alioune Sall.

The authors also wish to express their sincere appreciation to Thelma M. Awori, Assistant Administrator and Director of UNDP Africa, Abdoulaye Mar Dieye, Senior Economist and Head of the Policy Unit at UNDP Africa, and Caitlin Wiesen, Policy Advisor on Poverty at UNDP Africa, who supported this project from the outset and without whose assistance it would not have been possible. [1]

---

1. The analysis, recommendations and opinions expressed in this book do not necessarily reflect the views of the United Nations Development Programme, its Executive Board or its Member States.

Introduction

The eradication of poverty is one of the central objectives of contemporary development policy. The international community's determination to overcome poverty has been highlighted by the recent declaration of the first United Nations Decade for the Eradication of Poverty (1997-2006) and by the emphasis on poverty eradication in the Programme of Action adopted at the World Summit for Social Development.

The United Nations Special Initiative for Africa (UNSIA), launched in March 1996, is another example of concerted international action to reduce poverty. The eradication of poverty is also the overriding goal of UNDP, which all its experience and efforts are geared to achieving, particularly in Sub-Saharan Africa. The magnitude and expansion of poverty in Africa and the grave threat it poses to social, political and economic stability make it one of the biggest challenges facing the region.

Africa comprises 32 of the world's 48 least developed countries (LDCs) and 34 of the 45 lowest-ranked countries for human development in UNDP's *Human Development Report 1998*.

Recent estimates put the number of poor people living in Sub-Saharan Africa at 250 million, which is around 45% of the region's population. And poverty continues to spread in Africa at an alarming rate because of virtual stagnation of per capita income growth (2.1% over 1991-95) and limited prospects for economic growth (4% on average, compared with 5.4% for developing countries for the decade 1997-2006 and 6%-7% for 2010-2020). [1] Savings and investment ratios in Africa are the lowest of all the developing regions and the foreign debt burden is on average twice as high

---

1. World Bank, *Global Economic Prospects and the Developing Countries* (Washington, 1997).

as gross national income, reaching four times export revenues in some cases. As a result, it will probably take Sub-Saharan Africa another two generations to recover its average living standard of the mid-1970s. Underscoring this trend, the *Human Development Report 1998* points out an overall decline of around 20% in the consumption of goods and services over the period 1975-1995. [1]

Despite some gains, the human development challenges facing Sub-Saharan Africa are huge. Health and education indicators show severe deficiencies. Africa has the highest morbidity and mortality rates in the world. Health and nutrition standards have deteriorated and Africa is the continent worst affected by AIDS.

Recent armed conflicts have caused terrible damage and destruction. With six million refugees, Africa accounts for over half the world total. A further 20 million people are displaced within national borders.

Some striking successes have, however, been recorded. Between 1960 and 1995, life expectancy at birth in Sub-Saharan Africa rose from 40 to 51 years. Between 1970 and 1997, the adult literacy rate more than doubled. From 1960 to 1997, net enrolment ratios increased from 25% to 50% for primary school and from 13% to 38% for secondary school. The proportion of the population with access to safe drinking water rose from 25% in 1980 to 43% in 1998. There has also been significant progress in the advancement of African women: for example, female literacy as a percentage of male literacy is over 60, a higher proportion than in the Arab States and South Asia.

Slowly but surely, political liberalization and a stronger, more dynamic civil society are helping to found accountable and transparent political systems. Since 1990, multiparty presidential elections have been organized for the first time in 21 countries. Since 1980, opposition parties have been legalized in 31 countries.

The consolidation of peace in Mozambique and South Africa holds out hope for the emergence of a dynamic center of growth in Southern Africa, with positive consequences for the continent as a whole. The buoyant West African economies also raise expectations of development advances in that part of the continent. Other African governments are endeavoring to resolve political and economic imbalances and are implementing mechanisms for conflict prevention, mediation and settlement.

Subregional cooperation is also fraught with difficulty, although major changes offer room for optimism. New information technologies, which

---

1. UNDP, *Human Development Report 1998* (New York: Oxford University Press, 1998).

are changing the nature of competition, are opening up vast new possibilities for African countries. But if Africa is to seize these opportunities, new relationships between governments, the private sector and civil society need to be forged. New alliances, institutions and ways of perceiving and managing development should also be established, particularly in the area of poverty reduction.

The challenges facing the region over the next fifteen years highlight the urgency for Africa to consolidate peace and good governance, build the capacity to manage development, recover comparative advantages and create a new international competitiveness while asserting its own program of action for development centered on poverty reduction.

Despite their complexity, the general causes of poverty are now well understood. They are closely interlinked and reinforced by their consequences, thus perpetually exacerbating the phenomenon of poverty.

While situations vary from country to country, poverty is recognized as a multidimensional phenomenon, influenced by a wide range of factors. These include poor people's lack of access to income-earning and productive activities and to essential social services (health, education, safe water). Their low level of participation in political processes and their lack of influence on the political life of their countries are major obstacles. Compounding this are the direct and indirect consequences of external economic and financial factors, over which African governments have no control.

Poverty has often been aggravated by the incapacity of governments and the market to allocate resources efficiently and equitably so that poor people benefit from them. Despite affirmations to the contrary, African governments still have not made poverty reduction a central theme of their policy, as demonstrated by the limited allocation of budget and other resources to assisting the poor. Making basic social services available and accessible has rarely, if ever, been a development priority.

Even where African governments have drawn up general policy guidelines on poverty reduction, problems and lack of progress persist. This situation stems from poorly designed policies and insufficient or unrealistic attention paid to the implementation and monitoring of the policies set out in national plans and sectoral strategies. These problems are sometimes exacerbated by excessively dispersed or inconsistent donor support.

In most Sub-Saharan African countries, poor people have little or no say in the government decisions that affect them or in the choice of services designed for them. Poverty reduction policies continue to be top-down. Resources and decision-making are strongly concentrated in central government structures to the detriment of local authorities and communities where there is a direct interface between poor people and the available services.

Against this background, the United Nations Development Programme has undertaken an extensive investigation into the issues inherent in poverty reduction, the impact of action taken to date by governments and their external partners and the strategies and programs under way in Sub-Saharan Africa.

Through this report with a regional scope, UNDP seeks to sharpen the focus of its work, to recommend improvements and innovative approaches to ensure real progress against poverty and to assist governments and development partners in the broad sense, with a view to designing and implementing operational poverty reduction strategies.

PART ONE

Analysis and assessment of poverty in sub-saharan africa

CHAPTER 1

The poverty phenomenon in Sub-Saharan Africa

1. The general problem of poverty in Sub-Saharan Africa

The magnitude and expansion of poverty and the grave threat it poses to social, political and economic stability make it one of the biggest challenges facing Africa at the end of this century and into the next.

According to the estimates in UNDP's *Human Development Report 1998*, some 250 million people in Sub-Saharan Africa survive on around $1 a day. [1] With South Asia, Africa is the poorest region in the world. Approximately 45% of Africa's population is income-poor according to the national poverty threshold. The incidence of human poverty (defined by life expectancy, educational attainment and living conditions) is estimated at 42% and income poverty (measured according to a poverty line of $1 a day) at 39%.

Both human poverty and income poverty are increasing significantly in Sub-Saharan Africa in both relative and absolute terms. Slow income growth over a long period is one of the main causes of this situation. Between 1970 and 1992, per capita GDP grew by only $73 (PPP$) in the Sub-Saharan African countries, compared with $420 in South Asia and $900 in East Asia.

Over the same period, Sub-Saharan Africa's real growth in GDP at market prices changed direction: a 1.7% rise in over 1970-1982 was virtually canceled out by a 1.7% fall over 1982-1992. Between 1981 and 1989, the region recorded a cumulative decline of 21% in per capita GDP. This decline affected countries that had undertaken structural adjustments and

---

1. UNDP, *Human Development Report 1998* (New York: Oxford University Press, 1998).

Table 1.1. – Trends in Income Poverty in Developing Countries

Region or Country Group	Percentage of population living below the income poverty thresold [a]		Share of poor people in developing countries		Number of poor people (millions)
	1987	1993	1987	1993	1993
Arab States	5	4	1	1	11
East Asia, South-East Asia and Pacific	30	26	38	34	446
East Asia, South-East Asia and Pacific (excluding China)	23	14	10	7	94
Latin America and the Caribbean	22	24	7	9	110
South Asia	45	43	39	39	515
Sub-Saharan Africa	38	39	15	17	219
Developing countries	34	32	100	100	1 301

a. With poverty threshold of 1 dollar/day.

Source: Human Development Report Office, 1998.

those that had not, worsening the living conditions of the poorest people everywhere. According to a World Bank study published in 1996 on trends in developing countries, per capita GNP fell in 27 of the 35 countries for which statistics were available. The most severe drop was recorded in the intermediate and least developed countries (per capita income fell by 58% in Gabon, 50% in Nigeria, 42% in Côte d'Ivoire and 31% in Mozambique and Niger).

Between 1991 and 1995, real GDP at market prices in the region rose by 2.1%, which represented a negative annual growth of per capita income of around 0.7%, given Africa's rate of population growth (2.8%). However, these averages mask wide variation. Of the 43 countries examined in the World Bank's *World Development Report 1997*, only twelve posted positive per capita growth rates in 1995, with only six of these showing rates above 3.8%.

The only universal characteristics of poverty are low income and low consumption or, in other words, the only common feature of the poor as a category is a lack of resources for consumption.

Table 1.2. – Human Poverty in Developing Countries
(in millions of inhabitants)

Regions or groups of countries	Adult illiteracy, 1998	Population without access to health services, 1990–1997	Population without access to safe drinking water, 1990–1997	Mal-nourished children below the age of 5, 1990–1998	Maternal mortality rate per 100,000 live births, 1995	People not expected to survive to age of 40, 1995 [a]
All developing countries of which	844	766 [b]	1 213	159	473	507
Least developed countries	147	241	218	34	1 030	123
Arab States	59	29	54	5	380	26
East Asia	167	154	398	19	96	81
Latin America and the Caribbean	43	55	109	6	190	36
South Asia	407	264	230	89	554	184
South East Asia and the Pacific	38	69	162	20	447	58
Sub-Saharan Africa	135	206	249	28	971	125

a. Population age 0 to 39 years.
b. Not including Turkey and Cyprus.
Source: Human Development Report Office, 1997 and 1999.

Viewed from the angle of production, i.e. the conditions under which poor people have to work to earn their living, situations of poverty are extremely diverse. A clear understanding of this diversity is the first step towards designing appropriate instruments to tackle the problems faced by poor people and to enable them to take advantage of the opportunities available to them.

Conventional instruments for measuring economic growth, such as per capita GDP, contribute little to our understanding of the true nature of pov-

Table 1.3. – Classification of the Developing Countries of the African Continent South of the Sahara

Country	Human Poverty Index (HPI) (%)	Rank by HPI	Rank Gap between HPI and HDI	Rank Gap between HPI and Poverty Threshold at 1$/day
Zimbabwe	17.3	17	– 24	– 18
Botswana	22.9	29	4	– 8
Kenya	26.1	32	– 14	– 13
Lesotho	27.5	35	– 13	– 12
Congo	29.1	38	– 4	–
Cameroon	31.4	41	– 4	–
Ghana	32.6	43	– 1	–
Zambia	35.1	45	– 8	– 14
Rwanda	37.9	48	– 29	– 2
Togo	39.3	49	– 7	–
Tanzania	39.7	50	– 8	14
Zaire	41.2	52	0	–
Uganda	41.3	53	– 13	– 3
Nigeria	41.6	54	3	9
Central African Repub.	41.7	56	– 4	–
Guinea-Bissau	43.6	58	– 11	– 8
Namibia	45.1	59	24	–
Côte d'Ivoire	46.3	63	8	18
Mauritania	47.1	65	6	11
Senegal	48.7	68	1	0
Madagascar	49.5	70	9	– 1
Guinea	50.0	71	0	19
Mozambique	50.1	72	2	–
Ethiopia	56.2	75	2	14
Burkina Faso	58.3	76	1	–
Niger	66.0	78	2	3

Note: Ranks according to HDI and poverty threshold at 1 dollar/day have been recalculated to reflect the inclusion of 78 countries in the HPI ranking. The negative results in the classification gaps columns mean that the country concerned gets better results in terms of HPI than in terms of other measurement criteria; positive results mean the contrary.

Sources: PNUD, Human Development Report Office and World Bank, 1997.

erty. In recent years, these instruments have been enhanced with references to food security, income distribution and social development (encompassing health and education). While these composite indices allow for more comprehensive assessments and comparisons of poverty at the international and national level, they highlight the components rather than the causes of poverty. [1] Poverty is not a state, it is the result of a process. While it is important to locate the areas where poverty rates are highest, it is essential to determine the factors that cause poverty. Analyzing the general characteristics of poverty and poverty reduction in Sub-Saharan Africa is fundamental to a comprehensive understanding of the phenomenon of poverty.

Poverty in Africa is more than low income; it is the much broader problem of chronic human deprivation, both economic and social, that affects a majority of African people.

2. General characteristics of poverty and poverty reduction in Sub-Saharan Africa

2.1. Economic policies and poverty reduction

2.1.1. Economic performance and growth profiles

Sub-Saharan Africa's recent development performance has been examined at length by the World Bank in its annual reports and in a publication on adjustment in Africa. [2] The main conclusion of the Bank and subsequent work by the African Development Bank and the United Nations Economic Commission for Africa is that better macroeconomic policies lead to better economic performance. [3] However, over the period 1987-91, macroeconomic policies in most African countries were inappropriate. Average per capita income in the countries where reforms have been most successful — particularly Burkina Faso, Gambia, Ghana, Nigeria, Tanzania and Zimbabwe — grew by a mere 1.1% over 1987-91; agricultural output increased by only 2.0%, representing a continuous decline in per capita agricultural production. Countries that made only minor improvements in their policy recorded negative income growth of 0.1%, per capita and countries where economic policy worsened posted a much larger decline (– 2.6%). [4]

---

1. UNDP, *Human Development Report 1990-1997* (New York: Oxford University Press, 1990-1997).

2. World Bank, *Adjustment in Africa: Reforms, Results, and the Road Ahead* (Washington: Oxford University Press, 1994).

3. Frances Stewart, *Adjustment and Poverty: Options and Choices* (London: Routledge, 1995); K. Y. Amoako, "Les défis du développement en Afrique au vingt et unième siècle", Commission Economique pour l'Afrique, Conférences des Ministres chargés de la Planification, Ouagadougou, 30-31 janvier 1996.

4. World Bank, *A Continent in Transition: Sub-Saharan Africa in the Mid-1990s* (Washington, 1995).

The rate of increase in poverty has outstripped the pace of economic growth in African countries. At Africa's current rates of population growth, economic growth rates would need to double over a long period, to at least 6%-8% per year between 1999 and 2010, if they are to have a hope of alleviating poverty.

Box 1.1.
Growth and poverty: where to start?

Increases in GDP seem to be connected to reductions in poverty. Growth in real consumption, or GDP per person, is statistically associated with about 33-50% of the variance in the incidence and intensity of poverty. And in more than 85% of cases where there are data for changes in both growth and poverty over a period, one goes up while the other goes down.

This is usually taken to mean that growth is good for poverty reduction, but it explains only about half of it. Correlation is not causation, however, and there is no indication about which way the causation might work.

Might it be that poverty reduction causes growth? There are certainly reasons for it to do so:

• Poverty makes people risk-averse. Poverty reduction makes them more prepared to take the entrepreneurial risks necessary for growth.

• Poverty makes people immobile. Poverty reduction gives them more resources to move, look for jobs or wait for more appropriate jobs.

• Poverty is an obstacle to improving the health and education of children. Poverty reduction improves human productivity overall, but it also means that future investments in health and education are more evenly spread among those who can make best use of them — rather than being concentrated in a small group that can afford to pay for them.

Any evidence? Recent work certainly suggests the value of greater equality for growth. A number of studies show that the equality-growth pathway works partly through better schooling and more equal distribution of assets, particularly land. Equality is not the same as low poverty, but the evidence is highly suggestive.

Source: UNDP, Human Development Report, 1997.

The effect of different growth profiles on poverty reduction actions also needs to be assessed. Some processes of economic growth are more effective in alleviating poverty than others. Data available for Sub-Saharan Africa indicate extreme inequality both within countries and in relation to other regions in the world. Measures of inequality in studies on income distribution confirm considerable variation within countries, within large subregional blocs and between continents. The table below highlights the wide variation in the Gini coefficient[1] for per capita spending between Africa and some Asian countries and between West Africa and Southern Africa, all other things being equal.

The causes of these high levels of inequality in Sub-Saharan Africa are not clear for the region as a whole, although certain historical factors, such as apartheid in East and Southern Africa, can be considered to have played a key role. The persistence of these inequalities leads to systematic high demand for transfers, which in turn tend to reduce rates of capital accumulation, economic growth and the capacity to alleviate poverty.[2]

Table 1.4. – Compared Indices of expenditure inequality per inhabitant

Sub-Saharan Africa (%) 1988-1992		Asia (%) 1988-1991	
West Africa		**South Asia**	
Côte d'Ivoire	35	India	28
Ghana	41	Pakistan	31
Nigeria	44	Sri-lanka	30
Southern Africa		**East Asia**	
Botswana	55	Indonesia	45
Lesotho	56	Malaysia	49
Malawi	65	Philippines	41
Tanzania	54	Thailand	47
Zimbabwe	57		

Source: World Bank, The Social impact of Adjustment Operations: an Overview, 1995.

Adopting a specific growth model or strategy implies making choices in terms of policy and allocation of public resources. Recent experience shows that for adjustment programs to boost supply, macroeconomic policies need to incorporate pro-poor public spending and substantial investment in favor of producers, a majority of whom are poor women. In this regard, projects for the construction of roads and other economic and social infrastructure should favor rural rather than urban areas; universal schooling and adult literacy should take precedence over substantial investment in universities.

---

1. The Gini coefficient is a common measure of inequality. A coefficient of 0 represents perfect equality and a coefficient of 1 represents perfect inequality. The poverty line is based on purchasing power parity below or equal to $1 per person per day.

2. World Bank, *The Social Impact of Adjustment Operations: An Overview* (Washington, 1995).

One of the biggest challenges is to achieve and maintain high pro-poor growth rates over a long period. High overall growth does not suffice to reduce poverty. There is a need to design growth profiles that benefit poor people directly. The distribution of growth between sectors and regions highlights the population groups that should be targeted to benefit from employment and income distribution opportunities. The structure of poverty profiles in Africa suggests that growth needs to be targeted towards the development of rural areas, particularly poor rural areas. Pro-poor growth processes are not an act of charity — they are the pre-condition for lasting growth and the ultimate objective of sustainable human development.

Box 1.2.

Analysis of income distribution in Uganda

Income distribution in Uganda appears to be more equitable than in the other East African countries. For instance, the Gini coefficient for the rural areas in Uganda in 1992 was 0.35 against 0.49 in Kenya and that of the urban areas was 0.44 against 0.45 in Kenya. Nevertheless inequalities in income distribution seem to have increased slightly between 1989 and 1992. The analysis of the Gini coefficient shows a significant difference between rural and urban areas, i.e., inequalities increase in the urban areas and decrease in the different rural areas. It is important to emphasize that the Poverty Eradication Action Plan in Uganda takes these analyses and the increase in inequalities into account.

	1989	1992
National expenditure		
National	0.367	0.409
Urban	0.373	0.439
Rural	0.364	0.352
Expenditure related to poverty line		
National	0.368	0.383
Urban	0.371	0.439
Rural	0.364	0.353

Source: UNDP, National Report on SHD in Uganda, 1996

2.1.2. Savings and investment

Savings and investment are a key issue in Sub-Saharan Africa, because they are essential for growth. Domestic saving in Africa is extremely low because of the incidence and severity of poverty. After two decades of virtual economic stagnation, a combination of falling household income, capital flight, disinvestment and the outbreak of devastating conflicts has diminished overall saving. The gross domestic savings ratio for the continent as a whole is one of the lowest in the world at 12.3% on average over the period 1980-1995 in the intermediate countries and in some high-growth least developed countries and at less than 10% in the low-income countries. In many cases, particularly in countries in crisis, saving was negative. Yet, without a rise in the savings ratio, countries cannot increase productive investment to stimulate economic growth and employment.

Table 1.5. – Economic and Financial Indices of Sub-Saharan Africa
   ·   (1965-1995)

	1965-1973	1973-1980	1980-1989	1990-1995
GDP Growth Rate (as %)				
Low income countries	2.9	3.1	1.9	1.1
Intermediate countries	3.5	3.9	2.8	3.7
Sectoral development (annual average)				
Agriculture	2.6	1.9	2.5	2.6
Industry	10.0	8.1	0.7	1.3
Exports	8.2	1.8	2.2	2.8
Imports	6.5	7.3	5.8	5.9
Gross domestic savings (as % of GDP)				
Low income countries	12.5	14.3	10.1	9.9
Intermediate countries	15.3	17.9	12.2	12.5
Gross domestic investment (as % of GDP)				
Low income countries	14.0	15.0	12.5	11.3
Intermediate countries	16.5	20.5	15.0	17.5

Source: International Monetary Fund, "International Financial Statistics", Washington, IMF, 1989-1996, United Nations, Department of Economic and Social Affairs, "Statistical Yearbooks 1980-1995", New York, 1980-1996.

Average gross domestic investment has also remained comparatively low in Africa. The ratio of investment to GDP in Sub-Saharan Africa was around 15% on average over the decade 1985-1995. Some intermediate countries recorded average rates of around 18%-19%, but many LDCs showed rates below 10%-12%, which do not even make it possible to recover the cost of the infrastructure and the productive capital initially invested.

Over the past fifteen years, Sub-Saharan Africa has failed to attract foreign savings from non-public sources. In 1990-98, foreign direct investment and portfolio investment represented only 6.5% of total net resource flows to Africa.

Despite the continent's considerable potential, a lack of macroeconomic policies favorable to private enterprise has not helped to increase the rate of return and attract investors. The semi-public enterprises in which govern-ments have invested substantial fiscal resources and foreign loans have proved unproductive because of defective macroeconomic frameworks and policies. The poor quality of social and economic infrastructure on the whole is a hindrance to development. Compounding this, extremely high debt-service absorbs a large share of the resources needed for physical and social investment and jeopardize opportunities for growth and external development financing. Macroeconomic and sectoral adjustment responses to these problems must be found.

2.1.3. Access to markets and agricultural development

An analysis of the constraints on poverty reduction point at poor peo-ple's lack of control over income-generating assets and limited access to the market. The poor tend to have less land and less capital, to be less educated and in less good health and to have acquired fewer rights than people in higher income groups. In most Sub-Saharan African countries, 70% of the population work in rural areas and depend on agriculture for their liveli-hood. The types and quantities of goods produced by the vast majority (85%-90%) of farmers, 60%-70% of whose output is intended for self-consumption, relegate them to the margins of the market economy. The major macroeconomic development choices and measures only affect the rural poor to the extent to which they produce tradable goods and buy consumer products.

The location and accessibility of produce markets and employment opportunities have an influence on how much the poor benefit from growth. Studies on average consumer spending in a large number of Sub-Saharan African countries highlight unequal growth, underpinned by dis-parities between communities in (among others) access to markets and nat-ural resources.

Connection to the market is a decisive factor for agricultural develop-ment. This has been especially visible in the production of export crops. There was a genuine convergence of interests in societies towards taking advantage of the opportunities offered by these crops for wealth creation. Export crop cultivation often led to the development of well-organized industries, with direct intervention from governments, for whom these exports represented a significant source of revenue. It also resulted in the active participation of people, who in some cases derived appreciable income from these crops. In some cases, the expansion of cash crop cultiva-tion led to the distribution of equipment, production inputs and technical innovations in the rural areas concerned.

Connection with the market has also appeared, although more subtly, with the expansion of traded in food. For a long time, the food market was residual in relation to self-consumption. In the Sahelian region for example, where only 20% of people live in urban areas, there is still only one potential customer for every four producers. Moreover, not all producers have access to the food market: those who were well connected to towns seized the first market opportunities, widening the gap between different rural areas; others remained on the margins of the process. Government food policies, which gave priority to supplying towns at low prices, did little to encourage dynamic domestic markets.

Opportunities for potential producers have remained marginal on the whole, because the rapid modernization of agriculture in Sub-Saharan African has affected only a small proportion of farmers, while some farms in West and Southern Africa, for example, are now well integrated into the market and solely market-driven, for a large number of households, agriculture remains primarily a way of life or a means of survival. Even if markets develop rapidly, this duality in agriculture is likely to characterize the region and some of its sub-regions for a long time to come.

According to recent research, the Sub-Saharan African countries that had made real improvements in their policies showed weighted average growth in agriculture of 3.5% per year over the period 1986-93. The countries that had made only minor improvements in their rural development policies recorded growth of 2.5% per year, and the countries whose economic policy deteriorated showed growth of only 0.3% per year. [1]

Since most poor people live in rural areas, poverty reduction clearly depends on strong rural growth. Therefore, reestablishing growth in agriculture must be the absolute priority of any poverty reduction strategy in Africa.

One of the challenges in rural development is to ensure greater participation of rural people, particularly the poorest among them, in market opportunities. However, the influence of these people resides mainly in urban demand for their produce and labor. Access to infrastructure is therefore a priority in a situation where nontraded food accounts for 60%-70% of the poorest people's output. Access — to roads, to periurban and urban centers, to inputs and modern techniques, to subsidies for basic inputs such as fertilizers and to the labor market and/or to opportunities for expanding basic capabilities — is a key to poverty reduction in Sub-Saharan Africa.

---

1. IFAD, *The State of World Rural Poverty* (Rome, 1993); Graeme Donovan, *Agriculture and Economic Reform in Sub-Saharan Africa*, Working Paper No.18 (Washington: World Bank, 1996).

Box 1.3.

Socio-economic characteristics of poor households in Mali

Household poverty increases proportionally to household size

The results of the Malian survey on the Social and Economic Situation show that the percentage of poor households increases with the number of household members. For instance, 40% of the people in the category of households with 3-5 persons are poor whereas this percentages reaches 60% in the category of households with 5-9 and, reaches 70% in the category of households with more than 10 persons. The poor tend to have more children or more dependents.

The household is exposed to poverty as fast as the head of household grows old

A large number of poor people are found in households with elderly head of household (aged 40 and above). Poverty index is 40% in the 15-39 age group; it reaches 60% in the age group of 60 and above. Indeed, the older one grows, the less one is able to provide for the needs of ones dependents.

Educated head of household are generally less poor than uneducated head of household.

At national level, 83% of the uneducated heads of household are poor, while this percentage is about 60% of the headsof with household who have received Level 1 or 2 Basic Education and, 15% of the heads of household who have received secondary education.

Households with farm-employed heads are generally poorer than those with non-farm-employed heads.

The non farm occupations encompass wage-earners of the public or private sector, self-employed workers, traders, etc.

The annual expenditure of the poor is three times less than that of the non-poor

The average annual expenditure per capita was CFA F 79 011 at national level in 1994. This expenditure varies: it was CFA F 162 993 for the non-poor and CFA F 26 897 for the very poor, i.e., an expenditure of one sixth. The average expenditure per capita is higher in the urban areas (CFA F 164 037 in Bamako and CFA F 117 040 in smaller cities) than in the rural areas (less high in the South where is reaches CFA F 51 767 and higher in the North where it reaches CFA F 81 026).

Source: National Poverty Eradication Strategy, Government of Mali and UNDP, vol.1, 1998.

2.1.4. Participation of women in development processes

Around half of Sub-Saharan Africa's human capital is under-utilized, because poor people do not have the resources (land and credit) that would enable them to contribute to production and economic development. Efforts to reduce poverty must tackle inequalities, which vary between countries, cultures and ethnic groups. Special attention needs to be paid to the situation of women, who often do not enjoy the same access to resources as men, despite their considerable productive potential.

The contribution of women to the rural economy remains underestimated. Official statistics rarely measure this contribution, although it is clear that not only the unpaid household responsibilities, but also the farming and marketing activities of women represent a significant, even dominant, contribution to the well-being of low-income rural households. All the data indicate that the more disadvantaged a household, the more hours women spend working and the greater their involvement in economic production and family well-being.

The gender imbalance in the division of labor and in access to and control over productive resources originates in the inequality of rights and responsibilities between the sexes. The crucial role played by women in economic production in Sub-Saharan Africa contrasts with the systematic discrimination to which they are subjected in terms of access to education, to finance, to basic resources and to yield-enhancing techniques.

In Africa, as in West and South Asia, over 70% of women over 25 are illiterate. Even in the six-to-eleven-year age group, the proportion of girls not enrolled in school is over 25%, not counting those who drop out later. [1] The lack of childcare services puts an all-too-often ignored pressure on girls from poor families. If their mothers work outside the home, girls have to miss school to take care of their brothers and sisters, which perpetuates the cycle of low educational attainment and low income from one generation of women to the next. The legal and cultural barriers to women's entry to the labor market are often considerable.

Women produce between 70% and 75% of Sub-Saharan Africa's food crops but their productivity is significantly lower (by around 10%-15% on average) than men's, according to several surveys. [2] Yet their potential is considerable if these figures are considered in the light of the current gender imbalance in terms of access to and control over economically productive resources.

Taking advantage of this potential productivity gain by improving the situation of women and particularly women farmers, would lead to a considerable increase in Sub-Saharan Africa's food production and thus substantially reduce one of the causes of food insecurity in the region.

The current status of women in Sub-Saharan Africa is generally unenviable and the poverty profiles established in various countries show that predominantly rural poverty is also predominantly female.

---

1. UNDP, *Human Development Report 1997* (New York: Oxford University Press, 1997).

2. IFAD, *The State of World Rural Poverty* (Rome, 1993).

Table 1.6. – Profile of Women in African Countries

	% of women having an economic activity 1995	Men's share of Adult labour force (Age 15 and Above)	Women's share of Adult labour force (Age 15 and Above)	Women's share of labour force by sector 1995 — Agriculture	Industry	Services	% of female-headed households 1986-1995	Fertility rate 1995	% use of contraceptives 1986-1995	Maternal mortality rate (for 100,000 live births) 1990	School enrolment as % of age group 1993 — Primary Girls	Primary Boys	Secondary Girls	Secondary Boys	Adult literacy 1997 Females	Men	Women Administrators and managers 1985-1995	% of Seats in parliament held by women 1996	% of Women in governments 1996 **
South Africa	46	79	37	13	17	70	n.a.	3.9	50	230	110	111	84	71	82	82	19	25.0	7.0
Angola	73	90	46	87	2	11	n.a.	6.9	n.a.	1,500	87 a	95 a	n.a.	n.a.	29 c	56 c	n.a.	9.5	4.9
Benin	75	83	49	64	4	31	21	6.0	16	990	44	88	7	17	26	49	7	7.2	14.9
Botswana	65	83	46	78	3	19	47	4.4	33	250	120	113	55	49	60	80	26	8.5	13.5
Burkina Faso	77	90	47	85	4	11	7	6.7	8	930	30	47	6	11	9	29	14	3.7	11.5
Burundi	83	93	49	98	1	1	25	6.5	7	1,300	63	76	5	9	22	49	13	n.a.	5.4
Cameroon	48	86	37	64	4	32	19	5.7	13	550	84 a	93 a	22 a	32 a	52	75	10	12.2	4.5
Cap-Verde	44	88	39	14	31	54	38	3.6 b	n.a.	n.a.	130 a	132 a	26 a	28 a	64 c	81 c	23	11.1	11.1
Comoros	63	87	42	84	3	13	32	6.0	21	950	69 a	81 a	17 a	21 a	50 c	64 c	0	0	2.7
Congo Rep.	58	83	43	83	2	15	21	6.0	n.a.	890	n.d.	n.a.	n.a.	n.a.	67	83	6	1.6	6.5
Congo Dem. Rep.	62	85	43	92	2	6	16	6.7 b	8	870	58 a	78 a	15 a	33 a	33 c	60 c	9	5.3	3.4
Côte d'Ivoire	44	88	32	62	8	30	16	5.3	11	810	58	80	17	33	30	50	n.a.	8.3	7.1
Djibouti	n.a.	n.a.	n.a.	80	8	12	18	5.8 b	n.a.	570	33 a	43 a	10 a	15 a	68 c	87 c	2	0	0.9
Equatorial Guinea	45	88	35	82	3	15	n.a.	5.9 b	n.a.	820	n.a.	n.a.	n.a.	n.a.	68 c	90 c	2	8.8	4.9

Table 1.6. – Profile of Women in African Countries (suite)

| | % of women having an economic activity 1995 | Men's share of Adult labour force (Age 15 and Above) | Women's share of Adult labour force (Age 15 and Above) | Women's share of labour force by sector 1995 | | | % of female-headed households 1986-1995 | Fertility rate 1995 | % use of contraceptives 1986-1995 | Maternal mortality rate (for 100,000 live births) 1990 | School enrolment as % of age group 1993 | | | | Adult literacy 1997 | | Women Administrators and managers 1985-1995 | % of Seats in parliament held by women 1996 | % of Women in governments 1996 ** |
				Agriculture	Industry	Services					Primary Girls	Primary Boys	Secondary Girls	Secondary Boys	Females	Men			
Eritrea	75	87	47	80	8	12	n.a.	5.8 [b]	5	n.a.	43 [a]	54 [a]	13 [a]	19 [a]	n.a.	n.a.	n.a.	21.0	7.8
Ethiopia	58	86	40	80	8	12	16	7.0	4	1,400	19	27	11	12	25	45	11	2.0	8.9
Gabon	63	84	44	84	3	13	n.a.	5.2	n.a.	500	136	132	n.a.	n.a.	53	74	n.a.	n.a.	7.7
Gambia	69	90	44	91	3	6	n.a.	5.3	12	1,100	61	84	13	25	25	53	15	n.a.	18.9
Ghana	81	82	50	50	17	33	37	5.1	20	740	70	83	28	44	53	76	9	n.a.	9.6
Guinea	78	87	47	84	6	9	13	6.5	2	1,600	30	61	6	17	22	50	n.a.	7.0	13.0
Guinea-Bissau	57	91	40	91	2	7	n.a.	6.0	n.a.	910	42 [a]	77 [a]	2	10	42	68	8	10.0	11.9
Kenya	74	89	46	82	4	14	33	4.7	33	650	91	92	23	28	70	86	n.a.	3.0	5.8
Lesotho	47	85	37	86	3	11	n.a.	4.6	23	610	105	90	31	21	62	81	33	4.6	14.6
Liberia	54	84	39	82	2	16	19	n.a.	6	560	n.a.	n.a.	n.a.	n.a.	22 [c]	54 [c]	11	5.7	7.0
Madagascar	69	89	44	92	2	6	22	5.8	17	490	72	75	14	14	32 [c]	60 [c]	n.a.	3.7	1.8
Malawi	79	87	49	92	3	5	26	6.6	22	560	77	84	3	6	42	72	8	5.6	4.3
Mali	72	90	46	75	4	21	13	6.8	7	1,200	24	38	6	12	23	39	20	2.3	6.2
Mauritius	36	80	31	24	16	60	18	2.2	75	120	106	107	60	58	79 [c]	87 [c]	17	7.6	9.8

Table 1.6. – Profile of Women in African Countries (suite)

	% of women having an economic activity 1995	Men's share of Adult labour force (Age 15 and Above)	Women's share of Adult labour force (Age 15 and Above)	Women's share of labour force by sector 1995			% of female-headed households 1986-1995	Fertility rate 1995	% use of contraceptives 1986-1995	Maternal mortality rate (for 100,000 live births) 1990	School enrolment as % of age group 1993				Adult literacy 1997		Women Administrators and managers 1985-1995	% of Seats in parliament held by women 1996	% of Women in governments ** 1996
				Agriculture	Industry	Services					Primary		Secondary		Females	Men			
											Girls	Boys	Girls	Boys					
Mauritania	64	87	44	82	4	14	n.a.	5.2	3	930	62	76	11	19	26	50	8	1.3	5.4
Mozambique	83	91	49	97	1	2	n.d.	6.2	n.a.	1,500	51	69	6	9	23	58	11	25.2	12.8
Namibia	54	81	41	47	3	50	39	5.0	29	370	138	134	61	49	91	91	21	18.1	11.4
Niger	70	93	44	92	0	8	10	7.4	4	1,200	21	35	4	9	7	21	8	n.a.	10.9
Nigeria	48	87	36	67	7	26	n.a.	5.5	6	1,000	82	105	27	32	47	67	6	n.a.	6.2
Uganda	81	91	48	85	3	12	29	6.7	15	1,200	83	99	10	17	50	74	n.a.	18.1	8.9
Central Afr. Rep.	69	87	47	63	5	31	19	5.1	15	700	n.a.	92	n.a.	n.a.	52	68	9	3.5	4.9
Rwanda	83	94	48	98	1	2	25	6.2	21	1,300	76	78	9	11	52	70	8	17.1	10.7
Sao Tomé & Princi.	37	77	34	n.a.	n.a.	n.a.	33	n.a.	n.a.	n.a.	n.a.	n.a.	n.a.	n.a.	42[c]	73[c]	9	7.3	7.7
Senegal	61	86	42	87	3	10	16	5.7	13	1,200	50	67	11	21	23	43	4	11.7	5.6
Seychelles	57	79	42	n.a.	n.a.	n.a.	n.a.	n.a.	n.a.	n.a.	n.d.	n.a.	n.a.	n.a.	86[c]	83[c]	29	27.3	20.8
Sierra Leone	44	84	35	78	4	17	11	6.5	n.a.	1,800	42[a]	60[a]	12[a]	22[a]	18	45	8	6.3	5.9
Somalia	63	87	43	87	2	11	n.a.	n.a.	n.a.	1,600	n.a.	n.a.	n.a.	n.a.	14[c]	36[c]	n.a.	n.a.	0
Sudan	33	86	28	84	5	11	13	4.9[b]	8	660	48[a]	61[a]	19[a]	24[a]	35[c]	58[c]	2	5.3	1.7

Table 1.6. – Profile of Women in African Countries *(suite)*

	% of women having an economic activity 1995	Men's share of Adult labour force (Age 15 and Above)	Women's share of Adult labour force (Age 15 and Above)	Women's share of labour force by sector 1995			% of female-headed households 1986-1995	Fertility rate 1995	% use of contraceptives 1986-1995	Maternal mortality rate (for 100.000 live births) 1990	School enrolment as % of age group 1993				Adult literacy 1997		Women Administrators and managers 1985-1995	% of Seats in parliament held by women 1996	% of Women in governments ** 1996
				Agriculture	Industry	Services					Primary Girls	Primary Boys	Secondary Girls	Secondary Boys	Females	Men			
Swaziland	41	80	37	78	4	18	40	4.8 [b]	20	560	119 [a]	125 [a]	51 [a]	53 [a]	76 [c]	78 [c]	14	3.1	7.5
Tanzania	83	89	49	89	2	9	22	5.8	18	770	69	71	5	6	57	79	n.a.	17.5	9.6
Chad	67	88	44	80	2	19	n.a.	5.9	n.a.	1,500	30	62	n.a.	n.a.	35	62	n.a.	17.3	4.3
Togo	53	87	39	64	8	28	26	6.4	12	640	81	122	12	34	37	67	8	1.2	3.0
Zambia	66	86	45	82	3	15	17	5.7	26	940	99	109	19 [a]	31 [a]	71	86	6	9.7	8.4
Zimbabwe	67	86	45	80	4	16	33	3.8	48	570	114	123	40	51	80	90	15	14.7	11.6

a. data of 1990-95;
b. data of 1994;
c. data of 1995.

* Married women old enough to procreate
** Positions of Ministers and Deputy Ministers
n.d. : données non disponibles ou non applicables .

Sources: UN Africa Recovery from information provided by the UN Statistics Division. *Notes:* World Bank, World Development Report, 1997; UNDP, Human Development Report, 1997; n.a: data not available or not applicable. UNICEF, The State of the World's Children, 1998.

Women are less educated than men, have less access to health care, employment opportunities and credit, and participate less in national and local political life and decision-making. However, significant improvements are occurring in many countries, which suggests profound and irreversible qualitative changes in the short or long term.

While still noticeably underrepresented in the highest spheres, African women are gradually conquering an increasingly important place in national political and administrative systems in generalized democratization processes; more women are gaining access to posts of authority and power, taking on prominent political and executive office both nationally and locally.

However, this positive trend should not obscure the fact that in most African societies women remain a dominated social category, victims of prejudice and reactionary practices, often deprived of the right to speak out and a passive object of rather than an active player in national political life.

Several factors contribute to the problematic situation of African women:
   – status within the family as wife, mother and laborer; the value placed on having many children; ancestral practices such as excision, levirate marriages, polygamy, forced marriages and repudiation;
   – under-enrolment of girls and low literacy rates of women (8% in 1990);
   – precarious reproductive health, aggravated by exhaustion, malnutrition, close pregnancies, pregnancies too early or too late in life;
   – mass emigration of young productive men, increasing women's workload in and outside the home;
   – insufficient inclusion of the female dimension in the design of development projects and programs;
   – limited access to economic resources, i.e. land, credit and other factors of production.

To ensure the advancement of women, in the follow-up to the Fourth World Conference on Women held in Beijing in September 1995, many governments have endeavored to design and implement national strategies and plans of action based on access to essential social services and productive resources (land, credit, inputs, equipment, technology, etc.).

2.1.5. Globalization, regionalization and poverty reduction

The relationship between globalisation and the process of regional integration are essential for an understanding of the phenomenon of poverty.

• *Integration into the world economy*

In the current context of globalization, a number of developing countries have made substantial progress on economic development in the past three decades. Progress has been most remarkable in East Asia, but is not confined to this region since some intermediate countries in Africa, notably South Africa, are also pursuing a process of sustained growth.

But globalization, which is also a process of polarization and marginalization, does not yet appear to be benefiting Africa as a whole. A majority of countries, particularly the least developed African countries, have been relegated to the margins of the globalization process as shown by indicators of Africa's participation in world trade (1.8% of world exports), contribution to manufactured value added (0.3%) and attraction of foreign direct investment (0.02%) over 1990-1995. [1]

The poor economic results of Africa's least developed countries, both in absolute terms and in comparison with other developing countries, can be attributed to several factors. Approximately a third of African countries have been affected by serious civil strife and political instability, which have considerably hindered their development efforts and, in some cases, have had devastating economic and social consequences, particularly on the poorest people. In other LDCs, structural constraints, such as the nature of the economic situation and the level of technological development; damaging external shocks, such as low commodity prices and the debt crisis; and policy failure have arrested development efforts. In the past few years, most of these countries have applied reform programs designed to liberalize their economies and strengthen their integration into the world economy. The reforms have had some success in terms of economic stabilization, but have usually failed to stimulate the higher growth rates needed to breathe new life into countries' economies.

The requirements of global integration have favored the conclusion of the Uruguay Round of reforms to the multilateral trade system. This is likely to give an appreciable stimulus to world trade and can therefore increase African countries' trading opportunities. While it is too early to ascertain exactly the costs and benefits of the Uruguay Round agreements for particular countries, most of the gains will probably bypass the poorest countries, going instead to both old and newly industrialized countries and, to a lesser extent, to the intermediate countries in Africa that have already established internationally competitive industries and are thus equipped to compete in liberalized markets.

For the majority of African countries, the situation is particularly difficult. Following the Uruguay Round, the preferential tariffs that LDC exports enjoyed under the Generalized System of Preferences (GSP) and the Lomé Convention (for LDCs in the ACP group) will disappear.

---

1. United Nations, Economic Commission for Africa, *Critical Capacities for the Mobilization and Efficient Allocation of Domestic and External Financial Resources*, Eca Doc. 20/11 (Addis Ababa: UN, 1995).

Most Sub-Saharan African countries are still dependent on exports of primary products for their foreign exchange earnings. However, trends in world commodity markets since the 1970s have generally been unfavorable to them. The real prices of the most important products for LDCs, such as coffee, cotton, copper and tea, have been on a long downward course. The least developed African countries have also lost world market share for many of their main commodity exports because of local production problems and productivity gains in competitor countries.

Globalization and liberalization also have a major impact on economic policies in LDCs. These developments in the world economy have undeniably reduced the possibilities for countries to implement independent national economic policies. Governments can less effectively control economic activities within their own borders (e.g. general direction of economic activities and capital movements).

Meeting the challenges of globalization and liberalization will require major adjustments in economic policy, distribution of resources and productive structures in African countries, particularly the poorest among them. Most of this adjustment will have to be accomplished by the countries themselves, even if international support is essential. Domestic policies will play a crucial role in the capacity of the poorest African countries to adapt advantageously to the new requirements of the world economy.

The major challenge for African countries is to implement independent national and subregional development policies that condition integration into globalization, and not the reverse, as is the case now, where Africa's development policies are dictated by globalization.

African countries, particularly the LDCs, must maintain macroeconomic stability and adopt dynamic trade policies while protecting their markets from excessive fluctuations. Although countries do not have identical needs, some concerns will probably be important everywhere: consolidating sectors that are sources of growth for domestic and subregional needs without neglecting exports to distant markets, improving farm output and productivity and modernizing and expanding physical infrastructure. A major effort will also need to be made to enhance human resources, particularly by raising the general level of education, which is a pre-condition for higher productivity and a more competitive economy.

In this context, what Africa expects from the international community is more support for its adjustment efforts, particularly financing on sufficiently advantageous terms to fund governments' infrastructure and social development programs and balance of payments and budget support to facilitate economic reform programs. The international community should also ensure that market access for LDC exports not be hampered by protectionist measures, and that the expansion of regional trade agreements not be prejudicial to the trade interests of African countries, in particular in their relationships with the leading industrialized countries.

• *Regional development*

African countries have long recognized that stronger regional cooperation and integration is essential to their growth and individual and collective prosperity. Their determination to accelerate regional integration finds its expression in the Lagos Plan of Action and the Final Act of Lagos, which set the target of an African economic community by the year 2000.

The least developed African countries in particular are parties to several trade agreements in their own regions. ECOWAS, CEMAC and SADC [1] are some of the most important integration projects. However, these agreements have not yet succeeded in stimulating intraregional trade. There is limited complementarity between the economic structures of the member countries, intraregional transport is often poor and there are still numerous obstacles to trade between members, partly because governments lack the political will to pursue a determined policy of regional trade integration, mainly out of a fear of harming the interests of domestic producers. These regional trade agreements would, however, offer potential benefits if intraregional trade were effectively liberalized, particularly since many countries have only tiny domestic markets. Local enterprises would benefit from a larger regional market, which would enable them to enjoy economies of scale, even as increased competition would encourage greater efficiency. Regional markets can be a good springboard for enterprises that want to build up to international levels of productivity before launching into world export markets. The slowness of this process is also due to the lack or weakness of an entrepreneurial class spurring integration.

In a global economy marked by the formation of large trading blocks, regional integration would enable Africa to market itself as a major destination for trade and investment. The economies of scale and increased competition generated by a vast free-trade area would make Africa more competitive within the world economy.

Regional integration would have other effects. It would open the continent to the free movement of factors of production (skilled labor, capital and entrepreneurs), goods and services. A free-trade area on the continent would foster local specialization, taking full advantage of local comparative advantages and economies of scale. It would allow complementarities to emerge across the whole of Africa. It would create an enabling environment

---

1. ECOWAS: Economic Community of West African States; CEMAC: Communauté Economique et Monétaire de l'Afrique Centrale (Economic and Monetary Community of Central Africa); SADC: Southern African Development Community.

for the emergence of competitive transnational African companies in world markets. African countries need to find ways of creating large integrated economic areas that will benefit national and subregional entrepreneurs rather than major foreign investors.

2.1.6. Development financing and assistance for the poorest countries

The priority issues of the volume of assistance, foreign debt relief and financial sector reform are keys to achieving the external financing needed for sustainable development and poverty eradication in Sub-Saharan Africa.

* *Development assistance for the poorest countries*

Nominal flows of official development assistance (ODA) remained relatively stable in the first half of the 1990s, but fell in real terms from 1991 onwards. The share of ODA allocated to LDCs in the GNP of the member countries of the OECD's Development Assistance Committee (DAC) fell from 0.09% in 1990 to 0.07% in 1995, which is less than half the aid targets and commitments agreed at the Paris Conference in 1990.

Official development assistance is shrinking, is being concentrated on certain countries and is subject to conditionalities that are sometimes excessive for poor countries.

Relations between donors and recipients, particularly for access to World Bank structural adjustment loans and IMF structural adjustment facilities, now depend largely on LDCs meeting adjustment conditions imposed on them. Political conditions relating to "good governance", including respect for human rights, have recently taken on increasing importance.

The weak administrative and institutional capacities of many countries remain an obstacle to local appropriation and execution of reform and development programs. In most cases, this reduces countries' real absorption capacity and compromises the efficiency of assistance, particularly in terms of poverty reduction.

In addition to economic reform, since the beginning of the 1990s many governments have undertaken sweeping political reform, implemented mechanisms of democratization and increased people's participation in the development process. The simultaneous execution of economic and political reform has overstretched the weak administrative capacities of most countries and hampered progress on the economic front, slowing the pace of aid disbursement as a result. In other countries, political conflicts and civil strife have led to the suspension of development programs and projects.

Budget restrictions in donor countries should not automatically mean a fall in aid flows to the countries that need them. Rather, assistance pro-

Table 1.7. – Net Resource Flow and Transfer in Least Developed Countries 1990-1996, (in billion dollars)

	1990	1991	1992	1993	1994	1995	1996
ODA Assistance including technical assistance (A)	11.7	12.8	12.5	11.9	12.6	12.7	12.7
Net loans under ODA (B)	4.6	3.5	4.1	3.3	3.7	3.5	3.6
Net ODA (C = A + B)	**16.3**	**16.3**	**16.6**	**15.2**	**16.3**	**16.2**	**16.3**
Other net public capital flow (D) [except IMF]	0.7	– 0.1	0.0	0.3	0.2	0.3	0.3
Net private export credits [a] (E)	– 0.5	– 0.4	0.1	– 0.6	– 1.1	– 1.0	– 1.0
Other net flows of private capital [a] (F)	0.6	0.3	0.3	1.1	0.6	0.7	0.6
Total private flows (G = E + F)	**0.2**	**– 0.0**	**0.4**	**0.5**	**– 0.5**	**– 0.3**	**– 0.4**
Total net flows of resources (C + D + G)	**17.2**	**16.2**	**17.0**	**16.0**	**16.0**	**16.2**	**16.2**
Long term debt service	– 2.5	– 2.1	– 1.7	– 1.4	– 1.7	– 1.8	– 1.9
Net purchase under the mechanism of IMF loan on market conditions	– 0.5	– 0.3	– 0.2	– 0.1	0.0	– 0.1	–
Transfer of resources	14.2	13.8	15.1	14.5	14.3	14.3	14.3
For the record, accumulated arrears under debt service	4.6	5.2	4.2	4.7	5.3	5.5	5.7

a. From DAC member countries, 1995 data.
Source: UNCTAD Estimates, 1996 Report, according to OECD, IMF and World Bank data, 1997.

grams should be refocused and considered as a priority. Even a modest increase in the financing of multilateral aid programs and priority resource allocation to LDCs under bilateral aid arrangements would ensure adequate ODA funding of poverty reduction in line with the 20/20 Initiative.

At the same time, possible new sources of ODA funding should be explored: developing countries that have acquired a capacity for assistance in the past few years should be associated with the traditional donor countries in providing assistance to the least developed countries, in the form of South-South cooperation (TCDC). Contributions from non-governmental organizations and decentralized grassroots cooperation should also be encouraged.

To prevent the poorest countries being marginalized from ODA financing, donors and LDCs should focus jointly on the problems of procedure and absorption capacity. A number of difficulties stem from the complexity of aid procedures and practices, which vary between donors and institutions, from restrictions on public contracts, from regulations in recipient countries and from insufficient coordination of aid programs, particularly for poverty reduction. The other type of difficulty, related to excessively stringent aid conditionalities for many LDCs, calls for increased efforts to strengthen capacities and more realism in setting result targets: e.g. setting criteria in line with the management and execution capacities of the recipient countries and endeavoring to facilitate adjustment instead of suspending aid as soon as countries run into difficulties.

While the efficiency and targeting of aid are important issues, the volume of aid remains paramount to ensure financing for the priority actions of promoting good governance and rational resource management with a view to eradicating poverty.

• *Debt and the least developed African countries*

ODA financing must be accompanied by concerted efforts to reduce the poorest countries' foreign debt to sustainable levels. Several mechanisms have been created to ease the debt burden of low-income countries, such as relief of public debt owed to the Paris Club of creditors and repurchases of debt owed to commercial banks. The size and growing burden of debt-service make LDCs' multilateral debt a critical issue. The multilateral financial institutions' senior creditor status would, however, appear to reduce the range of options available for resolving the debt problem. Policy discussions on debt began some time ago at the IMF and World Bank, but little progress has been made, despite the heavily indebted poor countries (HIPC) debt initiative.

Many LDCs, particularly those where growth has stagnated and export earnings have fallen since the beginning of the 1990s and impoverishment is spreading, are unable to honor their debt-service obligations.

More radical measures are needed on this issue, including a substantial reduction in outstanding debt in many cases. A concerted, comprehensive approach is needed: a mechanism with sufficient resources to reduce multilateral debt, coupled with an extension of existing mechanisms, could contribute significantly to bringing overall debt to reasonable proportions, in the light of the extreme poverty of many countries.

• *Financial sector reform in poor countries*

Many African countries have implemented major economic policy reforms to adapt to the new conditions imposed by liberalization and globalization. Reform of the financial sector has been a key element of the adjustment process and is intended to reduce or eliminate interest-rate and loan controls, to base monetary control on market techniques and to relax restrictions on the entry of private capital. Liberalization has stimulated competition, at least in some segments of the financial markets, with the appearance of new banks and other financial institutions. One of the positive aspects of this reform is that banks are starting to improve and increase the services offered to the public, particularly through investment in new technology. Liberalization has also encouraged government financial institutions to take commercial principles into account in their lending decisions and business in general.

However, the Sub-Saharan African countries, with the exception of South Africa, suffer from various handicaps that are an obstacle to the development of sound financial systems: low creditworthiness, undiversified capital markets, the exclusion of key economic sectors from credit and other financial services; inefficient, oligopolistic practices in the banking markets; and the general fragility of banks and other financial institutions. These problems can be partly attributed to earlier policies in the financial sector, aimed at controlling the money and financial markets.

Financial sector reform has pursued several goals: increasing the efficiency of financial intermediation, attracting deposits, stimulating greater competition in the capital markets and overcoming financial fragility. The overall objective of the reforms in Sub-Saharan Africa is to promote the development of a competitive, efficient and well-managed financial sector, capable of providing the financial services needed for the growth of a dynamic private sector. The main components of reform are financial liberalization, restructuring ailing financial institutions and strengthening prudential regulations, which have been introduced relatively recently and are not yet complete in many countries.

Financial liberalization has had limited impact on the efficiency of resource distribution, mainly because of macroeconomic instability and financial fragility. The size of the budget deficit in many countries has driven nominal interest rates to extremely high levels, pushing the private sector out of the credit market. Some state-owned banks, which dominate the financial markets, need to undergo profound financial restructuring and reform of their management before they can operate as efficient financial intermediaries with a commercial outlook. Furthermore, some segments of the credit market in the African LDCs in particular, suffer from severe deficiencies, which prevent potentially significant borrowers, such as small farmers, from having access to the loans offered by commercial financial institutions. These deficiencies are mainly problems of information, a lack of adequate loan guarantees, legal loopholes that make it impossible to recover loans and high transaction costs. In most countries, effective institutional solutions have not yet been found for these problems, which continue to marginalize poor and disadvantaged development stakeholders.

To sum up, development assistance problems have worsened over the past ten years, particularly for the poorest countries.

2.2. Demographic and social issues: population growth, employment, education and health, particularly AIDS

2.2.1. Population growth and falling living standards

Sub-Saharan Africa has the fastest growing population of all the developing regions. The rate of population growth in Africa rose from 2.8% in the 1970s to around 3.0% in the 1980s. The most recent estimates by the United Nations Population Fund in its *1997 Annual Report* indicate a stabilization of growth rates around 2.8% for the decade 1995-2005.

Population growth forecasts for 2005-2025 range from 2.8% to 2.0% per year, which would see a return to the pace of population growth of the 1950s. These rates are still much higher than those forecast for other regions of the world. Despite the expected deceleration in growth rates, Africa's population will more than double by 2025. This is mainly due to a faster decline in mortality rates than in fertility rates and to the large proportion of young people in the age pyramid.

The growing population and social and political pressure from youth are formidable challenges for the Sub-Saharan African countries.

In the short term, the effects of population policy will remain stable, since the birth control programs implemented over 1975-1995 have already been taken into account in the projections.

In the medium to long term, substantial improvements are expected because of fast-changing lifestyles, especially urbanization. The relationship between fertility and education is also significant.

In Namibia, Niger, Tanzania and Zambia, it has been shown that fertility is affected by women's access to education: the longer women spend in education, the lower the fertility rate. In Angola and Burkina Faso, the total fertility rate (TFR) for women who have never been to school is 6.6; the TFR for women with secondary or higher education is 4.1 in Angola and 4.2 in Burkina Faso. Fertility is also sensitive to urbanization: in Tanzania, the TFR is 7.5 in rural areas but 5.9 in urban areas; a similar difference is recorded for Burkina Faso. [1]

---

1. UNDP, *Rapport sur le Développement Humain au Burkina Faso 1997* (Ouagadougou, 1997).

The fact that the population will double over a generation does not reduce the urgency of a rapid reduction in fertility. On the contrary, demographic scenarios for the very long term (50 years and more) are widely divergent. Action could mean the difference between a difficult situation (low hypothesis: fast short-term population growth, but a rapid decline in fertility) and an untenable situation (high hypothesis: only a gradual deceleration of fertility). [1]

AIDS will not stop the population from growing in the region. Hitting young, productive people hardest, the sickness will mainly affect the dependency ratio (size of the dependent population that has to be supported by the working population) increasing the difficulty for working people to meet the needs of the population as a whole. In this area too, urgent action must be taken.

It is also clear that the faster the population grows in an economy with a surplus of labor, the more difficult it is to raise living standards. One of the main indicators of poverty, besides low income, is a lack of access to social services, which is more severe in Sub-Saharan Africa than in any other region of the world, chiefly because of this demographic trend.

Population will therefore continue to be a priority in development and poverty reduction programs in Africa for at least the next two decades.

Table 1.8. –   Fertility Rate of 32 African Countries: source
               of a rapid population growth 1997-1998

Country	Fertility Rate	Country	Fertility Rate	Country	Fertility Rate	Country	Fertility Rate
South Africa	3.9	Ethiopia	7.0	Mali	6.6	Sierra Leone	6.1
Angola	6.7	Gambia	6.1	Mauritania	6.5	Somalia	7.0
Burundi	6.2	Ghana	5.3	Mozambique	6.1	Tanzania	5.6
Benin	5.9	Guinea	6.6	Namibia	4.9	Chad	5.6
Burkina Faso	6.5	Guinea Bissau	5.8	Niger	7.1	Togo	6.1
Cameroon	5.4	Liberia	6.8	Nigeria	6.0	Zaire	6.2
Central African Rep.	5.0	Madagascar	5.7	Uganda	7.1	Zambia	6.0
Côte d'Ivoire	7.4	Malawi	6.7	Senegal	5.6	Zimbabwe	5.2

Source: UNFPA, "The State of the World's Population 1998", New-York, 1998.

1. World Bank, *Confronting AIDS: Public Priorities in a Global Epidemic* (Washington: Oxford University Press, 1997).

2.2.2. Employment

The fast-growing population is exerting strong pressure on employment opportunities in Africa in both rural and urban areas.

The rapid increase in Sub-Saharan Africa's urban population in recent decades is cause for serious concern. The population of some cities, such as Kinshasa, Lusaka, Nairobi and Nouakchott increased sevenfold between 1950 and 1990, i.e. in less than two generations. On the whole, Africa's urban population is increasing by 6% per year, twice the rate of the urban population in Latin America or South-East Asia. By the year 2010, an estimated 40% to 50% of the region's population will live in urban areas. Currently, most of Africa's poor still live in rural areas, as shown by national household surveys and recent poverty assessments.

A shortage of employment in urban areas increases the number of poor people. The main income-earning activities are self-employment and small businesses, principally in the informal sector, where working conditions are unstable and employment vulnerable. The informal labor market is characterized by low pay, low productivity, temporary and sometimes illegal employment, unsafe working conditions and a lack of protection under labor laws. According to household surveys in West and Central Africa, participation in the formal sector, both public and private, is low for both sexes (less than 10% of the working population), while self-employment and small businesses are the only possibilities for regular employment. Family businesses are on the rise as men leave the formal public labor market for the informal sector and women leave exploitative informal wage employment. These changes stem from a combination of recurrent economic crises, a depressed formal labor market for men and increased pressure on women and sometimes children to contribute to household income.

In the past fifteen years, Africa's capacity to absorb labor has declined, mainly because of slack economic growth. At the same time, the labor supply has either increased or remained high, even as other specific imbalances exacerbate the shortage of modern employment.

First, in most Sub-Saharan African countries, there is a surplus of tertiary education graduates. In West Africa, for example, from 1980 to 1995, the labor market absorbed only 30%-50% of secondary and tertiary education graduates. Generalist courses and courses aimed at the service sector recorded the lowest rates of absorption, although some technical courses also suffered. The determinants of this imbalance lie on both the supply and demand sides. Fast population growth, an age structure heavily weighted towards youth, student grants and the attractiveness of stable employment in the public service have kept demand for education and supply of graduates high. These graduates are entering the market at a time

Table 1.9. – Population living below the Poverty Threshold
in some sub-Saharan African Countries

Country	Year	Rural areas	Urban areas	Total
Benin	1996	33.5	33.1	33.7
Burkina Faso	1994-95	45	8.6	44.5
Cameroon	1983-84	71	25	48
Gambia	1992	66	33	64
Guinea-Bissau	1991	58	24	49
Kenya	1992	47	30	41
Lesotho	1993	54	28	49
Mali	1994	69	49	68.8
Niger	1994	66	48	63
Nigeria	1992	39	23	33
Uganda	1989-90	57	8	55
Sierra Leone	1989-90	76	53	68
Zambia	1991	88	46	68
Zimbabwe	1990-91	31	10	25

Note: The figures in this table are numerical indices of poverty. Different poverty thresholds were used to establish these estimates, and accordingly the percentages for the different countries are not comparable.

Sources: Figures taken from the data of the national household surveys and the poverty evaluations.

when the modern sector has been cut by adjustment policies and the private sector is not yet strong enough to absorb the surplus into wage employment.

Secondly, while the education systems in African countries continue to produce graduates in relatively overfilled fields of study, there is a shortage of the technical skills needed for the productive economy. Two patterns are commonly observed in many African countries: the private sector employs a large number of untrained people in middle and senior managerial positions, while manufacturing enterprises lack technical staff with basic vocational or technical qualifications in areas such as mechanical engineering, electromechanical engineering and electrical engineering.

Thirdly, the decline of the share of agriculture in the economy is accompanied in many countries — particularly in the Sahel — by an almost excessive expansion of services. In Sub-Saharan Africa between 1965 and

1995, the proportion of the working population employed in industry stagnated on the whole (at around 6% to 9%), while the proportion employed in services increased from 10% to 18%. The share of vulnerable employment also seems to have risen. Several indicators common to most African countries indicate an increasing casualization of labor with a growing number of unemployed people, with or without work experience, taking on casual jobs and a rise in the number of second and temporary jobs.

Table 1.10. – Population and Employment Related Indicators (1960-1990)

	Labour force (as % of total population)	Women's share of about labour force (aged 15 and above)		Percentage of labour force in					
				Agriculture		Industry		Services	
	1990	1970	1990	1960	1990	1960	1990	1960	1990
South Africa	39	33	37	38	14	27	32	35	55
Angola	47	47	47	81	75	6	8	12	17
Burundi	54	50	49	95	92	2	3	3	6
Burkina Faso	54	49	47	92	92	3	2	6	6
Cameroon	40	37	37	89	70	4	9	7	21
Central African Rep.	49	49	47	93	80	2	4	5	16
Côte d'Ivoire	37	33	32	84	60	4	10	12	30
Ethiopia	44	42	41	93	86	2	2	5	12
Eritrea	50	47	47	87	80	4	5	9	15
Ghana	47	51	51	63	59	14	13	23	28
Guinea	49	48	47	94	87	1	2	5	11
Malawi	49	51	50	94	87	3	5	4	8
Mali	50	47	47	94	86	1	2	5	12
Nigeria	40	37	35	73	43	10	7	17	50
Uganda	51	48	48	93	85	2	5	5	11
Tanzania	52	–	–	–	–	–	–	–	–
Chad	49	42	44	96	83	2	4	3	13
Zaire	42	45	44	79	68	9	13	11	19
Zambia	42	45	45	85	75	6	8	10	17
Zimbabwe	46	44	44	81	68	10	8	9	24

Sources: UNDP, "World Human Development Report", 1991; ILO, "Estimates and projections of the labour force, 1950-2010", Geneva, 1996.

The urban unemployment rate has also increased considerably, more than doubling between 1975 and 1995, from 10% to around 20%-25%. Employment in the modern, mainly public, sector, has stagnated or declined. In 20 Sub-Saharan African countries, employment grew by an average 2.8% per year between 1975 and 1985, but by only 1% in the first half of the 1990s. [1]

These trends are not unrelated to the widespread persistence of poverty and growing inequality of income in Sub-Saharan Africa. Another central factor is the acceleration of internal and regional migration.

Rural exodus is often a survival strategy for the rural poor. In Mali, people leave the depressed economy of their villages in search of better prospects in towns, other villages or other countries. In Senegal, migration is usually from the center to the coast and from the north to the south of the country and towards Gambia and Europe. Movement towards the coast is posing increasingly critical economic and environmental problems. The coastal countries of West Africa have absorbed an estimated 10 million people in the past three decades, and this figure is expected to reach 20 million in 2020 according to the *West Africa Long Term Perspective Study.* [2] In Niger, rural people migrate to other rural areas with better prospects for commercial agriculture, to the oil fields of Algeria and Libya, to the coastal and gold-mining areas of Burkina Faso and to other coastal countries in West Africa.

Although the vast majority of the population, especially the poor, live in rural areas, urbanization has become one of the most visible causes of the transformation of consumption patterns and the decline of agriculture in Sub-Saharan Africa. Urbanization encourages the development of an individualist, trade-and-services-oriented culture, in which the proportion of poor people is increasing. Strategies used in the past to cope with problems are no longer valid. Traditional cultures are being abandoned and family and community networks of solidarity are disintegrating. Without an increase in the demand for labor, a large number of single women and uneducated young people, who have no way of contributing to a family business in agriculture or services, have to earn their living and provide for their children in an increasingly hostile social environment, where crime, drug use, prostitution and the risk of contracting AIDS are rife.

---

1. On Africa in general, see also D. Ghai, *Economic Growth, Structural Change and Labour Absorption in Africa* (Geneva, 1987) and J. Vandemoortele, *Labour Market Informalisation in Sub-Saharan Africa* (Geneva: ILO, 1991). On Mali, see J-P. Lachaud, *Pauvreté et Marché du travail urbain en Afrique subsaharienne* (Genève, 1994).

2. OECD, ADB, CILSS, *A Vision of West Africa in the Year 2020* (Paris: Club du Sahel/OECD, 1996).

2.2.3. Education and adult literacy

Of all the developing regions, Africa has the lowest gross primary enrolment ratio: 68% in 1995, compared with 88% in South Asia, and 107% in Latin America. Twelve African countries had succeeded in making primary education universal by 1990, but three others had enrolment ratios below 30%. The Sahelian countries lag a long way behind with average ratios of only 31% for girls and 53% for boys, compared with regional averages of 61% for girls and 73% for boys.

Primary school enrolments, which had increased during the 1960s and 1970s, stagnated and declined in the 1980s and early 1990s. The regional gross enrolment ratio for primary school, which rose from 36% of the school-age population in 1960 to 78% in 1980, fell back to 68% in 1995. The decline in household income, the deterioration of the quality of teaching and the increase in opportunity cost have reduced enrolment ratios, despite government efforts to maintain the share of education in national budgets.

While access to education has become an important measure of progress, the quality of teaching and its relevance to socioeconomic realities and employment should not be overlooked. There is a need for greater emphasis on what is done at school and on sectoral policies that give schools and communities more say in children's education and their integration into a changing economy and society.

Literacy rates in Africa are among the lowest in the world, only ahead of South Asia. On average, only 56% of adults in Sub-Saharan Africa are able to read and write, compared with 84% in Latin America. Literacy of adult women is 44% in Africa, compared with 83% in Latin America. The Sahel has the lowest average literacy rate, at barely 30% (19% for women). In Burkina Faso, only 9% of women are literate, compared with 29% of men.

The gender gap in education is central. Poverty is the reason most commonly given by parents for not sending their children, particularly their daughters, to school or for taking them out of school, as consistently confirmed by participatory surveys on the accessibility of education in Sub-Saharan Africa. Enrolment ratios rise as household disposable income increases. However, in many countries, the gap between enrolment ratios for boys and girls is relatively unaffected by the increase in household spending. This implies that raising household income alone is not enough to improve enrolment ratios for girls.

The vast benefits of educating girls — including a probable reduction in fertility rates — underscore the need to improve enrolment ratios for girls.

Table 1.11. – Education index in 20 African Countries 1970-1996

HDI Rank	Adult literacy rate (%)		Combined first-, second- and third level gross enrolment ratio (%, age 6-23 years)	
	1970	**1996**	**1980**	**1996**
South Africa	–	–	–	–
Angola	–	–	54	31
Burundi	20	34	11	31
Burkina Faso	8	19	8	20
Cameroon	33	62	48	46
Central African Republic	16	54	33	37
Côte d'Ivoire	18	39	39	41
Ethiopia	–	–	16	18
Eritrea	–	–	–	16
Ghana	31	63	48	44
Guinea	14	35	21	24
Malawi	–	–	33	67
Mali	8	29	–	–
Nigeria	25	56	50	50
Uganda	41	61	25	34
United Rep. of Tanzania	–	–	44	34
Chad	11	43	16	25
Zaire	42	76	46	38
Zambia	52	77	46	48
Zimbabwe	55	85	41	68

Source: Human Development Report, 1999.

While in most Sub-Saharan African countries, exemplified by Zambia, the prejudices against educating girls are strongest in the lowest income groups, these prejudices persist across all income levels. In Burkina Faso, Burundi, Gambia and Malawi, illiteracy rates for men vary from 40%-42% on small farms to around 46%-55% on large farms, whereas illiteracy affects 75%-79% of women, regardless of farm size. The literacy rates of public sector workers in the capital cities are the highest, but there is still a marked difference between men (80%-86%) and women (53%-59%). In

Burkina Faso, Mali and Niger, primary education shows up clear gender and rural-urban disparities. [1]

At household level, socioeconomic characteristics, cultural practices and social aspirations are all important factors in spending on education. In Niger and Guinea, farmers, whether they produce cash or subsistence crops, send significantly fewer children to school. On average, rural girls have only one chance in ten of attending primary school. In contrast, two-thirds of girls from households associated with the formal sector in urban areas go to school. In Senegal, female-headed households are more likely than male-headed households — especially polygamous households — to invest in the human capital of their members. The gender disparity is generally more pronounced in polygamous households than in monogamous households. In polygamous households in Mauritania, for example, the literacy rate of men is four times that of women. [2]

Low enrolment ratios for girls, compared with boys, are not limited to a small number of countries, but are widespread across Sub-Saharan Africa. In countries where average per capita income is $600 or more, primary enrolment ratios for girls and boys reach 100%. However, in countries where income is between $300 and $450, enrolment ratios are 60%-65% for girls and 80%-85% for boys and in countries where average income is below $300, enrolment ratios fall below 50% for girls and 65% for boys.

Statistical analysis shows that gross primary enrolment ratios tend to increase in line with per capita GDP. Household surveys corroborate the observation that primary enrolment ratios in Sub-Saharan Africa rise with household income. This correlation can be explained chiefly by the fact that the higher a family's income, the less it needs to send its young children out to work and the longer it can keep them in school. Increased education and adult literacy contribute actively to the economic and social integration of poor and vulnerable people and are thus a key issue for African countries.

Women probably offer the most powerful untapped resource for alleviating poverty in Sub-Saharan Africa. Investing in women's education and promoting women's access to productive resources, such as land and credit, will stimulate economic growth, correct imbalances resulting from uncontrolled population growth and make it possible to raise the living standards of the continent as a whole, thus achieving a reduction in poverty.

---

1. *Programme cadre national de lutte contre la pauvreté, Diagnostic général de la pauvreté au Niger* (Niamey, 1996); Ministère de l'Economie, du Plan et de l'Intégration du Mali, *Stratégie Nationale de lutte contre la pauvreté* (février 1998); Ministère de l'Economie, des Finances et du Plan, *Le profil de pauvreté au Burkina Faso*, (Ouagadougou, 1996).

2. UNDP, *Rapport National sur le Développement Humain en Mauritanie 1997*.

2.2.4. Availability and accessibility of health care: a crucial issue for Africa

The effects of education on poverty alleviation are substantial, but indirect, because people must be able to use their improved skills. In contrast, health care has a direct effect on poverty reduction. In the past, Africa made regular advances in health, but the improvement in health indicators is now under threat. Life expectancy, which rose by over ten years between 1960 and the end of the 1980s, has remained practically stable since then, at 51. Average life expectancy is 59 in South Asia and 68 in Latin America, with considerable variation between low-income and intermediate countries. There is much less of a range in Sub-Saharan Africa: the Sahel has the lowest life expectancy, at 48 years, and East Africa the highest, at 53 years. Recent studies by the WHO, UNFPA and UNICEF have highlighted the many ways to improve Africans' health status, by demonstrating that, despite severe budget restrictions, significant improvements are within reach of many countries if they apply certain policies. Policy recommendations consist mainly in adopting packages of cost-effective measures to tackle the most common health problems, in decentralizing the supply of health care, in improving the management of essential health care inputs and upgrading infrastructure and equipment in the health sector.

Since 1960, infant and child mortality in Sub-Saharan Africa as a whole has declined by almost a third. In 1990, the child mortality rate was over 140 per 1,000 live births in Guinea-Bissau, Liberia, Mozambique and Sierra Leone, compared with a regional average of 102 per 1,000 live births and under 20 per 1,000 live births in Mauritius and the Seychelles. The Sahel and Southern Africa show the highest rates of infant mortality (an average 118 and 117 per 1,000 live births, respectively), although in individual countries, particularly those in crisis, infant mortality is even higher, at between 120 and 180 per 1,000 live births. The proportion of children who die before their first birthday is higher in Sub-Saharan Africa than in any other developing region, yet vaccination of children against potentially fatal diseases, such as diphtheria and measles, has declined since 1980.

At the same time, AIDS has spread rapidly through most of Sub-Saharan Africa. In the past decade, more than 10 million adults and 1 million children (two-thirds of the world total) have been infected by the human immunodeficiency virus (HIV) in Africa. In many African countries, AIDS will slow economic growth by preventing a large share of the most productive age groups from working, across all income brackets. AIDS will also reverse advances in reducing infant mortality and raising life expectancy. [1]

---

1. UNDP, *Rôle du PNUD dans la lutte contre le VIH et le SIDA: Plan Directeur* (New York, 1996).

Box 1 4.
Poverty in Sub-Saharan Africa and HIV Aids

The aids pandemia cause a new wave of poverty and impedes medical and social advances. Many of the 30 countries with declining HDI must blame the propagation of the virus for at least part of this decline. This is the case in Botswana, Burundi, Cameroon, Congo, Kenya, Rwanda, Togo and Zimbabwe. Thus, Botswana and Zimbabwe had made real progress in the seventies and eighties but ever since, life expectancy has decreased by 5-10 years thus bringing these countries back to their human development levels of the sixties.

Forecasts to the year 2010 show that life expectancy could come down to 33 years (instead of reaching 61 in the absence of aids) in Botswana and to 35 years (also instead of 61) in Burkina Faso. Child mortality should reach 148 deaths per 1000 live births in Botswana (instead of dropping to 38 per 1000). In 18 out of the 22 countries studied, most of which are in Sub-Saharan Africa, the aids epidemic will reduce life expectancy by at least 10 years. In 14 out of these countries child mortality will also increase by at least 50 deaths per 1000 live births. These results are partly a direct consequence of aids — through the deaths it causes — but they are also related to the impact of the pandemia on development.

The impact of aids on poverty shows the two-way relationship existing between poverty and the disease.

Aids is closely related to poverty because the latter favors the propagation of the epidemic and HIV virus infection breeds a chain of factors of impoverishment and of economic and social disintegration..

The poorest are particularly exposed due to lack of education, information and access to social health services. These populations are also more threatened by social disintegration due to fast urbanization, civil strife and other armed conflicts.

Disease can have a catastrophic effect on the family unit. Besides income loss, health expenditure rapidly depletes the financial reserves of the household.

More than half of the family income can be swallowed up by expenditure towards caring for a sick member of the household. Families may be compelled to sell their economic resources such as land or cattle, which can only make them poorer or force them into high interest debt. The disease may also shatter all hopes of getting rid of poverty by forcing the families to withdraw their children from school. One of the most tragic consequences of aids is the increasing number of orphans. A study conducted in 15 countries of Sub-Saharan Africa anticipates that the number of orphans will double and might reach 4.2 millions in the year 2005.

Furthermore, the epidemic increases the burden that weighs already heavy on the national health services, with the consequence of reducing the quality of health care.

Slowing down aids requires that we endeavor to change mentalities and strengthen the resources of the populations so to help them cope better with the situation. Concerted efforts made at national level are beginning to bear fruit although the challenges remain very serious in this domain.

Source: UNDP, World Report on Sustainable Human Development, 1997.

Table 1.12. – Child survival and development index in Africa, 1990-1996

	Births not assisted by Health services (%) 1990 -96	Infants with low birth-weight (%) 1990-94	Under-weight children below the age of 5 (%) 1990-96	Infant mortality rate (per 1000 live births) 1994	Under-five mortality rate (per 1000 live births) 1995
South Africa	82	–	9	51	67
Angola	15	19	28	120	292
Burundi	19	–	37	122	176
Burkina Faso	42	21	30	101	164
Cameroon	64	13	14	62	106
Central African Republic	46	15	27	99	165
Côte d'Ivoire	45	14	24	89	150
Ethiopia	14	16	48	115	195
Eritrea	21	13	41	103	195
Ghana	44	7	27	79	130
Guinea	31	21	26	131	219
Malawi	55	20	30	147	219
Mali	24	17	31	156	210
Nigeria	31	16	36	82	191
Uganda	38	–	23	121	185
Tanzania	53	14	29	85	160
Chad	15	–	–	121	152
Zaire	–	–	34	94	185
Zambia	51	13	28	110	203
Zimbabwe	69	14	16	70	74

Source: UNICEF, 'The State of the World's Children', 1997 ", New York, Oxford University Press, 1997; UNDP, Human Development Report, 1997.

As in education, rural-urban disparity in health care is striking. Rural households in Sub-Saharan Africa are severely disadvantaged in terms of access to these services. The percentage of the urban population with immediate access to primary health care ranges from 44% to 99%. [1] In most of the Sahelian countries, less than 30% of rural people have easy

---

1. UNDP, *SMART Profiles. Socio-Economic Monetary and Resources Tables* (New York, 1996).

access to health services. In some of these countries, the proportion is as low as 18%, compared with 76% in urban areas. Only around half of the total population has access to safe drinking water, breaking down as 42% of the rural population and 70% of the urban population. In Zambia, the gap between town and country is extreme: infrastructure investment has provided access to safe water for 88% of the urban population, but less than 20% of the rural population.

2.3. *Political and institutional issues related to poverty eradication*

In the 1990s, a profound shift has occurred in Africa's political situation, even if African governments and society as a whole still have a long way to go before achieving genuine democracy and sound management of public affairs in the broad sense. In a number of countries, single-party governments and military regimes that monopolized power for 20 or 30 years, in a context of recurring instability where over 200 attempted coups d'état affected around 90% of the countries of Sub-Saharan Africa over 1960-1990, have given way to new governments elected in multiparty elections supervised by external observers (a total of 36 elections between 1992 and 1997). [1]

In some countries, a new constitution enshrining liberal values and the principles of the Universal Declaration of Human Rights, has been drafted by a constituent assembly. Steps towards a balance of powers have been taken with a view to defining the powers and responsibilities of the main organs of State (executive, legislative, judiciary) and to strengthening accountability, transparency and the primacy of the constitution. Some governments have also introduced new arrangements to devolve certain decision-making powers and responsibilities to regional, district and municipal level.

The process of democratizing African politics has not been smooth, however. In some countries, newfound freedom of association and freedom of speech after decades of brutal repression have sometimes led to heightened tension, even overt conflict. The affirmation of ethnic and religious differences, unless channeled effectively, can cause the fragmentation of existing States. In a number of countries, electoral procedures or results have been vigorously contested by the losing parties, whether justified or not, sparking long-lasting unrest or instability. Electoral winners have not always shown magnanimity or a spirit of reconciliation in victory. They have not sought to win the support of opposition parties, despite the need to forge a broad national consensus to rise to the sociopolitical and economic challenges of development. Political instability has strongly dis-

---

1. Coalition Mondiale pour l'Afrique, *Etude sur le passage à la démocratie en Afrique*, Note analytique, 1997.

rupted the processes of growth and adjustment and has exacerbated the situation of poverty that prevails in many African countries.

Instability excludes some 3% of Africans — around 12 million people — from the processes of human development, because they are refugees (7 million people according to 1996 UNHCR estimates) or have been repatriated (around 3 million people) or are displaced inside their own countries (approximately 2 million people). [1]

Since the beginning of the 1980s, civil wars in Angola, Chad, Eritrea, Ethiopia, Liberia, Mauritania, Senegal, Somalia, Sudan, Togo and recently Rwanda, Burundi and the Democratic Republic of Congo have killed thousands of civilians and created millions of refugees and displaced persons. These conflicts have hit poor families and communities particularly hard because most of the victims are civilians, particularly women and children. UNICEF estimates that during the current decade, more than one million children have been killed in armed conflicts and almost four million have become refugees or street children, 30% of whom are disabled. There are many more whose health and nutrition status have suffered from the destruction of health and education infrastructure. [2]

Instability and conflicts impede efforts to alleviate extreme poverty in African countries, because of the mass destruction and diversion of resources from development. The drain on budgets and other resources, particularly natural resources, stretch the already limited capacities of a number of countries. There is often a simultaneous loss of financing, in the form of external assistance other than humanitarian aid and domestic and foreign public investment.

In the past few years, public services have fallen off significantly in the whole of Sub-Saharan Africa. In real terms, per capita access to public services is estimated to have decreased by around 50% since 1980. [3]

This decline in public service forms a backdrop to a stabilization of overall staff numbers in the public administration and a drastic reduction in the working and fixed capital per public-sector worker. Constant deterioration in the value of public-sector pay has had serious effects on the availability of public services to poor people. In the past fifteen years, pay levels have fallen — sometimes significantly below the absolute household poverty line — for most public-sector workers, including professional and technical staff.

---

1. United Nations High Commissioner for Refugees, *Annual Report 1995* (Geneva, 1996).

2. UNICEF, *The State of the World's Children 1997* (New York: Oxford University Press, 1997).

3. Adebayo Adedeji, Reginald Green, and Abdou Janha, *Pay, Productivity and Public Service: Priorities for Recovery in Sub-Saharan Africa* (New York: UNICEF-UNDP, 1995).

The deterioration in services has often been attributed to an excessive number of public-sector workers, particularly those considered insufficiently qualified. The solution to the problem expressed in these terms has led to measures that are themselves problematic, but which are generally promulgated and strongly supported by donors, often despite vigorous opposition from African analysts and development specialists. These measures include: i) generalized public-sector staff cuts; ii) payment of premiums by donors and special grants for participation in conferences and workshops, encouraging absences from the workplace; iii) the implementation of parallel systems of services and disaster-relief programs, supported directly by donors or through foreign NGOs. The repeated failure of staff-reduction policies without comprehensive institutional reform have worsened an already bad situation.

Governance and institutional development play a decisive role in poverty reduction at three levels: central government, decentralized structures and communities and grassroots stakeholders. As a result, poverty eradication objectives are more focused, especially as a consensus seems to be emerging on the need to find a middle road between the paternalistic State and the unbridled free market, to encourage decentralized development and give more autonomy to local authorities and grassroots organizations.

The consolidation of democratic processes, sensible conduct of public affairs, transparency and accountability are vital issues for governments. Together with measures to strengthen grassroots action, these principles are the key to sustained socioeconomic development capable of reducing extreme poverty. Fighting corruption and incompetence ensures optimum utilization of the limited resources available for development. Under decentralization, transfers of power and grassroots decision-making and action can enhance the quality and cost-effectiveness of poverty reduction efforts. Local structures tend to identify less costly, more suitable ways of implementing priority services. The advantages of social control, common standards and the possibility of applying sanctions at local level offer a basis for social insurance and collective loan schemes. Decentralization also provides the remotest regions of developing countries with a more efficient transmission channel for warnings, facilitating timely reaction to events that risk becoming disasters, such as floods and epidemics.

When local authorities take genuine responsibility, decentralization tends to improve public services in all these areas. Decentralization can also contribute to better management of collectively-owned natural resources. In rural areas, poor people often depend directly for their survival on natural resources such as forests, pastures and water for irrigation or fish stocks. Communal land acts as a form of insurance for poor peasants.

A balance needs to be struck between two requirements. Policy coordination at central level is needed to generate economies of scale, decide the most cost-effective level of action and avoid jurisdictional disputes. At the same time, information-gathering and political and administrative responsibility need to be local to offer more autonomous development opportunities.

To resolve the complex problems of governance, empowerment and poverty reduction, countries will have to find answers to the following questions. How can governments implement necessary, but often painful, structural socioeconomic reforms and at the same time win regular elections, meet immediate social needs and compete with the opposition democratically? How can the fundamental rights of the individual be reconciled with collective rights in a poor country? How can the ethnic, cultural, linguistic and religious diversity of the African mosaic be preserved in a way that is compatible with building nation States and integrated development areas? How can poor people be involved more widely in designing and implementing policies and action programs to improve their living conditions?

Box 1.5.
Good governance, poverty and means of subsistence

Poverty, inequality and governance are inseparably related because poverty and inequality can still weaken a deficient governance. How can such a vicious circle be broken?

This can be achieved only by providing civic education which make people understand their individual rights and responsibilities. The problem is that the new interest groups coming up in many developing countries do not always reflect and express the needs of the poor, to the extent that the latter find it difficult to organize themselves and have a say in matters.

Poverty is not just a material situation; it is partly based on capacities and values. A better access by the poor to educational system is a good cure for poverty and inequalities. In many of the poorest developing countries illiteracy prevents people from finding jobs or from participating in decision-making.

Changes in the priorities of governments and of the private sector over the last decade have blurred the links between poverty, inequality, governance and sustainable human development. The legitimacy of the role of the State in poverty control is increasingly being questioned. Nevertheless a favorable environment as well as an equitable distribution of resources remain essential in terms of coping with poverty and inequalities and creating jobs. Formerly, the government was expected to eliminate poverty. Todays, people increasing recognize that the State, the civil society and the private sector must collectively take care of the problems of poverty and inequality.

Source: UNDP, "Governance and Sustainable Human Development", 1997

2.4. Food security

Food insecurity typically affects the poorest Africans, who are unable to produce, buy or trade enough food because of a lack of income, assets or rights. There are also transient factors that come into play in low-income economies and countries in crisis.

Transient food insecurity is caused by factors such as seasonal variation in the availability and price of food at household, regional or country level. Civil wars, drought and famine cause a particular kind of transient food insecurity that hits poor and vulnerable people hardest. Transient food insecurity can lead to chronic poverty and extreme poverty when temporary factors destroy assets such as land, food stocks and livestock. This situation is evident in a number of African countries, notably Burundi, Rwanda, Somalia and Sudan.

The link between poverty, hunger and malnutrition is obvious: people usually suffer from hunger and malnutrition because they are poor. Nutrition status is therefore a particularly sensitive indicator of current and past poverty.

While malnutrition is falling in every region in the world, the food situation has remained stable or has deteriorated in most of Sub-Saharan Africa over the past decade, which has had serious consequences for mothers and children in particular.

Poverty and malnutrition are a vicious circle, as poverty leads to malnutrition and malnutrition, particularly in young children, lowers future productivity by retarding the development of individuals and, as a result, of societies as a whole.

Malnutrition increases the risks of premature death. According to the WHO, on the basis of existing mortality rates, risks of death increase exponentially (at a cumulative rate of around 6%) with every drop of a point in the body weight index. [1] This is of particular concern in Africa, where moderate malnutrition is the main nutritional problem. Malnutrition increases the incidence and severity of disease by 50%, reduces the aptitude for learning by 10% and adult productivity by up to 20%.

Poor people are disproportionately affected by malnutrition. The consequences of their nutrition status are more likely to be passed on from one generation to the next and this situation can reduce their capacity to benefit from other social services, such as education. To strengthen the human capital of the poor, it is essential to break the link between poverty and malnutrition.

---

1. WHO, *World Health Report 1997* (Geneva, 1997).

Table 1.13. – Food security index in 20 countries of Africa South of the Sahara

African Country	Food Production per capita index (1979-81 = 100) 1993	Food consumption (as % of total household consumption) 1989-95	Daily calorie supply per capita 1996	Food aid in cereals (thousands of metric tons) 1994-95 [a]
South Africa	74	34	2,705	–
Angola	72	–	1,840	217
Burundi	92	–	1,941	48
Burkina Faso	132	–	2,284	19
Cameroon	79	24	1,981	2
Central African Republic	94	–	1,691	1
Côte d'Ivoire	89	39	2,491	56
Ethiopia	86	49	1,610	720
Eritrea	–	–	–	140
Ghana	115	50 [b]	2,206	101
Guinea	98	–	2,390	29
Malawi	70	30	1,827	204
Mali	91	57	2,276	17
Nigeria	129	48	2,125	–
Uganda	109	–	2,162	62
United Rep. of Tanzania	76	64	2,024	118
Chad	99	–	1,986	14
Zaire	100	–	2,060	83
Zambia	99	36	1,931	11
Zimbabwe	78	40	1,989	4

a. The temporal reference of food aid is the growing season that stretches from June to July.
b. Data refer to a year or a period different from the one specified in the column heading.

Source: FAO, 'The State of the World's Food and Agriculture', 1997 '', Rome, FAO, 1997.

Obstacles that must be overcome include a poor understanding of nutrition at household and national level, the lack of a specific institutional basis for action on nutrition, poor coordination between the ministries responsible for nutrition and sometimes even a lack of political will.

2.5. Access to natural resources and sustainable management of the environment

As a cause and effect of fast population growth, poverty is also a frequent cause and effect of environmental degradation. Sustainable management of natural resources is an essential condition for long-term growth
and poverty reduction in Africa. Conversely, persistent poverty is one of the
main causes of natural resource degradation. There are close links between
traditional cultivation and livestock farming methods, land tenure systems,
access to water and natural resources and methods of woodland resource
use.

Traditional land use and forestry have reduced the productivity and
resilience of natural resource systems. Despite the considerable investment
in yield-enhancing techniques, yields, especially of food crops, have
remained stable or declined in many countries. The resulting slowdown in
economic growth has not favored a transition to lower birth rates. The
swelling numbers of the rural poor are degrading and depleting ever faster
the natural resources of the rural environment that ensure their survival.
Degradation of fragile drylands is accelerating almost everywhere in Africa,
because of factors such as overgrazing, overuse, bad irrigation methods,
deforestation and climate change. Sixty-six percent of Africa's surface area is
made up of arid or desert lands and seventy-three percent of arid farmland
is already degraded according to the United Nations Environment Programme. [1]

Many, but certainly not all, of the rural poor live in areas where the
environment is extremely fragile, because the areas with more stable, more
productive resources tend to be controlled by the State, the private sector
or wealthy population groups. As a result, the poor are especially vulnerable
to erosion, which gradually diminishes productive areas. The threat is not
only due to natural causes. Poverty accelerates erosion. The poor often lack
the capital to invest even in traditional methods of land and water conservation. They also lack sufficient land and are forced to shorten fallow periods, putting further stress on resources. As with population growth, the
strain on the environment not only affects the poor, but the entire economy.

Attempts at agrarian reform in Southern and East Africa to facilitate
access to land have left serious loopholes, which in practice have enabled
powerful social groups to limit improvements in the situation of the poor.
On the crucial issue of land tenure, registration processes are excessively

---

1. UNEP, *Annual Report 1996* (Nairobi, 1997) and working papers for the Convention
on Desertification, Paris, October 1994.

complex and prohibitively expensive for the poor that programs to legalize land occupation have practically, sometimes unintentionally, become charters legalizing the eviction of poor people and leading to the loss of traditional rights.

Table 1.14. – Use of natural resources in 20 countries of Sub-Saharan Africa

	Arable land (as % of land area)	Irrigated land (as % of arable land area)	Gini coefficient for land distribution [a]	Annual rate of deforestation (%)	Annual rate of reforestation (%)	Household energy from fuel-wood
	1995	1995	1985-93	1981-90	1981-90	1994
South Africa	6.7	10.3	10.3	– 0.8	2	–
Angola	2.4	2.5	–	– 0.7	1	85
Burundi	40.8	1.2	–	– 0.6	59	77
Burkina Faso	13.6	0.6	–	– 0.7	13	84
Cameroon	12.5	0.4	–	– 0.6	29	74
Central African Republic.	3.4	–	–	– 0.4	–	–
Côte d'Ivoire	7.6	2.9	–	– 1.0	10	70
Ethiopia	10.9	1.6	0.32	– 0.3	17	86
Eritrea	–	–	–	–	–	–
Ghana	11.7	0.2	–	– 1.3	2	85
Guinea	2.6	15.4	0.19	1.1	6	87
Malawi	14.1	1.7	–	– 1.3	12	89
Mali	2.0	3.1	–	0.8	144	81
Nigeria	32.3	3.2	–	– 0.7	3	72
Uganda	21.4	0.2	0.62	– 0.9	0	86
Tanzania	3.3	5.0	–	– 1.1	13	89
Chad	2.5	0.4	–	– 0.7	8	82
Zaire	3.1	0.2	0.39	– 0.6	17	94
Zambia	7.0	0.9	–	– 1.0	8	86
Zimbabwe	7.0	6.8	–	– 0.6	2	–

a. The Gini coefficient measures inequality in land distribution. It ranges from zero (perfect equality) to 1 (complete inequality).

Sources: UNDP, Human Development Report, 1996, New York, 1999; World Resources Institute, "Annual Report 1994-1995", New York, 1995.

There are sometimes considerable constraints on access to water, which calls for a more equitable and rational approach and more decentralized management of scarce resources. The construction of dams for irrigation must be accompanied by specific measures to protect the people whose land is flooded. Furthermore, irrigation programs have tended to be concentrated in high-potential areas where the State, the parastatal farm sector and the wealthy classes predominate. Vast sums have been spent on large-scale irrigation schemes, but very little on water conservation and small irrigation works, which are more likely to meet the needs of small, marginal producers.

The poor often need to be assisted to reestablish a stable relationship with fragile resources. The processes under way in many regions are gradually, and sometimes rapidly, depleting natural resources to the detriment of all or most of the population. The solution lies partly in conservation and regeneration of resources and partly in making economically viable alternatives available to the poor to reduce their dependence on cultivation and livestock farming methods that hasten erosion and other irreversible damage to natural resources.

Given the extremely limited range of economic alternatives, it is not a question of prohibiting the poor from using ecologically fragile resources, but in changing the conditions under which resources are used. While early warning systems are important, secure land tenure and the volume of available investment resources are crucial. Poverty reduction requires not only raising poor people's production capacity, but also preserving and increasing the long-term value of the resources they control.

Conclusion

This chapter sought to provide an overview of the magnitude, trends and fundamental implications of poverty and the issues to tackle at various levels in order to alleviate poverty.

Poverty is a mass phenomenon in Sub-Saharan Africa, where it affects some 250 million people and continues to spread. Whether defined in purely monetary terms or according to the sustainable human development paradigm, poverty is increasing, as evidenced at once by the slow growth (or decline) in real GDP per capita over 1970-1992 and the severe lack of access to basic social services (health, safe water, education, etc.) for a substantial share of the population.

In addition to designing instruments for measuring and assessing poverty, there is a need to consider the diversity of situations of poverty and establish the causal relationships behind poverty.

Once the causes of poverty have been identified, recommendations can be made on the issues to tackle to alleviate poverty. An analysis of the general characteristics of poverty in Sub-Saharan Africa reveals many, multifaceted underlying issues. However, several major areas for action stand out.

• One of the causes of poverty in Sub-Saharan Africa is the poor performance of economic policies, illustrated by inadequate distribution of income and expenditure, low savings and investment ratios, absence — particularly of farmers — from the market economy, insufficient emphasis on the role of women in national development processes, the limited impact of export sectors, the faltering attempts at regional integration and the debt problem. Economic issues are thus at the heart of the problem of poverty. Keys to a solution lie in:

– designing and implementing pro-poor growth policies that favor poor rural areas in particular;

– undertaking macroeconomic reform and sectoral adjustment that will stimulate saving and private-sector investment;

– giving priority to agricultural growth as a major force for poverty reduction and enabling poor rural populations to benefit from market opportunities;

– taking steps to improve the economic, political and social situation of women;

– implementing policies to improve productivity and competitiveness and adopting a dynamic approach to trade, with a view to greater participation in regional integration and globalization;

– initiating substantive reform of the financial sector and supporting a comprehensive, concerted approach to the debt problem.

• Poverty in Sub-Saharan Africa is exacerbated by demographic trends. Africa has the highest rate of population growth (2.8%-3%) of all the developing regions. Over several periods, the population has grown faster than the economy, causing living standards to deteriorate. Rapid population growth, with its corollary of rural exodus, has contributed to a labor market characterized by chronic excess supply of labor. The difficulty of finding paid employment has swelled the ranks of the poor, particularly in urban areas. Access to education has been extremely limited and enrolment ratios and literacy rates are among the lowest in the world. Indicators of access to health services show severe deficiencies. Poverty reduction strategies and programs must give priority to the issues raised by population growth and its consequences for access to basic social services, focusing on:

– controlling the rate of population growth in line with economic growth;

– increasing educational attainment and adult literacy, with preferential emphasis on women and girls;

– increasing the actual use of basic health services.

• Political instability and internal and inter-country conflicts must be recognized as factors that reverse the gains in poverty eradication. Since the beginning of the 1980s, civil wars in Sub-Saharan Africa have killed or displaced millions of people. Many of the survivors of these conflicts are refugees or disabled, increasing the number of people severely affected by poverty.

Conflicts also dismantle traditional economic systems and institutional and organizational structures, rendering inoperable any attempts to design or implement poverty reduction policies or measures. The fundamental question for governments is how to achieve or maintain the peace and political stability needed to alleviate poverty. This raises other, more specific, questions to which countries will have to find appropriate responses if they are to make progression poverty reduction.

– How can the ambition to exercise political power be reconciled with the need to implement often painful and unpopular structural socioeconomic reforms?

– How can the logic and principle of changeovers of power between political parties be integrated and accepted democratically?

– How can national unity be preserved at the same time as ethnic, cultural, linguistic and religious diversity and in the context of regional integration?

– How can poor people be involved more widely in designing and implementing policies and programs to improve their situation?

• Food and nutritional insecurity are inherent to the situation of the poorest people in Sub-Saharan Africa. Inadequate or non-existent income deprives them of access to healthy food in sufficient quantities. As a result, malnutrition, by reducing the functioning and capabilities of its victims, decreases productivity and perpetuates the vicious circle of poverty. Therefore, to enhance the human capital of the poor, it is essential to break the link between poverty and malnutrition. Food security for poor population groups must become the priority human security.

This reinforces the idea that management of natural resources is an essential condition for long-term growth and poverty reduction. Population pressure and bad management of natural resources have led to environmental degradation and decline in agricultural output, particularly food production. But, out of necessity, poor people themselves sometimes contribute to further damaging the environment and available natural resources.

The issue is complicated by the limited range of alternative solutions. However, poverty reduction must remain a central consideration and appropriate responses to the survival needs of poor population groups must be found, namely by ensuring that the conditions for access to and use of resources are favorable to the poor and by reducing the dependence of the poor on methods that are harmful for the environment and agriculture.

An investigation of poverty and poverty-related issues in Africa will only be fruitful if the concept and dynamics of poverty are properly understood. The understanding of poverty has evolved considerably from a simple equation with material growth. Poverty is far more complex than monetary deprivation alone and the shortcomings of the "growth equals happiness" formula are now apparent. New concepts of poverty and methodologies to assess these concepts and translate them into action are invaluable. An examination of these approaches is an essential step towards finding responses to the issues outlined in this chapter.

CHAPTER 2

Definitions, measures and a comprehensive approach to poverty in Sub-Saharan Africa

1. Definitions of poverty

1.1. Current vision of poverty

There is no unanimously accepted definition of poverty. An understanding of poverty, on which the design and implementation of operational poverty reduction strategies are based, can be shaped by various economic, social, political or anthropological approaches or the standpoint of different international institutions, such as UNDP or the World Bank.

Poverty is almost never defined in itself, but through other concepts, such as growth, well-being, exclusion or equity. As a result, it is not easy to clearly identify the key elements of the concept of poverty, especially when it is often defined in relation to a specific context, whether global, regional, national or local.

However, despite country-specific conditions, the variety of conceptual approaches and the difficulties of identifying and defining poverty, a clear definition of the concept of poverty must be sought as a basis for designing national poverty reduction strategies. This definition should have an operational purpose and draw on the paradigm of sustainable human development devised by UNDP.

The principles of poverty eradication action expressed at the Copenhagen Summit for Social Development and in UNDP's *Human Development Report 1997* emphasize two essential features of the concept of poverty: i) its comparative nature — nationally and internationally and within specific situations of poverty; and ii) its complex and multidimensional nature. [1]

---

1. *Copenhagen Declaration on Social Development*, World Summit for Social Development, Copenhagen, 1995 and UNDP, *Human Development Report 1997* (New York: Oxford University Press, 1997).

The identification, measurement and perception of poverty are, by nature, comparative processes. International organizations have based their initial — implicit — approach to poverty on criteria related to growth, wealth or development. Two of the main indicators of countries' level of development — gross domestic product (GDP) and UNDP's human development index (HDI) — are of little value in themselves. Their main function is comparative, within a global or regional context. While it is not their primary objective, the calculation of these indicators leads to a development hierarchy or a ranking of countries as "rich", "poor" and "less poor". In the same vein, the category of least developed countries (LDCs) implies that other countries are considered more developed.

In parallel to these global comparisons, there are efforts to identify and understand poverty within each country. In country-specific approaches to poverty, indicators, comparators and other measures are calculated for internal comparisons and a country-specific definition of poverty. This national focus is essential for accurate analysis and designing strategies.

All the poverty lines and poverty profiles established in Africa comprise both comparative and specific dimensions. The comparative dimensions mainly concern geographical (rural/urban, national/provincial), gender, generational and socio-occupational aspects. The specific dimensions highlighted in poverty profiles may be the specific characteristics of rural poverty or of women's poverty, for example. On the basis of 31 African poverty lines shown in Table 2.2, it is difficult, although not impossible, to describe the phenomenon of poverty in Sub-Saharan Africa and its main characteristics, because of the variety of methodologies, conceptual standpoints and focuses used.

This new stage in understanding the concept of poverty leads to the other essential feature of poverty: multidimensionality, which needs to be incorporated into the vision of poverty and the design of operational poverty reduction strategies.

Concerns with identifying the population groups affected by poverty and the desire to measure it have sometimes obscured the fact that poverty is too complex to be reduced to a single dimension — namely monetary — of human life. It has become common for countries to set poverty lines based on income or consumption. While this approach considers an important dimension of poverty, it provides an incomplete picture of the many characteristics of poverty. Someone may be in good health and live a relatively long life, but be illiterate and thus cut off from learning, communication and interaction with others. Someone else may be able to read and write and have received a good education, but be prone to premature death because of epidemiological conditions or a physical predisposition. Yet another person may be excluded from participating in decision-making in the events that affect his life. The deprivation of none of them can be fully captured by the level of their income. [1]

Also, people perceive poverty in different ways — and each person and community defines the deprivation and disadvantages that affect their lives. Poverty of lives and opportunities — or human poverty — is multidimensional in nature and diverse rather than uniform in content.

In addition to emphasis on social, economic or geographical aspects, approaches to poverty also depend on the standpoint taken. Definitions vary widely according to whether a utilitarian/welfarist or other approach is taken and to whether poverty is viewed from the perspective of income, household consumption, basic needs or capabilities.

This plurality of definitions of poverty is no doubt due to the newness of the concept and related concerns. The conceptualization of poverty is still in progress, which explains the contradictions and disagreements over a definition, on which no consensus has yet been reached. However, since the main purpose of a definition of poverty is to achieve operational objectives, it should be based on an analysis of the characteristics and determinants of poverty specific to each continent, country or region.

1.2. Definitions of poverty

Beyond the theoretical value and the importance of having clearly identifiable concepts and methods on which to base poverty reduction strategies, it is worth examining the various definitions of poverty in more depth. [2] Indeed, the choice of a particular definition and approach will have crucial repercussions on the construction of poverty lines and poverty profiles and on the design and implementation of poverty reduction strategies. Furthermore, with a view to reaching the definition of human poverty advocated by UNDP, it is worth recalling the various concepts and definitions that contributed to its formulation.

The concepts and ideas described below are not exclusive. A combination of different standpoints and definitions has often been used in the construction of country poverty profiles and indeed in the formulation of UNDP's concept of human poverty.

---

1. UNDP, *Rapport National sur le Développement Humain Durable au Bénin 1997.*
2. See: Gilbert Aho, Sylvain Larivière et Frédéric Martin, *Manuel d'analyse de la pauvreté: applications au Bénin* (Université Laval, PNUD, 1997); M. Hopkins, *A Short Review of Contemporary Thinking about Anti-Poverty Strategies for Sub-Saharan Africa* (Geneva, 1997); S. Larivière & F. Martin, *Le cadre d'analyse économique de la pauvreté et des conditions de vie des ménages* (Québec, 1997); M. Ravallion, "Pauvreté et exclusion, la mesure de la pauvreté," *Problèmes économiques*, n°2508, 1997; World Bank, *World Development Report 1990: Poverty* (Washington: Oxford University Press, 1990); UNDP, *Human Development Report 1997* (New York: Oxford University Press, 1997).

1.2.1. Well-being and poverty

Definitions of poverty are expressed in terms of its most universally recognized comparator, well-being. While all the definitions are, of course, based on the concepts of well-being and poverty, there is no single definition of either in the abundant literature on the subject. Approaches to well-being can be broadly divided into "utilitarian/welfarist" [1] — those that emphasize people's perceptions of their well-being — and "non-utilitarian/non-welfarist" — those based on a range of possible degrees of well-being.

Utilitarians/welfarists define well-being as the degree of satisfaction derived by individuals from consuming goods and services. This approach emphasizes individual perceptions of what generates utility, or well-being. The degree of well-being is measured by neutral indicators that do not distinguish between types of goods and services, since what is important is that the person derives utility or satisfaction from them.

In contrast, non-utilitarians/non-welfarists define well-being more independently from individual perceptions by considering what is desirable for people from a social point of view. To measure well-being, they use selective indicators of particular goods and services considered to generate social utility.

Poverty assessments in developing countries are inspired variously by utilitarian/welfarist and non-utilitarian/non-welfarist thinking. For example, participatory surveys on the dimensions of poverty are utilitarian/welfarist, while studies emphasizing the nutritional aspects of poverty and well-being are mainly non-utilitarian/non-welfarist. Both approaches offer a valuable and complementary insight into poverty and therefore are not mutually exclusive. It is not operational to consider approaches to poverty in terms of an opposition between utilitarians/welfarists and non-utilitarians/non-welfarists. Rather, a definition of poverty should be based on the major themes that have emerged as thinking and practice have evolved.

1.2.2. Income or consumption perspective

The first conceptual approach to poverty was based chiefly on monetary poverty, measured in terms of household income or consumption. By this definition, people are considered poor if — and only if — they do not have sufficient income to enjoy a certain level of well-being.

Thus, from the perspective of household income or consumption, a person is considered poor if his income or consumption is below a predetermined poverty line. Many countries have set poverty lines to identify poor people and to monitor progress on poverty reduction. These thresh-

---

1. UNDP, *Rapport National sur le Développement Humain Durable au Bénin 1997.*

olds are often defined as the income or consumption level below which it is not possible to obtain or consume a specified quantity of food. No fewer than 34 Sub-Saharan African countries, generally on the initiative of the World Bank, have used these methods and set poverty lines based chiefly on food expenditure (see Annex 1 for a more detailed discussion of this point).

Despite the incompleteness of the monetary approach, the vast majority of tools used to assess poverty are derived from it. However, setting poverty lines based on household food consumption data does not take into account people's own perceptions and aspirations.

The monetary approach, in line with the World Bank's development paradigm, is basically utilitarian. It measures household income or consumption without taking into account how this income or consumption is used. But poverty lines, whether purely monetary or related to calorie intake, are also influenced by the non-utilitarian approach, since the poverty line is set "arbitrarily" and food is considered to be a priority determinant of poverty.

1.2.3. Basic needs perspective

This approach to poverty identifies certain basic needs — such as food, clothing and shelter — that must absolutely be fulfilled to keep people out of poverty. These needs are considered to be universal, even though their fulfilment will vary between countries, according to factors such as climate, culture or socioeconomic situation.

Developed principally by UNICEF, this definition defines poverty as deprivation in the material requirements for minimally acceptable fulfilment of human needs, including food. This deprivational concept goes far beyond a lack of private income: it includes the need for basic health and education and essential services that must be provided by the community to prevent people from falling into poverty. This concept served as a model at the Copenhagen Summit for Social Development and for the 20/20 Initiative that stemmed from it. [1]

This conceptual approach has been used in some countries to set absolute poverty lines that take into account needs other than food consumption. The poverty lines set in Ethiopia (1991), Namibia (1991) and the Seychelles (1994), for example, take into account spending on basic needs such as clothing, energy and transport. However, there is a lack of homogeneity in the definition of these basic needs. The sectors identified in the 20/20 Initiative could serve as a basis for a clear, operational definition of basic

---

1. UNDP, *Human Development Report 1997* (New York: Oxford University Press, 1997).

needs for the purpose of setting absolute poverty lines. The basic needs perspective is non-utilitarian in that it involves prior identification of the determinants of poverty.

The basic needs approach represents an initial extension of the concept of poverty to include both monetary and non-monetary factors and a concern for fulfilling needs, particularly food and access to social services.

1.2.4. Social exclusion

At the instigation of the International Labour Organisation, the theme of social exclusion has been used mainly to explain the re-emergence of poverty in industrialized countries. [1] In the 1970s, the concept of exclusion emerged to analyze the condition of people who are not necessarily income-poor — although many are that too — but who are kept out of the mainstream of society for other reasons. The inadequacy of traditional measures of poverty, based on income and consumption, was widely acknowledged to explain these new concerns.

The ILO published a study in 1996 that sought to link the concept of social exclusion to poverty reduction strategies. Case studies, notably in Cameroon and Tanzania, served as a basis for the formulation of this analysis. [2]

This theme further enhanced the concept of poverty with the notion of personal exclusion (e.g. the obstacles to social integration of vulnerable groups, such as the disabled, street children and the elderly) or social exclusion as a collective attribute of a society (e.g. racial, sexual or religious discrimination). This dynamic approach, more social than economic in focus, served as a conceptual basis for a definition of poverty during the preparatory stages of the Copenhagen Summit for Social Development in 1995. This approach does not require the setting of a poverty line. It is primarily a qualitative, social conception of poverty, which is often missing from other attempts to define poverty.

1.2.5. UNDP's definition of human poverty

Beyond a review of the different approaches to poverty, the Copenhagen Summit for Social Development sought to clarify and unify the concept of poverty. The principles of action and poverty eradication objectives formulated at the summit stress the multidimensional nature of poverty. *"Poverty has various manifestations, including lack of income and productive resources sufficient to ensure sustainable livelihoods; hunger and malnutrition;*

---

1. G. Rodgers, C. Gore and J. Figueiredo, *Social Exclusion: Rhetoric, Reality, Responses* (Geneva: IILS/UNDP, 1995).

2. IILS/ILO, *Social Exclusion and Anti-Poverty Strategies*, 1996.

ill health; limited or lack of access to education and other basic services; increased morbidity and mortality from illness; homelessness and inadequate housing; unsafe environments; and social discrimination and exclusion. It is also characterized by a lack of participation in decision-making and in civil, social and cultural life". [1] In other words, as emphasized in the conclusion of the Copenhagen Declaration, the manifestations of poverty should be apprehended not only in terms of income, but also in terms of access to social services.

This represented an initial convergence of concepts in an attempt to reach a definition of poverty. Alongside aspects related to income and productive resources, the summit addressed access to social services, social exclusion and lack of participation in decision-making processes.

The approach adopted by UNDP to the concept of poverty is derived from the paradigm of sustainable human development and from the declarations and resolutions of the Copenhagen Summit for Social Development and aims to reconcile and integrate the various existing definitions of poverty. It is a people-centered approach, in which economic growth is recognized as important for poverty reduction, but insufficient in itself. Economic growth must be considered as only a means to the end of human development.

The concept of human poverty developed by UNDP draws on previous definitions, integrates their fundamental elements and enhances the process with a focus on the concept of a lack of capabilities. [2] This form of poverty, captured partly by the notion of social exclusion, applies to people who do not have the opportunity to achieve minimally acceptable levels of the capabilities to function. These functionings can range from such physical ones as being well nourished, adequately clothed and sheltered, to more complex social criteria such as participation in community life and the opportunity to improve living standards. The capability approach reconciles the notions of relative and absolute poverty, since relative deprivation in incomes and commodities can lead to absolute deprivation in minimum capabilities.

In other words, human poverty encompasses both a monetary aspect — inadequate income and consumption — and aspects related to the accessibility of essential services and lack of capabilities. Poverty is, by nature, a complex and multidimensional phenomenon. This broad, consensual definition encourages the use of an extended range of tools to more effectively

---

1. "Poverty Eradication", *Copenhagen Declaration on Social Development*, World Summit for Social Development, Copenhagen, 1995.

2. UNDP, *Human Development Report 1997* (New York: Oxford University Press, 1997) and Renata Lok Dessallien, *Poverty, Module 1 - Poverty Indicators*, Technical Support Document (UNDP, SEDEP/BPPS, 1995).

assess and alleviate poverty. These include poverty lines, qualitative surveys on perceptions of poverty, public spending reviews and socioeconomic studies on the accessibility and availability of essential social services.

In most of the African countries where UNDP is supporting poverty studies or poverty profiles, people's perceptions of the dimensions of poverty are taken into account, beyond the construction of a poverty line and macroeconomic analyses. Following the exemplary initiative of Benin, the country offices in Burkina Faso, the Comoros, Guinea-Bissau, Lesotho, Mali, Namibia, Nigeria, South Africa, Zimbabwe and Zambia have fully integrated perceptive and qualitative aspects into their anti-poverty mechanisms.

This approach has also made it possible to standardize the definition of poverty. In Benin, the 1997 national human development report, themed on poverty, gives the following definition based on a human development approach: *"Poverty means that opportunities and choices most basic to human development are denied — to lead a long, healthy, creative life and to enjoy a decent standard of living, freedom, dignity, self-respect and the respect of others."*

At the country office in Nigeria, poverty is considered principally as a lack of capabilities in terms of income and fulfilment of basic needs. The 1996 national human development report indicates, *"By poverty is meant the inability to provide for physical subsistence to the extent of being incapable of protecting human dignity. These include food, clothing and shelter, potable water, health services, basic education, public transportation and work."*

In most African countries, approaches to poverty generally take into account UNDP's three main concerns: i) income poverty and economic growth; ii) fulfilment of basic needs; and iii) participation in decision-making. However, it would be optimal to standardize countries' viewpoints to reach a homogeneous, operational definition of poverty that would explicitly integrate these three essential aspects of the concept of human poverty. As expressed by UNDP Administrator James Gustave Speth in the foreword to the *Human Development Report 1997*, *"Poverty has many faces. It is much more than low income. It also reflects poor health and education, deprivation in knowledge and communication, inability to exercise human and political rights and the absence of dignity, confidence and self-respect."* [1]

UNDP's efforts to reach a comprehensive concept of poverty have gradually been recognized and the following consensual definition has emerged: poverty is a state of deprivation or denial of the basic choices and opportunities needed to enjoy a decent standard of living, to live a long, healthy, constructive life and to participate in employment and in the social, political and cultural life of the community.

---

1. UNDP, *Human Development Report 1997*, (New York: Oxford University Press, 1997).

Box 2.1.

Approaches to poverty in terms of sustainable capacity andlivelihood

The approach to poverty in terms of capacity focuses on possible conditions (potentialities) while distinguishing whenever possible, the choices that are available to a person but are deliberately neglected. For instance, a rich and healthy person who suffers from malnutrition due to excessive fasting must be distinguished from a person who is undernourished due to lack of means or to a parasitic disease. In practice, such a distinction is difficult to make when one deals with statistical aggregates (as opposed to detailed studies conducted at individual level), and the concrete application of the concept of capacity to the analysis of poverty has hitherto been based on unidimensional data. Likewise the World Human Development Report presents information essentially related to living standards and potentialities.

It would be desirable that the selection of particular aspects of existence as research basis for a study on poverty be debated in public. Indeed, such a choice is inevitably subjective. The criteria and balancing elements selected for the design of poverty indicators (such as human poverty indicator - or HPI) must be explicitly mentioned and clarified so that the public may assess all the ins and outs of the question. It is important that the criteria being used do not come from the elite or the authorities, but that they be determined through a democratic participatory process and even, if possible, that they be the outcome of that process. The promotion of this process is precisely one of the objectives aimed at by the World Reports on Human Development, and that also applies to poverty analysis.

Together with the notion of capacity, the approach by sustainable livelihood in the study of poverty is essential because it emphasizes specifically the need for the participation of the populations. In this approach, each community can define, with reference to its own environment, what it considers as criteria of well-being and key factors of misery. In this way, one highlights the concerns and anxieties of populations that are weakened and too often neglected by national statistics and by studies on poverty.

Source: World Human Development Report, 1997, UNDP, 1997.

---

2. Identifying and measuring poverty: poverty profiles

2.1. *From data collection to a poverty profile and an analysis of poverty*

The concept of human poverty should be used to identify and measure poverty in a country, region or community. There are various tools available for this. This stage in understanding the structure of poverty is an essential pre-requisite for designing an effective poverty reduction strategy.

Generally, the first stage in an analysis of human poverty involves constructing a poverty profile. This analytical tool incorporates all the information gathered on poverty and the structure of poverty in a country and seeks to: i) define poverty in the country; ii) identify and locate poor people; and iii) describe the main manifestations of poverty.

Box 2.2.
Major questions to be addressed by a poverty profile:

- What is poverty in the specific context of the profile achieved?
  - Who are the poor?
  - Where do they live?
  - What are the main signs of poverty?
  - What data are available to help assess poverty?
  - What are the (relative or absolute) poverty thresholds?
  - How many persons live in poverty?
  - What is the depth and incidence of poverty?
  - What is the migratory status of the poor?
  - What are the major income sources of the poor?
  - What do the poor produce and sell?
  - What is the situation of employment, under-employment and unemployment?

- What is the composition of the consumption basket of the poor and non-poor?
  - What is the family or household structure of the poor and non-poor?
  - How are the essential needs of the poor and non-poor characterized?
  - What are the major demographic features of the population?
  - What are the levels of availability and accessibility to basic social services?
  - What level of access to credit do the poor have?
  - What level of access to natural resources do the poor have?
  - What environmental problems are the poor facing?
  - What strategies do the poor use to get out of poverty?

Source: Technical Support Document, "Poverty, module 2: From Data Collection to Poverty Assessments", UNDP/BPPS, 1996.

The poverty profile is later supplemented with various data, studies and analyses to reach a comprehensive understanding of poverty. These include: i) an analysis of the general policy framework of the country from the angle of poverty reduction (public spending review, macroeconomic analysis, etc.); ii) a study of the institutional framework; and iii) a final analysis from a sustainable human development perspective to identify the causes of poverty. This comprehensive understanding of poverty in the country will provide a basis for designing a national poverty reduction strategy.

2.2. Objectives and stages of a poverty profile

Poverty profiles are often limited to the calculation of an income-based poverty line and related comments. However, the information provided by these poverty lines is insufficient to cover the many issues that contributed to human poverty.

The objective of a poverty profile is provide as complete a picture as possible of the phenomenon of poverty and the associated problems in a country or region. The profile analyses specific data to identify, locate, measure and describe poverty. It offers a better way to determine the structure of poverty in a country and the main beneficiaries of a poverty alleviation policy.

The construction of a poverty profile requires extensive information gathering, a data collection methodology and analysis based on quantitative and qualitative assessments. [1] The main stages in constructing a poverty profile are:

1. formulating a clear, consistent, operational definition of the concept of poverty within the specific framework of a country of a region;

2. collecting specific quantitative and qualitative data and identifying useful data;

3. setting a poverty line;

4. analyzing the perceptive and socioeconomic data on poverty;

5. constructing a poverty profile.

The analyses and results of the profile will then be used to reach a comprehensive understanding of poverty that will identify its causes and serve as a basis for the design of a national poverty reduction strategy.

From an operational perspective, this section will describe the stages of constructing a profile, from poverty lines and the data and surveys used to produce them to a comprehensive understanding of poverty.

2.3. Calculation of a poverty line

2.3.1. Objectives of a poverty line

Poverty profiles have often been considered synonymous with poverty lines, when poverty lines are in fact only one component of poverty profiles. This confusion stems from the World Bank's use of the term "poverty profile" to refer to the calculation of poverty lines. Unlike the World Bank, which considers poverty lines to be the most effective way to identify and measure poverty, UNDP views poverty lines chiefly as an instrument for identifying and measuring income poverty. It is important to be aware of

---

1. Renata Lok Dessallien, *Poverty, Module 2 - From Data Collection to Poverty Assessments*, Technical Support Document (UNDP, BPPS, 1996).

the limits of poverty lines for measuring human poverty: they do not analyze the aspects of poverty related to a lack of capabilities or access to essential social services.

Poverty lines are useful comparative tools for defining the incidence of poverty and the distribution of poverty across different social groups depending on region of residence, socioeconomic category, job status of the head of the household, etc. Based on household income or consumption, poverty lines quantify absolute poverty in monetary terms and characterize households in terms of their monetary income and consumption, particularly of food.

2.3.2. Role of quantitative surveys in the calculation of poverty lines

The calculation of a poverty line starts with quantitative household surveys. Despite intense debate in academic and development circles on the implementation of more manageable sampling methods to estimate the incidence of poverty in a country, there is still no data, methodology or study capable of replacing household surveys to measure and identify income poverty. Household surveys are thus one of the main sources of information on poverty. They use probability and sampling methods with statistical extrapolations and estimates on the reliability of the data.

The main household surveys used to set poverty lines in Sub-Saharan Africa are: living standards measurement study (LSMS) surveys, budget/consumption surveys, priority surveys and rapid participatory appraisals. A detailed analysis of the content, method and results of these surveys is proposed in the annex on poverty profiles.

Most of the poverty lines in Sub-Saharan Africa were calculated on the basis of one of these types of survey, which mainly offer an insight into income poverty. In addition to poverty lines, these surveys provide data and analysis for the third component of poverty profiles — the selection and analysis of socioeconomic indicators that will contribute to a better understanding of the structure and manifestations of poverty.

It is worth mentioning the cost of the surveys used to calculate poverty lines. A poverty line calculated on the basis of a budget/consumption survey costs around $1 million. It is therefore important to undertake a cost-benefit analysis of such an exercise before embarking on such expenditure. Priority surveys on household living standards, which are only sample poll, cost at least $300,000, and must be repeated regularly to ensure the validity of the results.

Table 2.1. – Objectives, cost and qualitative appraisal of various quantitative surveys

Types of studies	Countries	Objectives in a poverty profile	Strengths	Weaknesses	Duration	Cost
LSMS and Budget/consumption surveys	Botswana, Comoros, Cap Verde, Guinea, Guinea Bissau, Kenya, Lesotho, Uganda, Togo, Zimbabwe	– Establishing the poverty threshold – Creation of socio-economic data and indicators	– Data are rich and reliable – High credibility in decision-makers – Multiple possibility of analysis	– High cost in staff and money – Long to achieve – Not very flexible – Little national ownership	4 to 20 months	US$ 700 000 to 1 million
Priority surveys	Burkina Faso, Guinea, Mauritania, Niger, Senegal, Gambia	Same as above	– Low cost and poor flexibility – Multiple use	– Sampling errors – One passage survey No analysis of causes – Limited monetary poverty and access to social services	7 to 10 months	US$ 300 to 400 000
RASP	Cameroon, Madagascar, Mali, Côte -d'Ivoire	– Socio-economic data – Not completely adapted to the design of poverty thresholds	– Flexibility and weakness of costs. – Focused on poverty	– Limited to urban areas – Limited to monetary poverty and employment	6 to 8 months	US$250 to 350 000

2.3.3. Setting a poverty line

The criterion most commonly used to categorize people or households is food and non-food expenditure per adult equivalent. A cut-off line is established on the basis of consumption levels to distinguish between "poor" and "non-poor" households.

Box 2.3
The comparative value of absolute and relative methodologies

An absolute poverty line is sometimes considered to be a strict "survival" poverty line. In fact, this definition is too narrow to be of much use. Instead, an absolute poverty line should be seen as capturing a fundamental characteristic of poverty — its comparative nature. An absolute poverty line should be a constant line in terms of living standard and it should be the same across the whole area within which the comparisons of poverty are made. A relative poverty line, on the other hand, varies across an area and increases with average living standards. Comparisons of absolute poverty will class two people with the same standard of living in the same category — "poor" or "non-poor" — regardless of the time or place considered or of whether public action has been taken or not within the area investigated. Comparisons of absolute poverty are therefore "consistent", in the sense that individuals that are similar in all respects are treated in the same way.

The fact that many analyses do not recognize that comparisons of poverty are specific to an area can be a source of confusion. For example, when we seek to compare absolute poverty based on consumption everywhere in the world, there are convincing arguments for using the same level of real consumption as a poverty line for all countries.

This poverty line will probably be low for a rich country judged by its own standards, but the area for these comparisons of poverty extends beyond national borders. If, however, we try to establish a poverty profile for one country, the absolute poverty line set should be appropriate for that country. To determine what constitutes a reasonable absolute poverty line, we need to start by specifying the area to which it applies and recognizing that this poverty line can change if the area changes.

The attraction of having consistent comparisons within an area depends on the objective of these comparisons. If they are intended to determine allocation of resources to poor regions or countries, then they should be consistent. For example, the proportion of the population considered to be poor according to national estimates in the United States and Indonesia is roughly the same (around 15% around 1990). Such relative comparisons should not be used as a guide to aid allocation (and, fortunately, have never been). By whatever measure, there is little doubt that the incidence of consumption poverty is higher in Indonesia. If, however, we want to determine which country has the highest incidence of poverty, on the basis of criteria specific to that country, such estimates can be useful.

Source: M. Ravallion, "La mesure de la pauvreté", *Problèmes économiques*, n°2508, 1997.

Box 2.4.

Poverty threshold in Ghana

The poverty profile in Ghana is based on the results of a survey on LSMS type households initiated by the World Bank and conducted by the Ghanaian Statistics Office in 1987-1988.

On the basis of this data, the poverty threshold was determined at 2/3 of the average expenditure per capita. This line makes it possible to realize that 36% of Ghanaians live in what is considered as poverty, i.e., their expenditure does not exceed 2/3 of the average expenditure per capita. On the other hand, a line of extreme poverty what drawn at the level of 1/3 of the average expenditure per capita. Generally, consumption surveys and poverty profile have revealed that 69% of the expenditure of the poor and 66% of the expenditure of the non-poor are related to food consumption.

Source: A poverty Profile for Ghana, 1987-88, World Bank, 1990.

For the various types of poverty line set and used by no fewer than 35 Sub-Saharan African countries, an initial distinction can be made between relative and absolute poverty lines. Absolute poverty lines can further be divided into those used for international comparisons and internal poverty lines, and into those based exclusively on food expenditure and those that take into account all household food and non-food expenditure. [1]

Relative poverty lines are not as common and seem less relevant for assessing poverty in Sub-Saharan Africa. [2] In general, budget/consumption or priority surveys of average annual expenditure per adult are used to calculate a population distribution divided into five quintiles, with each quintile representing 20% of the population. The first quintile represents the 20% of the population with the lowest consumption and the fifth quintile the 20% with the highest consumption. The relative poverty line is usually set at the upper limit of the second quintile, arbitrarily classing as poor the 40% of the population with the lowest consumption.

The World Bank calculates another relative poverty line with a view to creating internationally standard indicators for international comparisons. This is a monetary value corresponding to two-thirds of the average consumption expenditure of all households.

---

1. See Annex 1 for a more detailed definition of relative and absolute methodologies.

2. On poverty lines, see S. Larivière & F. Martin, *Le cadre d'analyse économique de la pauvreté et des conditions de vie des ménages* (Québec, 1997); M. Ravallion, "Pauvreté et exclusion, la mesure de la pauvreté," *Problèmes économiques*, n°2508, 1997; World Bank, *Poverty Reduction Handbook*, 2nd ed (Washington, 1993); UNDP, *Human Development Report 1997* (New York: Oxford University Press, 1997).

Most of the countries that have benefited from the support of the World Bank in constructing poverty profiles have calculated relative poverty lines, usually in addition to absolute poverty lines. This is the case for Burkina Faso, Botswana, Cameroon, Cape Verde, the Comoros, Ethiopia, Gambia, Ghana, Guinea-Bissau, Lesotho, Nigeria, Rwanda, Senegal, South Africa, Uganda, Zambia and Zimbabwe. A combination of both methods, i.e. a cut-off at the last two quintiles and at two-thirds of average consumption expenditure, is generally used.

Box 2.5.

Relative poverty threshold in Comoros

On the basis of the 1995 priority survey on household consumption, various studies on poverty have revealed the multiplicity of the meaning given to this concept. The relative approach to poverty has made it possible to determine the significant percentages of poverty. The Comoros being composed of islands, it is the relative approach that is more adapted for measuring the significance of poverty in the various islands and environments. In this way, the distribution of per capita consumption was divided into classes of same strength ranging from the poorest to the richest through a quintile based distribution, giving five classes of 20% each of all the households. This procedure makes it possible to understand behavioral changes when one moves from the poorest to the richest.

Distribution of per capita consumption into classes of same strength (in Comorian Francs)

	Average consumption
Class 1 (poorest)	51.198
Class 2 (poor)	101.178
Class 3 (average income)	153.105
Class 4 (rich)	204.557
Class 5 (richest)	337.800

The majority of the poor and extremely poor households live in the rural areas. Average per capita consumption is CF 171,000 whereas it estimated at CF 190,000 in the urban areas. But the three islands of the Federation are diversely affected by this phenomenon. In the Big Comoro Island, per capita consumption amounts to CF 219,400 whereas in Moheli it amounts to CF 180,300 and CF 155,500 at Anjouan. The study of the distribution of the population through the five consumption classes confirms this situation in each of the islands.

Source: A.M. Sinane, "Poverty and Growth, the case of a small island economy: Comoros", 1997.

A combination of relative and absolute methods has often been used. This is the case in Zambia, where, in 1995, a poverty profile constructed with the support of the World Bank applied both absolute and relative methods to data from a priority survey on household income carried out in 1991. A relative poverty line was set at 70% of average expenditure per adult equivalent and a severe poverty line was set at 50% of the population. In addition, an absolute poverty line and an absolute extreme poverty line were calculated on the basis of average food consumption per adult equivalent. According to these two indicators, 69% of the population lives below the absolute poverty line and 55% are ultra poor.

The poverty lines used in Sub-Saharan Africa to identify, measure and define poverty have mainly been *absolute poverty lines*, which seem to be a more operational tool for understanding the phenomenon of poverty.

Absolute poverty lines can also be calculated for international comparisons. Most commonly, this is the poverty line set by the World Bank at $1 (1985 PPP$) per person per day. For various reasons, Guinea, Mauritania, Sierra Leone and Tanzania are among the countries that have used this method to calculate poverty lines.

Absolute poverty lines can also be set as a nutritional measure of poverty and can be based on the cost of basic needs, food energy intake or the share of food in consumption. [1]

Box 2.6.
Poverty profile in Mauritania

The poverty profile in Mauritania was determined on the basis of surveys on household living standards conducted in 1989-1990. Poverty was assessed on the basis of average per capita expenditure, in constant prices of 1988 deflated by a regional life cost index. Furthermore, two poverty lines were defined in reference to the world poverty thresholds proposed by the World Bank respectively 370 dollars and 275 dollars, in constant prices of 1985. Thus, in local currency these two thresholds, which are supposed to represent poverty and extreme poverty, are set respectively at MU 32,800 and 24,400 per capita and per year. The World Bank average was retained because of the difficulty to find a national consensus on a consumption basket. Finally, the aggregation of poverty was achieved in relation to the measurement of poverty incidence (proportion of households below the poverty line) and the depth or seriousness of poverty: the average gap between per capita expenditure and the poverty line expressed in percentage.

---

1. On poverty lines, see Annex 1.

Elements of poverty profile in Mauritania, 1989-1990:
incidence, depth and inequality of poverty in households according to
geographic zones and socio-economic groups

Parameter	Average per capita and per year expenditure in MU	Poverty threshold Poverty line = 24 200 MU			Poverty line = 32 800 MU		
Geographic zones							
Nouakchott	47 585	25.1	14.5	7.4	36.1	16.5	13.2
Zones divided into plots	57 582	11.1	–	3.0	20.8	–	6.1
Zones not divided into plots	36 749	37.4	–	11.3	49.6	–	19.5
Other cities	45 510	31.1	12.8	11.3	44.5	14.5	17.9
Privileged zones	69 330	7.7	–	1.0	12.2	–	3.2
Unprivileged zones	34 474	41.9	–	16.0	59.4	–	24.7
Rural River area	24 589	60.6	18.2	29.2	73.8	17.5	39.2
Other area	28 619	57.9	54.8	30.0	69.3	51.8	38.7
East	25 892	65.1	–	33.6	75.3	–	43.0
Center	31 977	49.1	–	25.5	62.0	–	33.4
Whole urban	49 700	27.7	(27.3)	9.0	39.7	(21.0)	15.2
Whole rural	27 531	58.7	(73.0)	29.8	70.5	(69.3)	38.8
Whole country	36 160	44.7	100.0	20.4	56.6	100.0	28.2
Socio-economic group							
Independent farmer	25 031	62.8	47.0	32.9	74.4	43.9	42.0
Independent non-farmer	44 864	27.6	10.9	9.2	42.3	13.2	16.1
Public wage-earner	47 567	29.7	11.7	11.9	39.4	12.3	17.5
Private wage-earner	39 582	43.1	10.3	15.8	56.2	10.5	24.4
Unemployed	33 903	43.5	9.1	18.1	55.8	9.2	26.1
Inactive	36 948	42.3	10.1	19.2	53.3	10.1	26.6
Head of household							
Men	36 217	46.7	–	21.2	58.2	72.3	29.3
Women	35 984	38.7	–	18.1	51.8	27.7	25.0

Sources: Report on Sustainable Human Development in Mauritania, 1996, UNDP, 1996.

Many Sub-Saharan African countries have set absolute poverty lines on the basis of data on food or non-food consumption or expenditure. This is the case for Benin, Burkina Faso, Cameroon, Côte d'Ivoire, Ethiopia, Gambia, Guinea, Kenya, Madagascar, Malawi, Mali, Namibia, Niger, Senegal, the Seychelles, Togo, Uganda, Zambia and Zimbabwe.

Box 2.7.
Establishing the poverty threshold in Zambia

The absolute poverty line in Zambia was obtained from two very close surveys: i) a 1991 study of the Price and Income Commission and ii) the 1991 Priority survey. The method used is based on the cost of a basket of goods that is required for reaching a certain level of feeding. This level of feeding was calculated on the basis of recommendations made by the WHO and by the Central Statistical Office of Zambia. On the basis of that food basket, a poverty line was drawn at 1380 Kwacha per adult per month. The cost of the food basket was calculated at 962 Kwacha per adult per month. The K 1380 line was thus obtained by dividing the food cost, i.e., K 962 (which is considered as the extreme poverty line) by 70 percent, which is considered as the average percentage of household food expenditure. Persons above K 1380 per month are then considered as non-poor. The persons between K 1380 and K 962 are considered as poor and those below K 962 are considered as extremely poor.

Based on these data, poverty in Zambia is very high. In 1991, 69% of Zambians belonged to households considered as poor, that is, unable to cater for its basic food needs and others basic needs. Furthermore, 55% of the inhabitants were below the extreme poverty line, a line that relates only to basic food needs.

Source: Zambia Poverty Assessment, World Bank, 1994.

Once a poverty line has been set, a whole series of indicators are calculated from it to give an accurate measure of poverty and to identify the poor. [1] The main indicators are: i) the rate or incidence of poverty, which shows the percentage of people living below the poverty line; ii) the depth of poverty, which calculates the average distance below the poverty line; and iii) the severity of poverty. A more detailed analysis of these indicators is provided in Annex 1.

---

1. Our aim here is not to describe the methodology used to calculate these indicators, but to give a brief overview.

Box 2.8.

Poverty threshold in Mali

Three approaches were used to assess the poverty threshold in Mali. The results vary a lot depending on the method used. However, all these studies highlight a great magnitude of poverty in the country.

• The first method used is based on the valorization of the level of food consumption of 2 450 calories per day. It made it possible to establish a poverty threshold of CFA F 137 000 and an extreme poverty threshold of CFA F 77 000 in 1989. This threshold indicates a poverty incidence of 73% in 1989 and of 91% in 1994 [1].

• The second method is based on the average per capita expenditure and sets the poverty line considering that the poor represent 40% of the popula-

tion whose expenditure is less high and that the very poor represent 15% of that population. This gave a poverty threshold of CFA Francs 89 170 and an extreme poverty threshold of CFA Francs 53 780 in 1989. The updating of these thresholds in 1994 raised them to CFA F 104 791 and CFA F 63 201.

• The third method used is based on the valorization of the consumption of 2 450 calories per day in "rice" equivalent. It makes it possible to calculate the annual expenditure in rice equivalent below which the individuals are unable to cater for their vital needs. On the basis of this method, the overall poverty threshold was estimated at CFA F 77 204 in 1994 and the extreme poverty threshold at CFA F39 500.

Source: "National Poverty Alleviation Strategy", Republic of Mali, 1998

2.3.4. Main results of poverty lines

Given the different concepts of poverty and the diverse methods used to calculate poverty lines, these measures have little comparative value on the scale of the region as a whole. Whether in relation to the incidence, the depth or the severity of poverty, the data collected in the different countries do not really make it possible to paint a valid quantitative picture of the structure of poverty in Sub-Saharan Africa. Indeed, it would be useless to try to compare relative and absolute poverty lines or poverty lines based on average expenditure and those based on average calorie intake.

---

1. This incidence is obtained by updating the 1989 data considering an 18% price increase rate during that period.

Box 2.9.
Poverty measurement indicators in Burkina Faso

The study of the poverty profile is based on data of the priority survey on household living standards conducted in 1994/1995 on 8 642 households distributed throughout the national territory divided into 8 strata (including 2 urban and 6 rural ones). This study made it possible to establish an absolute poverty threshold on the basis of which the scope (number of persons below the threshold), the depth (per capita average cost of total eradication of poverty) and the seriousness of poverty were measured.

On the basis of a daily adult food calorie need, estimated at 2283 calories and on the basis of the household expenditure structure (food and non-food), the national absolute poverty threshold in Burkina Faso was established at CFA F 41,099 per adult per year. Thus 44.5% of Burkinabè live below this national threshold. The national poverty depth, that is, the per

capita average cost of total eradication of poverty is then CFA F 5,753, or, 14% of the amount of the absolute threshold. But this amount varies according to the area of residence, the socio-economic group of the household leader and the type of household.

After considering the incidence and the depth, the analysis by socio-economic group (S.E.G.) of the depth makes it possible to state that poverty in Burkina Faso is essentially acute among farmers with a particularly alarming situation for food crop farmers. Indeed when one takes poverty aversion into consideration, it appears that poverty is particularly severe among the food crop farmers (0.07 "severity" index), the inactive and the unemployed (0.068) and among cash crop farmers (0.056). This severity is rather low among craftsmen and traders (0.012 "severity" index) and almost nil among wage-earners of the civil service (0.001).

Source: Poverty Profile in Burkina, INSD, Burkina Faso, 1996.

Data on the incidence of poverty, for example, vary widely. According to consumption-based poverty lines calculated from budget/consumption or priority surveys, poor people were estimated to make up 72% of the total population in Togo in 1995, 69% in Zambia in 1991, 68% in Mali, Sierra Leone and Uganda, 66% in Namibia, 64% in Botswana and 63% in Niger. In contrast, absolute poverty is estimated at 13%-15% in Benin and 30% in Cape Verde.

The average incidence of poverty in Sub-Saharan Africa seems to range from 30% to 50%, with extremes of 13% and 72% (see Table 1). This gives an idea of the difficulty of comparing these data. In Namibia, an intermediate country with an average level of human development, 66% of the population is estimated to be poor, while in Benin, ranked as one of the least developed countries with a low human development index, less than 20% of the population is considered poor.

However, an analysis of the different profiles does point up several major recurring characteristics of poverty in Sub-Saharan Africa. For example, there is a high prevalence of poverty in Sub-Saharan Africa, where an average 40% to 50% of the population lives in absolute poverty and 20% to 30% in extreme poverty.

In terms of the spatial distribution of poverty, most of the national poverty lines show it as predominantly rural, affecting subsistence farmers in particular. Women are also disproportionately poor. But the determining factor lies in the high incidence of extreme poverty: between a quarter and a third of the population of Sub-Saharan Africa cannot even meet its basic food requirements.

Countries in crisis are a special case. To begin with, poverty profiles for countries in crisis are unavailable, because poverty reduction is not among these countries' immediate priorities. When profiles do exist, as in Rwanda and Sierra Leone, they are out-of date and no longer apply in the situation of crisis or conflict.

While poverty lines have the advantage of clearly identifying poverty, they are nevertheless incomplete. They do not reflect local people's perceptions and pay little attention to national concepts of poverty or human poverty. They assess only income poverty, without considering the qualitative, human or social aspects of poverty. Also, poverty lines do not analyze the causes of poverty, an essential pre-requisite for designing national poverty reduction strategies.

Table 2.2. – Types of major poverty thresholds in Africa South of the Sahara

Country	Poverty threshold [a]
1. South Africa	Budget/consumption survey, 1993: – absolute poverty threshold: 53% – extreme poverty threshold: 29%
2. Bénin i) ii)	1986/87 survey, – poverty threshold: 15% (based on food consumption + non food consumption) 1996 survey, food poverty threshold: – rural: 16.3% – urban: 29.9% – together: 13.5% Overall poverty threshold (food + non food): – rural: 33.5% – urban: 33.1% – together: 33.7%
3. Botswana	Budget/consumption survey, 1985/86, absolute poverty threshold: 64%

Table 2.2. –   Types of major poverty thresholds in Africa South
of the Sahara *(suite)*

Country	Poverty threshold [a]
4. Burkina i) **Faso** ii)	Based on the priority survey on household living conditions, 1994: – absolute poverty threshold (food expenditure in terms of calories + other expenditure) = 47% – extreme poverty threshold food expenditure and minimum of other expenditure): 30% Based on the results of the same survey: – urban poverty threshold (food expenditure a + essential social ser- vices): 25%
5. Cameroon	Poverty survey, 83/84, – absolute poverty threshold: 49% (equal or less than 40% of average consumption per capita) – extreme poverty threshold: 26% (below 40% of consumption average)
6. Cap Verde	Based on the budget/consumption survey: – poverty threshold = 30% (2/3 of annual average consumption per capita) – extreme poverty threshold: 14%
7. Comoros	Household consumption survey, 95: – relative poverty threshold: 40% (quintiles 1and 2: related to con- sumption) – extreme poverty threshold: 20% (last quintile)
8. Côte d'Ivoire	Survey on standard of living, 85, poverty line related to food consump- tion: – urban poverty: 5.2%
9. Ethiopia	Poverty survey, 1993: – urban absolute poverty threshold: 60%; (based on a basket of minimal consumption of essential needs) – rural poverty threshold: 52% (based on vulnerability and general pov- erty)
10. Gambia	Poverty survey, 1991: – absolute poverty threshold: 40% (based on expenditure required for a minimum of calories) – "general" poverty threshold: 60% (adjusted with non food)
11. Ghana	Poverty survey, 87/88: – relative poverty threshold: 35.9% (set at 2/3 of expenditure average)
12. Guinea i) ii)	Urban budget/consumption survey, 1992: – urban poverty threshold: 48% (based on minimal food and non food expenditure) Survey on household living conditions, 94/95: – absolute poverty threshold: 300$/pers/year: 40,3% – extreme poverty threshold: 176$/pers/year: 13%

Table 2.2. –   Types of major poverty thresholds in Africa South
of the Sahara *(suite)*

Country	Poverty threshold [a]
13. Guinea Bissau	Household consumption survey, 91: – poverty threshold: 49% (consumption/pers at 2/3 of average) – extreme poverty threshold: 26% (1/3 of average) – poverty threshold, ASDI 1996: 60% poor including 75% in rural areas
14. Kenya	Priority survey on households, 95: – absolute poverty threshold: 46% – rural: 90% – urban: 10%
15. Lesotho i) ii)	Budget/consumption survey, 93: – relative poverty threshold: 49% (50% of consumption average) – extreme threshold of relative poverty: 25% (25% of average consumption) Census data, 96: – rural poverty: 59% (ultra: 29%) – urban poverty: 28% (ultra: 12%)
16. Madagascar	Employment and poverty survey, 1992 Urban poverty line 34% poverty based on household consumption
17. Malawi	Budget/consumption survey, 88/89: – absolute poverty threshold: 55% (based on food expenditure) – extreme poverty threshold: 20%
18. Mali i) ii)	Budget/consumption survey, 88/89: – absolute poverty threshold: 40% (based on calorie consumption) – extremely poor: 15% of the poorest Poverty survey, 1996: – absolute poverty threshold: 68,8% (based on calorie consumption "rice equivalent"
19. Mauritania	Survey on household living conditions, 89/90: – poverty threshold of $ 370/year = 57% – extreme poverty threshold of $ 275/year = 44% (no consensus on a consumption basket).
20. Namibia i) ii)	Poverty survey, 1991: – absolute poverty threshold: 66% based on household subsistence level in terms of food, clothes, energy) Budget/consumption survey, 1994: – poverty threshold: 50% (Income less than $130 per household) – extreme poverty threshold: 22%
21. Niger	Household consumption survey, 1994: – absolute poverty threshold: 63% urban: 48% rural: 66% – extreme poverty threshold: 34% urban: 18% rural: 36%

Table 2.2. – Types of major poverty thresholds in Africa South
of the Sahara *(suite)*

Country	Poverty threshold [a]
22. Nigeria i) ii)	Consumption survey, 1991: – poverty threshold: 45% (expenditure per capita per year) Poverty survey, 1995: – relative poverty threshold: 40% (2/3 of household expenditure)
23. Uganda	Budget/consumption survey, 89/90: – relative poverty threshold: 70% (expenditure at 70% of households) – absolute poverty threshold: 68% (food expenditure at 70% of the average) – extreme poverty threshold: 54%
24. Rwanda	Relative poverty threshold: 40% (40% lowest expenditure of a sample in terms of expenditure per capita)
25. Senegal	Priority survey on household living conditions, 1992: – absolute poverty threshold: 33% (base on a 2400 calorie intake equiv./adult) – relative poverty threshold: 53% (expenditure at 2/3 of average) – extreme poverty threshold: 26% (expenditure at 1/3 of average) – threshold of US $ 1/day: 61%.
26. Seychelles	Budget/consumption survey, 1984: – absolute poverty threshold: 30% (based on cost of food/transport/clothing)
27. Sierra Leone	Survey on household living conditions, 89/90 – poverty threshold of $ 1 per day: 68%
28. Tanzania	Poverty survey, 1993, – poverty threshold of $ 1 per day: 27 at 49% (based on different estimates)
29. Togo	Budget/consumption survey in 90 and 95: – poverty threshold: 72% (based on consumption) – extreme poverty threshold: 57%
30. Zambia	Priority survey on household living conditions – relative poverty threshold: 70% of population in terms of expenditure – severe relative poverty threshold: 50% of population in terms of expenditure – absolute poverty threshold: 69% (based on food expenditure) – severe poverty threshold, below food expenditure: 55%
31. Zimbabwe	Budget/consumption survey: – absolute poverty threshold of 25% (based on expenditure and implication of essential needs)

a. This table is based on the poverty profiles of the various countries listed, on national SHD reports or on summaries on poverty sent to UNDP.

Therefore, other tools need to be used alongside poverty lines to measure the phenomenon of poverty. The scope of poverty lines, limited to an absolute and mainly monetary assessment, does not cover all the dimensions of poverty. It is therefore important to conduct qualitative or participatory appraisals to supplement and refine the poverty profiles, in which the calculation of poverty lines and related indicators were only a first stage.

2.4. Qualitative appraisals of poverty

2.4.1. Objectives of qualitative or participatory appraisals

The weakness of the methods used to calculate poverty lines highlights the need to conduct participatory appraisals. Knowledge of people's perceptions of poverty and non-monetary aspects of poverty — i.e. denial of basic needs and deprivation of capabilities — is essential to an understanding of human poverty. This is why UNDP has supported, almost everywhere in Africa, initiatives to conduct qualitative surveys based on participatory methods to better grasp local perceptions and human aspects of poverty.

Box 2.10.

Method of diagnosing benefits in the health sector in Lesotho

An in-depth qualitative analysis of individual and household health related behavior was conducted. Participant observers were sent to study three communities for two months.

They found that the villagers did not use the services of the government health worker because there was no curative medicine and general treatment of patients was poor. An unsteady supply of contraceptives deterred women from making the long trek to the clinics. Fees were seen as too high by the poor, and considered too low by the well-off.

The direct impact of the survey method was: village health workers were supplied with aspirin and simple remedies, contraceptive supplies were improved and user fees were adjusted according to ability to pay.

Source: Method and Tools for Social Assessment and Participation, World Bank, 1995.

The results of surveys on the perceptions of poverty are not only a way of identifying, measuring and diagnosing poverty. They are also useful for the implementation, monitoring and evaluation of poverty reduction programs and for basic capacity-building.

2.4.2. Contribution of qualitative surveys to the construction of poverty profiles

Qualitative data, like quantitative data, is collected and analyzed through specific surveys. [1] The main qualitative methods used for poverty profiles are intensive sociological and anthropological methods, beneficiary assessment and rapid participatory appraisal (RPA). A more detailed analysis of these qualitative and participatory surveys is provided in Annex 1.

Since a qualitative understanding of poverty is a recent concern, these surveys have been rarely used to date, with the exception of RPA, which has been used in around 15 Sub-Saharan African countries, including Botswana, Burkina Faso, Chad, Ethiopia, Kenya, Lesotho, Mali, Nigeria, Senegal, Uganda, Zambia and Zimbabwe.

The inherent weaknesses of these methods — i.e. low validity of the sample, low quantification of results, impracticability and lack of standardization — has led to the introduction of a new method to remedy these deficiencies. Participatory appraisals are of little use if the results are not validated or are not complementary to quantitative studies.

A specific method of poverty analysis needs to be designed that is complementary to poverty lines. Participatory poverty assessments encompassing people's perception of the dimensions of poverty in rural and urban areas seem to respond best to the objectives of a full profile of human poverty and offer an initial analysis of views of poverty through interviews with focus groups with a ranking of themes during the interviews, through multiple choice pictures representing the themes. [2]

---

1. On participatory methodologies, see Gilbert Aho, Sylvain Larivière et Frédéric Martin, *Manuel d'analyse de la pauvreté: applications au Bénin* (Université Laval, PNUD, 1997); J.M. Cohen and N. Uphoff, "Participation's Place in Rural Development: Seeking Clarity through Specificity," *World Development*, vol.8, 1980; S. Paugam, "Représentation et perception de la pauvreté," *Problèmes économiques*, n°2508, 1997; World Bank, *Methods and Tools for Social Assessment and Participation* (Washington, 1995); Renata Lok Dessallien, *Poverty, Module 2 - From Data Collection to Poverty Assessments*, Technical Support Document (UNDP, BPPS, 1996).

2. See Gilbert Aho, Sylvain Larivière et Frédéric Martin, *Manuel d'analyse de la pauvreté: applications au Bénin* (Université Laval, PNUD, 1997); UNDP, *Rapport National sur le Développement Humain au Bénin 1997*; République du Mali et PNUD, *Stratégie Nationale de lutte contre la pauvreté*, 1998.

Box 2.11.

Nigeria: A MARP survey reveals the need
for redefining government programs

A MARP survey conducted in 10 States of Nigeria in 1993-1994 revealed that the populations were aware of the government programs implemented in favor of local communities. The program involved boreholes and wells, the construction of primary health care centers and roads, the promotion of self-employment among the youth, the immunization of children and the promotion of micro-credit.

However, the participatory interviews revealed that these programs were facing many problems: many projects were abandoned, some activities were conducted with the aim of embezzling public funds, the traditional authorities were not involved in the projects, the Government had attempted to increase its credit by lending support to community projects when these were already completed. On the other hand, the populations were obliged to pay taxes without receiving services in return. The Government had made promises but did not respond to the requests of the communities and there is no indication that the activities will directly benefit the poor.

Therefore it is not surprising that the poor persons do not trust the government programs. The communities insist on the fact that they themselves should be the ones to be in charge of these projects while the Government should assume their responsibilities by providing funding, technical assistance and supervision. In many communities, local mutual aid organizations have largely developed in order to face the difficulties and crises; such organizations could play a more active role in poverty alleviation programs.

Source: "Methods and Tools for Social Assessment and Participation, World Bank, 1995.

The information on perceptions of well-being and poverty is collected according to a participatory methodology in representative rural areas and the largest towns of a country. They involve on average between 2,000 and 3,000 people, in urban and rural areas. Benin, Burkina Faso and Mali have undertaken qualitative studies of this type to supplement and refine their national poverty profiles.

At a cost of around $100,000 to $150,000, these studies offer an inexpensive way to supplement poverty lines with qualitative data and to better appreciate human aspects and people's perceptions of poverty.

The importance of a qualitative approach is clear, both for not limiting poverty assessment to monetary and absolute concepts and for reaching as accurate a definition as possible of human poverty. Perceptions of poverty and a participatory approach are central to the human poverty approach.

Box 2.12.

Benin: Perception of poverty by the populations

In Benin, qualitative studies on the perception of poverty dimensions in the rural areas (SPPR) and in the urban areas (SPPU) led to a first analysis of speeches on poverty using interviews with focus groups and effort to rank the themes dealt with during interviews helped by a multiple choice of images corresponding to the themes.

The information on the perception of well-being and poverty was collected in four rural areas representative of the rural environment (four agro-ecological zones according to a division by the Ministry of Rural Development) and in the four major cities of the country (Cotonou, Porto-Novo, Abomey-Bohicon and Parakou).

The methodology used to measure the perception that the Beninese populations have about well-being and poverty has two components: the setting up of "focus groups" and "weighed individual vote". The objective of the focus groups was to highlight the basic dimensions of well-being and poverty as perceived by the populations. For each focus group, homogeneous groups were set up on the basis of three criteria: age (the youth, the adults and the elderly), sex (male and female) and the geographic location of the village or the district of each region/city surveyed.

The "weighed individual vote" method aims at establishing for each individual an order of priority in the determinants of improved well-being by socio-economic category. To that effect a series of images representing of the focus groups were prepared by a team of community development specialists. This type of survey takes place

in the same way as a vote whereby the participant is urged individually and privately to choose by order of priority the images that are most likely to increase his/her level of well-being and to reduce his/her level of poverty.

The results of the focus groups show that in the rural areas the conventional essential needs such as feeding, health, clothing and housing ranked first among the essential dimensions that characterize absolute poverty. Other dimensions of poverty were considered as essential by the rural populations along with basic needs. These are employment and economic activities, children, religion, moral health, means of transport, roads and tracks.

Thus one can distinguish three major classes of dimensions. These are first the dimensions related to the non-satisfaction of basic need such as feeding, clothing, housing and health. The second group of dimensions refers to the major means that would help directly satisfy these needs, that is, money. One could associate to that dimension a minimum income that would help satisfy the basic needs in order to get out of poverty. Finally, a third class of dimensions refers to the way of getting that money. In this last category for instance one finds employment, market, credit, agricultural inputs and children. The high monetization of economic and social activity in the rural areas is such that poverty is intimately related to money making opportunities.

The interviews with the different populations revealed that there was practically no differences in perception between ethnic groups, age groups, type of economic activities and level of formal education. On the other hand, at the level of agro-ecological zones, there were differences in the degree of relative importance given to some dimensions. These differences are related to the natural conditions of each zone but also to the economic peculiarities and cultural specificity related to tradition and to the evolution of the exogenous economic domination.

In urban environment, in the four big cities that were surveyed, the first five dimensions of poverty were identical to the ones identified in the rural environment, the most important one always being feeding. Then came the dimensions that are more or less important to the urban populations, namely wage-earning employment, education, environment/sanitation and culture (i.e., religion in this case). Just like in the rural environment, the poor looks for any employment but he/she prefers the "white people's employment". Work in the urban popular economy (informal sector) is not perceived as employment: "the trader, the tailor, the carpenter or the hairdresser" have occupations, not jobs; the "zemidjan" (motor-taxi driver) and the bush taxi driver, the shop assistant, the building site worker *have jobs*.

Based on the weighed vote, the dimensions which, according to the populations, were most likely to improve their well-being were identified. Depending on well-being improvement functions, one observes fundamental differences not only

between the rural and urban environments but also within the same environment (between the different agro-ecological zones, between the four big cities and sometimes between different socio-economic categories). Thus while in the rural environment dimensions such as "Means of transport", "Child", "Drinking Water" and "Clothing" were considered as most likely to improve the well-being of the populations, in the urban environment, on the other hand, it is dimensions such as "Health", "Road", "Employment/income" and "Credit" which are selected in priority.

Apart from the data related to these two studies, the perception of poverty may also be assessed through: (i) the analysis of common language that allows for the identification of the meaning of the words used and the construction of taxonomy for the poor on the one hand, and (ii) the phrases from the oral literature (proverbs and sayings, tales and songs), popular graphic art as well as cultural elements on the other hand.

In common language, in Yoruba and Fon for instance, there is a real taxonomy for the poor that shows that the different poor strata of the population do not necessarily share the same vision of poverty. Based on the meaning of the words recorded, poverty is very closely related to extreme inadequacy of material means and to deprivation, but also to misery and suffering, to difficulties in finding food. This perception of poverty is similar to the results of the SPPR and SPPU.

Source: National Report on Human Development in Benin, 1997, UNDP, 1997.

The majority of countries that have included a qualitative and participatory approach in their poverty profiles have done so with the support of UNDP. This is the case for Benin, Burkina Faso, Mali, Namibia, South Africa and Zimbabwe. The table below shows what people perceive to be the main dimensions of poverty.

It is interesting to note the choices and frequency of the themes expressed in countries with diverse situations. With the exception of Namibia, an intermediate country with an average HDI, the dimensions of poverty mentioned are similar across all the countries. The dimension of food appears in first position four times out of six, confirming the importance of the nutrition factor to an understanding of poverty in Sub-Saharan Africa, as already shown in the calculation of poverty lines. Employment appears five times, health four times and education three times.

Table 2.3. – Five major dimensions in the perception of poverty

Country	1st dimension	2nd dimension	3rd dimension	4th dimension	5th dimension
Benin	Food	Health	Clothing	Housing	Employment
Burkina Faso	Food	Health	Education	Employment	Water
Comoros	Education	Solidarity	Employment	Access to land	–
Lesotho	Food	Clothing	Employment	Agricultural equipment	Health
Mali	Food	Clothing	Health	Solidarity	Housing
Namibia	Employment	Agricultural equipment	Education	Social security	Income generating activities

While these qualitative surveys are not intended for comparisons on the scale of the region, they do confirm the relevance and validity of this type of analysis and action as a complement to quantitative surveys and analyses. Awareness of the way in which the people affected by poverty perceive the phenomenon contributes to the construction of definitive poverty profiles, by focusing on the most important dimensions of well-being and poverty, and to the design of effective poverty reduction strategies with the support and participation of the people concerned.

2.5. Construction of a poverty profile

2.5.1. Stages in the construction of a poverty profile

In addition to calculating a poverty line and conducting participatory appraisals, there is a need to ascertain the structure of poverty in a country, taking numerous other factors into account. It is only on the basis of these three components that a complete profile of poverty can be produced. The poverty profile must integrate all the relevant information on poverty if it is to answer the following questions adequately:

- What is poverty?
- Who are the poor?
- Where do poor people live?
- What are the main characteristics of poverty?

Figure 2.1. – Components of a poverty profile

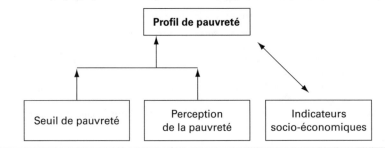

The *first stage* in the construction of a poverty profile is to formulate a national appraisal of poverty, which should be the subject of discussion and broad consensus in the country to ensure the validity of the data in the profile. This definition should take into account the various theoretical developments on the concept of poverty, the specific situation of the country and the concept of human poverty. The national definition of poverty will have to integrate a wide range of factors, including:

- theoretical approaches to poverty;
- people's perceptions of poverty and its causes;
- capacity-building, at the level of central government and grassroots communities;
- the overall environment of the country;
- the sustainable human development paradigm.

The second stage consists in setting a poverty line and identifying the main specific indicators of poverty.

The *third stage* involves conducting participatory surveys to ascertain the main dimensions of poverty and people's perceptions of well-being, poverty and the causes of poverty. The results of these surveys are then used to identify and analyze the main social, economic, environmental and governance-related indicators that will lead to a more comprehensive understanding of the phenomenon of poverty.

In the *fourth stage*, these data are used to construct a poverty profile that will serve as a basis for the *fifth and last stage*, a comprehensive understanding of poverty with a view to identifying its causes and preparing a national poverty reduction strategy.

2.5.2. Determining the main characteristics of poverty: choice and analysis of socioeconomic indicators

As a general rule, the socioeconomic indicators used should assess:
1. household income/consumption;
2. social services, including education, health, housing and nutrition;
3. governance;
4. capacity-building;
5. environment and natural resources;
6. gender.

Before analyzing the indicators chosen to enrich and complete the poverty profile, there is a need to identify the information and data available in the country and the various studies already undertaken that could contribute to the construction of the poverty profile. The surveys on household consumption (LSMS, budget/consumption surveys, priority surveys) mentioned previously can support the construction of indicators. Other types of survey, such as UNICEF's sentinel surveillance sites, can also be useful for these analyses and for establishing essential indicators. These surveys, which use a combination of quantitative and qualitative elements, can provide original data on the themes included in the poverty profile.

A poverty profile generally includes a characterization of poor people according to socioeconomic indicators. Many indicators can be used; the choice will depend on the objectives of anti-poverty action. Annex 1 lists the main themes to be considered, the most commonly used indicators for these themes and references to surveys and studies that can be used to establish these indicators. [1]

---

1. For more details, see Gilbert Aho, Sylvain Larivière et Frédéric Martin, *Manuel d'analyse de la pauvreté: applications au Bénin* (Université Laval, PNUD, 1997); United Nations Department of Technical Cooperation for Development, *Household Income and Expenditure Surveys: A Technical Study* (New York, 1989); UNICEF, *Monitoring Progress Toward the Goals of the World Summit for Children. A Practical Handbook for Multiple-Indicator Surveys*, 1995; Renata Lok Dessallien, *Poverty, Module 2 - From Data Collection to Poverty Assessments*, Technical Support Document (UNDP, BPPS, 1996).

Box 2.13.

An SSS survey in Liberia

In 1992 and 1993, in conditions of crises and conflicts, two cycles of SSS surveys were conducted in Monrovia. The objectives were relatively large, including areas such as health, education, water and sanitation as well as children's conditions under particularly difficult circumstances. The aim was to identify differences in terms of access to the different social services among the populations of Monrovia and those of the rest of the country during the civil war. The survey revealed that health services were more accessible in the country than in Mon-

rovia but that the rural health centers had less qualified health workers, probably due to differences in conceptual and methodological approaches with respect to the assistance given by the NGOs on the one hand and by emergency aid agencies on the other.

According to estimates, _ of children in Monrovia attended school against 50% in the rest of the country. When food became available in the schools enrolment doubled. Finally, the lack of money was considered as the main reason for not sending a child to school.

Source: Sentinel Site Surveys, UNICEF, March 1996.

Beyond thematic indicators, it is important to strive to achieve a better understanding of the concept of human poverty. The concepts, analysis and indicators developed around the sustainable human development paradigm are central to this. [1] At the heart of the concept of human development is the process of broadening people's opportunities and well-being. While the choices available to people are neither finite nor static, there are three essential human opportunities, regardless of a country's level of development: to live a long and healthy life, to have access to learning and knowledge and to have the resources needed to enjoy a decent standard of living. Human development does not stop there, however. Many people place great importance on other choices, ranging from political, economic and social freedoms to the right to be creative and productive, to enjoy self-respect and human rights.

Income is an important component of people's aspirations. But it is only one component, which is far from summarizing their entire lives. Income is a means to achieving human development. It is therefore important to consider the following indicators:
 – the Human Development Index (HDI),
 – the Human Poverty Index (HPI).

---

1. UNDP, *Human Development Report 1997* (New York: Oxford University Press, 1997).

Box 2.14.

Human Poverty Index - How helpful is it to decision-makers?

The human poverty index can be used in at least three ways.

1. As a tool for advocacy. If poverty is to be eradicated, public opinion and support needs to be mobilized to the cause. The HPI can help summarize the extent of poverty along several dimensions, the distance to go, the progress made. Income poverty also needs to be measured — but income alone is too narrow a measure.

2. As a planning tool to identifying areas of concentrated poverty within a country. The HDI has been used in many countries to rank districts or countries as a guide to identifying those most severely disadvantaged in terms of human development. Several countries, such as the Philippines, have used such analyses as a planning tool. The HPI can be used in a similar way, to identify those most seriously affected by human poverty. Though ranking by any one index alone would be possible — say, by illiteracy rate, lack of access to health services or the percentage in income poverty — the HPI makes possible a ranking in relation to a combination of basic deprivations, not one alone.

3. As a research tool. The HDI has been used especially when a researcher wants a composite measure of development. For such uses, other indicators have sometimes been added to the HDI. The HPI could be similarly used and enriched – especially if other measures of poverty and human deprivation were added, such as unemployment.

Although greeted with controversy when first launched in 1990, the HDI has found an increasing following as a simple measure of human development. The HDI provides an alternative to GNP, for assessing a country's standing in basic human development or its progress in human development overtime. It does not displace economic measures but can serve as a simple composite complement to other measures like GNP.

The HPI can similary serve as a useful complement to income measures of perverty. It will serve as a strong reminder that eradicating poverty will always require more than increasing the incomes of the poorest.

Further work is merited to explore how the HPI and the HDI could be enriched and made more robust in situations where a wider range of data on different aspects of poverty and human development are available.

What the HPI does not show. The HPI provides a measure of the incidence of human poverty in a country (or among some other group), say 25%. This means that judged by the HPI, an "average" of some 25% of the country's population is affected by the varous forms of human poverty or deficiency included in the measure, it is not possible to associate the incidence of human poverty with a specific group of people or number of people.

Source: World Human Development Report, 1997, UNDP, 1997.

An analysis of the indicators and data used to measure and identify poverty is thus the last phase in the construction of the poverty profile. The methodology used to date to construct profiles, generally with the support of the World Bank, should be extended to include the concept of human poverty. Poverty lines that mainly take into account income poverty and household consumption and indicators on household consumption and fulfilment of basic needs (food, water, health and education) do not cover the whole problem of poverty. Supplementing these tools with data on perceptions of poverty and the overall environment are an essential step towards a comprehensive understanding of the phenomenon of poverty.

In the countries where UNDP has supported the design of national poverty reduction strategies and been associated with identifying and measuring poverty, these complementary elements have always been taken into account. This has been done in Benin, Botswana, Burkina Faso, Guinea, Lesotho, Mali, Namibia, Niger and South Africa. It is to be hoped that other countries will follow this human poverty approach. In this respect, national human development reports on poverty are an effective instrument for moving beyond the narrow framework of income poverty to a comprehensive assessment of human poverty. The problem of poverty in Sub-Saharan Africa is an overall development problem that should be analyzed from the perspective of the sustainable human development paradigm.

3. A comprehensive approach to poverty

3.1. Introduction

As an excellent tool for identifying and measuring poverty, poverty profiles are a good way to begin approaching the structure of poverty. Based on the concept of human poverty, a poverty profile highlights aspects related to monetary poverty and fulfilment of basic needs. However, it does not encompass the dimensions of empowerment of the poor and their participation in decision-making.

The main purpose of reaching a comprehensive understanding of poverty is to identify the causes of poverty in order to design poverty reduction strategies and implement poverty alleviation programs. It is therefore essential to investigate the capacities of governments, civil society, NGOs and grass-roots communities to meet these challenges. A comprehensive understanding of poverty provides an operational frame of reference for the design of a poverty reduction strategy and the implementation of poverty alleviation programs.

3.2. A comprehensive approach to understanding poverty

A comprehensive understanding of poverty is an essential preliminary stage in the implementation of a national poverty reduction strategy. It includes identifying the causes of poverty and defining the institutional and social framework in which these strategies are to be designed. Unlike the World Bank, which limits its appreciation to identifying and measuring poverty, UNDP extends the frame of reference and the context of poverty reduction strategies. To reach a comprehensive understanding of poverty, countries need to enhance and further analyze their poverty profiles and public spending reviews from the perspective of sustainable human development.

To determine the multiple causes of poverty, a comprehensive understanding needs to include an analysis of:

1. national development policy from the angle of poverty reduction, and therefore of sustainable human development;

2. the institutional framework and capacity for implementing policy;

3. the capacity of poor people to help themselves and participate in decision-making;

4. the external environment and its impact on poverty.

The chart below illustrates the main stages and key information in the process of reaching a comprehensive understanding of poverty. This process does not require unwieldy and expensive studies and analyses, but rather consists in using relevant information from existing tools.

3.3. Analysis of national policy from the angle of poverty reduction

3.3.1. Objectives

Analyzing the national development policy framework in terms of poverty reduction is one of the foundations for a comprehensive understanding of poverty. The poverty profile and the analysis of policy form a homogeneous structure: they respond to each other, sustain each other and constantly interact with each other. [1]

The main objective of analyzing national policy from the angle of poverty reduction is to achieve a better understanding of the impact of policies, with a view to:

– promoting efficient, equitable economic growth;

– making social services more effective and more responsive to the needs of the poor;

---

1. See M. Hopkins, *A Short Review of Contemporary Thinking about Anti-Poverty Strategies* (Geneva, 1997); K. Subbarao, *Lessons of 30 Years of Fighting Poverty* (Quebec, 1997); Renata Lok Dessallien, *Poverty, Module 2 - From Data Collection to Poverty Assessments*, Technical Support Document (UNDP, BPPS, 1996).

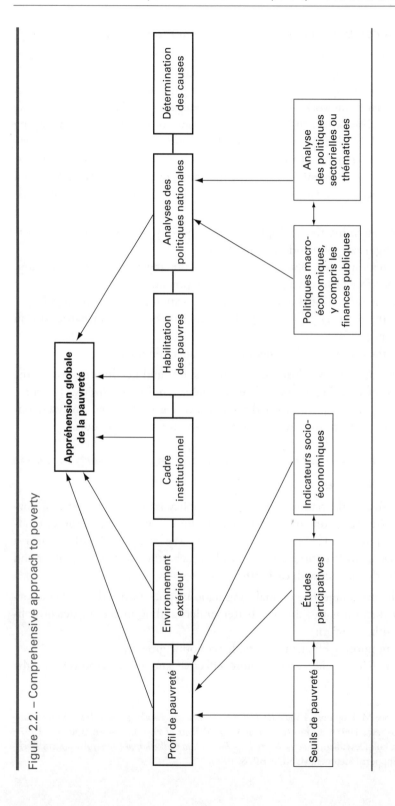

Figure 2.2. – Comprehensive approach to poverty

– giving the poor the opportunities to improve their living standards and well-being;

– integrating poverty into the design and implementation of policies.

Given the physical impossibility of analyzing and assessing every national development policy, some broad sectoral choices must be made. Hierarchies and priorities can be established on the basis of the main themes that emerged during the construction of the poverty profile. To reach a better understanding of poverty and respond effectively to it, the following areas for action should be examined, from the perspective of sustainable human development:

– macroeconomic framework,
– social services (education, health and safe drinking water),
– agriculture and infrastructure,
– employment,
– access to factors of production,
– capacity-building,
– environment and natural resources.

3.3.2. Macroeconomic framework and poverty

The macroeconomic analysis should consider the impact of the national macroeconomic framework and policies on poverty, the national development processes that include or exclude the poor and the choices made between economic growth and equity in line with the country's major development objectives. [1]

The impact of macroeconomic policies on poverty tends to be overlooked. Yet macroeconomic policies have a direct effect on the living standards of poor households, through the goods, services and capital markets. Regardless of the sector, poverty reduction strategies and programs are destined to failure if the macroeconomic environment is unfavorable. A project supporting the processing and marketing of agricultural products, for example, will not succeed in a highly inflationary environment, with prohibitive interest rates and a constantly depreciating national currency. [2]

It is important not to forget that overall economic growth remains critical to poverty reduction. [3] However, the positive impacts of poverty reduc-

---

1. On macroeconomic aspects, see P. Bardhan, "Efficacité, équité et lutte contre la pauvreté," *Problèmes économiques*, n°2520, 1997; G. Chapelier and H. Tabatabai, *Development and Adjustment* (BPPS/UNDP: 1989); D. Reed, *Macroeconomic Policies, Poverty and the Environment* (New York, 1997); T. McKinley, *The Macroeconomic Implications of Focusing on Poverty Reduction* (New York, 1997).

2. F. Martin et S. Larivière, *Cadre d'analyse économique de la pauvreté et des conditions de vie des ménages*, Québec, 1997.

3. See K. Subbarao, *Lessons of 30 Years of Fighting Poverty*, Québec, 1997 & P. Bardhan, "Efficacité, équité et lutte contre la pauvreté," *Problèmes économiques*, n°2520, mai 1997.

tion through growth are largely determined by income distribution. The impact of the growth rate on poverty reduction will depend on initial inequalities in income. Growth coupled with balanced income distribution is therefore an effective macroeconomic way to reduce poverty. Many projects can contribute to economic growth, while alleviating the severe deprivation of the poor, particularly by improving their living standards.

Taxation, budget, monetary and exchange-rate policy all have a major influence on poverty reduction strategies and programs. An analysis should take into account the following elements:
   – impact of structural adjustment on poverty;
   – efficiency and equity of growth;
   – impact of macroeconomic reform on access to basic social services;
   – impact of macroeconomic reform on employment;
   – tax, budget, monetary and exchange-rate policy and poverty reduction;
   – consistency between poverty reduction policy and macroeconomic policy.

3.3.3. Analysis of national policy from the angle of poverty reduction

Policy analysis first requires identifying and prioritizing the development policies that have a major impact on the living standards of the poor and that would therefore be most likely to either facilitate or hamper the implementation of a poverty reduction program. In addition to macroeconomic policy, an analysis should also cover the framework of sectoral and thematic development policies, with particular focus on:
   – social development policies: education, health, social protection, nutrition and employment;
   – policies related to access to the factors of production: capital, land, natural and environmental resources, information, infrastructure and technology;
   – policies related to capacity-building, including the legal framework for participation of the poor, freedom of association, and the process of designing and implementing national strategies and programs.

On the basis of this incomplete list, it is essential to identify the instruments for implementing these policies and to analyze their consequences on economic growth and the poor. Then it will be possible to assess how much impact these policies are likely to have on the current situation. [1]

---

1. A guide to analysing the national policy framework has been published by UNDP, SEDEP/ BPPS. See Renata Lok Dessallien, *Poverty, Module 2 - From Data Collection to Poverty Assessments*, Technical Support Document (UNDP, BPPS, 1996) for a complete metholodology of this type of exercise.

Box 2.15

Structure of the analytical study of national poverty eradication policies in Burkina Faso

I. National Development Strategy
 a. Major features of the develop-
    ment strategy
 b. Macro-economic   performance
    indicators
    – growth of the economy
    – employment, unemployment
      and informal sector
II. Poverty and inequality
 a. Indicators of poverty and ine-
    quality
 b. Inputs of poverty profile
 c. Evolution of income distribu-
    tion

III. Poverty alleviation strategy
 a. Objectives
 b. Policies and programs
    – Price and income polices
    – Supply of basic social services
    – Access to land and migration
    – Infrastructures,   employment
      and rural micro-achievements
    – Urban employment
    – Micro-credits
    – Planning familial
 c. Mechanism   for   implementing
    strategies and policies
IV. Coherence between macro-economic
    policies and poverty eradication

Source: M. Raffinot, National Poverty Eradication Strategies in Burkina Faso, SEDEP/
BPPS, UNDP, 1997.

Within the framework of the "Evaluation of Poverty Alleviation Programmes, Poverty Reduction Lessons Learned" regional project, UNDP has supported a series of studies and analyses on the major national development policies from a poverty reduction perspective. Such studies now exist in Benin, Burkina Faso, Cameroon, Côte d'Ivoire, Ethiopia, Madagascar, Malawi, Mali, Senegal, Tanzania, Uganda and Zimbabwe.

3.3.4. Analysis of public expenditure, through public spending reviews and the 20/20 Initiative

An analysis of public expenditure is an effective instrument for achieving a comprehensive understanding of poverty and the implementation of a poverty reduction strategy, because it is based on a consistent, practical methodology for identifying and monitoring poverty-related policies and strategies.

The main objective of the public spending reviews initiated by the World Bank is to i) improve governments' fiscal management; ii) assess the consistency of policies; and iii) analyze the impact of adjustment on the social sectors.

With reorganized and broadened objectives from the perspective of poverty reduction, public spending reviews are an effective way to:
– ascertain the levels of expenditure on priority sectors for poverty reduction;
– study the effectiveness and sustainability of expenditure on poverty reduction;
– ascertain the distribution of expenditure and identify the beneficiaries;
– determine the actual share of public budgets contributing to poverty reduction.

Most of these studies were initiated by the World Bank and focus on spending in the social sectors, primarily health and education, followed by social protection, water/sanitation and employment. From a sustainable human development perspective, it would be useful to extend these studies to new fields such as the environment and spending on gender. Within the framework of the 20/20 Initiative, it would be beneficial to establish the links and synergies between public spending reviews, impact studies and 20/20 studies. [1]

First, the government's income and expenditure must be assessed. With a view to reaching a comprehensive understanding of poverty, a public spending review must calculate total government spending on poverty reduction, identify the sources of financing used and their sustainability.

Following this, all expenditure must be itemized, including that of the central government, decentralized structures and State and parastatal enterprises. However, it is important to avoid posting any expenditure more than once. This exercise presupposes a detailed analysis of spending channels and the overall operation of the administration.

Distinctions must also be made between capital and recurrent expenditure. This is particularly important for spending on the social sectors, where operating costs generally account for a high proportion of total expenditure. This analysis examines the relationship between income and expenditure and seeks to determine both the financial sustainability and the impact of this spending.

It is essential to identify as accurately as possible the sectors to be studied. The results of the poverty profiles and analyses of the country's major development policies, including macroeconomic policies, indicate the sectors with the biggest impact on poverty reduction.

In the 32 Sub-Saharan African countries that have undertaken public spending reviews, 22 of these reviews have dealt only with the education

---

1. Chapter 3 gives a more detailed analysis of government expenditure, public spending reviews and the 20/20 Initiative.

and health sectors. Supported by the World Bank (jointly with UNDP in eight cases), the main objective of these reviews has not been poverty reduction, but an assessment of the impact of SAPs on the social sectors. [1]

Most of these studies have looked at i) the proportion of education and health expenditure in total expenditure; ii) the allocation of resources with these two sectors; and iii) wage expenditure in relation to other expenditure.

From a poverty reduction perspective, these reviews appear insufficient. However, under the 20/20 Initiative, implemented jointly by UNDP and UNICEF, the range of sectors will be extended and the analyses enhanced. The 20/20 Initiative analyses public spending on the essential social services of basic education and literacy, primary health care, reproductive health, nutrition and safe drinking water. While these areas do not cover all the aspects of poverty, they extend the sphere of investigation. This analysis includes both intrasectoral and intersectoral studies, with recommendations on reallocation of resources, including official development assistance, either within the same sector or towards other sectors.

The Sub-Saharan African countries currently completing 20/20 studies include Benin, Burkina Faso, Cameroon, Chad, Côte d'Ivoire, Kenya, Malawi, Mali, Namibia, Niger, South Africa, Tanzania and Zambia.

After analyzing the breakdown of expenditure within and between sectors, it is important to determine the beneficiaries of this spending. This means identifying the main beneficiaries in each category of expenditure in order to assess as accurately as possible the extent to which the groups identified as poor in the poverty profile actually benefit from this spending.

For each sector and sub-sector, this involves identifying the expenditure of most benefit to poor people and which groups of poor people. This targeting is essential to increase the effectiveness of public spending for poverty reduction. Here again, the results of the poverty profiles can be used to identify beneficiaries.

As for the overall framework of national development policy, the efficiency and effectiveness of spending needs to be evaluated, through a cost-benefit analysis and an assessment of the effects on growth and equity. This last exercise can be used to formulate recommendations for reallocating resources within the same sector or towards other sectors.

3.3.5. Analysis of the institutional framework for policy implementation

The World Bank tends to consider an analysis of the institutional framework as part of the public spending reviews. However, if the two do

---

1. See Chapter 3 for a more detailed analysis.

interact, it would seem important to analyze the institutional framework independently, so as not to limit the scope of investigation to the government's capacity for financial management only. From the perspective of sustainable human development, UNDP considers strengthening national capacities as a development priority. From this perspective, institutional analysis takes into account not only the government's capacity for financial management, but also its capacity to deliver quality products and services to the poor. It is thus a useful adjunct to the policy analysis and public spending reviews, with a view to providing a fuller picture of the government's capacity to design a poverty reduction strategy and implement poverty alleviation programs.

The term "institutional analysis" should be understood in the broad sense as referring to all organized groups and structures that provide services to the public, at macro, meso or micro level. Based on the concept of governance, i.e. an active partnership between the three major stakeholders — the State, the private sector and civil society — this exercise focuses on the following aspects of institutional analysis and capacity-building:

– on the basis of the poverty profile and the policy analysis, identify the most suitable institutions for delivering services to the poor that will have the most impact on their standard of living;

– analyze the respective role and responsibilities of the institutions identified;

– measure the efficiency and impact of the services offered or delivered by these institutions. In addition to the appropriateness and efficiency of the services provided, this part examines the sources of financing of these institutions, to assess their cost and sustainability;

– assess the extent to which the services provided meet the needs of the poor. Just as the public spending reviews include an assessment of the beneficiaries of services, there is a need to evaluate the extent to which the identified institutions target the poorest groups and meet their needs.

These studies from a sustainable human development and capacity-building perspective have rarely been undertaken. Apart from the World Bank's institutional studies, institutional analyses in relation to poverty are rare in the Sub-Saharan African countries, with the notable exception of Lesotho, which used this type of analysis to identify the institutional framework for its poverty reduction strategy. [1]

1. Government of Lesotho, "Poverty Reduction Within the Context of Good Governance," 8th Roundtable Conference, Geneva, 1997.

Box 2.16.

The institutional framework of poverty alleviation in Lesotho: the role of Community-Based Organizations

The Community-Based Organizations (CBOs) are service institutions that play two important roles in poverty alleviation: i) many poor people are members of such organizations and, ii) they help the poor to articulate their views and needs in ways that can be heard by decision-makers.

The major feature of the CBOs is mutual aid based on the principle of traditional community values, i.e., reciprocity and interdependence. Essentially composed of women, these organizations are divided into four major categories: the women's societies with income generating activities, the savings and credit societies, the societ-

ies for funerals and the cultural and traditional organizations. The members of these societies are, mainly in the rural areas, unemployed women or women with precarious employment, small farmers and workers belonging to the low income groups.

In general, the major strength of these organizations lies in the collective sense of responsibilities as well as in their collective guarantee. These efficient systems of good management at the grass roots level offers opportunities that have not yet been largely utilized by the development agencies in order to tackle poverty control.

Source: Poverty Reduction Within the Context of Good Governance, Government of Lesotho, 8th Round Table Conference, Geneva, 1997.

3.3.6. Strengthening the capacities of the poor

After an analysis of the institutional capacity to deliver adequate services to poor groups, it is as important to consider the other side: strengthening poor people's capacity to respond to the services delivered and to participate fully in the decision-making on poverty reduction that affects them. In this respect, the following questions should be considered:

– To what extent does the legal framework contribute to strengthening poor people's capacity to help themselves and to seize and broaden the economic and social opportunities offered to them?

– Do the poor participate in decision-making and are they really involved in participatory processes?

– What are the different forms of participation and who is mainly involved? Are the poor really taking an active part?

At the instigation of UNDP, several African countries have embarked on analyses of the participation of poor groups and civil society in poverty reduction action. In addition to Lesotho, which made it the major theme of its 8th Roundtable Conference held in Geneva in November 1997, these include Botswana, Guinea, South Africa and Zimbabwe.

Box 2.17.

The participatory aspects of designing a Poverty Alleviation Action Plan in Zimbabwe

Based on the experience of the drought of 1991-1992 and on the social dimensions of the structural adjustment, the Government requested the UNDP assistance in designing a Poverty Alleviation Action Plan. The implementation of the plan will start with a large social mobilization throughout the country, including massive public sensitization and information campaigns aimed at consolidating the interest and support of the communities with respect to the objectives and activities of the Plan.

The social mobilization process was focused on the Poverty Diagnostic Study which provided district level information on the following domains: i) poverty distribution in terms of land use and socio-economic groups; ii) the access by underprivileged groups to social nets and to employment market and; iii) the constraints and causes of poverty as perceived by the populations. This exercise of global appraisal of poverty served as a basis for community participation, for the formulation of a poverty control strategy, the design of policies and programs and for the monitoring/evaluation of poverty.

Source: "Poverty Eradication: A Policy Framework for Country Strategies", UNDP, 1995.

3.3.7. Impact of the international environment on the living standards of poor households

The impact of the international environment on national poverty is an important element in understanding poverty. The international environment influences national policies and poverty is determined by both internal and external factors.

Until now, the poverty profile and the comprehensive approach to poverty have involved describing, measuring, identifying and understanding poverty from an internal point of view. It is also important to investigate the external causes of poverty.

The main themes to examine are:
- the level and trends of external debt,
- international terms of trade and commodity prices,
- the composition of exports and imports,
- the balance of payments,
- foreign investment,
- difficulties encountered in regional integration,
- international migration,
- development assistance and poverty reduction.

3.4. *Identifying the causes of poverty*

After analyzing the poverty situation of a country, it is essential to seek the causes of poverty as a basis for designing a national poverty reduction strategy. The recommendations of the World Summit for Social Development in Copenhagen included national poverty eradication plans to *"address the structural causes of poverty"* stemming from both national and international factors. [1] The Programme of Action recommends *"developing, updating and disseminating... indicators of the national and international causes underlying poverty"*.

This part of the exercise — innovative in relation to existing profiles and analyses — can also contribute to consolidating UNDP's role in poverty reduction action. [2]

Both poverty profiles and a comprehensive approach to poverty involve describing the manifestations of poverty, without necessarily considering the structural causes of poverty. It is therefore useful to complete studies on poverty with an analysis centered on the causes. The national or international causes of poverty can be divided into three broad structural categories, plus a fourth — cyclical — category for countries in crisis or conflict.

3.4.1. Inequitable distribution of factors of production

The first main structural cause of poverty is unequal distribution of the factors of production. [3] Factors of production are any of the resources needed to produce a good or service. By this definition, the basic factors of production are land, Labour and capital, in the broad sense.

The concept of factors of production comes down to that of resources. Resources reduce people's vulnerability and enable them to resist poverty. A lack of resources or poor distribution of resources increases vulnerability and insecurity, and poverty in general. It is therefore crucial to consider the structural inequalities in the distribution of resources, particularly land and natural resources, credit, economic resources, social capital and technology.

1. "Poverty Eradication," *Copenhagen Declaration on Social Development,* World Summit for Social Development, Copenhagen, 1995.

2. UNDP, *Poverty Eradication: A Policy Framework for Country Strategies* (New York, 1995).

3. M. Hopkins, *A Short review of Thinking about Anti-Poverty Strategies,* Geneva, 1997; S. Larivière et F. Martin, *Cadre d'analyse économique de la pauvreté et des conditions de vie des ménages* (Québec, 1997); M. Todaro, *Economic Development in the Third World* (London, 1989); UNDP, *Human Development Report 1997* (New York: Oxford University Press, 1997).

3.4.1.1. *Physical, financial and human capital*

Economic and social resources are usually goods and services that can be used to produce other goods and services or generate income. These resources are often unavailable or difficult to obtain for the poor.

The main kind of *physical capital* is land, especially for rural people. Given that income poverty in Sub-Saharan Africa is three-quarters rural and mainly affects people and households who depend on agriculture for their livelihoods, the importance of land is clear. The following aspects of the land issue warrant analysis:
  – land tenure and title,
  – distribution of land,
  – productivity of land,
  – gender bias in the availability and accessibility of land.

The main issues regarding *financial capital* are the inaccessibility and poor distribution of credit and savings. [1] Credit and savings are essential resources for the poor, enabling them to seize opportunities offered by the market to invest and use inputs and equipment. Credit and savings also play a key role during cyclical downturns, such as droughts, recessions and illness. Poor people also have more limited access to financial capital. It is therefore essential to analyze the causes and consider the following elements:
  – availability of credit and savings to poor people through an overview of the microfinance systems in the country;
  – the different types of institutions offering financial intermediation at local level and their strategies.

By *social capital* what is meant are social resources. [2] The capacity of individuals to forge links with others is a vital form of social capital that begins within the family and community. Being healthy and educated are essential conditions for consolidating social capital, because they broaden people's opportunities in society.

Therefore, an analysis of endowment in social capital is a key to identifying the structural causes of poverty. The following issues should be examined in depth:
  – endowment in human capital (health, education),
  – factors contributing to social integration and social exclusion.

---

1. See J. Garson, *Microfinance and Anti-Poverty Strategies* (UNCDF, 1996); UNDP, *Credit for the Poor*, 1989.

2. IILS/UNDP, *Social Exclusion and Anti-Poverty Strategies* (Geneva, 1996).

3.4.1.2. *Contribution of the poor to growth and equity*

Poor distribution of wealth and the fruits of growth between rich and poor is a fundamental structural cause of poverty. Economic growth can be an effective way to eradicate poverty by raising the productivity and income of poor households and by increasing opportunities and choices. However, in too many countries, growth does not lead to a reduction in poverty, either because it is not high enough or because its nature and structure are not aimed directly at improving the living standards of poor households.

Therefore, it is important to consider the following key issues:
- the structure and pace of growth,
- the contribution of growth to reducing or increasing poverty,
- the relationship between efficiency and equity in growth,
- growth and job creation.

The fundamental issue is to broaden the bases of economic growth to ensure that poor segments of the population contribute to and benefit from growth.

Box 2.18.

Identification of the causes of poverty in Niger

Within the context of designing a National Outline Poverty Alleviation Program, the Government of the Niger assisted by the UNDP undertook a global diagnostic study of poverty. Beyond the analysis of the identification of poverty measurements, this study strives to make an exhaustive inventory of the causes of poverty. According to that study, the most general and probably the most profound reason for this situation lies in the inadequacy between the natural population growth and the growth of wealth. The simultaneous degradation of natural resource capital as well as the effect of other economic and socio-cultural factors worsen the process.

In that context, the following factors were highlighted:
1. Natural causes
   Population growth and distribution
   Limitation of natural resources
2. Economic causes
   Macro-economic imbalance
3. Socio-cultural factors and resistance to change
4. Institutional causes
   Inadequate administrative supervision
   Poor involvement of the private sector
   Poor organization of the agricultural sector
   Institutional capacities of the civil society

Source: Republic of Niger, "National Outline Poverty Alleviation Program", vol.1, "General Diagnosis of Poverty", 1996.

3.4.1.3. *Difficulty of access to technical knowledge*

Related to the unequal distribution of factors of production are problems of access to the technical knowledge needed to make optimum use of physical, financial and human capital. Productivity gains, better utilization of financial capital and enhancement of social capital, particularly in health and education, depend on the acquisition and implementation of technology and access to information and technical knowledge. [1]

The positive effects of education and investment on productivity depend on the technologies available. The issue is crucial because in a highly skills-intensive global economy, access to technology on reasonable terms gives countries and households the means to use their opportunities.

3.4.1.4. *Degradation of natural resources and population growth*

An analysis of the distribution of factors of production should take into account two relatively independent variables, but which are fully related to this problem because of their major impact on access to and distribution of factors of production and resources. These are environmental degradation and population growth.

The first chapter, on the issues inherent in poverty in Sub-Saharan Africa, highlighted the main effects of these two variables on poverty. Environmental and demographic factors can worsen existing deficits and inequalities in areas such as access to land, savings and credit and human capital endowment.

For many years, deforestation, prolonged droughts, soil erosion and diminishing reserves of surface and ground water have been aggravating factors that reduce opportunities for endowment in factors of production. The combination of growing claims on common property resources, low agricultural productivity and population growth create a poverty-accelerating spiral that in turn exacerbates environmental degradation.

Environmental degradation and population, often linked, are aggravating factors that must be taken into account in any examination of the causes of poverty.

3.4.2. Deficiencies in governance and empowerment

By assessing national development policy, the institutional framework and ways to strengthen poor people's capacities, a comprehensive approach to poverty can determine a country's capacity to design and implement a poverty reduction strategy and program. The second major cause of poverty can be found in the deficits in governance and empowerment. This

---

1. UNDP, *Human Development Report 1996* (New York: Oxford University Press, 1996).

involves more than a general analysis of the government's capacities or the failure to empower poor groups or households. It is a comprehensive approach at macro, meso and micro levels to policy design and implementation, which should clearly identify the causes of poverty linked to bad policies, lack of capacities or bad management.

3.4.2.1. Deficit in the design and implementation of national development policies

An analysis of major national development policies, whether macroeconomic or sectoral, highlights certain structural factors inherent in or responsible for poverty. Policies based on a development paradigm that is not people-centered, poorly targeted policies or a lack of national development policies — frequent in countries in crisis or conflict — can be causal or aggravating factors in poverty.

The same applies to poor implementation of policies and strategies. Inadequate monitoring and evaluation, corruption, lack of political will or failure to take people's aspirations into account can generate harmful effects that cause poverty.

3.4.2.2. Inequality before the institutional and legislative framework

The involvement or inclusion of the poor in decision-making processes and the institutional framework is a crucial element in poverty alleviation. If poverty reduction strategies and programs are to take account of poor people's aspirations through a participatory approach, it is essential to determine whether the institutional and legislative framework is not itself responsible for producing or aggravating poverty.

The effectiveness of poverty reduction action also depends on the way in which services are delivered. Effective policies must foster broad political participation, accountability and transparency in public action and take the aspirations of disadvantaged groups into account.

3.4.2.3. Poor people's low level of organization and capacity deficit

Empowerment, people's capacity to be included in development processes and their willingness to participate fully in poverty reduction programs are at the heart of the poverty problem.

It is extremely important to identify the factors for poverty in poor households' capacities or lack of capacities. While people are assumed to be able to choose freely how to allocate their resources, a lack of basic capabilities may mean that the choices made by poor households generate more poverty. Although people's choices should be respected, a poverty reduction perspective can be encouraged through actions to strengthen basic capabilities, empower poor households and include them in participatory development processes. These are key factors in identifying causes of poverty.

The marginalization of poor people from political power and civil society should also be considered. In addition to strengthening the capabilities of the poor at the level of individuals, there is also a need to determine the level of participation or influence that disadvantaged groups have on politicians and their decisions. In general, the voice of the poor tends to be marginalized or even usurped by a small, cultivated, urban élite, claiming to speak on their behalf. Special focus should be given to the place and role of women in this process.

Box 2.19.

Identification of the causes of poverty in Kenya

The National Report on Human Development in Kenya highlighted a series of underlying interrelated factors of poverty. The major causes of poverty are related to the following elements:

– low resource base, inadequacy of productive assets and lack of ownership in terms of land, capital, labor access to credit. This weaknesses are positively correlated to inadequate access by the poor to education, technical skills, entrepreneurship, employment, health, sanitation and water;

– destruction of natural resources which in turn reduces the productivity of agriculture, forestry and fisheries;

– marginalization and lack of participation by the poor in decisions that affect them;

– inappropriate or lack of assistance for the victims of transitory poverty;

– lack of access to markets and unfair trade/prices for local and domestic goods and services in sectors predominated by the poor (marginalized/remote geographical locations, lack of protection from unscrupulous middle men, poor terms of trade within the domestic economic, corruption, etc.);

– lack of legal protection;

– poor job security;

– lack of or ineffective social security systems;

– poor development of infrastructures that are supposed to strengthen the groups (water, energy, communications, roads, etc.).

Source: F. J. Mumina, "Economic and Social Aspects of Poverty and its Eradication in Kenya", UNDP, 1997.

3.4.3. Inequalities in development opportunities

The third structural cause of poverty is unequal access to opportunities to overcome poverty. These are opportunities to benefit from social services (health, education and safe drinking water), economic opportunities (access to markets, financing and employment) and access to housing and infrastructure. These issues are, of course, related to the design of policies in these sectors, which largely determine the quality and efficiency of these services. Most poverty reduction programs are based on this type of causality in their implementation.

3.4.3.1. *Inequality of access to basic social services*

The availability of basic social services, particularly primary health care, basic education and safe drinking water, has a significant influence on poor people's access to resources, particularly human and social resources. The poor quality, inadequacy or unsuitability of policies in terms of meeting the needs of the poor can seriously diminish their resources and worsen the living standards of disadvantaged households.

In Sub-Saharan Africa, social services are badly distributed. In contrast to wealthy urban groups, poor communities have little or no access to basic social services. According to the *Human Development Report 1997*, the average proportion of people without access to safe drinking water is 13% in urban areas, but over 40% in rural areas; female illiteracy rates are 28% in urban areas, but 66% in rural areas. Also, because of disparities in income and the cost of living, services such as water and energy are often proportionately more expensive for poor people than for the rich.

A precise study of the constraints on access to basic social services is therefore fundamental to an investigation of the causes of poverty.

3.4.3.2. *Inequality of access to economic opportunities*

The causes of poverty related to economic resources and capital have already been examined. A more dynamic analysis of the accessibility and availability of economic opportunities is a useful adjunct to this exercise. When seeking the economic causes of poverty, special consideration should be given to:
- access to microfinance,
- access to markets,
- imbalances in prices for goods and services produced by the poor,
- access to employment.

3.4.3.3. *Inequality of access to infrastructure and housing*

In addition to the key factor of land in rural poverty, housing is a vital element in both urban and rural areas. Income- and employment-generating activities are often home-based. An analysis of access to housing in urban and rural areas should focus on the types of housing and housing rights available.

There is a clear lack of access to infrastructure for poor groups and regions; remoteness and distance compound low availability of infrastructure. The accessibility of major infrastructure, such as roads, water supply/sanitation, communication networks and electricity, should be evaluated. An analysis should also take into account the considerable rural-urban disparities and the particular case of remote regions, which are often pockets of poverty.

3.4.3.4. The special case of countries in crisis or conflict.

Instability or conflict in a country generally reverse poverty eradication efforts. Apart from the direct impact of conflicts in terms of mass destruction of resources, significant resources are also diverted from development. It is not appropriate to embark on surveys, analyses and studies of poverty during particularly serious and urgent situations. Conflict prevention is the action most likely to influence poverty reduction. However, in these cases, it is important to consider four essential points:
- the overall problem of the crisis and aspects of social integration,
- assistance for victims,
- rapid conflict resolution,
- implementation of reconstruction programs.

3.5. Towards a comprehensive understanding of poverty

The themes approached in this study offer a basis for a comprehensive understanding of poverty in a country. The various stages of this process involved conceptualizing, identifying, measuring and profiling poverty in a country or region and determining the causes of poverty. However, it is important not to lose sight of the operational purpose of this approach, which is to provide the necessary information for designing a poverty reduction strategy.

All the themes approached so far contribute to the design of a coherent, operational poverty reduction strategy. Their originality lies in the consideration of factors inherent in the concept of sustainable human development and human poverty.

The stages of this approach can be recapitulated as follows:

1. Clarifying the concept of poverty and formulating a specific definition, based on the paradigm of sustainable human development.

2. Constructing a poverty profile aimed at analyzing, measuring and identifying poverty in a country by:
   2.1. Setting a poverty line based on the definition of human poverty and not limited to purely monetary or absolute aspects.
   2.2. Conducting participatory surveys on the dimensions of poverty and well-being, accessibility of social sectors, ways to reduce poverty and related socioeconomic indicators, to clarify and enhance the poverty line.

3. Reaching a comprehensive understanding of poverty that offers a full picture of the phenomenon, through an analysis of the national and international environment and an investigation of the structural causes of poverty.
   3.1. Analyzing and assessing the major national development policies, including macroeconomic policies, sectoral development policies and public spending reviews.

3.2. Analyzing the institutional framework for the implementation of poverty reduction policy.

3.3. Assessing ways to empower the poor and strengthen their capabilities.

3.4. Analyzing the international factors that influence national poverty.

3.5. Identifying the structural causes of poverty.

Box 2.20.

Stages of a global poverty assessment exercise in Burkina Faso

1. Definition of human poverty.

2. Design of a poverty profile.
   2.1. Setting of poverty thresholds.
      2.1.1. Absolute poverty threshold based on household food and non-food expenditure, supported by the World Bank.
      2.1.2. Relative poverty threshold based on annual average expenditure of adults divided into 5 quintiles.
      2.1.3. Objective well-being threshold taking expenses required for reaching a state of well-being into account (housing, clothing, access to basic social services and to natural resources, water and wood).
   2.2. Conduct of qualitative surveys.
      2.2.1. Participatory surveys on the dimensions of urban poverty (PSUP).
      2.2.2. Participatory surveys on the dimensions of rural poverty (PSRP).
   2.3. Design of socio-economic indicators with special emphasis on availability and accessibility to basic social services and to natural resources.

3. Global assessment of poverty.
   3.1. Analysis of national development policies.
      3.1.1. Studies on macro-economic policies with reference to poverty eradication.
      3.1.2. Studies on policies in favor of social sectors and employment in the context of preparing the Round Table Conference on the development of social sectors.
      3.1.3. World Bank sponsored review of public expenditure and analysis of the incidence of education and health expenditure UNDP and UNICEF sponsored, Diagnostic Study on the implementation of the 20/20 Initiative in Burkina Faso.

Thus, with the well-known exception of sets of themes related to governance and capacity strengthening at macro, meso and micro levels, the major features of this phenomenon of poverty in Burkina Faso are taken up as part of this poverty diagnosis.

Source: UNDP, Burkina Faso 1998.

It is encouraging to note that the countries where anti-poverty efforts have been supported by the UNDP country office have all, at least intuitively, used this approach to poverty. Ideally, this approach should be more clearly and more homogeneously related to the paradigm of sustainable human development.

The construction of a profile and the analysis of poverty should take into account both the operational purpose and sustainable human development paradigm, which are the basis for this approach.

The approach should be flexible, open and inexpensive. Many of the surveys and approaches described have already been undertaken in many countries. Over 33 African countries have set poverty lines on the basis of budget/consumption or priority surveys. In some cases, as in Benin, Burkina Faso and Mali, it has been possible to use and reanalyze existing poverty lines, refining the analysis from a sustainable human development perspective, without embarking on unwieldy and expensive methods. The same applies to the public spending reviews and work on the 20/20 Initiative, for which there are many existing studies. Analyzing their results from an anti-poverty perspective does not always require new surveys nor the deployment of major resources.

Since the main objectives are to provide the information necessary for the implementation of a poverty reduction strategy and to support the program to implement this strategy, the operational dimension of the exercise should always be at the forefront. A survey or an analysis should only be undertaken to meet an identified need and not for the mere conceptual pleasure of studying or analyzing. All the themes covered must therefore contribute actively and optimally to the objectives of the exercise.

Based on the paradigm of sustainable human development, this approach puts people back at the center of the problem of poverty, through a participatory approach focused on the construction of a long-term vision of development issues and the phenomenon of poverty.

The approaches to identifying and measuring poverty should be harmonized at the subregional or regional level. In the countries where UNDP supports an anti-poverty approach, this contains common elements: a definition of human poverty, participatory surveys, an analysis of the relationship between governance and poverty, 20/20 studies. However, it would be useful for UNDP to extend the potential synergies and consider developing an optimal methodological framework and an anti-poverty approach. The common and innovative elements in this study could serve as a basis for such an approach.

The publication of national human development reports on poverty are a new integrating factor. These offer a analysis of poverty, assert a sustainable, human vision of poverty and are a first step towards a harmonization of approaches.

Box 2.21.

The major outlines of poverty diagnosis in Namibia

1. Definition of human poverty.
2. Design of a poverty profile.
   2.1. Establishment of poverty thresholds supported by the World Bank:
      2.1.1. 1991 absolute threshold based on household subsistence
      2.1.2. 1994 absolute poverty threshold based on a budget/consumption survey taking household food and non-food expenditure into account.
   2.2. Participatory surveys on poverty perception and solutions to find, supported by the UNDP.
   2.3. Design of socio-economic indicators, especially focused on regional, racial and gender disparities, access to social services, the environment and access to natural resources.
3. Global assessment of poverty, including the drafting of the National Report on Sustainable Human Development devoted to poverty.
   3.1. Analysis of development policies
      3.1.1. Analysis of macro-economic policies
      3.1.2. Analysis of national development policies based on historical references to colonial past and apartheid in the country.
      3.1.3. Review of public expenditure and analysis of the incidence of the World Bank in the sectors of education and health and, Diagnostic Study on the implementation of the 20/20 Initiative sponsored by UNICEF.
   3.2. Institutional analysis of constraints within the legal and regulatory framework and centralization of powers.
   3.3. Identification of the structural causes of poverty.

Source: By S. Adei, "Poverty in Namibia, UNDP, 1997 & "Namibia: Monitoring the 20/20 Compact", UNICEF Namibia, 1997.

UNDP's regional Poverty Strategies Initiative (PSI) is another effective harmonization tool. It involves assessing poverty in the light of the major principles of sustainable human development. Implemented in the follow-up to the Summit on Social Development in Copenhagen, the PSI has a twofold objective that responds perfectly to the concerns expressed above, by:

– assisting country programs to formulate definitions, analyses, measures, criteria and indicators to determine the nature, the prevalence and the distribution of poverty in a country;

– assisting UNDP country programs to formulate national plans and the implementation of poverty reduction strategies.

Once this exhaustive analysis of the poverty situation of a country has been completed, the causes of poverty can be investigated with a view to ascertaining the key factors to be considered in the design of a poverty reduction strategy.

PART TWO

National poverty reduction strategies

Macroeconomic policy, institutional reform and social mobilization favorable to poverty reduction

Designing a national poverty reduction strategy should be seen as a process that fits into a country's existing development policy framework. The analysis stage described previously sought to identify this framework and the main development strategy and policy options in a country, with a view to determining the advantages and limitations of the environment in which the national poverty reduction strategy will be implemented.

While the overall framework is largely specific to the development objectives and priorities of each country, there are some general features that recur in most of the Sub-Saharan African countries. Apart from the special case of countries in crisis — where a development policy framework either does not exist or is not operational except for aspects related to rehabilitation and reconstruction or macroeconomic management during the crisis or conflict — there are common strategic elements, namely the implementation of structural adjustment programs and the need for an assertive renewal of strategic planning offering a long-term vision of national development prospects.

Before examining the main strategies specifically aimed at alleviating poverty, it is important to outline this frame of reference, which will have a considerable impact on the design and content of the national poverty reduction strategy.

1. Structural reform, strategic planning and long-term visions of poverty reduction

1.1. Structural adjustment programs and poverty reduction

Adjustment programs were introduced in response to the major internal and external imbalances experienced by African economies in the 1980s, characterized by unsustainable current account deficits, internal financial problems and extremely slow growth. To correct this situation, many countries adopted structural adjustment programs (SAPs), with the support of international financial institutions or on their own initiative. Structural adjustment pursued two aims: economic stabilization through policies to reduce demand and a restructuring of demand to re-establish growth.

Adjustment has often been considered a crucial stage on the path to sustainable, poverty-reducing growth in Africa. However, adjustment programs have failed to deliver their early promises: they have not shown a capacity for genuine poverty reduction through robust economic growth. Some proponents of adjustment believed that the reforms would rapidly put the African countries on the road to strong growth of the kind seen in Asia. Opponents of adjustment see it as an insufficient substitute for long-term development measures. The resulting confusion has sometimes led to unconstructive debates on the effectiveness of adjustment policies and economic recovery packages.

To evaluate the effect of adjustment on disadvantaged sections of the population, it is important to properly understand the dynamics that prompted African countries to embark on adjustment programs. The economic crisis in the early 1980s brought sharp reductions in per capita income, hitting the most destitute households hardest. The effect on the situation of poor people was determined by the existing distribution of income, the pace of growth and the impact of growth on income and household activities and by the existing breakdown of public spending. At the beginning of the 1980s, all these factors caused the situation of poor people to worsen in most African countries. Growth trends stabilized or turned negative.

By the mid-1980s, in reaction to this recession, governments introduced adjustment measures, which penalized the most disadvantaged groups. Rural people were the first to feel the unfavorable effects of the general slowdown in economic activity and the lower returns on their production, with a worsening of the internal terms of trade. In countries where the urban labor market collapsed, the urban middle class suffered the sharpest drop in living standards.

In some African countries, adjustment did help to increase per capita GDP growth. There was every reason to think that this growth would improve the situation of the most disadvantaged people, given the strong existing correlation between economic growth and a decline in poverty in other parts of the world. However, in many countries, these reforms did not reduce poverty. The aim of the structural reforms was not to reduce poverty, but to promote growth. According to the United Nations Children's Fund (UNICEF), many adjustment programs launched in the early 1980s either failed to target the poorest households or did not put sufficient emphasis on the provision of adequate services to the most disadvantaged groups. However, since the end of the 1980s, adjustment programs have taken more account of improving the distribution of public spending and the provision of social services.

In this respect, UNDP places great importance on the implementation of specific poverty reduction strategies to fill in the gaps left by structural reforms.

All countries aspire to a stable macroeconomic environment, with low inflation and low budget and balance-of-payments deficits and competitiveness in world markets, which requires adjustments to the structure of public spending, investment and production.

Structural adjustment policies can have beneficial effects for the poor in the medium to long term, particularly if a return to growth stimulates demand for labor. In general, however, structural reforms have had unfavorable consequences for the poorest households.

Businesses and the labor market in the least developed countries have taken time to adapt to the adjustment process: unemployment and under-employment have worsened during this period and labor income has fallen. At the same time, shrinking demand has had negative consequences on poor people's consumption. The impact of the shocks has been better absorbed, all other things being equal, in countries with a relatively high overall level of wealth, particularly the middle-income countries.

Stabilization policies have also contributed to a reduction in economic activity, hampering growth. In countries where the public sector plays a dominant role, a reduction in public spending sets off a chain reaction. Many small entrepreneurs and contractors — whose business ranges from road construction to provision of services — have been forced into debt as business has declined and the State has stopped paying its bills. Internal debt in many African countries has thus become substantial.

The need to cut public spending is likely to deal a serious blow to two essential elements of poverty reduction: the provision of social services and the implementation of transfers and safety nets for the poorest people. The simultaneous needs of stabilizing the economy and protecting the poor require a trade-off between often drastic fundamental measures aimed at creating the conditions for future growth and policies to assist the poor.

Box 3.1.

SAP and poverty in the context of Togo

The obligation to restore as soon as possible the Togolese State internal and external financial equilibrium as part of SAP (Structural Adjustment Programme) is not as such a cause for impoverishment. However, this obligation reveals at sectoral level the latent poverty that prevailed in the country which was masked by internal and external indebtedness and the imbalance of external accounts.

The first point of emergence of this latent poverty was the State budget that had to severely reduce public expenditure. This reduction affected all the sectors, but mainly the social sectors, even those considered as priority sectors.

Several programs for the construction or rehabilitation of maternity hospitals, health centers, for the purchase of drugs, training and sensitization programs have decreased by more than one third. It is particularly the rural areas, already underprivileged, that are most affected by these reductions, particularly in terms of supply of drugs distributed through the health centers. Despite the efforts to mitigate the social impact of adjustments, particularly by implementing SDA [1] type projects and the maintenance of a significant flow of assistance in the social sectors, the situation of health and education services was not significantly improved.

The second point where poverty brutally emerged after structural adjustments and reforms is that of employment and income. The freezing of recruitment in the civil service brought about lesser market expansion and sectoral decrease in employment and income. The number of people employed by the civil service has decreased by 4.9% moving from 35,516 persons in 1983 to 33,777 in 1989; and in the private and parastatal sectors the decline was 2.3% per year during the same period. Only the primary and tertiary sectors recorded positive growth rates in terms of employment (5% for employment in the sectors of trade, bank and insurance; and 0.6% for rural employment)

In many aspects, namely those concerning finance rehabilitation (reduction of staff expenditure, decrease in internal and external arrears, raising some tariffs of publics services, adoption of a new tax code, etc) as well as the rehabilitation of the parastatal sectors and State companies, the first SAP can be considered as a success.

However, during the second period, unexpected economic events, namely the collapse of markets for products traditionally exported by Togo, reduced or annihilated the assets of the first phase.

In summary, budgetary reductions and reforms led to the emergence of a latent poverty in terms of social consumption of the populations and in terms of their productive capacities the progress of which was reduced. The GDP that had dropped by 9% as compared to 1991 dropped again by 10-12% in 1993. The populations are even poorer (as their per capita income was reduced by 25-30% as compared to 1992).

Source: National Poverty Alleviation Strategy, Ministry of Planning of Togo & UNDP, 1995.

---

1. SDA = Social Dimension of Adjustment

Box 3.2.
The structural adjustment program spillover
in social domains in Zimbabwe

After its independence in 1980, Zimbabwe invested considerably in human development, by designing several innovative programs aimed at accelerating actions in favor of education, health, housing, water distribution and sanitation. However, in the late eighties, these investments grew weaker, on the one hand due to economic adjustments and, on the other hand because the public authorities were unable to develop economic opportunities allowing for the utilization of the improved potentials of the population.

Faced, from the eighties onwards, with a slow growth and with a considerable budget deficit, the public authorities embarked in 1991 on a structural adjustment program. This policy annihilated a number of achievements in social development and has not yet given any economic improvement. With respect to employment, the measures aimed at reducing the value of capital as compared to that of labor and at stimulating manpower substitution did not improve the situation. The public authorities were also unable to proceed to an efficient redistribution of the resources that were produced.

In the social domains, the institution of not free health services and the increase in the price of food products led to a degradation of health conditions. In 1993, the child mortality rate still represented 56 deaths per thousand live births and life expectancy had dropped to 53 years. In the education sector, the budget reductions and the introduction of school fees caused enrolment and education levels to drop.

Source: World Human Development Report 1996, UNDP, 1996.

Policy factors clearly have a decisive influence on the choice of strategies. Policy objectives can be at odds with poverty alleviation, particularly when they involve reducing demand or stimulating rural growth to the detriment of towns.

Market liberalization is supposed to offer more opportunities to entrepreneurs. However, for many people, particularly the poorest, the market does not offer equal access to the opportunities that these new policies should offer nor to the facilities that would enable them to take advantage of these opportunities. In Sub-Saharan Africa as in countries in transition, market opportunities are unequally distributed and do not benefit the poor.

Thus, while structural adjustment programs have been seen as the only way to lift Africa out of crisis, their limitations became apparent early on. Structural reforms have not brought any satisfactory response to the problem of poverty. By addressing purely macroeconomic concerns — such as debt, growth, employment and income — they seem to have overlooked the central element of development — people. Even under the later generations of SAPs that attempted to integrate this concern, adjustments have concentrated on economic and financial dimensions, neglecting the human aspects of poverty.

New development strategies, based on the paradigm of sustainable human development, are needed to encourage both economic growth and a reduction in human poverty. From an economic point of view, the consolidation of adjustment through redistribution of resources and growth, rather than through a reduction in economic activity, is a path to be explored.

Box 3.3.
A well advised intervention by the public authorities, the case of Ghana

Like that of other African countries South of the Sahara, the Ghanaian economy suffered serious distortions, a persistent degradation of infrastructures and institutions and external shocks in the mid-eighties. However, it evolution since that period shows what well advised action taken by the public authorities can yield.

In Ghana reviewing the basic guidelines meant a high increase in a large number of official prices. These price increases were necessary to correct the distortions between official and parallel markets, as well as between agriculture and the other sectors of the economy. They were supported by vigorous budget sanitation measures and by an effort to redirect expenditure towards the poor. This change made it possible to revitalize and expand some social services.

For Ghana, it was not possible to amortize the decline in consumption

by reducing fixed investments. These investments were already at a very low level at that period (gross internal investment amounted to 12% of GNP, whereas the average in Sub-Saharan Africa was about 15% in 1988). Foreign assistance played an essential role in maintaining and stimulating per capita consumption (consumption increased by 1.6% per year during the 1985-1988 period). Ghana thus received, for instance, 9.8% of GNP as ODA, a rate slightly higher than the average of Sub-Saharan Africa that year (8.8%)

Budget readjustment was sustained by improving tax collection which more than doubled fiscal revenue: from 5% of GDP in 1983 it increased to 12% of GDP in 1990. Social budgets increased later on. Hence education expenditure per capita increased by 51% in real terms and that of health increased by 66%.

Source: Boateng E.O., Ewusi, K., Kanbur, R. & McKay, A., *A poverty Profile in Ghana: 1987-1988*, World Bank, Washington D.C., 1992

Box 3.4.
SAP and employment in Burkina Faso

The structural adjustment policies implemented since 1991 do not seem to have caused any special problem in terms of employment. The negative consequences resulting from privatization were largely offset by programs of large scale public works. Official estimates indicate, for the 1991-1996 period, 38 500 job creations related to SAP (including 20 600 temporary workers). 6 490 teachers in particular were recruited from 1991 to 1994 (including 950 school teachers per year) in addition to the traditional recruitment by the Teachers' training college.

On the other hand, the structural adjustment seems to have had a negative effect on incentives to agents. The nearly total closedown of the civil service, for instance, did not encourage

parents to send their children to school (up to secondary level), at the risk of turning them into unemployed persons for whom they would have uselessly invested. This closing down as well as the rapid growth of numbers in secondary school now give rise to unemployed holders of diplomas from secondary and higher schools. Besides, the generally low incomes gives little chance to these diploma holders to develop self-employment.

Furthermore, the blatant differentiation in standards of living within the society and the civil service as well as the lack of control certainly contribute to reduce the quality of public services. This was even accelerated by devaluation, which compelled a number of civil servants to look for supplementary income.

Source: Rapport National sur le Développement Humain: Burkina Faso 1998, UNDP Groupe de Reflexion sur le DHD 1998.

1.2. Strategic planning and long-term visions of poverty reduction

Adjustment is not an end in itself for Africa, but, as has been observed in other developing regions, it should be one component in a poverty-reducing growth strategy. In Sub-Saharan Africa, past and present adjustment programs have followed an approach based on pursuing macroeconomic reforms, completing trade and farm sector reforms, restructuring public finances and creating favorable conditions for the development of the private sector in the production of goods and services. The success of these responses depends on a radical transformation of the role of the State, which is not without difficulties in the current context of fragile democratic processes, weak institutions and, often, considerable political resistance to change.

Even if the necessary reforms can be successfully implemented, adjustment programs will not solve all of African countries' problems. Adjustment can only lay the foundations for a return to growth. To reduce poverty and improve living standards, there is a need to continue to invest in human resources and infrastructure development, to strengthen institutional capacities and to empower people. What is needed above all, perhaps, for resources to be used as effectively as possible towards achieving development objectives, is determined, sensible management of public affairs and a strategic and consensual long-term vision of society.

Box 3.5.
National Long Term Perspective Studies

National Long Term Perspective Study (NLTPS) or "African Futures" projects aim to produce a shared vision of the plausible structural transformations in a country over a generation. Neither owned by governments, nor monopolized by opposition parties, nor dominated by experts, NLTPS are intended as a framework for strengthening social dialogue between all national stakeholders and for appropriating development strategies and policies with a view to action.

The study is an exercise entirely carried out by nationals that seeks to integrate development actions into a coherent, comprehensive vision.

In most countries, the NLTPS process consists of five chronological and complementary phases. The first phase involves compiling an inventory of people's aspirations and using these as a basis for mapping out themes of national interest for investigation. The second phase seeks to identify the variables and key factors likely to influence the country's evolution and to assess the positive and negative forces affecting the fulfilment of national aspirations. The information collected during this phase enables countries to highlight their strong and weak points and to gauge the opportunities and threats that may arise in the future.

The third phase aims to construct alternative scenarios of the future and to build a shared national vision. In the fourth phase, the team in each country drafts a national development strategy based on a national vision of long-term development. This process involves identifying the main development issues facing the country and the strategic actions and options within the country's reach and formulating a comprehensive national development strategy. The fifth phase, or operational development planning phase, involves designing and implementing plans and programs of action over successive periods with a view to concretizing the national vision. This phase has only been partly achieved in the countries that have completed their studies. To fully operationalize this process, the results of the studies, which are still being examined, need to be appropriated by governments and translated into action.

Source: *Futurs Africains: quelques repères. Cinq années d'études nationales de perspectives à long terme* (Abidjan: PNUD-NEI-SAFICA, septembre 1997).

This shared vision must enable people to participate in the design and implementation of policies in an open framework of sound governance and development management. It must contribute to a better understanding of the causes and processes of poverty to assist the design of consensual strategic development guidelines and appropriated poverty reduction strategies and programs.

UNDP's initiative to support National Long Term Perspective Studies in Africa (NLTPS or "African Futures") offers a valuable new approach in this field. Several lessons can already be drawn from the first phase of this project (1992-1996), particularly concerning the assessment and causality of poverty and social exclusion in Africa.

Currently, seven countries — Cape Verde, Côte d'Ivoire, Gabon, Guinea-Bissau, Malawi, Mauritius and Zimbabwe — have completed a NLTPS; four countries — the Seychelles, Swaziland, Tanzania and Zambia — are close to finishing; four others — Madagascar, Mali, Sao Tome and Principe and Uganda — are in the initial phase; and three — Benin, Burkina Faso and Congo — are in the preparatory phase.

In all the countries, the African Futures projects are based on five essential processes: integrating long-term strategic thinking into development management; producing a shared vision; involving people in policy design, decision-making and policy implementation; anticipating the future by constructing scenarios; and strategic development management.

The NLTPS are not a substitute for planning or adjustment policies. Their objective is to reinforce these two instruments of development management. They offer a new approach to development management, mainly by seeking to bring development closer to people and to involve them in decision-making processes, in contrast to past practice in which participation was only envisaged for the formulation and implementation of local projects.

In the NLTPS, poverty rarely appears as a distinct problem. Of the seven countries that have completed the theoretical phase, only Mauritius identified poverty as a specific theme.

In Cape Verde, poverty is only identifiable through a long list of "obstacles to development": scarce natural resources; small landmass; lack of financial and technical resources; poor-quality schooling and technical and vocational training; underdeveloped agriculture, livestock farming and fisheries; ecological vulnerability; lack of water; lack of a strong modern entrepreneurial class; disparities in levels of development between islands; rising unemployment, especially youth employment; underdeveloped national culture; mentalities and behavior incompatible with development; an insufficiently enabling political environment for development; deficiencies in the health system, etc.

In Guinea-Bissau, the study does not mention poverty either, but deplores the legacy of colonial policy, which has left a social sector characterized by fragile health and education infrastructure and a severe shortage of qualified human resources.

In Côte d'Ivoire, poverty is implicit in the description of the economic crisis of recent years. According to the summary document of the perspective study *Côte d'Ivoire 2025*, the crisis is illustrated by an annual 1.5% decline in real GDP between 1986 and 1990. "In a context of strong population growth", comments the document, "this results implies a severe deterioration in the average Ivoirian's standard of living". Still in economic terms, poverty is implicit in the description of the negative effects of the free-market option and the call for corrections, particularly the protection and encouragement of local initiatives. The surveys highlight an aspiration to greater economic and social equity for the regions and indicate that this will depend on genuine administrative decentralization and more assertive regional development.

Poverty is scarcely more explicitly described in the study from Zimbabwe. Here again, it has to be discerned, mainly through people's aspiration to benefit from quality service in the social sectors: health, social security, education and housing. These services are integral to socioeconomic development, according to the study, which advocates guaranteed access for the greatest number, mainly through a fee structure adapted to people's purchasing power. The education system is criticized for its excessive focus on academic knowledge, to the detriment of the practical skills likely to lead to a job and reduce unemployment. The study calls for an acceleration and transformation of rural development to eliminate or significantly reduce poverty and improve the living standards of farmers.

Poverty does not seem particularly present in the NLTPS. In the vast majority of cases, it is not explicitly approached as a specific theme for reflection. It is expressed through the diverse forms that it takes. It can be seen in unemployment and exclusion, which affect a substantial proportion of society, in inadequate social services, in the deprivation experienced by various population groups and in the precarious situation of women and youth. Most of the African countries that have conducted these exercises do not have a poverty reduction strategy.

Everywhere, the concept of poverty is interchangeable with the low purchasing power and social exclusion that stem from it. Everywhere, poverty means people's incapacity to afford social services. Poverty is the result of parents' financial inability to provide their children with the education that could guarantee their social integration and human dignity. Everywhere, poverty signifies food insecurity, life in an unhealthy environment and life characterized by every form of deprivation. Poverty is both an economic failure and the social abandonment of particular population groups and individuals.

Box 3.6.

The absence of a poverty alleviation strategy in Kenya is largely due
to the lack of a global strategic vision of the development in the country

The formulation of policies, strategies or programs in Kenya was never based on a global, strategic and operational approach, neither on clear implementation principles. Likewise no study on the numerous, structural and interacting causes of poverty was really initiated. The sectorial and punctual approach help to combat the symptoms of poverty, rarely its causes. Therefore, no global and multidimensional approach has ever been envisaged.

From an economic point of view, the fundamental issues of economic growth with equity and employment creation implies greater expenditure in the social sectors and the empowerment of other actors such as women, NGOs, private sector and civil society through greater participation in the management of the economy. The participatory process ensures sound social policy as well as increasing the opportunities and contribution of all stakeholders to economic growth.

On the other hand, the institutional structure blocks both the participatory processes and the design of a long term vision on development prospects. In Kenya, the five year planning process is more and more perceived as inefficient with respect to the number of objectives and targets reached by the Government. Also, the annual budgetary cycles and their programming are not better because they hardly meet the funding needs. What is in fact expected is a strategic targeting of the most destitute populations and the implementation of a poverty reduction strategy.

Source: F. J. Mumina, "Economic and Social Aspects of Poverty and its Eradication in Kenya", Nairobi, 1997.

The examination of the proposals in the NLTPS lead naturally to a holistic approach to poverty alleviation.

The study from Côte d'Ivoire notes that the increase in the State's own resources following the devaluation of the CFA franc now makes it possible to raise the subsidies to existing development funds, to undertake wide-ranging social actions and to consider the implementation of a support fund for new graduates, a national guarantee fund for coffee and cocoa producers' cooperatives, a fund for women and development, etc. The study asserts that strong economic growth depends on the continuation and consolidation of State support to the social sectors.

In Malawi, the proposed poverty reduction strategy is similarly comprehensive. The vision that emerges from the study there recommends that traditional values and culture serve as a springboard for the promotion of economic and social development. One of the strategic options necessitated by the high rate of population growth is the improvement of the status of women through increased access to income-generating activities. The opportunities identified by the study in the health sector include the willingness of donors to provide support. Concerning the education system, the study recommends that strategies be developed to improve the working conditions of teachers.

A comprehensive approach is also advocated in Zimbabwe to solve the problems posed by poverty: as elsewhere, the economy is only envisaged as a means to improving people's social condition, and culture is seen as offering ways to reach social objectives. The study asserts that the participation of communities in their socioeconomic development depends on society's recognition of the diversity and equality of cultures and on each community's willingness to accommodate different views. Tolerance is thus seen as essential to economic and social development.

The economy must intervene by making financial resources available to farmers, women, youth and disadvantaged groups. The Zimbabwe study stresses the need to set up a rural development fund to hasten the emancipation of the countryside. It also recommends favoring equal opportunities for all in access to the factors of production — i.e. land, capital, training, employment — and promoting women, youth and disadvantaged social groups. People, particularly women, must be given access to financial resources to seize the opportunities that arise.

The study emphasizes women, youth and disadvantaged groups because of their precarious financial situation and ensuing social vulnerability. These two aspects can be considered as poverty reduction objectives. This shows the way in which poverty reduction is envisaged in the NLTPS through combined solutions, always considered comprehensively.

It is too early to assess the validity of the poverty reduction strategies recommended in the studies, as confirmed in Frédéric Grahmel's excellent analysis, [1] because of these countries' complete lack of experience in this area. Ways to operationalize the NLTPS strategies are being examined. The transition from the theoretical dimension of these studies to the inclusion of their recommendations in national development programs is also one of the objectives of the second phase of the "African Futures" regional project, which began recently. Here again, current attempts at analysis can only be speculative or abstract.

There is a need for a genuine renewal of planning and policy instruments, because capacity for economic and social planning and programming in Sub-Saharan Africa is clearly deteriorating.

---

1. F. Gramhel, *La pauvreté à travers les Etudes nationales de perspectives à long terme* (Abidjan: PNUD-Futurs Africains, 1998).

Box 3.7.

The promotion of growth focused on the economic realm
of the poor in Togo

Growth and poverty control policies are far from being anything new in Togo. However, for a long time, poverty has been perceived as the poverty of the Nation and not that of the citizens. For that reason, the objectives were expressed in terms of national economic growth. When at a later phase it was realized that, notwithstanding growth, the number of poor did not decrease significantly, policies aimed at "catering for basic needs of the populations" were initiated. The major investment programs that were initiated and implemented in the social sectors date back to that period.

In order to guarantee continued resource allocation to the poor and poorest, there seems to be no better way than that of promoting the generation of new resources among the poor themselves by improving the productivity of their existing jobs and, by creating new jobs and incomes in the sectors where poor constitute the majority of the population. It must be noted that such a strategy also in the long run to bring about better mobilization of internal savings for "proximity" investment.

The strategies, in that perspective, would consist in promoting measures that are likely to improve the productivity and income of the existing jobs in the agro-pastoral sector which encompassed the greatest number of poor and, in the urban and peri-urban areas such strategies would consist in creating new job and income opportunities, especially in the various non structured and informal sectors.

For the traditional policies of sectoral investment, training, structuring, organization and support coordination and synchronized implementation which conditions success in terms of growth and diversification also reach their objective of concrete reduction of poverty; it is important that they be guided on the one hand by the principle of selective targeting and on the other hand by the establishment of priorities in the allocation of the available limited resources.

If it is relatively easy to identify priority regions in poverty terms, the accurate targeting of poor and very poor human groups who must have priority in terms of allocating growth resources is more difficult. It is particularly, but not exclusively, for that reason that the setting up of decentralized communities that are able to design and take care of a considerable part of development activities takes on a capital aspect in poverty control.

The growth strategies that have been formulated will therefore integrate the expression of the general policy of the authorities in the country: a willingness to target and take growth actions as priority. They also integrate the proposals for poverty control that seem reasonable at that level and at this formulation stage. But beyond that, they also propose institutional and operational means to guarantee that they will be materialized.

Following recommendations the growth policies and strategies will also integrate the dimensions of rational management of natural resources and preservation of the environment.

Source: Government of Togo, "National Poverty Alleviation Strategy", 1995.

2. Macroeconomic policy and poverty reduction

The poor make up over 50% of the population in many Sub-Saharan African countries. They belong to diverse socioeconomic groups, in both rural and urban areas. In their efforts to assist them, governments and various development organizations often treat the poor as though they were the passive agents of their own development. In fact, the poor use a whole range of survival strategies and mechanisms to adapt or react to unexpected situations of crisis and/or famine to maintain and, if possible, to improve their short-term situation. It appears especially important to understand the survival strategies and adaptation mechanisms of poor women — not to mention their economic potential — because there are more poor women than men and they tend to be poorer.

Box 3.8.

In Uganda: persisting poverty despite growth
and the implementation of specific programs

Since 1986, the Ugandan economy has resumed growth and the agricultural sector has been growing considerably, a fundamental element in poverty control. Indeed the agricultural sector has the potential to feed the whole country and must serve as a driving force to growth.

However, notwithstanding an average growth of about 6% per year since 1986, no significant effect can be recorded in terms of poverty reduction. The expenditure gap between the rural world and the urban world has widened and inequalities have significantly increased over a short period of time. The non-agricultural sectors have recorded the strongest growth and urban households were the main beneficiaries of growth. Thus, by nature that growth has not favored poverty reduction.

In the face of the persisting poverty, the Uganda Government set up in the early 1990 a poverty reduction program related to social costs and to the adjustment (PAPSCA). On the other hand a $ 98 million particular program to rehabilitate the northern provinces was implemented in order to finance infrastructures and agricultural development in the 10 poorest districts in the northern part of the country.

Despite these special efforts and despite a strengthening of the terms of trade in agriculture, only the poor working in the coffee sector recorded some improvement of their living standard. In general, the agricultural producers have been too slow to react to the rise in agricultural prices due to lack of technological means and to the poor access to markets. Thus, it is clear that poverty elimination must be a national priority and growth must be more beneficiary to the poor.

Source: "Uganda Human Development Report 1996", UNDP, Kampala, 1996.

The challenge for African governments is to find ways to develop and not hinder poor people's economic activities, and to implement reforms that respond to the needs of the poor and that are accepted by them. This would entail:

– more actively seeking ways to support poor people's survival strategies by encouraging the beneficiaries to participate in planning and implementing reforms;

– examining the public regulations that have had the most direct impact on the poor, to mitigate the effects of rules and regulations that impede opportunities for the poor in terms of everyday economic and income-earning activities;

– studying the options for identifying poor people in critical situations and enhancing targeting of vulnerable groups.

2.1. Macroeconomic policies favorable to poverty reduction

To achieve healthy economic growth, which remains the pre-condition to reducing poverty, African governments have recognized the importance of conducting economic reform and eliminating structural obstacles. However, while these reforms are necessary, they are an insufficient condition for poverty reduction. Governments and donors pay too much attention to the overall macroeconomic results of structural reforms, in the short and medium term. They do not give sufficient consideration to the difficulties of implementing new policies nor to the effects of both pre- and post-reform policy on distribution and equity, so that the winners and losers are not always those expected from economic reform.

Many African countries continue to see structural adjustment as a condition imposed from the outside on which their continued access to official development assistance depends. There are many opportunities for governments and donors to pool their efforts with a view to appropriating the adjustment process so that it fits more closely with national and local perceptions and demands, and so that responsibility for implementation falls more clearly to the government and society as a whole. When disagreements arise between governments and donors on the speed and pace of reforms, the short-term economic costs of slowing certain adjustment measures can be offset by the greater long-term advantages of more profound and better designed change resulting from adjustment that has been designed and implemented from the inside.

To integrate poverty-related concerns more effectively into the macroeconomic policy framework, governments and donors should put more emphasis on monitoring the results of reforms downstream. This applies to two types of policy:

i) Macroeconomic policies in general, which should be examined to identify any effect that might penalize the poor, so that appropriate changes can be made to the choice of priorities or the sequencing of measures (without harming the objectives of "growth and equity") or compensatory measures or programs be implemented, such as social funds and revenue transfers.

ii) Macroeconomic or sectoral policies expressly designed to assist the poor, which should be monitored to ensure that they contribute effectively and efficiently to supporting the most disadvantaged. On paper, many apparently pro-poor policies have little impact on them.

Box 3.9.

The national poverty alleviation program in Senegal

In April 1994, the Senegalese Government initiated the process of national dialogue for the purpose of designing a National Alleviation Strategy and a National Poverty Alleviation Action Plan.

In this context, cooperation bodies interested in the theme were contacted in order to draw from their experiences and have their support for the future program. In that respect, the United Nations System, including the Bretton Woods institutions, got actively involved in the dialogue process. Two major national emissaries enable all the development actors to agree on the following:

– a logic of the causes and effect of poverty;

– the ways and means for a poverty control strategy in Senegal;

– an organization of objectives into a hierarchy.

Thus a consensus was reached concerning the essential causes of poverty:

– the populations are poor in resources;

– the results of growth are inequitably distributed;

– the essential needs are inadequately catered for.

Insofar as the long term objective is to reduce poverty rates (end goal of the strategy), the following mid term objectives were assigned to the national strategy:

• *Increasing the populations' income*, through a voluntarist policy of economic growth recovery focused on increasing job opportunities for the strata most affected by unemployment and underemployment, on a rational utilization of natural resources and a policy for the transfer of modular resources to prevent from the dislocation of the social fabric.

• *Better control of exogenous factors* through measures aimed at limiting the effects of natural environment degradation, regional conflicts. The management of the external debt will also be taken into account in order to avoid uncertainties and increase the self-reliance margins of the governmental policy.

• *Equitable distribution of the results of economic growth* by using more efficient instruments of economic policy more adapted to the requirements of sustainable human development; mechanisms in terms of regulation and budget measures contributing to reduce inequalities in chances of access to the benefits of growth requiring the participation of the populations in the management of resources, in education and sensitization actions in order to reduce the negative impact of some traditions and bring about better conditions of access to land.

• *Better coverage of the populations' needs,* through better coherence of sectoral policies, improvement of conditions of access to social services for the larger strata of the population, a voluntarist policy for the control of population growth as well as effective participation of the populations in decision-making and managing basic services.

The implementation of this poverty alleviation strategy will be part of an overall national strategy that aims at maintaining, even strengthening the competitiveness of the economy resulting from the major change in currency parity and from more rigor in the implementation of economic policy reforms.

The Poverty Alleviation Strategy described above is supported by a program of action focused on income and job generating activities through the promotion of micro-enterprise, micro-development and the implementation of community infrastructures through labor-intensive activities. The components of the program (they are four: income increase and diversification and job creation; improvement of access to basic social services; security nets; social and civil actions; strengthening of the system for monitoring household living standards), the targeted populations and zones as well as the institutional implementation framework are globally well articulated. Furthermore, the external partners of Senegal are well prepared to assist the country in implementing the program. However, the administrative procedures for the approval of the program are serious constraints to its start.

Source: UNDP, "Poverty in Senegal: Manifestations and Alleviation Strategy", 1997

Moreover, pro-poor objectives are sometimes overly optimistic or unrealistic in the light of existing resources and should therefore be aligned with what can be done with available resources.

To achieve this appropriation and integration:

– governments should study the best way to ensure the support of grassroots groups and stakeholders for the process of adjustment and reform, preferably before, and not during, the stage of negotiating the programs;

– governments and their development partners should agree on the practical criteria for measuring poverty and on social objectives for macroeconomic policies, to ensure that the results sought can be achieved. They should also extend the analysis of macroeconomic policies to identify and resolve their unfavorable consequences on the poor; and calculate the expected costs of this policy monitoring to determine viable, sustainable, operational ways to implement them.

2.2. Social Dimensions of Adjustment

The limited impact of the poverty reduction programs implemented in Sub-Saharan Africa in the late 1980s in complement to stabilization and structural adjustment efforts cast doubt on the underlying analytical and operational approach. The Social Dimensions of Adjustment (SDA) projects focused on the short-term mitigation of the negative effects of adjustment on mainly urban poor groups. The initial results obtained at the beginning of the 1990s proved that the policies of compensatory transfers or assistance (particularly safety nets) were insufficient.

Box 3.10.
Social security nets in Senegal

Following the devaluation of the CFA Franc by 50% in 1994, the immediate reaction of the Senegalese authorities aimed at limiting the inflationist trends related to such a measure of political economy was to establish a CFA F 15 billion security net under the State Table of Financial Operations to support the prices of high consumption products, i.e., rice, sugar, drugs and school stationery which are essentially imported. This price support program on a sliding scale covered the 1994-1995 period. Presently the prices of those products have been completely liberalized.

This social security net program suffered particularly from lack of targeting. The most destitute groups of the population benefited from it in the same way as the rest of the population. This program erred in terms of targeting efforts, which remains a determinant criteria of poverty control programs in terms of cost-effectiveness. This security net, funded by international assistance, raises again the problem of the efficiency of this assistance as compared to objectives aimed at. Indeed wouldn't the objective be a search for social stability soon after such an important change in parity, rather than a resolute option to combat poverty?

Source: Momar-Coumba Diop, *Poverty Alleviation in Dakar. Towards the definition of a municipal policy,* Dakar, 1996.

While SDA projects did not reduce poverty in Africa — this was not their objective — they did generate studies and research that paved the way for new proposals on long-term poverty reduction. The SDA analytical research and field experience had three major effects.

First, the SDA projects reopened the debate on poverty, which became the focus of several consultations and technical workshops at international and regional level. These forums, organized by various agencies of the United Nations system, were an opportunity to enhance concepts and approaches to poverty, which is now viewed in its various dimensions, both monetary and non-monetary. [1]

Secondly, the SDA projects disseminated the idea of country poverty profiles and thus contributed to introducing permanent research on living standards, on the characteristics and causes of poverty and on the accessibility of basic social services. Few African countries do not now have a poverty profile, whether constructed by the national government or by a development institution, such as the World Bank or UNDP.

Lastly, the SDA projects proposed a series of mechanisms for transmitting and targeting policy measures. Even if the proposed analytical framework is not yet unanimously accepted by all the participants, it has shown technical experts and policy-makers the need to focus on policy and strategy choices and on operational approaches to ensure maximum impact on the poor.

The formulation and implementation of poverty reduction policies and strategies depends finding ways to reconcile the need for adjustment and economic recovery with the objectives of raising the income of the poor and financing transfers to the most disadvantaged.

2.3. SAPs and the social sectors

Because of a lack of data on trends in living standards, development analysts have difficulty evaluating directly the effects of adjustment programs on the poor and distinguishing these effects from long-term economic and social trends. The method consisting in evaluating the impact of adjustment programs by analyzing trends in social indicators does not produce accurate results, because these indicators react with a considerable lag to changes in income and other trends (such as literacy rates and women's educational attainment).

More empirical research is needed to define reliable indicators that can distinguish between short-term economic trends and long-term development processes and to obtain data that will contribute to settling the debate over whether adjustment is beneficial or harmful for the poor.

The World Bank and the International Monetary Fund (IMF) have intensified their work in this area with mixed success, notably the study of the 23 countries that have applied an Enhanced Structural Adjustment Facility (ESAF) and the study published in March 1998 on a sample of 66 countries that implemented an IMF-sponsored program over 1986-1996. [2]

---

1. UNDP, *Human Development Report 1997* (New York: Oxford University Press, 1997).

2. "Countries with ESAF-Supported Programs show Progress in Social Spending and Social Indicators" (study of 23 countries with ESAF-supported programs), *IMF Survey* 21 July 1997; "Sample of 66 Economies: Social Spending Rises and Indicators Improve With IMF-Supported Programs", *IMF Survey* 23 February 1998.

These results should be interpreted with caution. It is difficult to gather consistent data on social spending because of delays in releasing figures, differences in statistical coverage between countries and the fact that spending by local authorities is sometimes not included. All this renders comparisons between countries problematic. Furthermore, the social indicators are influenced by many factors other than social spending, such as the overall sociopolitical and economic situation, improvements in medical technologies and the intensification or decline in the activities of NGOs and other private service providers.

2.4. Public spending policies

2.4.1. Restructuring of public spending during adjustment

Reducing the budget deficit is one of the cornerstones of a policy of stabilization of demand. The State has two ways to restore balance to public finances: cutting spending or increasing revenue. Many countries have opted for cutting spending, because of the State's limited capacity to raise tax revenue.

In a context of necessary public spending reductions, some countries have tried to promote the social sectors by reallocating spending. But faced with an acute public finance crisis, these sectors have generally not been spared by the overall spending cuts.

The 1990s have seen a slight change in priorities in the allocation of public spending. The World Bank's realization of the need to integrate a social dimension into the SAPs has protected the social sectors more effectively.

However, given the overall constraints on public spending, the shrinking resources for the social sectors have affected the situation of the poor. It would therefore be appropriate to take steps to:
– protect consumption: poor people have few savings, do not have access to credit and are thus unable to protect the level of their consumption;
– protect poor people's physical and human capital: health, education, irrigation works and rural roads are examples of investments that should be protected to favor activities that will enable the poor to generate income. If the crisis and the effects of adjustment have reduced the level of these investments, it should be restored as rapidly as possible.

However, it is not enough to protect the poor. Genuine poverty reduction policies should also be implemented. A poverty reduction objective must be systematically included in economic policy. Poverty alleviation must be integrated into the objectives and processes of adjustment policies. In terms of fiscal policy, this means more efficient management of spending aimed at poverty reduction to enhance its impact and to justify its subsequent increase.

Box 3.11.

Social Spending Rises and Indicators Improve With IMF-Supported Programs

Government spending on education and health has increased since the mid-1980s in countries with IMF-supported programs, especially in those supported by ESAF.

Education Expenditure

In a sample of 66 countries with IMF-supported programs for the period 1986-96, education spending rose by 0.1 percentage point as a share of GDP between the preprogram year and the most recent year for which data are available (a period averaging eight years). Changes were larger for a sample of 32 countries supported by ESAF, with education spending rising by 0.2% of GDP. Although modest, these changes occurred in the context of countries' efforts to secure fiscal adjustment through reductions in total government outlays. As such, these small increments in spending as a share of GDP led to proportionally larger increases in education spending as a share of total spending. Such outlays rose as a share of total government spending by 2.0 percentage points for the sample of 66 countries, and by 1.8 percentage points in SARF countries. Since the preprogram year, real per capita spending has increased on average by 0.9% per year for the full sample of countries and 2.8% a year in SARF countries.

The increase in education spending varied substantially between regions. For example, real per capita spending increased sharply (5.9% a year) in Asia, while real per capita outlays declined in Sub-Saharan Africa (0.5 percentage point).

Health Expenditure

Health outlays rose as a share of GDP by 0.3 percentage point between the preprogram year and the latest year for which data are available, and by 1.7 percentage points as a share of total government spending. Comparable increases were experienced in the sample of SARF countries. Real per capita government health outlays increased on average by 1.5% a year for the whole sample and 2.8 percent per year in ESAF countries. As with education spending, there was considerable variation between country groups. Real per capita health outlays rose strongly in Asia and the Western Hemisphere (4.1% and 3.8% per year, respectively), and increased slightly in Sub-Saharan Africa (2% a year).

It appears that rising social spending was accompanied, on average, by improvements in social indicators (as reported by the World Bank and UNESCO) for countries with IMF-supported programs. The illiteracy rate fell by an average of 2.4% per year, and gross enrolment rates in primary education rose by 0.9%. Health indicators also improved, as life expectancy increased by 0.3% per year and infant mortality rates fell by 1.8% per year. Progress was especially substantial with respect to increases in access to health care (4.6% per year) and immunization rates (approximately 6% per year).

Source: Bulletin of the International Monetary Fund, March 2nd, 1998.

From this perspective, public spending reviews merit closer attention. The implementation of a policy of efficient public spending must be based on a consistent and practical methodology for identifying and monitoring the policies and strategies designed to this effect. The public spending review is an effective instrument for this purpose. Although its objective is not poverty reduction, it has nevertheless contributed to discussion and to focusing the attention of policy-makers on social spending.

In the *World Development Report 1990* themed on poverty, the World Bank began to address the need to integrate a social dimension into the SAPs and to reduce structural poverty. To facilitate the formulation and implementation of the social dimension of the SAPs, the bank has developed several instruments.

The public spending reviews have been the main instrument for strengthening capacity to plan and monitor spending. In Sub-Saharan Africa, they have been used to build capacity for fiscal management and monitoring in the countries that benefit from the Special Facility for Africa (SFA). The main objectives of the public spending reviews are:
— to draw conclusions with a view to improving the process of managing the State budget;
— to assess the consistency between policy announcements and actual fiscal policy, in particular in the social sector;
— to evaluate the relationship between the World Bank's assistance and the efforts of the countries in terms of social services;
— to make policy recommendations allowing an improvement of social services through efficient and sustainable public spending.

Public spending programs are both an economic and a social policy instrument. They include both a macroeconomic dimension, through the level of spending and the impact of fiscal policy on the overall economic environment, and a mesoeconomic dimension, through the intersectoral and intrasectoral allocation of resources. Although strictly speaking not a poverty reduction instrument, the public spending reviews can nevertheless:
— link spending levels and the intersectoral and intrasectoral breakdown of spending to the poverty profile and identify mechanisms that reduce or aggravate poverty;
— study the effectiveness of public spending on the social sectors;
— study the effectiveness of safety nets in meeting economic and social objectives.

Broadly, public spending reviews analyze public spending policy at two levels. First, at macroeconomic level, they analyze the planned overall reduction in spending, i.e. the reduction in the budget deficit.

Secondly, at mesoeconomic level, they concentrate on three areas: i) the intersectoral allocation of spending, in particular the proportion of social spending in relation to other spending, the objective being to ensure that the overall reduction in spending has not led to a disproportionately large reduction in social spending; ii) the intrasectoral allocation of resources, which involves identifying the priorities of a given sector, for example, in education, the breakdown of spending between basic education and higher education; and iii) the composition of spending, which consists in analyzing the breakdown in spending between capital expenditure and recurrent expenditure, and in showing the share of certain expenditures, such as wages, in total expenditure.

In more detail, the public spending review should clarify:

– The level of spending and intersectoral allocation. This information should not be restricted to the central government budget; it should integrate all the other budgets — provincial and local authorities and state-owned enterprises. This requires a consolidation of the public budget by incorporating all the other budget components into a single budget.

– The impact of spending, to identify the beneficiaries through comparisons between regions (rural/urban) and socioeconomic groups.

– The effectiveness and efficiency of public spending on social services.

– The potential role of other sectors, such as the private sector and non-governmental organizations.

– Means of financing and their sustainability.

All the public spending reviews offer a general analysis of the social sectors, infrastructure and agriculture. Theoretically, all the sectors can be analyzed within this framework. However, several factors can influence the choice of priority sectors in the study: the results of the poverty profile, the government's priorities or the country's capacity for reaction and analysis.

In practice, however, the public spending reviews have generally been limited to two sectors — education and health — and focus on three main points:

a) The proportion of health and education expenditure in total expenditure. The objective is to ensure that the overall public spending cuts to reduce the public deficit have not caused a disproportionately large reduction in spending on the social sectors.

b) The intrasectoral allocation of resources in these two sectors. The public spending reviews have indicated that intrasectoral priorities need to be changed to benefit the poor.

c) The proportion of wage expenditure in relation to other expenditure. The public spending reviews have shown that a high proportion of spending in these two sectors is allocated to wages, to the detriment of spending on equipment.

Table 3.1. –   Diagnostic review of Public Expenditure and analysis
              of incidence in Africa South of the Sahara, 1988-1997 [a]

Country	Years of public expenditure reviews	Analysis of incidence	Social sectors considered	Technical support
South Africa	1995	1996	Education/ Health	World Bank
Benin	1989, 1991,1994	–	–	World Bank/ UNDP
Botswana	1985, 1989, 1995	–	Education/ Health/Water	World Bank
Burkina Faso	1991,1994, 1996	1996	Education/ Health	World Bank
Burundi	1991, 1992	–	Education/ Health	World Bank
Cameroon	1995	–	Education/ Health	World Bank
Cap Verde	1995	–	Education/ Health	World Bank
Comoros	1994, 1995	–	Education/ Health	World Bank
Côte d'Ivoire	1997	1996-97	Education/ Health	World Bank
Ethiopia	1993	–	Health	World Bank
Gambia	1991, 1993, 1996	–	Education/ Health	World Bank
Ghana	1992, 1995, 1997	1995	Education/ Health	World Bank
Guinea	1992, 1994, 1997	–	Education/ Health	World Bank/ UNDP
Guinea Bissau	1994	–	–	World Bank
Kenya	1993, 1995	1993, 1995, 1996	Education/ Health/Water/ Infrastructure	World Bank
Lesotho	1993, 1995, 1996	1996	Education/ Health	World Bank/ UNDP
Madagascar	1992, 1994, 1996	1996	Education/ Health	World Bank/ UNDP
Malawi	1989, 1992, 1994, 1997	1994, 1996	Education/ Health	World Bank

Table 3.1. – Diagnostic review of Public Expenditure and analysis
of incidence in Africa South of the Sahara, 1988-1997 [a] *(suite)*

Country	Years of public expenditure reviews	Analysis of incidence	Social sectors considered	Technical support
Mali	1989,1993, 1996	1993, 1996	Education/ Health	World Bank/ UNDP
Mauritania	1990, 1994	1995	Education/ Health	World Bank
Namibia	1991, 1994, 1997	1995	Education/ Health	World Bank/ UNDP
Niger	1991, 1993, 1995	1995	Education/ Health	World Bank/ UNDP
Nigeria	1991, 1995	–	Education/ Health	World Bank
Uganda	1989, 1993, 1995	1995	Education/ Health	World Bank
Rwanda	1991, 1994	–	Education/ Health	World Bank
Senegal	1989, 1992, 1995	1995	Education/ Health	World Bank
Seychelles	1994	–	Education/ Health/Water	World Bank
Sierra Leone	1989, 1993	–	Education/ Health/Water/ Infrastructure	World Bank
Tanzania	1993, 1995	–	–	World Bank
Togo	1990, 1993, 1995	–	Education/ Health	World Bank
Zambia	1994, 1995	–	Education/ Health/Water/ Infrastructure	World Bank/ UNDP
Zimbabwe	1995	1995, 1997	Education/ Health/Water/ Infrastructure	World Bank

a. Data are taken from different years of public expenditure review. See relevant bibliography.

Public spending reviews should be used to supplement studies on poverty. Unfortunately, there has not yet been any genuine synchronization of the two approaches.

2.4.2. Allocation of public resources to social services

An analysis of the allocation of resources to the social sectors must take into account two essential elements: i) the volume of financial resources needed to attain objectives such as bringing down the under-five mortality rate to 70 per 1,000 live births or allowing 80% of children to benefit from at least five years of primary education; and ii) the constraints that influenced the allocation of resources.

There are two methods to estimate the amount needed to finance these sectors. The first, developed by the World Bank, consists in calculating the unit cost of providing a service to attain a specific objective. In the *World Development Report 1993*, the World Bank estimated at $12 per person the spending needed to ensure access to a package of minimum health services. [1]

The second method is based on the proportion of resources allocated to the health and education sectors in countries that have already attained the desired objective. This approach led the WHO to call for 10% of budgets to be allocated to health [2] and UNICEF and UNDP to develop the ratios underpinning the 20/20 Initiative.

Calculating the level of spending per capita is an example of the unit cost approach and allows for comparisons on the basis of a benchmark cost. The actual allocation of resources to the social sectors depends on the country's initial resources (per capita GDP), on the capacity of the State to raise public resources (rate of taxation) for public spending after debt-servicing and on the tradeoffs between and within the state-subsidized sectors. The impact of the volume of financial resources deployed also depends on the efficiency of the health and education systems.

In Africa, the intermediate countries spend three times as much on the health and education sectors as the least developed countries. Niger allocated CFAF1,333 per capita in real terms (base 1987) to health in 1994, which covered 22.2% of the cost of the minimum package of public health services and basic clinics calculated by the World Bank. In contrast, Côte d'Ivoire allocated CFAF3,605 per capita in 1994 (in real terms, base 1985), representing 70% of the basic minimum.

---

1. World Bank, *World Development Report 1993: Investing in Health* (Washington: Oxford University Press, 1993).

2. WHO, *World Health Report 1996* (Geneva, 1996).

Military spending is equivalent to 44% on average of combined spending on education and health in Sub-Saharan Africa. [1] In Guinea in 1992 education accounted for 22.6% and health 7.6% of total spending, while defense totaled 12.5% of the State budget. These figures reflect an imbalance in public resource allocation that is unfavorable to the social sectors.

The allocation of public spending to the social sectors in the 1990s have been strongly affected by the crisis in public finances. Without massive support from donors, all the adjusting countries have had to reduce allocations to social spending (health and/or education). Because of insufficient public revenue, public spending programs in some of the least developed African countries are around 60% dependent on external resources.

The ratio of health and education spending to GDP measures the macroeconomic importance of the social sectors and provides an indirect indication of the efforts made to develop human resources.

In the countries committed to implementing the 20/20 Initiative, which are usually adjusting successfully, changes in the share of public spending allocated to the social ministries in the past few years are a good indicator of governments' real priorities.

The ratios available range on average from 12% to 38% over 1990-97. These disparities may be due to dissimilar content of research undertaken nationally and should be compared with caution. [2] They can also result from different situations or policy choices — following a decrease in public resources, Cameroon and Niger chose to drastically reduce the financing allocated to social services, while other countries, such as Benin, Côte d'Ivoire and Malawi, allocate 30% to 40% of their budgets to the social ministries.

In more general terms, an analysis of social sector financing shows that the resources allocated to basic services are inadequate in the light of needs and the objective of poverty reduction. Actions to improve coverage and access of the poorest groups to social services must solve three problems:

– resource allocation — securing a substantial volume of financial resources to ensure sufficient production of social services in the light of needs;

---

1. UNDP, *Human Development Report 1996* (New York: Oxford University Press, 1996).

2. While the health and education ministries are the core managers of social services, other ministries may have a minor part of their activities in these sectors. For example, the drinking water supply in rural areas may be the responsibility of the ministry of agriculture, the ministry of the environment or the ministry of capital works.

– internal efficiency — ensuring that the social systems make the best use of the resources available to them;

– equity — allowing the most disadvantaged users to benefit from basic services without compromising economic rationality and social efficiency.

Table 3.2. – Proportion of Public Expenditure allocated to Social Sectors

	1990	1992	1994	1996	1997
Benin					
Ratio Public expenditure/GDP		20.2	19.8	19.5	18.8
Ratio social expenditure/Public expenditure		28.7	29.7	33.1	30.7
Ratio ESS expenditure/social expenditure				38.0	33.1
Ratio ESS expenditure/public expenditure (I20/20)				12.6	10.2
Burkina Faso					
Ratio Public expenditure/GDP	19.1	22.0	30.7	31.0	34.1
Ratio social expenditure/Public expenditure	14.0	12.5	12.8	13.0	12.8
Ratio ESS expenditure/social expenditure	68.8	77.2	79.4	74.5	81.1
Ratio ESS expenditure/public expenditure (I20/20)	15.1	19.4	23.5	17.5	19.5
Cameroon					
Ratio Public expenditure/GDP	14.4	17.9	13.9	15.5	
Ratio social expenditure/Public expenditure	27.9	27.6	15.9	13.7	
Ratio ESS expenditure/social expenditure	36.8	31.2	31.1	30.2	
Ratio ESS expenditure/public expenditure (I20/20)	10.3	8.6	4.9	4.1	
Côte-d'Ivoire					
Ratio Public expenditure/GDP		35.3	29.9	28.0	
Ratio social expenditure/Public expenditure		36.3	28.0	35.2	
Ratio ESS expenditure/social expenditure		37.2	41.8	32.2	
Ratio ESS expenditure/public expenditure (I20/20)		13.5	11.7	11.3	

Table 3.2. – Proportion of Public Expenditure allocated to Social Sectors

	1990	1992	1994	1996	1997
Mali					
Ratio Public expenditure/GDP			27.4	23.1	
Ratio social expenditure/Public expenditure			25.9	26.7	
Ratio ESS expenditure/social expenditure			61.1	63.0	
Ratio ESS expenditure/public expenditure (I20/20)			15.8	16.8	
Namibia					
Ratio Public expenditure/GDP		42.5	35.9		
Ratio social expenditure/Public expenditure [a]	29.4	29.7	36.9	33.5	
Ratio ESS expenditure/social expenditure					
Ratio ESS expenditure/public expenditure (I20/20) [a]	14.0	21.0	22.0	19.0	
Tanzania					
Ratio Public expenditure/GDP	18.2	23.8	21.4	18.2	19.0
Ratio social expenditure/Public expenditure	19.8		28.5	20.3	20.1
Ratio ESS expenditure/social expenditure					
Ratio ESS expenditure/public expenditure (I20/20)					
Zambia [a]					
Ratio Public expenditure/GDP					
Ratio social expenditure/Public expenditure	16.3	8.4	19.4	19.9	
Ratio ESS expenditure/social expenditure					
Ratio ESS expenditure/public expenditure (I20/20)					

a. For countries marked with an asterisk, the financial years last from July to June: the 1990 column is for financial year 1990/91.

Source: UNDP-UNICEF 20/20 Studies conducted at national level, 1997-1998. National Reports on Initiative 20/20, 1996-1998.

Table 3.3. – Public Health and Education Expenditure as % of GNP

Country (LDC)	Public health expenditure as % of GDP en 1990	Public education expenditure as % of GNP	
		1980	1993-94
Benin	2.8		
Burkina Faso	7.0	2.6	3.6
Burundi	1.7	3.0	3.8
Ethiopia	2.3		
Gambia		3.3	2.7
Guinea	2.3		
Lesotho		5.1	4.8
Madagascar	1.3	4.4	1.9
Malawi	2.9	1.9	
Mali	2.8	3.8	2.1
Mozambique	4.4	4.4	
Niger	3.4	3.1	3.1
Uganda	1.6	1.2	1.9
Central African Republic	2.6	3.8	2.8
Tanzania	3.2	4.4	5.0
Chad	4.7		2.2
Togo	2.5	5.6	7.1
Zaire	0.8	2.6	
Zambia	2.2	4.5	2.6
Other countries			
South Africa	3.2		7.1
Botswana		7.0	8.5
Cameroon	1.0	3.2	3.1
Congo		7.0	8.3
Côte d'Ivoire	1.7	7.2	
Gabon		2.7	3.2
Ghana	1.7	3.1	3.1
Kenya	2.7	6.8	6.8
Namibia		1.5	8.7
Nigeria	1.2	6.4	1.3
Senegal	2.3		
Seychelles		5.8	7.4
Swaziland		6.1	6.8

Source: Human Development Report, 1997.

Box 3.12.

The influence of Official Development Assistance on resource allocation to social sectors in Guinea

Until 1988, the results obtained in terms of resource allocation to the sector of education revealed the inadequacy of means required to achieve objectives, or the poor allocation of State resources to priority sectors in Guinea. However, since the Education Structural Adjustment Program (ESAP) was initiated in 1989, some improvement has been recorded.

During the pre-ESAP period (1986-1989), the current average expenditure was GF 1615.6 against 5426 for the period of ESAP implementation (1990-1992). If education current expenditure per capita amounted only to GF 743.4, i.e., US $ 2 in 1986, it reached 8,338 GF, i.e., US $ 9.2 in 1992. Regarding investment, education expenditure amounted to GF 353.3, i.e., US $ 1 in 1986, the figure reached GF 1,565, i.e., US $ 1.7 in 1992. This increase in education expenditure per capita mostly reflects donors' effort to allocate more resources to this sector. Indeed, consid-

ering the evolution of most of the budget devoted to the education sector, one notes a moderate performance of State budget allocation in favor of this sector. The proportion of State education expenditure as percentage of total expenditure was 8.3% in 1988 and 7.8% in 1992.

Since the beginning of the economic recession in 1983, the availability of external resources is one of the major determinants of the evolution of the general level of public expenditure in Guinea. The periods during which the country has access to external resources through economic reforms supported by the Bretton Woods institutions correspond to the highest levels of public expenditure. Thus between 1984 and 1989, total expenditure steadily increased. On the other hand, with the interruption of the structural adjustment programs during the 1990-1993 period, expenditure recorded a steady decline in commitment.

Source: UNICEF, "Social sectors and budget restructuring", Conakry, 1994.

The education sector in Sub-Saharan Africa suffers from serious internal inefficiency. The average unit cost of a primary school pupil is 1.5 times higher in Africa than in Asia, the unit cost of a secondary school student is 2.5 times higher and the unit cost of a higher education student is 3 times higher. As a result, African enrolment ratios are far below Asian averages.

Studies on the impact of education spending have highlighted a need to strengthen the State's commitment to reallocating resources in favor of the poorest people. In Côte d'Ivoire, the poorest quartile accounts for 30.5% of children aged 6 to 11, but only 23.9% of school pupils in this age group, while the richest quartile accounts for only 18.3% of children aged 6 to 11,

Table 3.4. – Comparison of unit costs per student between Africa and Asia

	Unit cost as % GNP per inhabitant	Enrolment rate
Average for Africa, 1989		
Primary	16.3	56.4
Secondary	47	14.6
Tertiary	546.8	1
Average for Asia, 1989		
Primary	9.9	94
Secondary	18.5	42
Tertiary	148.9	10.1

Source: Studies on Initiative 20/20 conducted at national level and submitted during regional workshops of Cotonou at Pretoria with UNDP and UNICEF support.

but 26.9% of school pupils in this age group. The disparities are even sharper in secondary education where 51.7% of students come from families in the richest quartile, although only 31.5% of young people aged 12 to 30 belong to this quartile.

The direct cost of sending a child to school is the chief determinant of demand for education. Most surveys on this issue conclude that the main factor discouraging poor parents from sending their children to school is the cost of education, including school equipment, and transport. The opportunity cost of these private education expenses is clearly higher for poor families. In South Africa, the direct cost of primary education absorbs more than 40% of household non-food spending per child sent to school. The corresponding figure for the richest families is only 6%. This cost is even higher for a secondary student, accounting for 50% of the poorest families' non-food spending.

While the share of the State in the total cost of sending a child to school is often higher for poor families than for rich families, the distribution of public spending between the different social categories still largely favors the well-off. In Madagascar in 1993, the first quintile benefited from only 8% of public spending on education, compared with 41% for the last quintile. The same disparities were evident in South Africa in 1993.

Table 3.5. – Unit cost per student in some countries of sub-Saharan Africa

Pays	% of GNP per capita		% GNP per capita	Primary Education		
	Unit cost of a primary school student	Unit cost of a secondary school student	Unit cost of a higher education student	Student: teacher ratio	Salary of a primary school teacher (as % GNP per capita)	Rate of repeating a grade
Botswana	9	51	284	32	290	5
Gambia	11	26	0	32	350	16
Ghana	5	17	250	29	150	3
Kenya	13	47	680	31	400	
Lesotho	7	43	192	55	390	22
Malawi	7	94	1,030	64	450	21
Mauritius	10	18	117	21	210	5
Namibia	26	48	300	29	750	25
Sierra Leone	3	17	366	31	90	
South Africa	35	81	191	24	840	
Swaziland	8	28	262	33	260	15
Tanzania	11	193	1,180	35	390	5
Zambia	4	33	207	44	180	
Zimbabwe	21	40	137	36	760	
Average	13	55	400	35	390	

Source: UNESCO, World Education Report, 1994.

Table 3.6. –   Incidence of public expenditure in some countries
of sub-Saharan Africa

Country	Year	Incidence education expenditure	
		20% poorest	**20% richest**
South Africa	1993	14	35
Côte d'Ivoire	1993	14	35
Ghana	1992	16	21
Kenya	1992/3	17	21
Madagascar	1993	8	41
Malawi	1994/5	16	25
Tanzania	1993	13	23

Therefore, it is essential to find ways to improve the distribution of education spending. The measure most commonly proposed to increase public spending in favor of the poor is targeting. The theoretical effectiveness of this instrument no longer needs to be proved. However, an optimum degree of targeting needs to be found in the light of factors that can influence its effectiveness: the characteristics of the poor, the socioeconomic environment or the country's administrative capacity. When poverty is scattered and administrative capacity insufficient, it is preferable to opt for broader targeting through an increase in spending on basic education.

2.4.3. 20/20 Initiative: a framework for raising financial resources and a mechanism for monitoring poverty reduction efforts

2.4.3.1. Origin and objectives

The 20/20 Initiative was the first concrete poverty reduction measure adopted at the World Summit for Social Development in 1995. This initiative endorses a mutual commitment between developed and developing countries whereby at least 20% of official development assistance and 20% of public spending from countries' own resources are to be allocated to social services.

In 1996, at the Oslo meeting on implementation of the 20/20 Initiative, ten African countries volunteered for a pilot trial: Benin, Burkina Faso, Chad, Côte d'Ivoire, Malawi, Mali, Namibia, Niger, South Africa and Tanzania. In October 1997, a regional technical workshop was held in Cotonou for the French-speaking countries to design a common methodology. A similar workshop was attended by the English-speaking countries in Pretoria in February 1998.

The 20/20 Initiative is one instrument in a broader policy of economic and social poverty reduction. It focuses on the expansion of essential social services — basic education, primary health care, reproductive health, nutrition, drinking water and sanitation. It aims to improve the physical and intellectual condition of the poorest people by facilitating their access to basic services and to achieve more equitable distribution of public spending.

The 20/20 Initiative has three main objectives:

– a financial objective: increasing the public resources allocated to essential social services to secure sufficient production of services in relation to the needs identified;

– an objective of internal efficiency: ensuring that the systems make the best use of the resources available to them;

– an objective of equity: directing services to the poorest population groups.

The 20/20 Initiative is a key instrument for dialogue between governments and development partners on policies to expand basic social services. It provides essential support for the design, implementation, monitoring and evaluation of poverty reduction strategies and programs. It is also a pragmatic framework for raising domestic and external resources to facilitate access for the poorest people to four essential social services. This financing is likely to generate positive externalities benefiting society as a whole.

The 20/20 Initiative chose to focus on essential social services because of: i) their good cost-benefit ratio; ii) their strong impact on the main social indicators; and iii) their potential use as a tool for reducing inequalities. Validated by international consensus, essential social services are a powerful instrument (although necessarily limited) [1] supported by all the governments represented at the Oslo meeting.

The social services defined under the 20/20 Initiative are:

Basic health care: primary health care, prevention, maternal and child health, district hospitals, district health administration, training of nurses in fields other than third-level hospital specializations, health education.

Basic education: primary schooling and training of primary-school teachers, early-childhood development and pre-school education, literacy for adults and youths who have dropped out of school.

Drinking water and sanitation: low-cost technologies for drinking water supply and sanitation, hygiene education.

Nutrition: activities most directly supporting an improvement in the nutrition status of vulnerable groups.

---

1. Several East African countries wanted spending on social housing for the poorest people to be included as essential social services. South Africa devotes 8% to 9% of public recurrent expenditure to social action for the most disadvantaged groups.

Reproductive health: family planning, reproductive health, HIV/AIDS prevention, population programs.

Box 3.13.
Why basic social services?

The basic social services have some specific features that make them different from other priority fields of human development and justify the special attention paid to them through the 20/20 Initiative; the basic social services are particularly important in reducing the worse aspects of poverty. Ignorance, disease and hunger are the major factors that perpetuate the cycle of poverty. Basic education, primary health care, family planning, nutrition, drinking water supply and sanitation are therefore the crucial themes that may contribute to break this cycle. From the economic standpoint, all the basic social services show a high yield rate and are associated to very positive externalities. In other words, the whole society will benefit from the expansion of the coverage of these services and from the improvement of their quality. Thus the 20/20 Initiative appears as a pragmatic framework for mobilizing both national and external resources that will enable the populations to have access to quality education and basic health care system, to better nutrition and to good reproductive health, to drinking water and to a sound environment through the sanitation of their living environment. The end goal of all these efforts is nothing but making poverty eradication and sustainable human development operational.

Source: "20/20 Initiative: reaching the objective of universal access to essential social services for sustainable human development" UNFPA, WHO, UNDP, UNESCO & UNICEF, 1995.

2.4.3.2. *Progress to date*

In the countries that volunteered for a pilot trial, the first stage of implementing the initiative consists in conducting studies to assess the priority given by the government and donors to the basic social sectors and to identify possibilities for raising additional resources to support basic social services. These studies form the basis for a national plan of action to achieve the 20/20 objective.

For their plans of action on the 20/20 Initiative, all the countries adopted the common framework established at the Cotonou and Pretoria workshops and consisting of four sections:

– an economic and financial analysis: the macroeconomic context and its impact on public resources, trends in budget allocations and official development assistance in favor of the essential social services, an estimate of the funding needed to reach the threshold of 20% of public spending and ODA;

– a functional analysis: the activities of the essential social services and their impact on human development and equity;

– a prospective analysis: the possibilities for raising additional resources and increasing the efficiency and impact of financing;

– operational guidelines: the mechanisms for implementation, monitoring and evaluation.

Box 3.14.
The 20/20 Initiative in Burkina Faso

The international community took the phenomenon of poverty as its top concerns and globally gave rise to a series of conferences on the theme of poverty eradication The most important of these conferences was unquestionably the World Summit on Social Development held in Copenhagen from 6th to 12th March 1995. This summit adopted the implementation of the 20/20 Initiative as a first concrete poverty alleviation measure. This initiative, for the developed and developing countries, seals the mutual commitment to respectively allocate at least 20% of the official development assistance and 20% of the national budget to basic social services.

As a follow-up to the Copenhagen world summit of social development,

Burkina Faso volunteered to conduct a pilot experiment on the implementation of the 20/20 Initiative.

Based on the available first results, the Burkinabè State has allocated in 1995 and 1996 an average of 13.6% of its budget to basic essential social sectors, i.e., 11.8% in 1995 and 15.4% in 1996. Out of more than CFA Francs 23 billion allocated to the sectors of the 20/20 Initiative in 1995, basic education received more than 13 billions, i.e., 57% of the total against 36% to health; the remaining 7% were divided between drinking water and reproduction health. This preponderant portion allocated to health an education accounted respectively for 38% and 55.6% of the total allocation to the basic social sectors.

Government efforts to promote the social services of the 20/20 Initiative

	1995 % Budget	1996 % Budget	1995 % Revenue	1996 % Revenue	1995 % GDP	1996 % GDP
MEBA	6.8	8.6	9.9	9.7	1.2	1.2
HEALTH	4.3	5.9	6.3	6.7	0.7	0.8
Social action and family	0.4	0.5	0.5	0.5	0.1	0.1
Drinking water	0.4	0.5	0.5	0.6	0.1	0.1
Initiative 20/20	11.8	15.4	17.3	17.5	2.0	2.2

As for the development partners of Burkina Faso, the resources that they allocate to basic social sectors represent an average of 17.3% of the total assistance for the 1995-1996 period. This percentage was 18.3% in 1995 against 16.5% in 1996. The distribution between sectors there is

somehow different from that of the State. Thus, taking the cumulated disbursement of 1995 and 1996 into account, i.e., US $ 149 million, the water and sanitation sector represent 36.6% against 30.8% for basic education, 24.5% for health and 7.9% for reproduction health.

Additional steps were taken to further diagnose the analysis of social expenditure in terms of efficiency and effectiveness of investments in favor of the essential social sectors. Similarly, steps were taken to look more in-depth into the opportunities for infra and inter-sectorial budget restructuring in favor of the 20/20 Initiative and the reduction of extreme poverty. Finally, a reflection on the modalities for mobilizing additional resources in favor of basic social sectors as well as for monitoring and evaluating the 20/20 Initiative was initiated by the Government and its major development partners, namely on the occasion of a national workshop on this initiative organized in Ouagadougou in September 1998.

Source: "20/20 Initiative in Burkina Faso", Ministry of Economy and Finance & UNDP, Ouagadougou, 1998.

2.4.3.3. *Results of the studies and options for reform*

The share of public spending (from own resources) allocated to the essential social services in these countries ranges from 4% to 20%. Several countries — Burkina Faso, Niger and Namibia — are close to the objective of 20% advocated by the 20/20 Initiative. Others, such as Mali and South Africa, are not much further off. All these countries implemented a policy of redistribution in favor of basic social services more than a decade ago.

These budget ratios should also be assessed in the light of per capita spending on essential social services. With half the ratio, Côte d'Ivoire allocates three to four times the per capita amount to social services as Burkina Faso and Niger. The weakness of these social indicators is that a high ratio suggests a political commitment to enhancing the impact of the amounts allocated, which is not always the case.

In countries with a low level of development, investment in essential social services is mainly financed by external project aid, leaving the ensuing operating costs to the government and users. [1] The share of investment in spending from own resources rarely exceeds 10%-15%.

---

1. The relative accessibility of donor financing for investment leads to "relative overinvestment" in the poorest countries: some facilities are not functional because of a lack of financial and human resources. There is irreversible deterioration of the working condition of facilities, which are not cost-effective as a result. When budgets are not sufficient to ensure the proper operation of existing infrastructure, spending on maintenance of facilities in remote areas tends to be the first to be cut. Some official development assistance to the poorest countries could be allocated to the operation of essential social services, i.e. to *maintaining* facilities. This would lengthen their lifespan and lead, in time, *for the same amount of expenditure,* (i) to providing more working infrastructure and to engaging a process of *sustainable* development and (ii) to increasing the financial accessibility of essential social services.

Table 3.7. – Share of total public expenditure (on own resources) allocated to essential social services [a]

As % of public expenditure	Year	Basic education	Basic health and nutrition	Water and sanitation	Total ESS	ESS per capita [b]
South Africa	1996/97	10.0	3.5	0.5	14.0	938
Namibia	1996/97	11.5	5.9	1.7	19.1	589
Zambia	1997				20.0	
Malawi	1997				20.0	
Tanzania	1997				15.0	
Cameroon	1996/97				4.0	2 311
Côte d'Ivoire	1996	9.0	1.8	0.6	11.4	10 712
Benin	1997	7.0	2.2	0.3	9.5	3 801
Mali	1996	12.2	3.4	0.3	15.9	2 783
Burkina Faso	1997	10.6	8.3	0.6	19.5	3 349
Niger	1992	14.7	4.3	1.4	20.4	2 604

a. According to the documents, total public expenditure used to calculate percentages sometimes include donations, and even some loans. There is need to define a single calculation method.
b. Amount allocated to ESS per capita is labeled in country currency: FFCA, South African Rand, Namibian $…

Source: National documents on Initiative 20/20.

The distinction between capital investment and recurrent expenditure is useful in that there is a need to maintain a balance between these two components to avoid under-financing of operating costs and abnormal depreciation of infrastructure. But an accurate assessment of this break-down can only be made by examining the combined own resources and official development assistance spent on essential social services.

2.4.3.4. *Possibilities for raising additional resources*

To achieve the objective of allocating 20% of all public spending to essential social services, and to surpass this objective once achieved, [1] all the volunteer countries have investigated possibilities for raising additional resources, through an intra and intersectoral restructuring of public spending and by seeking new sources of financing.

Raising additional resources must be associated with the involvement of stakeholders to ensure that the funds are more effectively and efficiently spent on essential social services.

In addition to increasing external assistance, there are several other ways to raise the funds needed to expand essential social services: i) increasing public revenues; ii) debt relief; iii) intersectoral restructuring; iv) intrasectoral restructuring; and v) raising private or household financing (for-profit and not-for-profit private sector, household contributions).

i) *Increasing public revenues*

All the governments are committed to a policy of reducing budget deficits. Therefore, an increase in public spending can only come from an increase in public revenues, i.e. by raising the rate of taxation (which is possible in a country like Benin, where the tax rate is 12%).

More effective collection procedures would also raise tax revenues. Several countries have taken vigorous steps to improve tax collection in the past few years (Tanzania, which recently introduced VAT at a uniform rate of 20% is trying to broaden the tax base and is waging a public campaign against corruption; Mali and Malawi have implemented specialized agencies for tax collection).

With no change to the rate of taxation, countries with sustained GDP growth will enjoy surplus tax revenues, some of which could be used for essential social services. However, when the existing tax rates in these countries are around 17%-20%, the Bretton Woods institutions advise reducing

---

1. The objective of 20% is an intermediate stage. With 20% of total public spending allocated to essential social services in Burkina Faso, basic health care accounts for 8% of the budget, corresponding to per capita spending of CFAF2,700, or $4.50, which falls far short of the $12 recommended by the WHO.

tax pressure (Côte d'Ivoire plans to reduce its tax rate from 21% in 1998 to 20% in 1999). This source of financing can therefore only be envisaged in countries where existing tax rates are low.

The countries that have not yet completed their privatization programs can also generate privatization revenues. In principle, fiscal orthodoxy requires privatization revenues to be assigned to reducing the government deficit. However, in Côte d'Ivoire for example, where over CFAF100 billion is expected from the privatization of 40 enterprises over 1998-2000, some of these revenues could be allocated to investment in essential social services. Similarly, in Cameroon, it has been proposed that 10% of privatization revenues be earmarked for essential social sectors.

The decentralization process under way in most countries offers considerable scope for transferring management of essential social services to local authorities. The central government can secure the participation of local authorities with appropriate tax incentives.

Increasing local taxation revenues is a possibility, at least in regions with strong economic potential. Raising decentralized public resources would allow the central government to withdraw from the richest regions and concentrate on the most disadvantaged. This is one of the options currently being explored by Burkina Faso (introduction of municipal taxes) and South Africa to reduce inequality.

In South Africa, spending on essential social services is high and growing faster than other social spending, reflecting the real priorities of the government. However, the territorial distribution of this spending is proportional to the population, although the inequality of wealth between regions ranges from 1 to 8. Ways to redistribute spending between regions are currently being investigated.

Some measures that may cause social tension require gradual implementation. The financial return of single measures may be low, but their combined return can be substantial.

ii) Reducing debt

Internal and external debt-service is usually considered non-discretionary spending. Nevertheless, numerous steps to relieve or forgive debt have been taken (Toronto, Trinidad and Naples Agreements in 1988, 1990 and 1996 respectively). All the 20/20 volunteer countries are concerned by these debt-relief measures.

Box 3.15.
Putting debt into the service of development

Debt reimbursement often absorbs between one quarter and one third of the already limited public revenue in the Sub-Saharan African countries as in many other developing countries and thus supplant public investments in favor of human development which are crucial. In some countries such as Guinea Bissau, Mauritania, the Democratic Republic of Congo and Zambia the service of debt fallen due represents three to six times the level of public expenditure devoted to education. High indebtedness and unpaid arrears also dissuade foreign private investments and encourage the drain of national savings, which are a vital finance source required for human development, economic growth and the improvement of living standards.

Over the last few years, measures have been taken to tackle the debt issue. Multilateral organizations and bilateral donors are sponsoring plans for the reduction of commercial debt. Creditor countries have agreed on a number of measures in accordance with the terms of the Toronto Convention, of the Trinidad Convention and of the 1995 Naples Convention. Although these measures contribute to reduce indebtedness, many low income and highly indebted countries have still not gotten rid of a large portion of their debt. Moreover, these measures are inadequate.

The initiative in favor of the highly indebted poor countries appears as an innovative solution compared to the other former techniques that were likely to help solve the persistent problems posed by the African debt. It takes up debt reduction in a global, integrated and coordinated manner that covers all groups of creditors and all debt categories (bilateral, multilateral or commercial) in order to make the debt service sustainable and bring out resources to be invested in the social sectors. The countries that are eligible to benefit from this initiative are those having a current net debt value over exports higher than 200 - 220%, and having recorded success with successive SAPs over the last 6 years. These solutions can technically be used to solve the debt problem but their application is being delayed, even in low income and highly indebted countries what are making considerable efforts to reform their economic policy. Consequently, as early as 1995, the UNDP supported the idea that, as a matter of urgency, international measures should be adopted in view of finding a sustainable solution to the problems of indebtedness of the low income and highly indebted countries.

Source: Human Development Report, UNDP, 1996

The initiative launched in 1996 by the World Bank and the IMF in favor of the heavily indebted poor countries (HIPCs) is an innovative solution that approaches debt reduction comprehensively, covering all groups of creditors and all categories of debt (bilateral, multilateral and commercial). Eligible countries are those with a net present value of debt-to-exports ratio of between 200% and 220% and a debt-service-to-exports ratio of between 20% and 25% and at least six years of successful SAP implementation. Indicators of economic and financial performance are complemented by social indicators. The HIPC debt initiative is expected to take effect from 2000. All the revenues generated by a reduction in multilateral debt — and therefore of debt-service — are earmarked for essential social services. The countries now eligible include Burkina Faso, Cameroon, Mali, Mozambique and Uganda [1].

iii) Intersectoral restructuring of discretionary spending

All the volunteer countries have experienced several structural adjustment programs and restructured their budgets in favor of the social ministries. Burkina Faso, Côte d'Ivoire and Ghana have slashed subsidies to loss-making state-owned enterprises; some countries have reduced the defense budget (e.g. Burkina Faso, with a reduction of CFAF1 billion per year since 1993); and some have made general public-sector staff cuts, excluding the social ministries — after Côte d'Ivoire, Cameroon and Kenya, Tanzania recently cut 20% of the staff of its public service.

On closer examination, there is little spending that can be transferred without major problems. In several countries, the share of public spending allocated to the social sectors has significantly increased (35%-37% in Côte d'Ivoire and Zambia) to the detriment of the other ministries and the margin for possible transfers has become minimal. Only when social spending is below 25% can countries consider a reallocation of resources in favor of the social sectors.

Concerning sovereign expenditure, all the countries that have undertaken SAPs have reduced staff in the ministries of defense, security and justice and in the general administration, through voluntary redundancy and early retirement schemes. Public-sector wages are under surveillance. Non-wage operating budgets are now rarely overencumbered, although some of this spending could be more efficient.

No country yet envisages a significant reduction in spending on security. In some countries, it is possible to reduce defense spending further (Mali and Namibia after the current redeployment of redundant military personnel, and Tanzania). Where reductions in credits for the sovereign ministries still appear possible, these should be gradual.

It would be useful to ascertain how far to reduce security spending, which is the favorite target of resource redistribution. Security budgets certainly reached high levels in the 1970s. The example of South Africa is edi-

---

1. Luc-Joël Grégoire. Le Burkina Faso et l'initiative PPLE : Défis de l'Allégement de la dette au profit du Développement Humain Durable. Working Paper, PNUD, vol 3, Août 1999.

fying: the share of public spending allocated to the social services rose from 34% in 1983 to 39% in 1995, while security spending fell from 22% in 1990 to 16% in 1997 (of which defense spending fell from 14% in 1990 to 6% in 1997, with the end of the wars in Namibia and Angola). A twofold trend is evident in budget allocations: i) an overall reduction in security spending large enough to conceal ii) slow but steady growth in the police and justice budgets aimed at combating crime related to urbanization and unemployment and at reintegrating former prisoners.

Cuts to the economic ministries (agriculture, industry, trade, capital works) risk harming the development of economic activities and job creation in a context of high unemployment and under-employment. It should be possible, however, to identify unproductive spending in these ministries and to envisage transfers to the essential social services. The amounts concerned should be low.

iv) Intrasectoral restructuring of spending

An intrasectoral restructuring of social expenditure in favor of basic social services has been occurring for a number of years in almost all the 20/20 volunteer countries (Burkina Faso for education, Benin and Côte d'Ivoire for health, etc.). In health, the impulse for emphasis on basic services was given by the International Conference on Primary Health Care in Alma Ata in 1978 and by the Bamako Initiative in 1987. Budget restructuring in favor of essential social services is supported by donors, which sometimes make it an aid conditionality (e.g. European Union budget support).

Reallocations should continue, because there is still room to do so. Generally, restructuring within the same ministry means differentiating the rates of growth of credits: a higher rate for district clinics than for hospitals in Burkina Faso, for example.

In education, Tanzania and Zambia envisage increasing fees for secondary and higher education and transferring the savings to primary education. Other ways to transfer resources between levels are possible in Benin, Cameroon, Mali and Malawi. In Namibia and South Africa, teachers' salaries are gradually being reduced and the savings used to improve quality.

A similar effort is observed in the health sector. Côte d'Ivoire plans to increase the share of basic health services in health spending, from 29% now to 50% in the medium term. Tanzania is examining the possibility of reducing the share of resources allocated to hospitals and reallocating them to primary health care.

However, restructuring of budget allocations is limited by a concern for balance. In public health, the levels of primary, secondary and tertiary health care form a pyramid whose optimal operation depends on maintaining spending ratios.

South Africa is the only country that believes it has reached a balance between the different levels, in both health and education. Further transfers are considered detrimental to the efficiency of the health system.

In some extremely poor countries, non-essential social services are so underfunded that it is hard to envisage any budget reallocation (in Niger, non-essential services absorb around 50% of social spending, but the amounts are too low to be reduced further). Other countries, such as Zambia, plan to introduce fees to cover the whole cost of some services and even to privatize some non-essential services.

v) Raising private financing

Other possible sources of additional financing include the private sector, mutual schemes and user-pay services.

Concerning the mobilization of the private sector, the central government and/or local authorities could implement public service contracts with professional associations (health care personnel and teachers) to establish and/or manage essential social services, through a series of appropriate measures (access to credit, taxation, various forms of support). This way of raising additional resources has its limits, however, since the social services must be at once accessible to the poorest people and financially sustainable. Therefore, there is a need to examine precisely the conditions for achieving a balanced budget through fees, customer segmentation, taxation and subsidization of some costs by the State.

The contribution of potential users through mutual health insurance should expand in the future in various forms, some of which have yet to be developed. Those in operation now mainly target middle-income groups.

The extension of user-pay systems must take into account the contributive capacity of the poorest people. In Zambia, where primary schooling is free, the introduction of fees without taking account of families' income would harm the poorest people, who already have to pay for books and uniforms. In contrast, an improvement in the quality of services [1] would raise the utilization rate of facilities with almost no change in the level of public spending. In Malawi, people seem to accept the idea of fees when it is accompanied by a tangible improvement in the quality of services.

2.4.3.5. Improving efficiency, effectiveness and equity

In almost all the countries, the operating budgets in the social sectors have high execution rates (e.g. 90% in Burkina Faso in 1997), partly because of the European Union's budget support. But the goods and ser-

---

1. Including medicines, by enhancing the efficiency of health care protocols and availability.

vices purchased with the credits allocated to essential social services in the budget are sometimes absorbed by other national or regional structures. This distortion is particularly evident in health. There are also cases of staff being paid from essential social services budgets, but who are in fact employed in services of a higher level. Only a detailed examination of actual spending would show up the amounts genuinely consumed by essential social services.

To reduce this type of distortion, [1] accounting procedures specific to the 20/20 Initiative — and, in time, appropriate budget nomenclature and indicators — should be implemented alongside the usual accounting procedures.

In almost all the countries, efficiency can be enhanced by tackling the main sources of overcost: unwieldy, slow donor procedures that increase the "transfer costs" of projects; treasury payment delays that affect prices, which incorporate interest payments and recovery costs incurred by suppliers; and a lack of transparency in the award of public contracts. [2]

The appropriation of budgets for the essential social services is conditioned by the liquidity of the treasury rather than by the fiscal year. Funds are often released in the middle of the fiscal year and commitments closed five or six months later; advances are not sufficient to cover needs. Corrections have been made in some countries, but payment delays generate overcost.

Investment budgets have lower execution rates than recurrent expenditure, although they have risen (in Burkina Faso: from 78% in 1995 to 83% in 1996, and in Mali to 60% over 1991-97). This situation can be attributed to the insufficient absorption capacity of the social ministries.

A reduction in the unit costs of investment and utilization in Africa would also appear important. In education, to reduce the unit cost primary school per pupil and to increase the utilization of facilities and human resources, some countries plan to systematize multigrade classes in sparsely

---

1. Some fraudulent practices — such as the non-materialization of goods or services duly recorded as delivered and paid for by the treasury — are fortunately rare. Such incidents occur when devolution of the administrative services is recent, when the monitoring system is not yet sufficiently operational. The amounts involved are sometimes high and the essential social services are deprived of the resources they need to operate.

2. A combination of factors increase the normal cost of goods and services financed by projects: (i) unwieldy, slow administrative procedures of donors; administration of projects by financiers who sometimes lack professionalism; (ii) a lack of competent local enterprises and recourse to enterprises located in distant towns; (iii) a lack of transparency and rigor in management leading to abuses in the award of contracts. There are no accurate estimates of these additional "transfer" costs that reduce the efficiency of projects. They are higher for projects implemented in remote areas.

populated areas and double sessions in highly populated urban areas (Burkina Faso, Côte d'Ivoire, Namibia). Where possible, the number of pupils per teacher will be increased, without exceeding 50 however.

Regarding health sector, countries are turning to operational district health centers and minimum packages of activities (MPAs) in the basic services and the extension of the use of essential generic medicines, which has substantially reduced the unit cost of medicines.

Countries have suggested various ways of reducing the unit costs of facilities, such as the use of local materials and maintenance policy.

The main actions designed to reinforce the efficiency of essential social services are: the redeployment of health personnel and teachers to rural areas and small urban centers; improved availability of working tools and educational material; in-service staff training and enhanced supervision; reform of teaching programs; and native-language literacy.

The policy of cost recovery for health services and essential medicines represents a major change in the relationship between users and providers of health services. It means that users contribute to the financing of services in exchange for a guarantee of availability and quality. It takes time for people to appropriate these mechanisms. Therefore, special support from the government is required.

It would be useful to pursue discussions and experiments on ways to use the revenues from cost recovery, which are sometimes appropriated or frozen by the treasury, and on the competence of management committees to improve the quality of essential social services, implement an essential medicines policy and rationalize health protocols.

The objective of equity requires positive discrimination measures to promote access to social services for the poorest people. The areas with the largest population living under the poverty line are also those the least endowed in infrastructure, staff, equipment and operating resources and consequently those that receive the lowest-quality services. The most obvious way to strengthen equity is to correct this imbalance by densifying services [1] and making them more functional. However, this might not be

---

1. In large poor countries (Burkina Faso, Chad, Mali, Niger) that lack transport infrastructure, it is difficult to envisage an extension of coverage when the State can allocate only $5-$6 per capita per year to the operation of basic health and education services and when cost recovery covers barely 20% of health spending.

From the point of view of efficiency of spending, an equitable distribution of resources to the whole population for financing social services would not be desirable, because it would lead to a dilution of resources, which, below a certain critical mass, have virtually no impact. In contrast, a temporary concentration of resources on the more densely populated areas could be generally positive, because of the eventual knock-on effect on the temporarily neglected areas. Efficiency and equity are sometimes difficult to reconcile.

enough because in urban areas, where services are available and accessible, the poorest people use them less frequently than others.

Similarly, positive discrimination measures to promote the education of girls should be considered, as in Benin and Zambia.

Several countries intend to implement or extend cost recovery in education and health, with compensatory mechanisms so that the poorest people are not excluded (e.g. exemptions in Tanzania and Zambia).

2.4.4. Conclusions and recommendations

The public spending reviews and the studies conducted under the 20/20 Initiative show various methodological shortcomings and a lack of connection to poverty reduction strategies and programs. To improve their implementation, it is important to:

1. systematize public spending reviews and annual inventories of external assistance;

2. integrate the 20/20 Initiative into further sectoral and poverty reduction analyses.

Without substantial commitments to increase resources and execution capacity, many, if not most, of the components of a poverty reduction strategy are destined to failure. Governments need to raise new financial resources both domestically and internationally to combat poverty. Revenue can be increased by broadening the domestic tax base and improving tax collection. An increase in domestic saving, debt relief or rescheduling and an increase in domestic and international private investment are also key factors for improving revenues.

There are also many opportunities to increase the resource base by reallocating public spending, either between different sectors or within sectors, in favor of the poorest people. Research shows that the poor receive only a small fraction of the resources available per capita, in terms of access to basic social services, credit and extension programs. Many African governments still have not taken the political decision to decrease the resources allocated to loss-making state-owned enterprises or to defense in favor of more productive spending that could benefit the poor through local structures. Not enough funding has been transferred from higher education and health services to primary and functional education and basic health care. There is also a need to increase the non-wage share in ordinary spending and the volume of spending transferred from central structures to peripheral services and local authorities.

In all these areas, the redistribution of resources in favor of the poor is only one part of a solution. Pro-poor spending in sub-sectors and intermediate-level services should be assessed according to the same criteria of efficiency and achievement of social objectives as other public- or private-sector activities.

In addition to raising resources through efforts to increase revenues and redirect expenditure, more attention should be given to capacity-building in relation to poverty reduction. Strengthening capacities is more than the training, development and efficient management of human resources — the rational utilization of staff, training incentives, adequate pay, equipment and administrative inputs to improve staff performance.

To enhance internal resources and the management of funding, governments should pay more attention to ways to raise new domestic resources for poverty reduction by redistributing resources between sectors and within each sector, in line with the recommendations of the 20/20 Initiative.

Governments and donors should seek new ways to strengthen capacity to combat poverty by enhancing national public spending reviews and impact assessment studies. Priority must be given to introducing more transparency and rigor into the planning and management of public spending. In this respect, it is essential to ensure that: i) programs are measured by performance indicators or objectives; ii) fiscal integrity and discipline are maintained or reinforced; iii) the breakdown between investment and recurrent expenditure is more rational; and iv) budget control is more widely delegated to regional and local structures.

The international community should actively seek ways to consolidate development assistance in favor of the most disadvantaged and the essential social sectors and to ensure substantial relief of the debt burden weighing on African countries in exchange for a commitment from governments to spend the proceeds from lower debt repayments on expanding basic social sectors.

2.5. Tax, monetary and exchange-rate policies

Most African countries have experienced severe budget imbalances, due to the widening gap between high levels of public spending — inherited from the commodities boom at the end of the 1970s — and the decline in tax revenues from trade, following the collapse in commodity prices at the beginning of the 1980s.

Over the period 1985-1995, the budget deficit in a sample of 30 African countries was an average 9%-12% of GDP, representing a serious obstacle to development, particularly when compared with the average rates in Asia (7%) and Latin America (6%). Sound macroeconomic policy paid off in East Asia and it will also in Sub-Saharan Africa. There are already signs of progress in some intermediate and least developed countries.

However, most of the countries in the region still need to reduce their deficits and indirect budget losses (covered by the banking system) and resort less to inflation and external loans for their financing needs. Although many countries are unable to reduce public spending, the breakdown of this expenditure can and must be improved.

The budget and tax policies of these countries have had considerable effects on living standards and on poverty in general, particularly under the stabilization policies and structural adjustment implemented from the early 1980s.

Public revenue in Africa remains low, at an average 18% of GDP. This is due to inadequate tax collection, which is in turn attributable to tax evasion and inefficient State financial administrations. Yet taxation systems play a major role in the economy and finance because of their influence on the level of demand, relative prices, allocation of resources and income distribution. For example, high import taxes can confer effective but undesirable protection and encourage inefficient import substitution. Export taxes and implicit taxation through state marketing boards can discourage production and exports. In many countries, the implicit and explicit tax burden on agriculture remains high. In 1975, direct and indirect taxation of agriculture as a percentage of agricultural value added was between 50% and 65% in countries such as Côte d'Ivoire, Ghana and Tanzania. [1] In 1995, adjustment efforts and the liberalization of the productive sectors and trade cut these rates by 35% to 45% depending on the sector.

In Ghana, official prices for many goods were raised under macroeconomic reform. These hikes were needed to correct the distortions between the official markets and the parallel markets and between agriculture and the other economic sectors. They were accompanied by energetic fiscal consolidation measures and an effort to redirect public spending towards the poor. This shift in priorities made it possible to revitalize and expand some social services.

At the end of the 1980s, other countries followed a different path and chose to ration imports to avoid a change in the nominal exchange rate. This caused an appreciation in the real exchange rate and the expansion of parallel currency markets. Measures taken to control domestic prices generally led to destabilization in the markets where prices were more strongly influenced by the black market exchange rate than by the official rate. This situation occurred in Zambia before the introduction of reforms, and in Tanzania. In countries where the effects of general rationing and price controls were exacerbated by other sources of serious instability (such as war in

---

1. Maurice Sciff and Alberto Valdes, *A Comparative Study of the Political Economy of Agricultural Pricing Policies* (Baltimore: Johns Hopkins University Press, 1990).

Angola and Mozambique), rural markets — comprising at least 80% of the poor — disintegrated.

Rationing imports and lowering official procurement prices are clearly harmful to rural areas. But what consequences did the radical reforms in Ghana and other countries have on the living standards of the rural poor?

Price reform serves the interests of the rural poor by increasing the income they derive from their output. However, in some cases, even a substantial change in prices and official exchange rates has barely any effect on poverty. The potential benefits of a lower exchange rate have not always been passed on to producers. Sometimes, as in Tanzania, these benefits have been absorbed by ineffectual marketing channels. Also, many of the poorest farmers produce crops that are largely unaffected by changes in the exchange rate and world prices, even as they suffer from the fall-off in economic activity (a factor that played a key role in Nigeria). These short-term effects do not dampen the justification for using price incentives on agriculture, but they support one of the major conclusions of this report, i.e. that there is a need for a coherent comprehensive strategy — involving improvement in marketing and rural infrastructure — to support rural income growth, increase saving and build household financial capacity.

Tax systems vary considerably between countries, according to their level of development. The most common problems are difficulties identifying a tax base and governments' poor administrative capacities, including their territorial authority to levy taxes. Indirect taxation (taxes on the consumption of domestic goods and services and on international trade) usually makes up the bulk of tax revenue in developing countries, particularly in Sub-Saharan Africa. The main source of direct taxation revenues (personal income tax, corporation tax, property tax) is corporation tax.

Despite the reduction in deficits, the budget situation in Sub-Saharan Africa is still precarious. Most countries are still heavily dependent on aid to avoid imbalances and, excluding external financing, deficits remain high at an average 8% of GDP in the LDCs and 10%-15% in the countries in crisis.

The balance between income and expenditure influences macroeconomic stability and the development of the private sector, to which the vast majority of the poor belong. Public spending conditions the improvement of economic and social infrastructure. The State can use its powers of taxation, spending and borrowing to encourage economic activity and to allocate resources to promote growth and equity. Achieving these objectives depends on raising tax revenues and implementing an appropriate tax system and establishing an order of public spending priorities that is compatible with development programs and growth profiles.

Public spending can be subdivided into three main categories: human capital (education, on-the-job training and health); physical capital (infrastructure, utilization, maintenance and other forms of capital investment); and all other spending (subsidies, transfer payments, debt-service and military spending). The importance of spending on physical and human capital for growth is now recognized. However, the impact of public spending in these areas is crucially dependent on the selection of appropriate projects and on an enabling overall economic environment.

Public spending in most African countries accounts for an average 28% of GDP. The breakdown of spending is also a matter for concern, because a disproportionate share of budgets is absorbed by interest payments.

Avoiding an overvalued exchange rate and reducing inflation and budget deficits as far as possible are essential economic policy directions. Monetary policy also has significant effects on living standards and poverty through its influence on the financing of the economy, on prices and inflation, on interest rates and hence on the real exchange rate.

Because of the influence of interest rates on overall demand and the balance of payments, the immediate objective of interest rate policy is to adjust the nominal interest rate to eliminate excess demand in the economy and control inflation, to attract net capital inflows and, as a result, to improve the balance of payments and secure more efficient allocation of productive resources.

At the end of the 1980s, changes in the economic and financial environment and the crisis in banking systems led many countries to turn increasingly to indirect instruments of monetary management (Burundi, Gambia, Ghana, Kenya, Madagascar, Malawi, Nigeria, Uganda, Zambia, Zimbabwe and the WAEMU countries). After 1989, the WAEMU used incentive regulation techniques. These are the money market, the system of minimum reserve requirements and the liberalization of banking operations.

Exchange rate policy has major repercussions on the living standards of poor households through its influence on:
 – prices, inflation and consumer purchasing power;
 – the relative share of the tradable goods sector and the nontradable goods sector in production;
 – the competitiveness of domestic products in export markets and in domestic markets in relation to imports; and financial flows with the rest of the world;
 – decisions to make capital- or labor-intensive investments.

In Africa, no precise trend in monetary policy appeared during the adjustment period. The median inflation rate, generally low to start with, fell by several percentage points, but there was wide disparity between countries. At the same time, strongly negative real interest rates, which discourage saving, were either reduced or became positive. However, in some countries, inappropriate or inconsistent macroeconomic policies resulted in the appearance of strongly positive real interest rates, which are not favorable to growth either.

Strongly negative rates indicate high inflation, which penalizes depositors and discourages domestic saving. Strongly positive rates are a sign of excessive monetary austerity and surplus demand for credit — unless rates have been raised to stem capital flight caused by expectations of a currency depreciation. Strongly positive rates are more risky for banks' financial balance, because, to stay profitable, they have to lend at high real rates, which leads them to take more risks than what is advised by the rules of financial prudence and to discourage private enterprise and opportunities for the economic participation of low-income groups. In Africa, interest rates are not a good indicator of monetary policy because they are not market-led.

How have macroeconomic and financial policies developed in relation to poverty reduction? It is not easy to answer this question because of the complexity and specificity of some national situations and policies and because of the difficulty in interpreting accurately the changes in fiscal, monetary and exchange-rate policy in many African countries and in measuring their impact on poor people. Is the decrease in inflation smaller or larger than the reduction in the exchange-rate premium on the parallel market? Does the legislative and regulatory framework improve significantly if this premium falls to a low level while inflation remains high? Is there a clear advantage in bringing the inflation rate down from 20% to 5% if this leads to the appreciation of an already overvalued currency? What is the effect of reducing an initial budget deficit of 15% of GDP by 3 percentage points or by 5% of GDP? No method offers a satisfactory answer to these complex questions and the work undertaken to date remains debated. Reflection and research must be pursued on these issues, particularly in relation to alleviating poverty and exclusion.

In the recent past, and still today, many governments hindered certain economic and financial policy measures under the cover of helping the poor. To support local producers, they applied high customs duties, imposed quotas, overvalued the exchange rate, subsidized loans and kept the price of energy, water and other inputs supplied by the public sector artificially low. They used price controls and customs barriers on agricultural products to allow the poorest people to obtain food at the lowest cost. They subjected entrepreneurs and investors to administrative authorizations, to dampen the appetite of the large producers and to encourage small ones, although the latter were notoriously under-productive. To reduce the concentration of income and assets, they set high marginal tax rates and established public-sector control of productive activities. The experience of the past four decades has shown that these policies were usually counter-productive, in terms of both efficiency and equity. Economic growth has generally been low and inequalities, instead of diminishing, have tended to worsen.

There is now a tendency to recognize that policies that contribute to growth by improving the allocation of resources (e.g. by reducing the distortions of relative prices, exchange-rates and trade policies) can be favorable to the poor. This is particularly so when traded output employs a higher share of labor than non-traded output and when exports have a higher labor-output ratio than import substitutes (on the condition that workers have the minimum education and skills required). Under-pricing of intermediate goods (capital, energy, natural resources, etc.) encourages capital-intensive projects, which are harmful to the environment and have negative consequences in terms of distribution.

A change in the terms of trade in favor of agricultural products and the removal of customs barriers on these products can be favorable to poor people if the agricultural sector mainly consists of small producers who market a significant share of their output and if farm wages increase apace with prices.

When the capital market is particularly imperfect, it can be extremely difficult for people without skills and resources to lift themselves out of poverty, especially when growth favors capital-intensive projects (or projects that require highly-skilled labor). As many economic geography studies have shown, the centripetal forces of an economy of increasing returns do little to encourage investment in under-developed regions, spurring regional polarization instead. Major industrial and commercial projects can uproot whole swathes of the poor population and deprive them of access to community goods and essential services. Although the winners usually have the resources to compensate the losers, this rarely happens in the current political context.

However, many integrated programs and projects can contribute to economic growth and to alleviating the severe constraints on the poor, by improving their living standards. This idea goes against the dominant current of economic theory, which emphasizes the compromise between efficiency and equity, stressing the costs of redistribution in terms of incentives and economic performance.

Redistribution policies can also contribute to economic growth by correcting the market failures most harmful to the poor — particularly imperfections in the credit and insurance markets — because people are forced to make costly adjustments and become trapped in the vicious circle of poverty. [1] Opening up new credit opportunities appears likely to encourage the poor to invest in education, which is a way out of poverty. It can also increase the economic viability of small farms and cottage industries, by enabling them to produce on a larger scale, to launch into higher-risk and potentially more profitable activities, and, in general, to avoid short-term strategies. Redistribution policies can also increase the overall potential of a society in terms of productive investment, innovation and utilization of human resources.

2.6. Employment policies and poverty reduction

In Africa, the main hindrances to development and employment promotion stem from the low productivity of the agricultural sector and the unfavorable conditions for enterprise development, particularly that of SMEs and microenterprises, in both rural and urban areas.

There are many different constraints, chiefly related to the following factors:

– The high cost of factors of production, particularly energy, inputs (in rural areas) and transport, which considerably increases enterprises' production costs and reduces the competitiveness of their products.

– Limited access to credit for microenterprises to finance investment or working capital. The terms and conditions of the conventional banking system are too stringent for microenterprises; and decentralized financial systems also fail to meet the credit needs of microenterprises.

– Limited recourse to labor-intensive techniques, which slows the pace of job creation.

– Inadequate supply of training: not suited to the reality of microenterprises (high cost, inappropriate programs, etc.).

In the past fifteen years, Sub-Saharan Africa has shown a decline in its capacity to absorb labor, particularly with regard to the deceleration of the rates of economic growth and an increase in demand for employment. Other specific imbalances exacerbate the problem of modern employment. In most Sub-Saharan African countries, there is a surplus of tertiary education graduates. In West Africa, for example, from 1980 to 1995, the labor market absorbed only 30%-50% of secondary and tertiary education graduates. As described in the first chapter, generalist courses and courses aimed at the service sector recorded the lowest rates of absorption, although some technical courses also suffered. The determinants of this imbalance lie on both the supply and demand sides. Fast population growth — which determines the age structure of the population — student grants and the attrac-

---

1. On this issue, see the theoretical models of Banerjee and Newman (1993) and Galor and Zeira (1993).

tiveness of stable employment in the public service have kept demand for education and supply of graduates high. At the same time, however, the size and growth of the modern sector have been reduced by adjustment and restructuring of the productive sectors. Moreover, this reduction in demand for graduates is occurring during a period of emerging free enterprise where the private sector is not yet dynamic enough to absorb the surplus of skilled labor. [1]

As a result of these conditions, several changes have occurred in the urban labor market in recent years in most Sub-Saharan African countries. [2] The urban unemployment rate has risen considerably, more than doubling between 1975 and 1995 from 10% to 20%-22%. Secondly, employment in the modern, mainly public, sector has stagnated or declined. In 20 Sub-Saharan African countries, annual growth of wage employment was 2.8% between 1975 and 1985, but only 1% in the first half of the 1990s.

The wage freeze and decline in nominal wages in the public sector under rationalization have led to the impoverishment of some sections of the population, particularly in urban areas. Between 1980 and 1987, the share of public sector wages in public spending in Africa fell by a seventh.

Employment growth in the informal sector, both urban and rural, has been a key determinant in the absorption of surplus urban labor. Annual employment growth in the informal sector was estimated at 6.7% between 1980 and 1985, [3] the most likely consequence of which is a worsening of income distribution in urban areas. In some countries, emigration to other countries has also been a factor in labor market adjustment.

These adjustments are clearly linked to the persistence of poverty and the growing inequality of income in almost all the Sub-Saharan African countries. Country-specific trends aside, available data shows that three-quarters of urban poverty affects households whose head or main economic support has a vulnerable employment status. Exclusion from the labor market is another dimension of poverty — particularly urban poverty — that economic and social policies should address.

The status of the head of the household also influences the participation in the labor market of secondary income-earners — married women and

---

1. Jean-Pierre Lachaud, *Pauvreté et Marché du travail urbain en Afrique subsaharienne* (Genève, 1994).

2. On Africa in general, see Dharam Ghai, *Economic Growth, Structural Change and Labour Absorption in Africa* (Geneva, 1987) and J. Vandemoortele, *Labour Market Informalisation in Sub-Saharan Africa* (Geneva: ILO, 1991) and ILO, *Jobs for Africa* (Geneva, 1997-1998).

3. J. Vandemoortele, *Labour Market Informalisation in Sub-Saharan Africa* (Geneva: ILO, 1991).

young people in the household: their participation rate is higher if the household head is in paid employment. A household head in paid employment, particularly wage employment, increases the likelihood of factors such as access to capital to start self-employment/a small business; a qualification; or a network of personal relationships offering access to a job.

These differences in access to wage employment may explain the gap between the aspirations and the employment opportunities of the poor and the vulnerability of marginal groups.

Traditional social institutions play a major role in disseminating information about employment, while employment offices are of decreasing importance, accounting for only around 8%-10% of hiring in Africa. In Central and West Africa, more than 80% of hiring in the modern sector takes place outside official channels.

In this context, access to employment is partly the result of a long process that endows people with human capital and shapes their social environment from school onwards, largely conditioning the acquisition of technical skills and their utilization on the market. [1]

According to regional surveys conducted by the ILO, the main determinant of access to employment are knowledge of the job (in 60%-75% of cases) and availability of capital (in 50% of cases). Gender-specific investigations show that knowledge of the job is a predominant requirement for men, while capital is essential for women.

Most manual trades require some type of formal or informal apprenticeship and a minimum amount of capital, while many other jobs can be done without training, but require a minimum of capital. In some situations, these barriers in terms of technical and human capital are compounded by institutional obstacles to certain types of self-employment/small business. In varying degrees according to the type of activity, these three factors — technical capital, human capital and institutional context — are key determinants of access to self-employment/small business opportunities.

The decline in real income of microenterprises and the gradual transformation of social structures have resulted in a diminishing supply of free or low-cost apprenticeship, limited opportunities for stable employment and the segmentation of poverty, particularly in urban areas. Although apprentices receive some compensation in more than half of cases, the cost of this type of training is an increasingly untenable burden for poor households. In West Africa, the growing use of apprentices in the workforce of microenterprises is probably a way to limit the fall in real income, but at

---

1. Jean-Pierre Lachaud, *Pauvreté et Marché du travail urbain en Afrique subsaharienne* (Genève, 1994).

the same time considerably reduces the proportion of apprentices from poor households. [1]

In these situations, although apprenticeship — whether formal or informal — is a fundamental determinant of access to employment, the quality of this training may not always be suitable. Without an improvement in the educational and technical aspects of apprenticeship in Africa, which is often limited to transmission of skills by observation, the role and sustainability of apprenticeship in offering access to employment may need to be re-examined.

It has been shown that the level of education and training of the head of the household, together with the family's educational and employment status, determine to a large extent access to particular types of employment.

Training — particularly apprenticeship in small and large enterprises — is positively correlated with participation in the labor market.

Box 3.16.
Poverty and labor market in Yaoundé

The pilot household employment survey conducted in Yaoundé in 1990-1991 as well as some other available fragmentary information can help understand the impact of the destabilization of the Cameroonian economy on poverty and more generally the relationships between the latter and the operation of the urban labor market.

The first major result of the survey was to underscore the existence of a relatively high average unemployment rate: 29.3%. The vulnerability of the poor on the labor market is not only related to the mode of employment. It is also a function of the degree of insertion into the labor market. In that respect, the analysis shows that unemployment rate within households is inversely related to the living standards — the poor and non-poor households respectively include 47.5% and 19.9% of unemployed people. A similar relation is obtained with respect to the head of household — 31% of heads of poor household are unemployed. It must also be added that the prevalence and duration of unemployment during a professional career are all the more high since the households are poor, and since the workers are vulnerable. Thirdly, unemployment rates — which is higher for men — significantly increase with the level of education. In average, one third of higher education graduates and, one quarter of secondary education diploma holders are unemployed. On the other hand, the percentages are half as important for the uneducated people or for the people who have received only a first cycle primary education. Furthermore, marked gender related differences are observed.

Source: J. P. Lachaud, "Poverty and urban labor market in Sub-Saharan Africa: Comparative Analysis", I.I.E.S., Geneva, 1994.

---

1. See J. Dawson and B. Oyeyinkin, *Structural Adjustment and the Urban Informal Sector* (Geneva: ILO, 1993).

For unprotected wage employees, traditional institutions play a key role in access to employment that offers on-the-job training or casual jobs that require no training. In contrast, workers in the modern sector must have the required technical skills, which can be enhanced by subsequent training and on-the-job experience.

An examination of people's occupational patterns is further evidence of segmentation in the labor market. The extreme stability of protected wage employment, the high mobility within vulnerable groups and the upward or downward mobility of unprotected wage employment — which leads alternatively to casual employment or to protected employment — and of self-employment suggest that the segmentation of the labor market may be partly related to demand. Apprentices in small enterprises often become wage — or quasi-wage — employees in the same enterprises before embarking on regular or non-regular self-employment. People who are trained in larger enterprises or who are directly recruited into junior positions in the public sector can hope for promotion to more protected forms of employment. As a result, the number of jobs held over a working life is higher in unprotected employment, particularly casual employment.

The socioeconomic transformations occurring in urban areas thus virtually exclude poor people from upward occupational mobility. The incidence of unemployment over a working life tends to be higher among poor households and/or those with vulnerable employment status. In recent years, the slowdown of economic transition and the withdrawal of the State have increased the vulnerability in the labor market, which is a major source of household poverty.

The prevalence and spread of vulnerable employment and high rates of unemployment — including marginal unemployment — are adjustments partly related to new economic policies. Strategies to reduce urban poverty would therefore benefit from better preliminary analysis and more pragmatism in the implementation of structural adjustment programs.

The theoretical interpretation of adjustment is that wage and price flexibility and the absence of structural rigidities will lead to a reallocation of resources that will generate economic growth and employment. In reality, in the developing African countries, adjustments in terms of income and distribution of income are probably as important as those achieved by relative prices. Thus, despite the considerable fall in real wages, major imbalances persist in the labor market. An excess supply of labor reduces household demand, limiting the opportunities for developing the goods and services markets, which in turn brings down the level of employment.

Most of the working population is located in the rural sector and, despite a narrowing of the gap between rural and urban incomes, strong migratory flows remain a major determinant of the imbalance in the urban labor market. Rural development envisaged mainly in terms of variations in relative prices tends to underestimate the rigidities of supply and overestimate the applicability of the orthodox model. Increasing agricultural income — a factor for stabilization in rural areas — depends as much on price policies as it does on structural reforms to enhance infrastructure, access to land and credit, marketing networks, etc.

Although structural adjustment programs narrowed the gaps in urban incomes in the 1980s, the pursuit of policies aimed at cutting public sector wages have become counterproductive. With the decline in real wages, the relative advantages of the public sector in Africa have gradually diminished. More seriously, these low wages mean that public sector wage employees are now heading households that are poor or fast becoming poor. [1] Any further reduction in public sector wages could have two negative social consequences: an increase in the incidence and depth of poverty in certain occupational categories — since more than half the wage employees of the African public sector are heads of households — and a reduction in the supply of basic goods and services for the population. [2] The relationship between wage employment (in the public and private sectors) and poverty suggests a need for greater focus on formal labor market institutions: training conditions, types of contract, wage policies, social security systems, hiring and firing procedures, etc. Socio-institutional reforms in the field of labor relations can clearly have powerful effects on the incidence of poverty.

To begin with, the promotion of self-employment/small business in Africa merits re-examination. For approximately 20 years, projects supporting the "informal sector" have focused on relatively viable activities already endowed with capital. While these policies are worth pursuing, it should be recognized that, in many situations, this type of action has not favored the poorest people (casual and marginal workers). Under these conditions, the social promotion of these groups requires more systematic support. Possible ways to achieve this include: the gradual integration of certain marginal self-employment activities into projects supporting the informal sector or the development of SMEs; the design of new forms of capital financing; the development of microprojects within a new institutional framework; and reconsideration of the regulations governing self-employment.

Secondly, SMEs are set to become a growing source of wealth creation, income distribution and employment and should be promoted as a way of

---

1. UNICEF/UNDP, *Pay, Productivity and Public Service in Africa*, Working paper (New York, 1995).

2. D. Lindauer, O. Meesook & P. Suebsaeng, "Government Wage Policies in Africa: some Findings and Policy Issues", *Research Observer*, vol.3 -1, 1988.

compensating for the lack of a pool of African entrepreneurs. However, effective promotion of SMEs will depend both on consolidating existing support (capital, training, markets, etc.) and on introducing major innovations. In particular, promotion needs to be more targeted towards sectors likely to intensify links between employment and value added, both in urban areas and with the rural sector. Self-organization of activities is a useful way to overcome economic and social constraints and increase people's participation, as demonstrated by the projects run by UNDP, UNCDF and the Africa 2000 Network in the segments of building materials and small-scale, economical construction and in the informal sector in West Africa. However, the dynamism of marginal self-employment and SMEs in Africa is also closely related to increasing rural income. Therefore, meso or microeconomic policies supporting these forms of employment must be accompanied by appropriate actions in favor of rural development.

In this respect, it would be beneficial to:

– Establish, promote and support specific legislation favoring the development of small businesses and cooperatives and encourage them to raise capital, design innovative loan programs and promote an entrepreneurial spirit.

– Enhance the productivity of the unstructured sector and local enterprises by promoting access to affordable credit, information, broader markets, new technology, appropriate technical and management skills and the means to build their skills and physical infrastructure, and by gradually extending labor standards and social protection, without compromising the capacity of the unstructured sector to create jobs.

– Foster the establishment and development of independent organizations and self-help institutions for small enterprises in the structured and unstructured sectors.

Thirdly, the issue of apprenticeship warrants special attention. It has been shown that a shortage of offers of apprenticeship reduces the supply of employment for men and women, even if the quality of this training is variable. Yet, in most African countries, particularly the French-speaking countries, the development of apprenticeship will be hindered by two trends.

First, access to apprenticeship is likely to become increasingly difficult, particularly for the poorest people. Since the role of the State in this field is relatively marginal, access to apprenticeship depends mainly on the capacity of the family circle to provide training and funding.

Thus, despite growing use of apprentices in the workforce of microenterprises, the proportion of apprentices from poor households will probably decline. Because of the economic crisis, apprentices are likely to remain longer in microenterprises in extremely vulnerable jobs.

Secondly, there is a shortage of technical skills and a surplus of general qualifications of little value on the market. These two features stem from poor understanding of the training available and the needs of the productive system. While microenterprises continue to play a key role, it would also be beneficial if the government and large enterprises became more involved in training, through partnerships. This would require a more extensive preliminary analysis of the types of training available — and their efficiency in transmitting skills — and an assessment of medium to long-term training needs — particularly in fields with the greatest shortages of technical skills. This type of action is necessarily linked to a complete rethinking of the education and training system. Given the low participation of women in the labor market, policies on apprenticeship should target women.

In the context of a surplus of labor and a shortage of technical skills, particularly in the modern sector, the creation of suitable integration mechanisms could help reduce youth unemployment and increase the efficiency of enterprises. It could be useful to promote job integration programs with the aim of adapting the profile of jobseekers to suit particular job vacancies in enterprises. This type of program has recently been implemented successfully in Asia and Eastern Europe with the establishment of funds for occupational integration and adaptation.

A priority for poverty reduction is the design of policies to target particular vulnerable groups. The vulnerability of women on the labor market is clear, given the informal mechanisms of traditional society, the lack of education and training, and possible discrimination from employers. In this context, improved access for girls to schooling, expansion of self-employment in specific microprojects, a reorganization of marketing infrastructure and, in some cases, a change in business legislation, could considerably increase the participation of women in the labor market.

In general, it is important to promote policies that aim to strengthen the economic and social position of vulnerable groups. Most self-employed and casual workers are not organized, with the exception of street traders in some big African cities. Promoting the organization of the poor through legislation, cooperatives or local or regional ad hoc associations can be a way to enhance the bargaining power of poor groups and, in some situations, to overcome ethnic discrimination.

In the short term, the vulnerability in the labor market and the magnitude of poverty call for a re-examination of public spending programs. In most African countries, despite the compensatory action of traditional social security systems, cuts in social spending have been a factor in worsening poverty. It is now important, taking account of macroeconomic constraints, to develop a package of direct measures to redistribute income and wealth, by targeting public spending towards the poorest people — whether chronically or temporarily poor — and by establishing basic needs priorities. A large share of public spending should be directed to the rural sector. However, increasing urbanization justifies vigorous action in favor of towns in the key areas of infrastructure — housing, transport, water and sanitation — and education and health, because exclusion from the labor market is often closely correlated to precarious access to these basic services.

Despite the new directions of development strategies, the State has a central role to play in investment; the current incidence of poverty and social exclusion calls for a reinforcement of the State's redistributive function. While urban poverty reduction depends in part on the implementation of public strategies, there is a need to determine the forms of state organization most suited to promoting policies that are independent from the immediate economic interests of the élite in power, the concern for survival of political regimes and from the predatory action of lobby groups.

In general, macroeconomic policies must:

i) Foster employment by directing investment towards labor-intensive public infrastructure and urban and rural works programs that benefit local communities. These works should use local resources and local labor and skills, making it possible to create the maximum number of jobs and income for the poor.

ii) Enhance the competitiveness, productivity and profitability of local enterprises by creating the conditions for fair competition in the award of public contracts in particular.

iii) Provide technical assistance and increased transfer of technology to poor countries, with a view to integrating employment and technical development policies into their social objectives and establish new local and national technical institutions while strengthening those that already exist;

iv) Advocate adequate regulation to promote the improvement of working conditions and the application of fundamental labor standards (including a ban on child labor, forced labor, servitude and discrimination against women) within the framework of employment-generating works programs.

v) Strengthen labor market information systems, in particular appropriate data and indicators on employment, underemployment, unemployment and income.

In this respect, organizations such as the ILO and UNDP provide external support in the form of technical advice and capacity-building within the framework of labor-intensive action, particularly various types of infrastructure (such as roads, irrigation, soil conservation and water supply). [1]

---

1. K. Griffin, *Macroeconomic Reform and Employment: An Investment-led Strategy for Structural Adjustment in sub-Saharan Africa* (Pretoria: ILO, January 1997).

2.7. International development cooperation policies

2.7.1. Debt relief and poverty reduction

Many African countries remain heavily indebted and have no viable solution to this problem in view. Although debt is still restructured on a country-by-country basis, the general practice is to reduce debt across the board by a certain percentage, as provided for in the Toronto and Trinidad Agreements and even in the more recent HIPC multilateral debt-reduction initiative with the Bretton Woods institutions.

However, by the measure of a net present value of debt-service below 200% of export revenues — a ratio now unanimously agreed as an approximate indicator of viability — these agreements will put only a small number of countries in a viable situation. Only six of the twenty-one heavily indebted low-income countries in Sub-Saharan Africa could bring their debt to a tolerable level; nine of them still have a net present value of debt-service payments above 300% of the value of their exports.

Reducing external debt alone will not be enough to stimulate private investment and commercial loans. However, if debt relief is supported by energetic reforms, it can contribute to creating a favorable climate for investment and growth, and allow governments to concentrate on structural problems. Two points should be emphasized. First, debt relief efforts to restore countries' external viability should be related to sound domestic programs, so that debt reduction fosters sustained, equitable economic growth that benefits the whole population, rather than encouraging countries to dispense with energetic domestic policy reforms. Secondly, the objective of debt reduction should be to bring outstanding debt to a sustainable level, so that countries can continue to have access to the concessional financing they need to supplement domestic saving and to develop the social sectors and alleviate poverty.

2.7.2. Domestic financing

Without substantial commitments to increase resources and execution capacity, many, if not most, of the components of a poverty reduction strategy are destined to failure. Governments need to raise new financial resources to combat poverty. Revenue can be increased by broadening the domestic tax base and improving tax collection, by expanding domestic saving, by obtaining debt relief or a rescheduling of debt and by increasing foreign private investment.

Another equally important factor are the many opportunities to increase the resource base by reallocating public spending, either between different sectors or within sectors, in favor of poor or vulnerable groups. Statistics show that the poor receive only a small proportion of the resources available per capita, in terms of access to basic social services, credit and extension services or by any other measure. Too many African governments still have not taken the difficult decision to reduce the resources allocated to loss-making state-owned enterprises or to defense in favor of more productive spending that could benefit the poor through local structures. Not enough funding has been transferred from higher education and health services to primary and functional education and basic health care. There is also a need to increase the non-wage share in ordinary spending and the volume of spending transferred from the center to the district or local level.

Redistribution of resources should not only reinforce the institutions of the social sectors, but also act on other sectors situated at an intermediate level of the economy, such as economic infrastructure and other institutions that serve both poor and non-poor people. It is essential to improve the operation and efficiency of market mechanisms — particularly in the factor markets and goods and services markets — to improve the income prospects of the poor.

In all these areas, the redistribution of resources in favor of the poor is only one part of a solution. Pro-poor spending in sub-sectors and intermediate-level services should be assessed according to the same criteria of efficiency and achievement of social objectives as other public- or private-sector activities.

In addition to raising resources through efforts to increase revenues and redirect expenditure, more attention should be given to capacity-building in relation to poverty reduction. Strengthening capacities is more than training and facilities. It covers a vast range of activities related to the development and efficient management of human resources — deployment of staff, incentives, skills development, adequate pay, material and administrative inputs to improve staff performance in the central government and decentralized structures — as well as the rational, efficient operation of institutions.

2.7.3. External assistance and poverty reduction

When external assistance reaches or exceeds 10% of GDP, as in Sub-Saharan Africa, it has a strong influence on many aspects of the economic life of the recipient countries. At a macroeconomic level, it should favor growth and support consumption. However, massive external support can encourage fiscal laxity and lead to distortions in the labor and capital markets. The countries attempting to strengthen their institutional capacity can also experience difficulties in managing complex assistance programs financed by different donors, each of which imposes particular conditionalities.

Table 3.8. – Indicators of the debt burden of highly indebted poor countries 1996 [a]

| Country [b] | NPV Ratio of debt/ exports [c] | NPV of public or state guaranteed debt in percentage of GDP | External Debt of the public sector to be settled in 1996, in percentage of [f] | | 1995 Percentage of exports represented by | | Export vari- ability [d] | Reserve coverage (months of imports) [e] | Budget indicators in GDP percentage [h] | | |
			Public Revenues [g]	Public Expendi- ture	The first Product	The first three Products			Tax reve- nues	Offi- cial Assis- tance	Pri- mary balance
Benin	–	50.7	17.3	11.9	35.9 Cotton	37.9	15.0	– 0.6	12.2	5.4	– 6.7
Burkina Faso	275.2	30.5	17.0	10.5	38.7 Cotton	54.7	23.1	Zone CFA	11.2	7.3	– 8.7
Cameroon	352.7	–	93.5	–	–	–	–	Zone CFA	–	–	–
Congo	261.0	144.4	27.2	25.2	83.6 Crude Oil	93.1	–	Zone CFA	–	0.9	10.7
Demo. Repub. of Congo	742.7	181.7	223.9	56.1	21.8 Diamonds	45.7	26.6	0.1	–	0.9	–
Côte-d'Ivoire	360.6	143.2	–	–	28.6 Cocoa	47.5	10.5	Zone CFA	–	–	–
Ethiopia	599.7	74.1	26.8	18.3	36.8 Coffee	46.5	17.9	8.7	12.8	6.3	– 5.5
Ghana	253.1	–	29.1	–	–	–	–	–	–	–	–
Guinea	177.9	33.5	32.6	20.9	37.4 Bauxite	58.2	11.9	2.8	7.1	3.1	– 4.5
Guinea-Bissau	1,293.2	199.9	68.9	30.6	56.3 Cashew nut	64.0	30.8	2.8	7.9	11.1	– 10.2
Kenya	147.8	45.3	27.8	26.6	7.3 Tea	15.7	18.3	3.6	25.1	1.3	5.3
Madagascar	514.1	90.6	102.6	49.6	12.3 Coffee	25.6	20.2	2.3	7.8	3.1	– 1.1
Mali	254.2	47.6	17.4	11.6	47.1 Cotton	75.1	20.6	Zone CFA	12.7	7.1	– 6.9
Mauritania	282.6	134.1	12.6	15.4	52.0	–	–	2.6	17.5	2.2	8.6
Mozambique	780.8	158.7	50.8	27.4	15.5 Shrimps	21.8	32.6	3.2	12.8	7.8	– 9.9
Niger	303.4	42.5	25.5	13.4	50.6 Uranium	69.3	19.3	Zone CFA	7.4	4.0	0.6
Uganda	293.8	31.0	18.2	11.3	68.4 Coffee	74.0	35.2	3.6	10.5	4.5	– 1.0

Table 3.8. – Indicators of the debt burden of highly indebted poor countries 1996 [a] (suite)

Country [b]	NPV Ratio of debt/exports [c]	NPV of public or state guaranteed debt in percentage of GDP	External Debt of the public sector to be settled in 1996, in percentage of [f]		1995 Percentage of exports represented by		Export variability [d]	Reserve coverage (months of imports) [e]	Budget indicators in GDP percentage [h]		
			Public Revenues [g]	Public Expenditure	The first Product	The first three Products			Tax revenues	Official Assistance	Primary balance
Rwanda	745.9	38.3	38.5	10,1	55.8 Coffee	66.9	38.2	3.2	7.8	16.3	– 2.7
Sao Tome & Principe	1,454.6	342.8	127.4	24.7	50.2 Cocoa	80.3	11.6	–	9.0	23.5	– 4.7
Senegal	147.7	42.0	30.4	27.1	17.8 Fish	32.2	11.7	Zone CFA	13.9	1.9	0.6
Sierra Leone	492.8	58.7	22.2	13.3	52.8 Rutile	97.3	18.6	1.4	10.4	3.7	– 1.2
Tanzania	551.2	112.7	63.6	47.9	12.8 Coffee	26.8	32.7	1.9	12.8	2.5	– 1.2
Chad	160.5	32.7	22.9	9.5	43.7 Cotton	67.7	13.6	Zone CFA	9.0	6.9	0.2
Togo	211.8	54.9	31.0	28.7	19.5 Phosphate	46.0	22.4	Zone CFA	14.0	2.8	– 3.4
Zambia	326.5	96.2	33.5	25.1	48.0 Copper	–	20.0	1.5	14.9	2.1	4.5

a. Unless otherwise indicated, all figures refer to 1996 (1995/96).
b. Excluding countries for which the debt variability analysis was not carried out (Angola, Burundi, Liberia, Central African Republic and Somalia).
c. NPV Ratio of the debt service: updated paid out value of (public or state-guaranteed) external debt service in percentage of the average of exports of goods and services over the three year period ending in 1996. For the debt service ratio, the exports for a year (1996) are considered as a basis.
d. Defined as standard deviation of export values over the ten year period 1986-1995 (financial years 1985/86 - 1994/95), in percentage of the average.
e. Imports of goods and services.
f. After taking into account the expected debt rescheduling or alleviation, as well the possible operation of the Paris Club on the debt stock under the Naples conditions.
g. Excluding donations.
h. Central Administration for Burkina Faso, Madagascar and Mali.

Source: Estimates by IMF Services.

Donors must ensure that their support does not crowd out domestic saving. The increase in total net transfers — an indicator used here to measure the extent of recourse to external saving — has led to an increase in investment and consumption. The fact that some foreign saving has financed a rise in consumption is neither surprising nor regrettable: in poor countries, donor support aims to smooth fluctuations in consumption and offset certain exogenous constraints (e.g. emergency assistance and assistance for the most disadvantaged).

However, external assistance must be adapted to the situation of each country, so that it contributes to the implementation of policy and investment conditions favoring an accumulation of capital and an increase in public saving.

The external support from which the Sub-Saharan African countries benefit must be maintained to avoid a fall in living standards, which would compromise the gradual creation of the conditions for sustainable growth. A strong reduction in net transfers over 1995-2005 would reverse the recovery in growth now emerging.

External aid programs need to be designed so that aid accelerates growth instead of hindering it. A prudent approach should comprise three parts:

– An overall development strategy, including the implementation of a financial framework designed to allow, in the long term, a change in the profile of official development assistance for poverty reduction.

– Conditions to link external assistance closely with structural reforms designed to gradually restore balance to the external account and increase domestic saving — particularly public saving — while ensuring pro-active development of the social sectors and basic infrastructure. Reforms aimed at stimulating investment and improving the efficiency of the public sector are particularly important.

– A financing plan to bring debt-service payments to a tolerable level. The international community would be well advised to forgive the external debt of the poorest countries in order to create the conditions for sustainable growth, while making external assistance closely dependent on the implementation of viable and equitable policy, particularly in the social sectors.

3. Institutional reform and social mobilization favorable to poverty reduction

3.1. Role of the State

Since the late 1980s, the role of the State has been constantly evolving in Sub-Saharan Africa. More and more governments are being democratically elected, gaining in credibility within and beyond their borders. The democ-ratization process is changing the role of the State, particularly as govern-ments are withdrawing from public enterprises and other productive sectors and taking more interest in the major development policy choices and the ensuing sociopolitical and economic tradeoffs. They are beginning to focus their action on the provision of goods and services in the public interest, limiting intervention in the economy to correction of market failures.

Although the measures needed to eradicate poverty are now better under-stood, no action will have lasting impact unless there is genuine political will. Individuals and groups can do much to alleviate poverty, but the effectiveness of their action will depend on the environment created by the public author-ities. Thus, the State has an essential role to play in poverty reduction, through its own action and its influence on other sectors of society.

Some governments devote much of their power to policies that run counter to the interests of the poor. In 1995, military spending in Sub-Saharan Africa totaled approximately $8 billion, which is roughly the annual amount needed to ensure universal access to safe drinking water and sanitation in all the developing countries. [1] During structural adjust-ment, some governments did not hesitate to reduce their social budgets, arguing that community self-help would make up the difference. In most cases, this has led to the introduction of cost recovery in health services in countries where the poorest people cannot afford to pay even minimal fees. A lack of financial resources should not be used by governments as an excuse to shirk their responsibilities.

However, many governments can and do now act in the common inter-est and in the interest of the poor by taking measures that have positive impacts on them. Experience has shown that a strategy aimed at eradicat-ing poverty requires a strong and active State committed to expanding the capabilities of the poor, not to depriving them of capabilities.

African governments must spearhead efforts to reduce poverty in their countries and yet their policies and strategies show insufficient political will to take the necessary measures.

One of the main obligations on governments is to formulate a develop-ment program. As genuine democratization progresses, this program should be conditioned more by the requirements of the electorate and less by those of the donor community, which is more concerned with promot-ing economic development in the broad sense. This rebalancing will raise new challenges for governments and donors and justifies the adoption of a broad-based participatory process for policy-making. Each government

---

1. UNDP, *Human Development Report 1996* (New York: Oxford University Press, 1996).

should ensure that its development program corresponds to national poverty reduction objectives and is effectively applied.

Although African leaders have often expressed a general aspiration to reduce poverty, few governments have formulated detailed, specific policies to this effect. Government policies that contribute to reducing poverty are systematically referred to in the World Bank's poverty assessments. Below is a brief overview of the poverty reduction policies that had been adopted in various countries when the last poverty assessment was conducted.

The new government of Malawi is strongly committed to poverty reduction and is in the process of designing a strategy to achieve this. A workshop attended by representatives of the government, the private sector, academic circles, donors and NGOs was held with the objectives of formulating a plan of action to reduce poverty and setting poverty reduction priorities. One of the advantages of the plan is that the various participants were given and accepted responsibility for implementing actions. In November 1995, the Malawian government and the World Bank produced a report on human resources and poverty, which confirms the validity of many aspects of the strategy, outlined in the box below.

At the Consultative Group Meeting held in Paris in December 1993, the government of Zimbabwe presented a paper outlining its plan of action for poverty reduction. This policy paper set out the government's new policy directions, based on the experience and execution of the SDA program. The government aims to expand and improve the scope, reach and impact of targeted social programs, by emphasizing job creation and self-sufficiency (box 2.2.). A poverty forum was set up recently in Zimbabwe to consolidate poverty reduction actions by focusing on ways to increase the efficiency of poverty assessment and alleviation and to foster intersectoral debate on poverty-related issues.

In the past few years, public services have fallen significantly in the whole of Sub-Saharan Africa. In real terms, per capita access to public services is estimated to have decreased by around 50% since 1980. [1]

The decline in public service forms a backdrop to a stabilization of overall staff numbers in the public administration and a drastic reduction in the working and fixed capital per public-sector worker. Constant deterioration in the value of public-sector pay has had serious effects on the availability of public services to poor people. In the past fifteen years, pay levels have fallen — sometimes significantly below the absolute household poverty line — for most public-sector workers, including professional and technical staff.

---

1. Adebayo Adedeji, Reginald Green, and Abdou Janha, *Pay, Productivity and Public Service: Priorities for Recovery in Sub-Saharan Africa* (New York: UNICEF-UNDP, 1995).

Box 3.17.

Process of formulating a national poverty reduction strategy in Malawi

Despite its remarkable economic performance, Malawi lags far behind its close neighbors in terms of social indicators. In an effort to find a solution to this "development paradox", the Government, supported by the United Nations System, undertook in 1993 an "Analysis of Poverty in Malawi" which served as a basis for poverty eradication actions in the country. This report revealed that poverty affects 60% of the rural population and 65% of the urban population. The most vulnerable groups include subsistence farmers with little land acreage, casual workers, female household leaders and the poor people in the urban areas. The key factors of poverty identified are poor agricultural production, low income, lack of education and health, rapid population growth and weak institutional structures. It is important to specify that these factors are interconnected. Based on this diagnosis, it was recommended that the human development strategy of Malawi should go beyond the framework of economic reforms in order to focus on structural constraints and institutional weakness in designing and implementing anti-poverty programs.

Following this report, a national workshop was held in 1994 in order to initiate a participatory process for poverty reduction. At the same time, an inter-ministerial committee was established and assigned the duty to provide the major guide lines of the national anti-poverty program. A presidential anti-poverty committee was also created and required to supervise all studies and exercises related to poverty reduction, with the support of several donors including the UNDP, UNICEF and the World Bank. It is in that context that the national anti-poverty strategy of Malawi was designed.

Source: Government of Malawi & UNDP, "Situation Analysis of Poverty", Lilongwe, 1993.

The deterioration in services has often been attributed to an excessive number of public-sector workers, particularly those considered insufficiently qualified. The solution to the problem expressed in these terms has led to measures that are themselves problematic, but which are generally promulgated and strongly supported by donors, often despite vigorous opposition from African analysts and development specialists. These measures include: i) generalized public-sector staff cuts; ii) payment of premiums by donors and special grants for participation in conferences and workshops, encouraging absences from the workplace; iii) the implementation of parallel systems of services and emergency programs for disasters, supported directly by donors or through foreign NGOs.

Following the repeated failure of staff-reduction policies to raise the quality of service, to improve the performance of remaining staff or to achieve significant budget savings, some countries have introduced more fundamental public-sector reforms, although these tend to be extremely slow to implement. These reforms, initially intended to identify programs and set targets for required numbers and qualifications of public-sector workers, have generally involved an examination of training/skills development, performance criteria and the design and implementation of reforms of institutional procedures. Although these reforms have some validity, this approach is unlikely to produce rapid results and, unless it is supported by other action, may even cause an irreversible erosion of capacities and skills before measures to improve them have been adopted and implemented.

Box 3.18.
Process of formulating a national poverty elimination strategy in Botswana

In 1991, the UNDP and UNICEF assisted the government in analyzing the state of human development in Botswana and in planning development activities for the following 15 years. It was discovered that four major key issues were to be taken into account: population growth, poverty, environmental degradation and HIV/AIDS. Since 1995, the government has defined the steps of the poverty elimination strategy: after this phase of elucidating the problem, the second step will consist in conducting a complete diagnosis of poverty in Botswana and the third one will consist in formulating a national poverty reduction strategy.

To that effect, the UNDP and the Botswana Institute for the analysis of development policies together measured the scope of poverty in the country and reassessed the instruments used to identify the determining factors causing poverty. The "Study of Poverty and Poverty Alleviation in Botswana" was finalized in 1996 and involved the central and local governmental authorities and groups at all levels of the civil society of Botswana, including the universities and NGOs. The study, in many aspects, is considered as a model in its kind mainly because of its strong internalization by the national authorities.

In this context, the poverty reduction strategy in Botswana capitalizes the results of the diagnosis and should take the following major aspects into account: reduction of social and income inequalities, improvement of household food security and rural development, preservation and development of the environment and natural resources, basic education, primary health care and support to population policies. At all levels, special measures will be developed in order to obtain maximal impact on women's situation.

Source: "Planning for People. A Strategy for Accelerated Human Development in Botswana", Government of Botswana, UNDP & UNICEF, 1993.

The drop in quality of public services is the result of adaptation strategies to ensure household survival. These practices cannot be eradicated while the majority of public-sector workers who provide front-line services, particularly in urban areas, have no other way to survive than to earn extra income to supplement their wages.

This indicates the urgency of raising public-sector wages to a level that will enable public-sector workers to enjoy a decent standard of living. This is a necessary pre-condition to improving the performance of the public service.

Africa must enhance access to public services and the productivity of public-sector workers if it is to restore dynamic growth, development and competitiveness. Basic health care, education, water supply, agricultural extension, law and order and maintenance of infrastructure are the conditions that will enable people to produce today and increase their productivity in the future.

Improving management of the public sector is another major objective for the future, but it probably surpasses what adjustment reforms can accomplish alone. The most difficult task may be for countries to create a sufficiently efficient public service at the central and decentralized levels to ensure the conditions for the proper operation of a market economy, notably sound macroeconomic and legal frameworks and a system of basic social services in line with the objective of growth through equity.

It is becoming increasingly obvious that, faced with the concerns to contain anti-democratic backsliding and the costs of the public service, adjustment programs and economic and social reforms have had little success in tackling the fundamental problems of the public sector — a lack of transparency and accountability, hiring and pay practices unrelated to productivity and competence, regressive financing methods, spending that is counter to human development priorities, and limited capacity for policy analysis. There is a need for a broader approach to the difficulties of strengthening administrative structures and creating the necessary conditions to improve development management, including decentralization.

Poor people will benefit more from an increase in growth and development opportunities if investments in human resources are protected during periods of democratic transition and adjustment and if measures are taken to eliminate harmful distortions on the labor, land and product markets. The situation has been changing in recent years with the efforts undertaken to strengthen national capacity for economic management and to enhance public spending on the social sectors. However, one of the biggest development challenges in Sub-Saharan Africa consists in improving institutional capital and human resources, which requires more than just a change in policy. A sustained effort is needed in terms of investment and institutional capacity-building, particularly to consolidate governance and expand the services accessible to poor people.

Box 3.19.

Good governance, decentralization and poverty reduction in Lesotho

Good governance has serious implications both on poverty reduction and on the capacity of a country to ensure long term sustainable economic and social growth. Three special components of good governance drew the attention of the Government and of the donor community: i) reforms of the public sector, ii) privatization and development of the private sector and, iii) decentralization.

With respect to decentralization, the Government highlights the importance of a redeployment of civil service staff at decentralized levels and of locally elected leaders in order to strengthen decentralization and local initiatives. The objectives consist essentially in changing the bureaucratic behavior of the civil servants and get them to take better care the needs and concerns of the grass roots communities.

Indeed, most projects and programs related to poverty control activities strongly imply the participation of the grass roots community. In that context, it is important to make the decentralization process a really effective one. Indeed, it is fundamental that the grass roots communities should consider theses new decentralized structures as responsible, transparent and dynamic in their relationships with the grass roots and able to meet their expectations. Failing that, the participatory efforts of the grass roots would be vain because of the distance established between the Government and the Basotho society.

Source: Government of Lesotho, "Poverty Reduction in the Context of Good Governance", Geneva, 8th Round Table Conference, 1997.

To strengthen the capacity of governments to plan and implement poverty reduction measures, special attention should be given to various new practices:

– Establishing consistent, targeted poverty reduction policies and strategies that focus particularly on raising resources and consolidating institutional capacities.

– Institutionalizing efficient systems to assess poverty and the various dimensions of human development and to guide development policies and strategies. In several African countries, this capacity remains limited, despite recent initiatives by the World Bank, UNDP, the UN Economic Commission for Africa and the African Development Bank to strengthen statistical systems and national observatories.

– Strengthening governments' capacity to plan and execute targeted programs aimed at overcoming the difficulties encountered by some of the poorest groups by involving them in the design and implementation of programs and projects. Participatory appraisals, which take account of poor people's own views, can provide useful information on the way in which poor people perceive the changes to their livelihoods and the services and programs designed to help them.

   – Developing institutions to provide services to the poorest regions and communities, to reach specific social groups (defined according to sex, income, age, ethnicity or other factors) and to respond to the needs and priorities of the poor. The management of services such as health care, education, water supply and sanitation, and agricultural extension should be decentralized so that decisions are participatory and reflect local priorities.

Box 3.20
Strengthening Good Governance

« Governance » generally describes the exercise of political, economic and administrative power in the management of public affairs. « Good governance » implies managing public affairs in a transparent, accountable, participatory and equitable manner showing due regard for human rights and the rule of law. It encompasses every aspect of the state's dealings with civil society, its responsability for the equitable division of resources.

Within this overall approach, good governance has two dimensions:the political dimension concerns strictly political action by the government, and the institutional dimension concerns the economic and social management of resources.

Article 5 of the revised fourth Lomé Convention introduces good governance as an objective of co-operation for equitable and sustainable development. Good governance features alongside and complements the aims of respect for human rights, democratic principles and the rule of law.

The concept of good governance takes specific account of the role of the authorities in managing resources, pro-moting a favourable climate for economic and social initiatives and deciding how to allocate resources.

Good governance therefore implies the existence of competent and effective institutions respecting democratic principles. The concept therefore extends the aims of democratization into the sphere of resource management.

Transparent and accountable resource management for equitable and sustainable development has four related and complementary aspects:

   – Equity and the primacy of law in the management and allocation of resources.

   – The institutional capacity to manage a country's resources effectively in the interests of economic and social development.

   – Transparency which entails being accountable and organizing effective procedures and systems for monitoring the management and allocation of resources.

   – Public participation in the decision-making processes. This dimension also concerns the scope to be given to private initiative, enterprise and civil society in development.

Source: European Commission. The Challenges of the partnership between the European Union and the ACP States, 12 March 1998, COM(98) 146.

– Developing the capacity to achieve emergency or crisis programs even in times of relative security, because of the least developed countries' vulnerability to exogenous factors. This recommendation applies particularly to countries in crisis where there is a lack of instruments to prevent and manage crises and where deficient administrations make it difficult to introduce structures and mechanisms to assist the design of programs of national reconciliation, rehabilitation and economic and social reconstruction.

3.2. Role of the private sector

The role of private-sector activities in poverty reduction policies has rarely been considered. National economic policies and strategies are based on the idea that the majority of poor people do not belong to the private sector. This includes small farmers, despite the fact that they are key stakeholders in development. Many small farmers need credit for their productive activities. This need is particularly acute among women, who perform or manage many agricultural or craft activities or run small trading or service businesses. It is generally recognized that loans — even small loans — are a vital way of stimulating the private sector and contributing to growth and poverty reduction.

In the past 20 years, specialists in company financing, banking and poverty reduction have found new ways to involve the poor from the private sector in poverty alleviation actions by organizing broad groups of borrowers, making it possible to reduce the cost of micro-transactions in favor of the self-employed poor. These experiences show that there are large-scale ways to increase the participation of the poor in the national economy. Investing in self-advancement organizations that finance these grassroots stakeholders is a sensible way to use subsidies.

By lowering the costs of information through a specialization in local financing and by reforming service systems, banks and credit institutions can operate profitably in these markets with small transactions and low-income customers.

Economic growth should promote the integration of the poor into a development process that stimulates private initiative and generates employment opportunities. To achieve this, it would appear essential to establish an appropriate legislative and financial framework to improve the business climate, attract foreign investment and foster entrepreneurship, particularly among women, through improved access to microfinance and targeted capacity-building for the economic advancement of new entrepreneurs.

The objective is to take advantage of economic reform to attract more capital to African markets and expand the productive sector. The main activities should include: a) supporting business associations, investment promotion organizations, capital market authorities and other groups in the private sector; b) supporting countries' efforts to design programs in favor of the private sector, particularly those whose objective is to integrate SMEs into the formal economy and to facilitate the integration of African countries into the world economy; c) forming networks of talented entrepreneurs to encourage private enterprise and vocations, disseminate regional experiences and attract foreign and domestic investment; and d) developing regional marketing strategies. These actions should ensure technical cooperation and more appropriate training through the establishment of regional databases on African entrepreneurs, the creation of links between small, medium and large enterprises and with transnational enterprises, and improved policy coordination in this field.

To support private-sector promotion in Africa with a view to reducing poverty, UNDP Africa launched the regional program Enterprise Africa. The program and related initiatives aim to provide a regional institutional framework for the coordination of SMEs in Africa and the promotion of African entrepreneurship. The program offers training in entrepreneurship and consultancy services for management and identifies sources of credit for businesses and service providers and consultancies for African governments.

The initiative aims to assist 20 African countries in implementing new programs to promote entrepreneurship or consolidating existing programs; 5,000 entrepreneurs — at least 40% women — will receive training; 150 links will be established between African SMEs and foreign firms; 90 local trainers will be certified with a view to organizing workshops on entrepreneurship (200 to be held over 1997-2000). Successes to date include more interaction and partnership between small, medium and large enterprises and an increase in viable enterprises and new jobs.

Another objective of the new program is to establish a dynamic network of groups of women entrepreneurs, a structured training module for the development of women's entrepreneurship and formal courses through which women entrepreneurs can access world markets.

The formal modern sector plays or could play a significant role in supporting strategies to reduce poverty or develop local economies, through activities such as training/skills development, promotion of subcontracting and the implementation of distribution networks. Some large enterprises in the petrochemical, pharmaceutical and mining sectors are initiating innovative activities, particularly the establishment of foundations for local development and poverty reduction. The modern private sector should instigate more initiatives of this type.

3.3. Role of civil society

In the process of democratization and general expansion of development opportunities, civil society has an important role to play, particularly in defining and assessing priorities and actions that should be included in poverty reduction policies and programs.

The importance of civil society's action is now recognized. Support should aim to give local stakeholders real responsibility and enable them to acquire genuine potential for action in favor of development. No matter how great their efforts, poor people are rarely able singlehandedly to resolve the problems of regenerating the environment and promoting development. Therefore, external assistance — in the form of financial resources and technical expertise — and the involvement of non-governmental organizations remain essential.

3.3.1. Non-governmental organizations

As the role of the State evolves, NGOs are increasingly called upon to act as intermediaries between governments and poor and vulnerable groups. Governments are now more aware of the importance of the role of NGOs in poverty reduction and are beginning to involve them in some essential activities to improve the living standards of the poor.

NGOs are a powerful instrument for promoting poverty reduction in Sub-Saharan Africa. They have introduced innovative and participatory methods in the design and execution of projects and are ardent proponents of strategies that consider the poor as economic and social stakeholders, rather than as passive recipients of aid. NGOs are also involved in most emergency programs for victims of sudden shocks, such as drought, ecological or epidemiological disasters and civil strife.

Box 3.21.

Promotion of people's involvement in the development process in Togo

Participatory approach to development is based on the double conviction that sustainable development requires on the one hand that the perceptions and expectations of the poor be catered for and, other hand that the spirit of initiative of women and men, of their groups and communities be a prerequisite to self-maintained development.

In the prospect of promoting growth focused on the economic realm of the poor, the necessity to release the creative potential of people and that of their participatory groupings towards initiating development activities based on needs expressed by the beneficiaries appears nowadays to be inescapable.

This spirit of initiative was hitherto largely stifled by excessive centralism and concentration of powers to design, decide, organize and implement. This situation is undoubtedly the root cause of the prevailing "wait-and-see atti-tude" of the populations. Since they were assigned very little responsibility, the populations logically expect the State to provide them with ideas and resources to improve their lot.

One of the reasons for including participatory approach in the overall development and poverty control strat-egy was that of changing the attitude of the development beneficiaries by pro-moting participatory institutions and mechanism at all levels. In concrete terms, the emphasis will be laid on:

i) promoting citizens' participa-tion in the design, formulation and implementation of development pro-grams concerning them most directly through strong support to policies and programs of decentralization and estab-lishment of really democratic and well endowed territorial communities;

ii) creating and "redynamizing", for demonstration sake, increased represen-tativeness and efficiency of producers' professional institutions by favoring the emergence of their federative structures (chambers of commerce, agriculture and craftsmen, etc.) to enable them to efficiently play their role of defending the economic interest of interface pro-fessions to facilitate dialogue with the public authorities;

iii) promoting, rehabilitating and improving the legal and institutional environment of grass roots participatory organizations (non-profit-making orga-nizations), just as well in the directly

productive sectors (various collaborative groups, pre-cooperatives, mutual aid funds, etc.) as in the cultural sector and that of support organizations such as the NGOs. The latter are increasingly developing various initiatives in the field and their role in poverty control will be strengthened by the setting up of a flexible and progressive collaboration between them and the State.

Positive effects on the macro-eco-nomic variables may be expected from these improvements through stronger involvement of the citizens at the core of the development process, widening the economic basis of growth and at the same time a more equitable redistri-bution of gains. Furthermore, with the best way of promoting the populations' participation in the development pro-cess, the strategies to promote commu-nity initiatives could be facilitated by the following:

– stimulating, designing and implementing integrated programs of grass roots development;

– developing a community based information system to help take deci-sions adapted to local contexts;

– changing the mentality of the State agents who must consider their role as that of technical advisers to the community groups instead of insisting on excessive administrative procedures (a setback to development);

– developing inter-community interactions both inside and outside the country.

Source: "Poverty Alleviation Strategy in Togo" Government of Togo & UNDP, 1995.

Clearly, there is also a need to strengthen the organizations that make up civil society. Experienced, responsible, efficient NGOs — be they national and local media, religious organizations, unions, research groups on policy choices or support groups — can bolster the process of good governance and human development actions aimed at equity, poverty reduction and sustainability. NGOs can assist the various sections of society to participate in the formulation of poverty alleviation measures.

3.3.2. Community structures and organizations

Dynamic institutions working for and run by the poor are a way for poor rural and urban communities to help themselves and apply measures to solve problems and overcome obstacles that they consider to be priorities. Better organization in favor of the poor can:

– increase production through more efficient use of labor and physical resources;

– improve the sustainable management of natural resources through participatory planning;

– support social infrastructure at community level by pooling resources and labor;

– assist local institutions to be more attentive to the needs of the poor;

– offer a framework for concerted action to help poor households and vulnerable people;

– assist grassroots communities to build, to help themselves and to ensure people's self- advancement as a way of reducing poverty.

The value of supporting sound community organizations has been demonstrated. Traditional leaders and community support groups often fill in the gaps left by inefficient or non-existent public services. As community groups have performed this task well in the past, their action should be used as a basis for future programs. These groups have often been ignored or bypassed by government measures to help the poor, with disappointing results. Now, more and more of these structures are playing a key role in projects and programs that benefit the poor directly.

While the need for local organizations is unanimously recognized, it can be difficult to know which organizations to support. Some organizations have neither a real social base nor a well-defined function and were simply set up in response to a particular opportunity, often a grant. Other organizations that claim to be local were set up entirely by external parties without agreement with local stakeholders. Yet other organizations were implemented on behalf of the population by public institutions, as a result of political decisions that are not always shared or explained. This is the case of the many "cooperatives without cooperators" set up by some African governments. Some local public organizations claim to represent the local population but are perceived as external institutions that represent the central government. The representativeness and legitimacy of all these types of organization are low. Therefore, support for grassroots activities must go to legitimate organizations that genuinely represent the most disadvantaged groups.

3.3.3. Governance, empowerment and poverty reduction

Efforts to reduce poverty will not be successful if they are designed in purely technocratic terms. Poverty does not exist in a social void. Approaches to poverty alleviation must take into account cultural considerations, changing social relations and access to and participation in political expression. Despite the emerging democratization in many African countries, the majority of poor people still have little influence on the decisions that affect their lives; poor women are particularly disadvantaged.

"Demarginalization" is the term often used to describe the complex process by which the poor must be allowed to have their say in issues that affect them. This consists mainly in increasing the economic and political opportunities of the poor, so that they can take essential initiatives to overcome their difficulties, whatever they perceive these to be and so that their opinions and concerns are taken into account by those they deal with — particularly governments. African governments — particularly the democratic African governments — will be increasingly called upon to respond to the needs of various groups of citizens, including the poor, with the limited resources at their disposal. This is the democratic dilemma facing any country that wants to give proper place to considerations of equity and social justice. Governments must recognize the fundamental importance of democratic, contradictory debate, of access to information for all and of the right of groups and communities to organize themselves. These considerations can pave the way for consultations sensitive to gender and to intergenerational ties and obligations and for the definition of a consensual long-term vision of society.

The most useful way to serve the interests of the poor is to give them active support by encouraging local communities to express their concerns and to establish self-help organizations that bring people closer to local authorities, service providers (public sector, NGOs, development partners) and available financial resources. Governments should not feel threatened by this approach which, on the contrary, can help them to respond better to expectations and gain in popularity.

To foster a governance framework favorable to poverty reduction and greater empowerment, it would be useful to:

– Consolidate the national approaches to sustainable human development likely to favor public awareness and broader discussions on the causes of poverty, particularly policies and practices responsible for the disproportionately large numbers of women, young people and ethnic and religious minorities among the poor.

– Pay sustained attention to ways to ensure greater devolution of power from the central government to the local level and to allow genuine and active participation of the poor, by encouraging them to form civil self-help organizations, which are an important and dynamic grassroots counterpart to the governments.

– Within the current processes of decentralization, encourage the participation of local communities and community groups in defining policies and strategies for grassroots development.

Box 3.22.

The Africa 2000 network and empowering populations to alleviate poverty

One of the major lessons learnt from the Africa 2000 Network experience is that strengthening the capacities of grass roots communities is a prerequisite to the success of projects and to the sustainability of grass roots actions.

Increasing the grass roots communities' own potential may lead to different types of interventions including the following:

– strengthening staff through training;

– improving efficiency through better internal organization, managerial procedures and programming;

– improving infrastructures and equipment by establishing structures the durability of which may be guaranteed by these organizations;

– increasing own financial resources by opening access to diversified resources;

– jointly choosing and fixing priorities.

The development process is not an automatic one, especially with respect to the communities in which individual and family interests are often conflicting with the priorities/objectives of the group. Indeed, when the members of the group do not feel committed to the common objectives determined by the group itself, the individual interests tend to prevail over collective interest. In communities in which individual interests are tied to priorities and objectives defined by the group, a self-regulation mechanism is established within the project and that initiative may be sustainable insofar as the new members - waiting to benefit individually from the project - will put pressure on the older members to either pursue or maintain the investments made in that field.

Empowering the populations may also be achieved by replicating the most successful projects and experiences: nearly all the groups supported by the Africa 2000 Network have given rise to other groups involved in activities that are similar or associated to those of the reference group. The latter then provides the technical support required for the newly created group. This internal training capacity is an important element of the process of grass roots self-promotion.

Source: F. Museruka, Regional Coordinator, Africa 2000 Network, UNDP, Ouagadougou, 1998.

Box 3.23

Generating Pro-Poor Growth, Reducing inequalities
and enhancing Human Capabilities

To generate growth the main policy components are ensuring sound macro-economic management and macroeconomic stability, boosting domestic demand by appropriately

adjusting real interest rates, adopting fiscal discipline, accelerating industrial production, reforming financial sector institutions and promoting good governance. But economic growth alone is not enough. It must be pro-poor growth – expanding the capabilities, opportunities and life choices of poor people. To ensure the generation of pro-poor growth, national action should :

1. Restore full employment and expansion of opportunities as a high priority of economic policy.
2. Remove anti-poor biases in the macroeconomic framework.
3. Invest in the capabilities of poor people by restructuring public expenditure and taxation.
4. Ensure access of poor people to

productive resources, including credit.
5. Increase the productivity of small-scale agriculture.
6. Promote microenterprises and the informal sector.
7. Emphasize labour-intensive industrialization to expand employment opportunities.
8. Build human capabilities through education and ensure access of poor people to education, health services, safe water and housing.
9. Make more financial assets and productive resources available to poor people and create productive and remunerative jobs for them.
10. Reduce inequality through progressive income taxation and other redistributive policies.
11. Provide income transfers and other social protection during adjustment and crisis.
12. Pursue national antipoverty integrated programmes.

Source: PNUD. Rapport de l'Atelier régional sur l'harmonisation des stratégies nationales de réduction de la pauvreté en Afrique de l'Ouest et Centrale. Ouagadougou: 6-9 avril 1999. (Rapport de synthèse).

CHAPTER 4

Poor people's access to productive resources and basic social services

Strategies to give poor people access to productive resources and social services generally include strands for improving access to natural resources — mainly land, wood and water — and financial and human capital, the latter being supported by specific policies on education, health and social protection.

These accessibility strands generally focus on the micro level and on standard operations that make the most impact on poverty reduction. Very often, poverty reduction strategies are interpreted as concerning only this micro approach: poverty alleviation then simply means grassroots operations directly affecting the poorest. While operations of this kind are essential, it must be borne in mind that they are part of a wider situation and that macro, meso and micro level operations must be interlinked (the meso level concerning mainly governance and participatory processes).

Empowering grassroots communities, building their capacities and strengthening their initiatives and their participation, are not merely powerful instruments for reducing poverty, but are essential conditions for the success of poverty reduction programs and strategies. We shall now look at the issue of access to productive resources and basic social services on the basis of strengthened local participation and capacities.

Poverty reduction depends on involving the communities primarily concerned, in identifying, implementing, monitoring and evaluating projects that directly offer services to the poor and provide them with ways of raising their living standards. The poor must be directly targeted and offered social services that meet their needs and their demand. It is not a matter of reinterpreting general development policies and extending everyone's access to social services and productive resources, but of finding ways to specifically give the poor and vulnerable access those productive resources and social services that have been identified as having the most positive impact on their living standards.

This means taking an comprehensive, multidimensional approach, looking not only at access to natural resources, financial capital and social services for the poor, but also at food security and rural development, without neglecting gender and environmental issues.

1. Access to natural resources

Poverty in Africa is a mainly rural phenomenon. Its structural causes lie in a lack of productive resources and the lack of access to them. Strategies to alleviate poverty therefore often stress poor people's access to land and related means of production.

1.1. Poor people's access to land

Although few policies to reform land tenure law or give access to land are put into practice, they are essential for any poverty reduction strategy. [1] The distribution and ownership of land, cropland especially—including attribution of title deeds—have a decisive impact on the output, incomes and living standards of poor rural households. Besides its use as a productive resource for farming, land can be used as capital by poor owners—their main asset, and often their only one. It can be given an exchange value to favor more efficient allocation among different possible uses, and can be used as security against loans to finance microenterprises or income-generating activities.

In Sub-Saharan Africa, access to land seems to be a practical problem mainly in Southern Africa and the Great Lakes region. The essential problems in these areas are poor land distribution or heavy population pressure on the usable land. In Southern Africa, for example, land ownership or utilization are very unequal, with a minority of rich landowners and a majority of poor, landless farmers. This is particularly the case in Namibia, South Africa and Zimbabwe, where land reform proposals are included in most poverty reduction strategies, or at least considered.

In the Great Lakes region, on the other hand, the main problems are heavy population pressure and competition between crop and livestock farming. Nonetheless, traditional land use and reallocation systems here have resulted in egalitarian land distribution, while the possibility of pass-

---

1. On the subject of land, see G. Aho, S. Larivière et F. Martin, *Manuel d'analyse de la pauvreté* (Québec, 1997); K. Subbarao, *Lessons of 30 Years of Fighting Poverty* (Québec, 1997); IFAD, *The State of World Rural Poverty* (Rome: 1992).

ing on land within a family has made it possible for people to make fairly long term investments and so improve productivity.

Elsewhere in Africa, especially in the Sahel, land problems could worsen in the coming years. Population pressure on depleted land is increasing continually and tensions are beginning to emerge as people seek to settle or work the best land.

Lastly, almost everywhere in Africa, it is especially hard for women to gain access to land, whether to work it or to own it: land is simply not available to women. This can cause major problems as it is often the women who are mainly responsible for crop production.

Box 4.1.

Land access and ownership in Namibia

One of the most sensitive problems in Namibia is that of land. The situation must be appraised in the light of the forced land expropriation operated by the Germans during the pre-apartheid colonial period and of the reinforcement of racial segregation under the South African domination. It is generally acknowledged that forced expropriation and transfer of the lands of the black majority in favor of white farmers have created a most disastrous situation in the country. 44% of the land are held by 4,200 white farmers, most of whom own cattle ranches while 145,000 households own 41% of the land, i.e., hardly half of what is required for farming. However, a UNDP sponsored perception study revealed that the absence of land is listed fourth only among then causes of poverty, whereas another similar study lists this problem fifth. This is due to the fact that given the arid or semi-arid nature of the lands the reallocation of these lands without technology, training and means to farm would not necessarily lead to poverty reduction.

Source: S. Adei, Poverty in Namibia: Structure, Causes and Reduction Strategies, 1997.

Nonetheless, access and rights to land are rarely seen as priority problems in Africa, and few concrete measures specifically targeting the poor are taken to solve them. As a rule, land policies are of two kinds and are designed to:

– strengthen land ownership rights, as in the Senegalese land reform of 1991;

– reallocate land, using undeveloped land as far as possible.

In recent years South Africa, with World Bank support, has taken a new approach and introduced market-oriented land reform. Potential buyers have been encouraged to negotiate for land with potential sellers. The government facilitates the negotiation process by providing assistance and support to sellers and helping potential buyers acquire the means to buy and develop the land.

1.2. Poor people's access to domestic energy and wood

Poor people's access to domestic energy and wood is another major challenge in the fight against poverty. Apart from being an energy source and building material of prime importance, wood, and poor people's access to it or to alternative energy sources, is an important issue for environmental protection and sound natural resource management. [1]

As pointed out in the section on environmental issues, deforestation is one of Africa's biggest problems. At the heart of this problem is a vicious circle: poverty is caused and worsened by a degraded environment, but causes environmental damage in its turn. Africa possesses 25% of the planet's forested land area, but carries out 30% of its deforestation and barely 2.8% of reforestation. And most deforestation in Africa is due to clearing forest for farming or cutting fuelwood for the home, both of which activities are largely carried out by poor people.

In this situation, poor people's dependence on traditional energy sources such as wood (straight or in the form of charcoal) is an essential factor for poverty reduction strategies. Studies have shown that it is the poorest countries, and within those countries the poorest households, that are most dependent on fuelwood.

Strategies to deal with this must confront a contradiction that is inherent in the multidimensional nature of poverty. Should priority be given to environmental protection, or to protecting the small degree of access poor people have to natural and productive resources? Radical environmentalist positions take the former option, with no regard for basic human needs, and have no answer to the problems of the poor. On the other hand, energy substitution policies have shown their limitations. They have never had a major impact as long as the poverty problem has not been solved. Whether it be energy substitution using gas or solar power or techniques for better use of natural resources such as improved cookstoves, these policies have clearly shown their limits and are only a very partial response to poor people's lack of access to natural energy resources.

Since the Rio Conference in 1992, the international community has mostly opted for an approach based on rational, community management of resources — land, wood and water especially — taking the village as the basic management unit. Grassroots communities must be made aware of

---

1. FAO, *State of the World's Forests* (Rome: 1997); UNSO, *Aridity Zones and Drylands Populations*, 1997; Club du Sahel Newsletter N° 16, 1997; UNDP, *Rapport sur le développement humain durable au Burkina Faso 1997* (Ouagadougou, 1997).

environmental problems, but must also continue to have access to natural resources. Participatory management of natural wealth and reserves is therefore recommended, including grassroots communities and village groups in the decision process while trying to maintain a balance between environmental protection and poor people's access to natural resources.

National Environmental Action Plans or national Agenda 21s are clear examples of this approach. They have been set up in many African countries with help from UNDP, UNEP and donors, keeping the poverty problem at the center of their strategy. They try to make the most of natural assets and their productive potential, while also maintaining a balance between the growing population and the environment's carrying capacity. The community-based natural resource management programs launched in many African countries are aimed at better organization and greater responsibility of rural communities in the management of natural resources, to ensure sustainable natural resource management and more secure land tenure.

Box 4.2.
The problem of water and wood in Botswana

Water is the most critical natural resource affecting all the facets of development. The limited surface water supply makes the country heavily dependent on groundwater. Since these natural groundwater resources are not renewed as fast as their consumption, the water problem is a crucial one.

Average water consumption is 116.9 million cubic meters per annum and is growing steadily. The leading consumers are livestock, mines and irrigation. However, with rapid population growth, domestic demand is expected to overtake that of livestock by the year 2020. The pressure on water resources results from the rapidly growing demand due to fast population growth, rapid urbanization, increase in human activities and rising incomes and standards of living.

On the other hand, wood is the main energy source both in the rural and urban areas. Fuel wood represents 60% of the domestic energy supply. Like water in the case of water, wood consumption is rapidly increasing due to population growth and in some regions fuel shortage is already being experienced. This shortage has brought about an increase in wood price to the detriment of the poor who cannot easily afford the substitutes. Thus, in the absence of cheap renewable energy, a situation arises in which poverty, population and the degradation of the environment boost one another. Indeed, population increase leads to increased demand of arable lands and fuel wood and, the poor families are obliged to chop more wood in order to increase their income. Thus the combination of poverty and demographic pressure will lead to natural resource decline and environmental degradation.

Source: Planning for People, A strategy for accelerated Human Development in Botswana, Republic of Botswana, 1993.

In Mali, for example, application of the principles of community-based natural resource management began with a scheme to stop erosion in farmers' fields by building stone lines and planting trees. Over time, this scheme developed into support for the management of all the village's natural resources, including fuelwood, compost-making and tree planting, and even literacy classes for villagers. In Zimbabwe, this approach was used as one way of helping local communities to manage wildlife and vegetation, allowing them to generate and manage income from hunting rights and sale of hides and trophies.

These seem to be the approaches best able to take account of the severe constraints affecting poor people's use of natural resources, be it in West Africa (Burkina Faso, Côte d'Ivoire, Ghana, Mali and Niger), Central Africa (Congo, Central African Republic), or Southern Africa (Botswana, Lesotho). [1]

1.3. Poor people's access to water

Access to water is a third essential element in strategies to reduce poverty while controlling natural resource use. There have been many water schemes launched as part of the fight against poverty, some concerning water for productive use in crop farming and livestock, others concerning water for domestic and drinking purposes. [2]

As regards safe drinking water, the amount available per capita in Africa is fairly small: 16% less than in the rest of the world. Twenty-one Sub-Saharan African countries have an average below the world average. [3] The relative scarcity of water mainly affects poor countries and, within these countries, the poorest households. These not only have more difficulty obtaining safe drinking water, they are also the most vulnerable in case of a water shortage because they have neither food stocks nor savings to make up for any shortfall.

Mostly policies in the 1970s and early 1980s focused on building major infrastructure, with dams and supply pipelines to the cities. In terms of poverty reduction, these strategies rarely reached the poorest people; the urban poor were unable to pay for the water, and this infrastructure was

1. UNDP, UNICEF and Republic of Botswana, *Planning for People. A Strategy for Accelerated Human Development in Botswana*, 1993; Government of Lesotho, "Poverty Reduction Within the Context of Good Governance", 8th Roundtable Conference, Geneva, 1997.

2. UNDP/UNICEF, *The 20/20 Initiative*, 1996; World Bank, *World Development Report 1990: Poverty* (Washington, 1990); IFAD, *The State of World Rural Poverty* (Rome: 1992).

3. UNDP *Human Development Report, 1997* (New York, Oxford University Press, 1997).

never intended for the rural poor. While 2% of total official development assistance was devoted to safe drinking water supply in the seventies and early eighties, that figure has risen considerably and now stands at 8% of the total. [1]

Indeed, improved access to safe water is one of the fields in which progress seems to have been most rapid since 1980. Access to safe water for all has been recognized as a basic need to for health, food and hygiene purposes. In other words, as one of the essential determinants of improved living standards.

Since the 1980s, as awareness of the importance of this issue has grown, the number of people in Sub-Saharan Africa with access to safe water has doubled in ten years, rising from 25% to 43%. Nonetheless, despite notable progress, there are still many shortcomings. The two biggest problems are lack of political commitment and the fact that access to water is rarely identified as a development priority. Thus, despite the progress made, access to safe water in rural areas, and urban sanitation, still require considerable effort.

The international community is aware of this situation and now includes access to safe drinking water and sanitation among basic needs in the objectives of the 20/20 Initiative. This should make it possible to give higher priority to these issues and bring in financing to match the problem.

As with wood, energy and land, access to productive water comes under the heading of rural development and food security as much as natural resources, if not more. As a rule, productive water mainly means irrigation systems to improve farm productivity. It may also mean installing water points and small dams to give livestock access to water. Here, only the aspects relevant to natural resource management for poverty reduction will be considered.

Sound, rational natural resource management implies local community management not only of land and wood, but also of water. So alongside the big irrigation and water supply projects for crops and livestock, more and more micro-projects are emerging, to meet the specific needs of the poor and provide them with infrastructure that matches their needs, and which they can manage themselves.

Because the rural poor live in sparsely scattered settlements and in the most remote or inaccessible regions, it is not easy to provide access to productive water or irrigation. It is mainly small-scale facilities that are needed, and these involve fairly high costs for public management and maintenance services. Therefore small village schemes involving local people are spread-

---

1. DAC-OECD, *Development Co-operation, 1996 Report* (Paris,1997).

ing. It is a question of allowing disadvantaged rural groups access to productive water, while stressing the fact that the water users will gradually take over an increasing part of the management and maintenance of the system. In Senegal, for example, the Matam agricultural development project is based on the principle of rehabilitating existing irrigation systems by training water user groups who then become responsible for maintenance of the facilities. The same approach, at village or local community level and with increasing local involvement in management and upkeep, can be found with water supplies for crops or livestock in most African countries. Very often, this type of activity involves NGOs who have the necessary technical know-how and the contacts with intermediaries on the ground that are essential for success.

Thus, to favor poor people's access to natural resources, programs must follow recent examples, correctly targeting poor communities and population groups and identifying the resources that are available and that poor people need. It is also imperative that the communities concerned participate in the programs, from the stage of identifying needs, through the execution of the program to managing and maintaining the infrastructure. Nonetheless, access to natural resources is conditioned by one more component that we must now address: providing appropriate technologies and infrastructure for the poor.

1.4. Poor people's access to technology, research results and extension services

As in the case of water, it is not possible to improve access to productive resources, and hence productivity and household living standards, without investing, on however small a scale, in technology and infrastructure. But the effect of such provision depends, once again, on how well the projects are targeted and how they are designed and executed. [1]

As a rule, the principles for implementing these strategies are similar to those for natural resources: targeting the poor, involvement and participation of grassroots communities, provision of infrastructure or technology that are suitable for the poor and that meet their needs.

The basis of this approach is to adapt technology and infrastructure to the needs of the poor and of small farmers, enabling them to increase their productivity. Until the 1980s, agricultural and infrastructure strategies favored large-scale irrigation schemes for large-scale mechanized, high-yield farming — a system that was out of the reach of smallholders and above all the poorest smallholders. In Malawi, for example, after twenty years of

---

1. World Bank, *World Development Report 1990: Poverty* (Washington, 1990); IFAD, *The State of World Rural Poverty* (Rome: 1992).

research and agricultural extension work on a high-yield hybrid maize variety, only 5% of farmers had adopted it. The reason is the massive scale of the projects and the failure to target small farmers. The new approaches, based on involving and giving responsibility to organized groups of farmers, of the poorest farmers especially, seems to be having a positive impact.

Zimbabwe's national agricultural research and extension project, for example, tried to make up for these deficiencies. The task in hand was to boost the country's adaptive agricultural research capacity, focusing efforts on benefiting small farmers. The result of this shift in focus was support for research into farming systems that were of obvious, specific interest to small farmers, especially when the work involved local experiments with suitable technology. A national extension project in Kenya is mainly trying to establish links between the agriculture ministry, the research centers and small farmers, with a view to supplying the appropriate technology needed by the latter. Grassroots training components and active participation by farmers in the management and implementation of these projects has led to an increase of some 85% in maize output, thanks to appropriate technology that matched the needs of the small farmers and was jointly managed by them.

Problems are similar to those of water supply. The infrastructure and technologies used must meet the same criteria, with constant attention to their accessibility to the poor. IFAD's Special Program in Niger, for example, was designed to reduce farmers' vulnerability to drought and desertification. The water conservation component was designed to improve water harvesting and retention and soil moisture using simple, efficient methods that the farmers could reproduce. A process of dialogue and participation was established with the dual purpose of explaining the new techniques to farmers and understanding farmers' perceptions and views of the issue. Strategies must always be designed to transfer a technology that meets needs as perceived by the poor population groups themselves.

Access to natural resources and related technologies and infrastructure must be placed at the core of poverty reduction strategies; this has rarely been the case to date, except for drinking water supply. It is a matter of including the poor in the development process, and giving them access to natural resources so they can increase their productivity and improve their living standards. To do this, resources and investments must be directed towards the poor. In fact, the access to natural resources is particularly connected with investment projects and rural development where the flows are generally appropriated by those with local or national power. It is rare that the poor are the primary beneficiaries. The basic principle is to ensure that those who possess least in terms of productive assets should benefit from access and investments. In some cases, for example, special forms of investment will be set up for the benefit of women or particularly vulnerable groups.

2. Access to productive capital, employment and financial services

To improve the living standards and income of the poor, it is essential to give them access to capital, be it productive capital for investing in infrastructure and appropriate technology as a basis for income-generating activities, or financial capital, particularly credit.

Anti-poverty measures at the micro level have three purposes: capacity-building, fulfilling basic needs, and improving living standards and incomes. This third goal can only be attained with stronger capacities, improved access to natural resources, and easier access to productive and financial capital enabling people to work or create jobs.

Here we see the interrelation and synergy between all the programs, activities and objectives of a poverty reduction strategy. In fact, the access to productive capital, employment and the financial market is conditioned by the possibilities for access to natural resources, infrastructure and technology discussed earlier in this chapter.

2.1. Strategies that improve poor people's access to productive capital and employment

By facilitating poor people's access to productive capital, including such natural resources as land, it is possible to change production technologies or choose methods appropriate to the resources, capacities and needs of the poor. This way they can produce more with less drudgery and improve their living standards more easily. The policies discussed above on access to land, on improving poor people's access to infrastructure and technology, on rural development operations and urban policies are fundamental aspects of this issue.

However, specific measures must also be taken to increase the incomes of the poorest groups and households or create jobs for which they are eligible.

2.1.1. Incentive measures that improve access to markets

Poor households' incomes cannot be increased simply through projects giving them access to natural resources and providing infrastructure and technologies that meet their needs. They must also have appropriate incentive measures or structures. For example, reducing import taxes on inputs and on supplies for building infrastructure destined for the poor is a highly effective measure. Big reductions in farm taxes were an essential component for increasing production and promoting agriculture and small farmers in several African countries, including Benin, Guinea, Mauritius, Nigeria, Tanzania and Uganda; all these countries substantially reduced farm taxes in the 1980s. Since then, for the first time, these countries have enjoyed agricultural growth of around 3% to 5% a year. In Tanzania, removing restrictions on private purchases of food commodities in 1990 increased competition, improved farmers' access to the markets, and triggered a revival in production of cashew nuts and some other crops. Because farmers saw their crops collected on time and paid for quickly, cashew nut output rose from 29,000 tonnes in 1990-91 to 41,000 tonnes in 1992-93.

More flexible legislation on farm produce markets and making access to these markets possible, or easier, for the poor, is another essential factor for poverty reduction policies. In many countries, poor people's access to markets is hampered by legislation, geographical distance and unfair practices that discriminate against them. Experience has shown that with strengthened capacities and access to information, the poor can take advantage of a more open market in many ways and can respond rapidly to this new economic situation. Incentive measures for trade and export, lower transport costs and adequate development of their basic capacities can significantly increase poor people's access to markets and, as a consequence, their incomes. In Central Africa, for example, a project to improve households' capacities for management and marketing of livestock enabled the herders to organize themselves in structured groups and become involved in developing policy in this area, while it also set up savings and loan organizations, and facilitated cattle marketing.

Box 4.3.
Price increases and their impact on poverty in Nigeria

Between 1990 and 1995, the average rate of increase in consumer price index was about 43% per annum. This is indicative of a high rate of inflation which normally should not be higher than 10% per annum. Worse still, the rate of inflation has been accelerating over time, accelerating from 13% in 1991 to about 72% in 1995. The rate of inflation has been accelerating faster in the rural sector than in the urban sector in recent years. While the rate of inflation in the urban sector increased from about 18% in 1991 to about 62% in 1995, the rate in the rural sector increased from about 12% in 1991 to about 75% in 1995.

It is also interesting to note that the rate of inflation in food prices has been accelerating faster in the rural sector than in the urban sector. Hence, from 1995 onwards, food prices have become higher in the rural sector than in the urban sector. Therefore, the cost of living in Nigeria has increased astronomically between 1991 and 1995, affecting mostly the rural sector and food prices, i.e., both the sector with the greatest number of poor households and the products most consumed by the poor.

Source: Human Development Report, Nigeria 1996.

However, the market liberalization introduced under the structural adjustment programs has aimed at strengthening large-scale farming. Only rarely have the poor been especially targeted by these adjustments. The Ugandan and Nigerian examples show that spectacular agricultural growth engendered by market deregulation has mainly benefited large farmers and urban dwellers. However, it should be possible in the same way to introduce policies to improve poor people's access to markets by changing the legislation, prices, discrimination and physical obstacles to access that operate against them. In general, poverty reduction strategies include this type of measure only in embryonic form. Efforts should be made in this direction so that opening up markets will no longer penalize the poor and it so often has in the past.

2.1.2. Incentive measures for job creation

To improve incomes and living standards, one of the main factors of production available to poor people is their labor. Where the labor force is greatly under-utilized owing to lack of opportunity, unemployment, underemployment or low productivity, there is generally poverty and social exclusion. To combat poverty, therefore, policies must promote employment.

The macro and mesoeconomic components of such policies have already been analyzed in this chapter. But, in addition to macroeconomic and sectoral policies to improve the employment situation, institutional reform of employment policy, building institutional capacity at all levels, and strengthening the capacities of the poor in this field, it is imperative to develop micro-policies to create jobs among the poor population groups at the grassroots level.

Again, this type of grassroots action must target its beneficiaries precisely, identify their needs in this field, and respond to their expectations through a participatory approach. Facilitating poor people's access to natural resources and productive capital, making available appropriate infrastructure and technologies, and introducing sectoral policies to promote employment, are all necessary and indispensable measures to promote employment. In general, however, they are not sufficient. Taking account of the particular aspirations of poor groups means supporting their efforts and activities through specifically targeted programs. Here too there are generally three complementary approaches: promoting labor-intensive technologies, setting up social funds to create jobs, and giving access to financial capital, loans especially, to promote job creation and income-generating activities and integrate disadvantaged groups into the labor market.

Measures to support employment at grassroots level require a thorough knowledge of the labor market and its structure in the country or region. It requires specific measures to combat poverty through special targeting. Broadly speaking, employment problems and their relationship to poverty concern formal urban unemployment (lack of jobs), lack of opportunities in the informal or unstructured urban sector, and under-employment in rural areas.

The role of employment in poverty reduction is paramount. It gives people the opportunity to become active development stakeholders and above all to earn an income that will give them access to a whole range of goods and services necessary for a decent standard of living. It has been shown in Burkina Faso that a household's well-being is highly sensitive to the employment status of the household head, who provides 80% of the household's total income. Besides the benefits of the income it brings in, employment enables people to make a productive contribution to society and exercise their skills and creativity. It is a means of self-fulfilment and helps to maintain human dignity and self-respect.

Job creation and higher incomes must therefore be among the priority objectives of a country seeking human development and poverty reduction; and only if the relationship between employment and poverty is analyzed can job creation policies be properly targeted as part of a poverty reduction strategy.

i) Implementing labor-intensive technologies

Labor-intensive technologies mainly benefit the poor, for whom their own labor is their main factor of production. The most usual measures to create jobs this way are building infrastructure with public funds and labor-intensive methods, providing information and training to economic agents on the potential offered by a labor-intensive production approach, and introducing greater flexibility into the formal labor market to make it more attractive to employers to hire more staff.

In most Sub-Saharan African countries, the social dimensions of the structural adjustment programs and the main social safety-net measures for the very poorest, include a component on labor intensive methods. Backed by the World Bank, African Development Bank, UNDP, ILO and bilateral donors such as Germany, most applications of labor-intensive methods under SAPs are short-term policies designed to quickly provide paid employment for the unemployed and help meet the people's infrastructure needs. They usually involve setting up a public works agency. It must be stressed that these programs are essentially short-term urban projects; they aim to temporarily boost poor people's incomes but offer no prospect of lasting employment or stimulation of the local economy.

Box 4.4.

The promotion of income generating activities and self-employment
in favor of the poor in Mali

The government considers that one sustainable way of alleviating poverty is to increase the capacity of the poor to generate enough resources to cater for their basic needs and to finance essential social services. The income generated by these activities will enable poor households to sustainably meet their demand for private goods and public services.

Sustainable income generation for the poor depends on the development of viable activities in the economic realms in which they are active. The promotion of self-employment for the poor is a requirement where the labor market does not absorb the abundant unskilled manpower. Micro and small enterprises are the real driving forces for job creation and income generation for the poor.

However, supporting the creation of income generating activities for the poor requires that judicious choices be made in order for the impact to be sustainable. There is a need to promote activities that generate goods and services required in priority by households. Furthermore, there is a need to make sure that the activities being supported are financially and economically profitable.

The government intends to support the initiatives of the poor in terms of creating micro and small enterprises in the most promising sectors. This particularly concern agro-food processing, small stockbreeding and off-season cropping. The government also intends to promote labor intensive programs generating jobs and incomes for the poor. These programs will focus in priority on improving public infrastructures most related to the economic opportunities of the actors.

The objectives of this strategy are the following:

– To promote unskilled labor intensive economic activities by targeting the most underprivileged zones and the off-season periods;

– To stimulate private investments in unskilled labor intensive sectors;

– To reduce rural exodus of the poor during the off-season period;

– To enable the poor of the land-locked areas to have access to more economic opportunities;

– To reduce unemployment and under-employment rate among the youth;

– To improve the coordination of the labor market in order to create more jobs for the poor.

In that context, the following priority actions have been identified:

1. To initiate labor intensive public works programs similar to AGETIP (Public Works Implementation Agency) by giving priority to the most underprivileged regions.

2. To design a program to support private sector investment in the economic realms of the poor, particularly the agro-food sector (processing, preservation, marketing and exportation).

3. Support the development of small stockbreeding and off-season cropping in favor of the poor.

4. To reduce the isolation of under-privileged zones through labor intensive works.

5. To improve the quality of technical and professional training of the youth in underprivileged areas.

6. To involve the labor market coordination structures in poverty eradication strategy.

Source: "National Poverty Eradication Strategy in Mali", Government of Mali & UNDP, 1998.

However, in line with the objectives of the public works agencies, part of the work is subcontracted to small private firms, to foster both employment of an abundant labor force and the development of the local private sector. In Senegal, during its first year of operation in 1991, the public works agency carried out 119 sub-projects for a total of $8 million, used 78 contractors and created nearly 2,000 person-years of employment. In view of the success of this type of public works agency or AGETIP (Agence d'exécution des travaux d'intérêt public), a number of others were set up in Sub-Saharan Africa, e.g. in Burkina Faso, Benin, Mali, Mauritania and Niger. In Burkina Faso, the agency Faso baara is an AGETIP set up in 1991 and using labor-intensive methods. Its aim is to promote small local enterprises using a plentiful workforce. Since its creation, it has paid out nearly a billion CFA francs in wages and provided roughly 5,000 person-years of work. The work mainly concerned improving urban infrastructure and environment in the capital. On the other hand, the jobs created are generally low-paid and insecure.

These projects have mostly provided short-term hiring and a brief increase in urban employment, a few longer-term jobs in management and maintenance of the new infrastructure, work training for some poor people, training in labor-intensive methods for entrepreneurs, and increased use of local techniques, raw materials and tools. As regards poverty alleviation and the need for stable employment, the AGETIP approach is just a tenuous, short-term palliative.

ii) Setting up social funds

Given the inherent limitations of the AGETIP approach, many countries have sought ways to apply labor-intensive methods in the medium and long terms. This partly means providing training and information for private entrepreneurs, wholesale use of such methods in all public or private infrastructure work, and more flexible labor legislation; or, once again, promoting appropriate, labor-intensive technologies. Lastly, it means no longer restricting these methods to public infrastructure and urban areas but extending them to rural areas, where the poor are most numerous.

In general, this type of longer-term sectoral policy involved setting up a social fund to start building social, economic or productive infrastructure for the poor and having them built by the poor themselves, using labor-intensive methods. For example, in a rural area this might mean ending the isolation of a village by building roads, markets or any kind of village infrastructure, productive (market, mill, grain bank, etc.) or social (school, health center, etc.). Exactly the same type of policy is applied to urban areas. As a general rule, this type of fund finances a series of related activities including:

– job creation through such activities as building or mending roads, irrigation systems or anti-erosion structures;

– income-generating activities through capacity-building and training programs, loans and technical assistance for microenterprises.

Until the beginning of the 1990s, such funds were managed by central government and gradually became virtually independent entities, autonomous public services. This development led on the one hand to weakening the government's own capacity in the social development field as resources and know-how were channeled to the social funds, and on the other hand to neglecting the need to target these funds. Centralized management naturally led officials to intervene first and foremost in urban or central areas, without any particular targeting of the most disadvantaged groups.

To remedy this situation, since the early 1990s the African countries, with donor support, have tried to decentralize these funds, along with all the other major decentralization measures and government reforms. Usually managed by local authorities, with the participation of the beneficiary communities and the intervention of local private business people for infrastructure building, these funds now pursue the following goals:

– financing small-scale rural infrastructure that meets local priority needs;

– building the capacities of local institutions in micro-project planning and management;

– promoting effective decentralization of the State and of investment budgets;

– promoting contractual relationships between private firms, communities and local authorities.

Decentralized or local social funds have been set up experimentally in Ghana, Mali and Mauritania, Tanzania, Zambia and Zimbabwe. The main functions of the Zambia Social Fund, for example, are now handled by district or village authorities, so that beneficiary communities participate and local authorities' management and implementation capacities are strengthened. The local development funds are responsible for financing microprojects launched at the initiative of grassroots communities in such fields as water and sanitation, building or renovating dispensaries, schools, community access roads, or trading or storage premises.

In Ghana and Zimbabwe, these decentralized funds aim to reduce poverty sustainably by fostering investment and boosting poor people's capacities. Based on the principle of active participation by beneficiary groups and effective decentralization of decision-making and management, the funds mainly operate in health, education, food security, water, and economic infrastructure requested by the poor. The main executors of the projects identified are NGOs and the private sector. In Mauritania, local development funds are mainly concerned with infrastructure for flood recession cropping or irrigation schemes, and reserve part of their investments for micro-projects to improve food security. They also fund water management schemes and help build the local administration's capacities, especially with regard to local investments. [1]

This gradual transformation of the social funds provides for a better response to the needs of the poor, while helping to strengthen grassroots communities' capacities. Also, less focused on simply creating jobs, they are more effective for the overall purpose of poverty reduction.

iii) Promoting microenterprises and the informal sector

In town and country alike, and apart from farming, most of the poor in developing countries depend on the informal sector for their livelihoods, especially microenterprises in the service sector, processing and trade. Throughout Africa, the informal sector gives individuals a chance to express their creativity. Yet governments rarely create an enabling environment for these microenterprises. They do very little to facilitate access to savings or loan arrangements, to provide security for business endeavor, or to improve infrastructure such as roads, water supply and energy. And yet all these factors are essential for the success of a microenterprise. [2]

These enterprises are the nurseries from which grow the SMEs of the formal sector and a fair proportion of a country's economic fabric. They contribute significantly to economic growth, accounting for 20% of GNP in Africa and 60 to 70% of jobs. In this respect, the informal sector has a vital role to play in alleviating poverty, by intensifying agricultural activity, creating more labor-intensive firms and integrating the poorest or giving them some social protection. For many poor households and disadvantaged groups, economic activities and mutual self-help developed within the informal sector provide a veritable social security safety net and are the sole source of income. Because of its dynamism and its potential in terms of employment and productivity, the informal sector has a crucial part to play in reducing poverty in Africa.

---

1. See UNCDF, *Poverty Reduction, Participation and Local Governance* (New York, 1995).

2. See UNDP, *Human Development Report 1997* (New York: Oxford University Press, 1997); United Nations, *Développement du secteur formel en Afrique* (New York, 1992); Leila Webster and Peter Fidler, eds., *The Informal Sector and MicroFinance Institutions in West Africa,* (Washington: World Bank, 1995); UNDP/RBA, *Private Sector Guide Creating the Action Agenda and Establishing the African Business Executives Programme* (New York: Oxford University Press, 1996).

Box 4.5.

Participation of the informal sector in growth

According to a study conducted in 1992 by the Economic Commission for Africa, the contribution of the informal sector to GDP in the African countries is estimated at about 20% and its contribution to the GDP of the non agricultural sector at 34%. For example, its contribution to GDP was 38% in Guinea, 10.3% in Tanzania, 30% in Burkina Faso, 24.5% in Nigeria and 20% in Niger. The sectorial analysis of available data shows the trade represents about 50% of the production of the informal sector, manufactured production represents 32%, services and transport represent 14 and 4% respectively.

In most African countries, the contribution of the informal sector to GDP is much more considerable than that of the manufacturing sector. For instance, in Guinea, 96% of manufactured agricultural products, i.e., food crops, drinks and tobacco, textiles and leather, wood products, non-iron ore and iron works come from the informal sector. There are only three fields - basic metallurgy, chemical products, paper production and printing - in which the informal sector does not play any role. It also plays a leading role in sectors such as trade, 92% of the added value, and real-estate, 71%. In construction, public works and transport, the contribution of the informal sector in terms of added value has been 36 and 45% respectively.

The situation described above also prevail in Burkina Faso and in Niger. For instance, in manufactured production in Burkina Faso, the contribution of the informal sector is 71 and 63% of the added value in 1980 and 1986 respectively. The activities of the informal sector, in those countries, cover the same fields as in Guinea. But in so crucial sectors such as construction and transport, the contribution of the informal sector is more significant: 65% and 49% respectively of the added value for the two sectors. In those same countries, the non structured industrial sector is a development basis that needs to be stimulated, modernized, rehabilitated and integrated into the overall development process.

In both urban and rural areas, the informal sector plays an important role in production. For instance, surveys conducted in Madagascar and in Niger have shown that agricultural income does not represent more than half of the total amount of rural households' gains. Another example is that in the Center-South of Cameroon 72% of family heads have secondary income sources that double their agricultural income.

A notable proportion of urban income totally comes from the informal sector: about 30% in Cameroon, 44% in Madagascar, 58% in Senegal and 68% in Mali.

Source: "Development of the informal sector in Africa", United Nations, 1993.

Box 4.6.

Case study on institutional transition: Kenya Rural Enterprise Program

The Kenya Rural Enterprise Program (K-REP) is a micro-enterprise development project considered as a success story. The major mission of K-REP is to help low income entrepreneurs to increase their participation in the development process and improve their standard of living. The specific objectives of the program consist in strengthening the institutions involved in the informal credit sector and, in increasing job opportunities and incomes for the poor through provision of loans, training and technical assistance to the groups and organizations offering micro-credits.

The development of K-REP took place in several stages. During the first five years, the strategy focused on strengthening K-REP's institutional capacity by providing financial services to a target population together with the social services traditionally provided by the NGO. However, it was realized that the approach to integrated services had less impact and high operational costs. In 1989, the institution abandoned its social service supply oriented approach and adopted an approach focused on sustainability and financial independence. The institution joined the four best partners among the local NGOs. In addition the institution adopted a Grameen Bank type approach. The financial assistance to the partner NGOs, that was totally subsidized, was reviewed. In order to ensure viability and valorize its own expertise, K-REP retargeted its financial services nearly exclusively towards juhundi and Chikola credit programs:

• The juhundi credit is a personal loan with market interest using the approach of solidarity group as a guarantee. The entrepreneurs set up solidarity groups and meet every week to deposit money, receive loan, disburse money and discuss their problems.

• The Chikola credit program offers loans to Chikola groups (rolling savings and credit associations) and to business associations, just like the jua kali cooperatives and associations. These loans are targeted on low income individuals and given at commercial interest rate for a period of 1-2 years.

In addition to these two credit programs, there are other programs that contributed to success. These are the credit institution support program that assists NGOs with loans so that they may in turn give personal loans and, three other services which are micro-credit support programs (training program, research and evaluation program and finally, consultation service program).

With this new strategy, K-REP was able to achieve good performance. After 2 _ years, the volume of loans given moved from 15.7 million shillings (with 2 500 transactions) to 70 million shillings (with 9 000 transactions). Transaction cost for each loaned shilling was reduced by 75% and recovery rate increased by 78%. The monthly revenue covers about 90% of operation costs excluding that of management. In addition, the program made it possible to mobilize more than 12 million shillings as savings.

Source: A. Nteziyaremye, S. Larivière, F. Martin & P. Larocque, "Micro-credit practices in developing countries", Ottawa, 1996.

Most informal sector enterprises are created and managed by poor people in their struggle to survive. At present, over 40 million Africans work in the informal sector and their income provide for over 200 million people in all. The informal sector thus helps reduce poverty by creating jobs for huge numbers of otherwise unemployed or under-employed people, by the knock-on effect of its growth, the social stability it engenders, the relationships it forges or can forge with the formal sector, and the advantages that result from women's employment. It also contributes to professional training, develops entrepreneurial spirit, and helps structure and consolidate traditional networks of solidarity and mutual self-help.

The current weaknesses of Africa's informal sector can be summed up as follows:

– government policies are not at all favorable to the unstructured sector,

– support and promotion infrastructure are insufficient,
– institutional support is lacking,
– there is little access to appropriate technology,
– human resource training is weak,
– access to credit and finance is lacking.

Most poverty reduction strategies include a major component to promote microenterprises and informal sector employment. This includes the legal and regulatory framework aimed at making it more flexible or introducing better targeted laws; capacity building activities for small business people; and major provision for microfinance, be it through loans or guarantees or by arrangements to help entrepreneurs make up bankable applications. This type of policy also often includes specific strands to promote employment or training in women's microenterprises, or targeting young people.

At the present time, most Sub-Saharan African countries have specific policies and instruments for supporting or promoting microenterprises and the informal sector. And in many countries, multilateral or bilateral donors have introduced support arrangements. The big problem threatening this type of activity is the multiplicity of initiatives and instruments introduced, mostly without much collaboration between the different stakeholders.

Several countries have introduced policies to promote the potential they have identified in the sector. Burkina Faso and Kenya, in their recent development plans, have included programs to support informal sector businesses and socioeconomic development institutions operating at local level. Côte d'Ivoire and Senegal have introduced a special patenting formula for informal sector enterprises, to help them build stronger links with the commercial institutions and markets of the structured sector. In some African countries, the informal sector now has access to credit and financial markets.

The best example is Nigeria, where the People's Bank provides credit without security for small business people who would never qualify for a loan under conventional banking practices. In Kenya, the government recognizes more and more the needs of "jua Kali" workers ("those who work in the sun"). Egyptian government policy encourages the growth of the informal sector and its integration into the structured sector by providing credit; loan amounts are limited by market conditions, but no security is required.

In this context, the main aspects of a specific policy to support or promote microenterprises and the informal sector must:

– support the development of a favorable institutional framework, especially as regards taxation and strengthening local credit institutions;

– give women and young people access to training, employment, credit, markets and commerce;

– invest in basic infrastructure and facilitate marketing of goods produced in the informal sector;

– facilitate access to appropriate technology for local conditions;

– make partnership and subcontracting agreements with formal-sector enterprises.

Without going into the details of strategies to support the informal sector and microenterprise, it is important to stress that such arrangements generally included a core component providing for microfinancing: loans, obtaining guarantees, etc. Indeed, whether the measures concern natural resources, market access, employment and microenterprise creation, microfinance is a central part of the provisions. This type of anti-poverty measure must therefore be examined with particular care.

2.2. Measures facilitating poor people's access to financial capital

Only 0.2% of commercial loans go to the billions of people who make up the poorest 20% of the world population. At present, only about eight million very poor people in the developing world benefit from microcredit programs.

And yet credit and savings mobilization services for the poor are an especially effective way to reduce poverty. [1] Until recently, loans were used to finance income-generating activities, to help households gain access to basic social services, to promote the private sector or finance local infrastructure. But this approach is not enough for combating poverty. Poor beneficiary groups must be better targeted, the focus must be on activities and services

---

1. See J. Garson, *Microfinance and anti-poverty strategies* (UNCDF, 1997); UNDP, *La politique de microcrédit du PNUD et Microstart I* (New York, 1998); UNDP, *Credit for the Poor* (New York, 1989); Women's World Banking, *The Missing Links: Financial Systems that Work for the Majority*, 1995.

that meet the needs of the poor and a specific instrument must be developed to reach poor groups: in other words, microfinance. Microfinance, a term which covers both savings and loans, must target and have an impact on the poorest household categories, to both mobilize poor people's savings and provide credit for the poor and for people in disadvantaged regions.

Since the early 1990s, many countries have adopted microfinance as a central element in their poverty reduction strategies. At the Washington summit on microfinance in 1997, the donors offered to considerably extend their microfinance services as a main tool for reducing poverty. This enthusiasm for microfinance was made possible by the resolution of a basic contradiction of the 1970s and 1980s: how to reconcile poor people's access to microfinance with a sound financial system. Now, microfinance institutions are required to be financially sustainable, and most of them are so. To achieve this, the new financial institutions base their work on the common assumption that success and sustainability depend on discipline in repayment.

Further, it is now recognized that when the services proposed and the microfinance instruments respond to the needs of poor communities, local institutions and communities can indeed raise financial and human resources to implement their projects. Provided village communities take part in management and the project is executed at grassroots level, then loans to the poor can help to make sure it is the poor who benefit from the advantages, that the area's specific needs are met, and that projects remain financially realistic and viable.

Box 4.7.

The heritage of Beninese households

In terms of quantity of goods and assets making up for their heritage, the Beninese households appear to be extremely destitute. Indeed, a significant percentage of the population (31% to 89% according to zones) lives in thatched mud houses, contrary to their own aspiration which is to live in corrugated iron roofed houses.

Far more than 70% of the Beninese population live in rural areas, very few households have agricultural imple- ments, even in the cotton zones where the degree of mechanization seems to be highest in the country. There are only one yoke for 1.7 households and one processing device for 5 households are available. Very few households own a cart. Similarly, hullers, graters and mills remain very rare equipment. This situation expresses more especially the difficult nature of the standards of liv- ing and working conditions of the households.

Source: National Report on Human Development in Benin, 1997, UNDP, 1997.

With a view to poverty reduction, microfinance instruments combining savings and loans should finance a wide range of activities, enabling recipients to improve their living standards,

- by creating microenterprises or SMEs,
- through self-employment and income-generating activities,
- through access to productive resources,
- through access to local infrastructure and appropriate technology,
- through access to essential social services.

These new institutions, based on examples of NGOs in Latin America and the Grameen Bank in Bangladesh, have adopted a closely targeted approach aimed mainly at:

- concentrating on small-scale savings, small loans and related activities,
- applying high interest rates and making sure loans are repaid,
- reducing transaction costs by going straight to the customer with no intermediary,
- developing institutional and operational capacities to reach as many people as possible.

Most of the new African microfinance institutions have adopted systems of this kind. Examples are the Kenyan Rural Enterprises Program which supports and finances small business; the Caisses Vilageoises d'Epargne et de Crédit Autogérées in the Dogon homeland of Mali, which has over 160,000 customers; Sahel Action in Burkina Faso, which puts the accent on income-generating microcredit for poor women; the Credit Union Movement in Ghana; and FECECAM in Benin.

Below we give details of some of the more significant examples of credit from these various types of institution. [1]

The Kafo Jinew in Mali is a fund linked to a network of small savings and loan funds in the cotton-growing region in the South of the country. It offers three types of loan:

- Farmers can obtain crop loans during the dry season at a 2% a month interest rate for nine months. Borrowers give personal security, but the villages take responsibility for recovering any unpaid debts.
- Short-term loans are provided for highly profitable trading activities for period of one to three months, at 4% per month interest. The interest is payable at the end of each month and the capital at the end of the loan period. Security arrangements are the same as above.
- Capital equipment loans for buying farm equipment are provided for three years at 1.2% interest per month. Security includes the equipment in question, as well as the same guarantees as in the above two instances.

---

1. A. Nteziyaremye, S. Larivière, F. Martin et P. Larocque, *Les pratiques de microcrédit dans les pays en développement* (Ottawa, 1996).

In Senegal, the Crédit Mutuel du Sénégal has developed several loan formulas at a standard interest rate of 2% a month or 24% a year:

– Crop loans, the biggest item in the whole network (80%), help farmers buy seed. They are granted in June and paid back as a lump sum six months later.

– Ordinary loans are subject to a savings plan. Borrowers can get up to three times the amount of the savings they have built up in the six months preceding their application. A quarter of the loan amount is kept in the savings account as security, until the total amount is repaid.

– With the project savings and loan arrangement, a member must save at a certain rate for six months to qualify for a loan of at least three quarters the amount saved. The loan is for six months and a quarter of the loan must be kept in the savings account until the total is paid back.

Loans enable the poor to obtain the cash they need to seize opportunities for work or for generating income, or to cope with crisis situations without having to dispose of their assets. Savings also provide this kind of flexibility, and this is an option often chosen by poor women. For saving does not create debts, and seems like an easy way to build up assets or capital. Microfinance projects and programs that combine savings and loan arrangements thus give the poor better opportunities. In fact this is the more widespread formula in Sub-Saharan Africa. For example, the Caisses Populaires network in Burkina Faso and the Caisses Villageoises d'Epargne et de Crédits in Mali both based their strategy on collecting savings before they started to offer loans. Compared to Asia or Latin America, it does not seem to be a priority for the African microfinance institutions to increase savings services; most of them already combine savings and credit services. According to a study conducted by Women's World Banking in 17 African countries, 85% of the institutions covered procure savings services for their customers. [1] They serve an average of 2,400 borrowers and 10,500 savers. These are very high figures compared to microfinance institutions in other parts of the world.

Over and above the acknowledged impact of savings, credit and loans for alleviating poverty and increasing poor people's incomes, the key question for the development of microfinance is that of financial intermediation by specific institutions that bring together financial supply and demand.

---

1. Women's World Banking, *Report of the Workshop of African Microfinance Practitioners*, 1996. The seventeen countries concerned are Benin, Burkina Faso, Cameroon, Côte d'Ivoire, Ethiopia, Ghana, Kenya, Mali, Mozambique, Niger, Nigeria, Senegal, South Africa, Tanzania, Togo et Uganda.

Box 4.8.
Alternating funding systems in Burkina Faso

The alternating systems of development funding essentially refer to alternating savings and credit systems and/or facilities of access to credit concerning funding alternatives for the activities of the rural populations and/or of the most underprivileged in general.

Alternating funding meets essential criteria, i.e., the willingness to help the most underprivileged portion of the population benefit from productive resources, namely the poorest population which all the same is the major productive force within the country. Giving them access to credit is one of the best alternatives to have access to the available economic resources. It is also essential to facilitate the respect of the socio-cultural values of the recipient populations so as for the economy to serve social needs and de facto increase their prosperity and well-being. Hence the need to accept and stimulate a plurality of funding systems.

Thus the system can be based on integral self-financing by the group in case the local populations decide to set up an independent alternating system without external support in institutional or financial terms. This case is still witnessed at traditional level with tontines or partial self-financing by the group in case the local populations request the establishment of an alternating funding system with external institutional of financial support.

The alternating system has three major functions: mobilizing local savings, giving loans and improving the liquid assets of the underprivileged populations.

The funding methods rests on two mechanisms. The first mechanism is the savings and credit system among the populations. It consists in modifying local savings to turn it into a credit. There are variants in terms of approach. The second mechanism includes access to bank credit through the alternating bank security fund.

• **The savings and credit system (SEC)**

The SEC approach consists in using locally identified means to finance the needs of the population. The first lever being the availability of savings. There is need to mobilize or to discuss its mobilization. That is why the first task consists in mobilizing savings before granting a loan. For instance in Burkina Faso, the savings and credit funds play an important role in the financing of activities in rural areas. Their promotion is ensured by development support organizations the most known of which are: the Desjardins international society (SDID) through the popular funds network and, CESAO through the Savings and Credit Cooperative Union of Burkina (UCECB). Other important groups are the "Naam" through the Traditional Savings and Credit Banks (BTEC).

• **The alternating security funds system (SFAG)**

The mechanism consists in sponsoring a partner with a bank by taking care of part of the security through a fund that will be managed as a fixed term deposit by the borrowing bank and will be released after the total loan has been refunded by the partner. In general, the fund covers part of the security and the partner has to endeavor to establish his/her own security as operations take place. In Burkina Faso, this mechanism is used by many organizations but it yields poor results. The maximum rate of success recorded in 1996 was 90%. The system has tremendous inadequacies; the banks that cover their risks with the funds at the outset do not make enough effort to recover the loan.

Source: F. MUSERUKA, Africa 2000 Network, Ouagadougou, 1998.

In general, to date, the poorest areas and households have had little access to financial intermediation. The poor still work with cash because no banks exist at their level and microcredit institutions are few and far between. They can therefore neither save nor borrow. To combat human poverty, the supply of microfinance must be increased so as to offer a varied range of essential activities to improve poor people's living standards, help them meet their basic needs and expand their capabilities. Non-banking institutions, especially NGOs, local informal associations and savings and loan cooperatives, have a key role to play in this regard. As they are the only local financial infrastructure providing financial services to the poor, they provide the foundations on which microfinancing programs for the poor could develop.

In Sub-Saharan Africa, the types of institution involved are the following:

- *Mutual funds and loan cooperatives*

These are formal institutions for collecting savings and granting loans, but are governed by specific laws covering cooperatives rather than by banking legislation. Their main problems are (i) that they are not sufficiently capable of adapting to managing modern financial activities, (ii) that their activities are totally unsupervised, and (iii) that their sole source of funds is the deposits of their members, who are also their customers—a situation which limits their lending activities.

However, they fulfil an important role in mobilizing savings and can be an integral part of the banking system, acting as local correspondents for banks. In this respect they have the same shortcomings as banks, mainly as regards cash overload. Lastly, their main customers are mainly the more dynamic sections of the rural population and the informal sector: large farmers, traders, etc.

- *Loan projects supported by donors or NGOs*

The role of these projects used to be restricted to giving advice and seeking funds. They also encouraged people to form credit groups. Now, as they have easier access to government resources and donor assistance, they have extended their scope of operation to granting loans. There are four main kinds of project that offer loan services:

− Savings and loan projects for specific target groups, these often being disadvantaged groups. Logistical and operating costs for these projects are paid by the donors, a factor that does not always ensure a long lifespan for such initiatives. Loans and guarantees are based on solidarity groups; loans are short-term and involve fairly small sums. Activities range from generating income to meeting essential needs and capacity building by promoting solidarity groups or setting up parallel social activities such as literacy classes and vocational training.

– Loan projects for SMEs and microenterprises in the informal sector, mainly in the cities, and small formal sector firms.

– "Grameen Bank" type projects giving small solidarity loans, often implemented by NGOs.

– Integrated projects that include a credit component and often have multiples aims, usually in connection with rural development or food security.

• *Local bank branches*

Banks are indispensable points of entry into the financial intermediation system. All financial transactions go through them, even funds granted to microcredit organizations by the State or international donors. It is therefore important to integrate the banks into the operation of the microcredit system; this will make it possible to exercise stricter control over the use of funds and avoid any subsequent national crisis.

The WWB study mentioned above gives a better understanding of how important microcredit is in Sub-Saharan Africa. For the 17 countries covered, the survey identified institutions with at least 500 active customers, applying current market interest rates and with repayment rates of over 85%. On these criteria, the WWB found 98 rural finance or microfinance institutions. [1] Of these, 85% offered both savings and credit services. Sixty-seven per cent of active borrowers from these institutions were women. The general average repayment rate was 85.2%; indeed, for 50% of the organizations concerned it was over 90%. As regards the institutional structure of these organizations, 51% were NGOs, 34% were savings and loan associations, and 13% were banks or other financial institutions. But there were sharp differences between regions. NGOs predominated in East and South Africa (62% of the total), savings and loan associations accounted for 79% in French-speaking West Africa, and banks and financial institutions were predominant in English-speaking West Africa (69% of the total).

Broadly speaking, local financial intermediation in Africa suffers mainly from the following weaknesses:

a) They are structurally highly fragmented, because of their isolation and lack of a coherent policy.

b) There is sometimes a cash overload. The poorer an area is, the more cash circulates since these areas are most likely to be in receipt of aid from donors or government.

---

1. Women's World Banking, *Report of the Workshop of African Microfinance Practitioners*, 1996.

Box 4.9.
Security based funding of small industry in Lesotho

Lesotho, with an essentially agricultural economy and limited natural resources, faced with a soaring population growth and largely dependent on funds sent by workers employed in the mines of South Africa, is trying to increase its economic independence, namely by facilitating the creation of enterprises and jobs in the country. The reduction of the credit shortage suffered by the small and micro-enterprises is considered as one of the means to reach this objective insofar as these enterprises represent the essential part of the manufacturing sector. The UNCDF and the UNDP initiated in 1989 a credit and assistance project in favor of small enterprises to which they granted US $ 1.1 million and US $ 900 000 respectively. In 1994, following the evaluation of the mid-term evaluation of the project, it was decided to reform it so as to strengthen it institutional framework and introduce a more decentralized approach.

The project aims at enabling small industries — 60% of which are headed by women of whom 30% own their business — to obtain loans more easily. To that effect, a security fund was made available to a local commercial bank (Lesotho Bank) to enable it to grant loans to these enterprises without running excessive risks. The program also aims at familiarizing enterprises with credit and at bringing small enterprises and banks together.

The project has several elements: a security fund, made available by installment to the Lesotho Bank to cover part of the losses incurred through loans to small enterprises in order to stimulate it to respond to the demand of small borrowers; a credit facility for granting loans at basic rates to small enterprises, either directly by the bank with the assistance of contact agents, or through selected financial middlemen who then redistribute this credit to their members in the form of loans; a con-

tact agents network that liaises between the bank and the small enterprises by looking for potential borrowers, assessing demand for credit, negotiating with the bank, ensuring the regularity of reimbursements and assisting the borrowers. Since 1994, specially selected local financial middlemen have been authorized to redistribute credits to small enterprises. These middlemen assume part of the risk. The project also has a technical assistance element with a three-pronged objective: to develop for contact agents a method for evaluating small industries, to assist the bank in managing micro-credit operations, to ensure the management of the whole plan and the monitoring of contact agents.

The project evaluation mission having noted that in order to efficiently reach the small industries scattered throughout the country and cater for their needs it was necessary to decentralize the loan and security system, the UNCDF authorized local middlemen themselves to grant loans under the project, on condition that they respect the principles of sound management and make sure they recover their expenses. Part of the security fund is henceforth kept aside to guarantee the loans to middlemen, the other part is till used to guarantee loans granted to borrowers. For reasons of long term viability, each middleman must create and manage a local security fund supplied by its members with enough funds to cover risks in case of a member's default. A first contribution is provided by the security fund in order to establish these local funds. The interests produced by the fund deposited at Lesotho Bank will be reinvested in the project. They will contribute to the capital which is to guarantee the loans to middlemen and will serve to finance a technical assistance plan meant to strengthen the project.

Source: "Poverty reduction, participation and better local governance", UNDCF, New York, 1995.

c) Lack of any government policy on credit for the poor and the state of the local economy both obstruct access to financial resources. The banks are obliged to keep cash as counterpart for the loans they grant because their customers only work with cash, and this limits the number of loans they can grant.

d) The savings deposited are not sufficient to allow for medium-term lending.

e) The decentralized credit system is very much concentrated in rural areas, while banks are concentrated in the towns.

In view of these obstacles, microfinance components of poverty reduction strategies must take account of the strengths and weaknesses of the system and provide a comprehensive response, both to the policy obstacles and to the difficulties poor people have in gaining access to credit. What is needed is a comprehensive view of the region or country as a whole, to encourage the development of microcredit services to the poor and establish links between the banking system and non-bank institutions operating in a similar field. This implies strengthening local capacities and integrating microfinance policies into governments' development strategies.

Secondly, there is a need to foster cooperation among the many different microcredit institutions and between these institutions and the banks. For the system to survive and effectively reduce poverty, a coherent, complementary framework is needed.

Thirdly, efforts must be made to harmonize donors' positions and activities in this sphere. For the donors are partly responsible for the fragmented nature of the microcredit sector and its excessively wide variety of activities, without any functional links or standardization among them, making it impossible to target the most promising activities and beneficiary groups for poverty reduction.

Lastly, activities must be refocused on the poor. In Sub-Saharan Africa, there are three main types of beneficiary to be targeted:

– Poor urban dwellers working in the informal sector, to encourage the creation of microenterprises and promote self-employment. For this, credit services for business formation, advisory and support services, and offering guarantees are the most commonly proposed services.

– Women in town and country, by supporting income-earning activities, helping women diversify their activities and meeting families' basic needs. In fact, over half of all microcredits in Africa go to women. This is because when it comes to repayment, women are considered to be more disciplined, honest and thrifty. This type of action also favors women's advancement and strengthens their capacities. Incidentally, the NGOs covered by the WWB survey managed far better than the other types of institution to reach a female customer base. For 88% of NGOs, more than half their borrowers are women. Taking all institutions together, women made up an average 62% of the borrowers.

— Poor people in rural areas in general, to develop farming or off-farm income-generating activities, or to set up productive or social infrastructure. For this purpose, setting up local social funds for rural areas is one interesting possibility. To do this villagers must be encouraged to participate in decentralized management of resources that are destined both for small-scale infrastructure projects and for providing individual microcredits for income-generating activities. Set up and managed locally, these funds have a very good chance of reaching the poorest groups or households.

Box 4.10.
Spectacular growth of rural credit in Guinea

The Rural Credit of Guinea was established in 1988 under the Agricultural and Rural Credit Project (PCAR) steered by the Ministry of Rural Development. Its approach is inspired by the principles of the Grameen Bank. Given the high rate of inflation that was prevailing at the time (26% per annum, IMF source), and the relative weakness of the demand expressed for savings services, it lays special emphasis on credit distribution. The network now receives support from CFD, the European Union and USAID.

The Rural Credit Funds propose several credit products inspired from the Grameen Bank [1]. Thus the granting of credit is based on the prior establishment of 5-10 member interdependent groups, with similar economic and social status, gathered on the basis of affinity. The "Interdependent Rural Credit" (CRS) is meant to finance economically profitable and diversified commercial operations, handicraft and

agricultural activities. It is a one year progressive credit with upper limit and monthly reimbursements. At 31/12/1994, it represents 60% of total outstanding credits distributed. The "Interdependent Agricultural Credit" (CAS) is a variant of the rural credit: redemption dates are designed in relation to agricultural cycle and installed after the harvesting period in order not to oblige the farmers to sell all their harvest at a low price. Its outstanding credit is equal to 27% of overall credit distributed in late 1994. The "Off-season Credit" (CCS) lasts six months. Its upper limit is lower than that of the CRS because it is meant to finance off-season market gardening. The interest rate applied to CRSs, CASs and CCSs is 3% per month on the remaining outstanding balance due. In case of delay, in addition to penalties, a GF 1 000 per month is payable by each of the members of the defaulting group. The granting of credit is blocked at the district level if

---

1. Adjustments were made in order to take Guinean reality into better consideration. Thus, a "Council of Wise People" is in charge of the quality of the composition of interdependent groups, and of ensuring the credibility of credit applicants.

the rate of reimbursement of outstanding credit is lower than 100%; it is blocked at fund level if that rate is lower than 90% (in actual fact, this rule applies on a case to case basis).

The National Food Security Support Project (PNASA) received the support of rural and mutual credit. The traders (collectors, wholesalers and semi-wholesalers) receive credits for the five month growing season at 2.5% interest per month, agreement protocols are established between the PNASA and the rural or mutual credit that manage the credit line made available to them by the PNASA and remunerate it. The design is that of the an in-channel integrated circuit.

Saving is facilitated by two types of society members: "free saving" or "voluntary saving" concern society members who do not have the right to get credits, essentially big traders and civil servants. Its remuneration is 17% per annum as per the most reliable balance of the quarter. In late 1994, the outstanding voluntary savings contributed for 73% to the total outstanding collected savings. The "security saving" is deducted from the total credit (10% of the amount borrowed) at the time of disbursement. It is no longer remunerated. It contributes for 27% of total collected savings.

A strong differentiation is observed within Rural Credit partnership. Civil servants and big traders who do not have access to credit represent respectively 56% and 17% of voluntary savers. Loans, mainly granted to farmers have multiple use: they most often finance activities that mobilize a small fast rotating capital.

Between 1989 and 1994, a spectacular growth was observed. Thus, in late 1994, the Rural Credit Network of Guinea included 40 funds covering all the regions, against 2 funds in 1989. In 1994 35310 society members were involved (31220 borrowing society members and 4090 "voluntary savers"), against 110 society members in 1989 (all borrowers). The outstanding credit amounts to GF 2.185 billion, and the outstanding saving amounts to GF 1.44 billion.

Thus Rural Credit is the fist credit system in Guinea, in terms of penetration and number of loans outside Conakry. However, the outstanding credit that it distributes only represent 1.4% of the outstanding credit granted to the private sector (amounting to 3% of GDP). Similarly the savings collected by the Rural Credit (GF 1 billion) corresponds only to 1.1% of checking deposits. Finally, the fund made available to the Rural Credit only account for 0.5% of public investments. If the micro-economic impact appears to be limited, the local effects are not negligible. The rural credit would tend to reduce the monetary constraint of the economic agents excluded from the official financial systems, by substituting themselves to usurious systems in the context of monopoly.

Source: P. Hugon & C. Richard, "Decentralized financing in Benin, Burkina Faso and Guinea", 1995.

Where a strategy of giving poor people access to microcredit is adopted, the impact is considerable. In Burkina Faso, Guinea and Benin, where decentralized financial systems are already tried and tested, they have proved very beneficial for poverty reduction. [1]

For example, especially in rural areas, local savings are mobilized for productive purposes and the knock-on effect on employment is considerable. Taking both direct and indirect job creation due to microcredit, 20,000 to 30,000 jobs have been created in each of these three countries. Incomes have also risen significantly in regions where microcredit organizations are well established and easily accessible to the poor.

Besides the economic and material aspects, microfinancing also has a big impact on poor households' capacities. Literacy rates rise and demand for training increases, especially where the projects include training among their objectives. Lastly, microfinance has a noticeable impact on poor people's integration into economic and decision-making networks. Communities are emerging that wield effective counter-power to such traditionally dominant groups as traders and money-lenders.

However, to make sure that microfinancing acts as an engine for poverty reduction, it is important to apply the following principles more strictly:

— better targeting of the poor, and special measures to reach the most disadvantaged among them, who are still usually excluded from microfinance networks;

— special attention to the danger of saturating the market, mainly in remote or outlying regions or in the poorest communities;

— strengthening the microfinance institutions' sustainability;

— thorough, detailed analysis of the real economic and social impact of microfinance on poverty levels.

For such programs to succeed, complex strategies must be designed and all the partners involved in the process — governments, banks, grassroots communities — must be willing. International organizations and the donor community must give their support in this field, especially during the early years. The task in hand is to create new structures or less rigid instruments, so that links are forged between the microcredit programs and funding sources, especially via the private sector. The challenge here is to get these complex activities under way while targeting them more precisely on the poor and on the activities that will best help beneficiaries out of the poverty trap.

---

1. P. Hugon et C. Richard, *Le financement décentralisé au Bénin, au Burkina Faso et en Guinée* (Paris, 1995).

3. Food security, environmental protection and poverty reduction

3.1. Rural development and food security

The green revolution, begun in the 1960s in India and in many Asian countries in the early 1970s, has improved food balances, increased and diversified production and reduced the pockets of extreme poverty, although in some countries, chronic under-nourishment still persists in places.

The situation in Sub-Saharan Africa is more complex given present yields, the level of solvent demand, environmental conditions and problems of access to productive resources.

Furthermore, competitive economic globalization and the rules of the World Trade Organization will not make the task any easier for the poorest countries. Already disadvantaged in terms of agroclimatic potential, solvency and access to markets, they will need a much higher level of organization and knowledge today to embark on their own green revolutions. Yet it is the only obvious way to combat poverty and food insecurity.

However, several examples — maize in Zimbabwe and cotton in West Africa especially — show that Africa is up to the task. The "white revolution" in cotton, grown as a rainfed crop in savanna regions where the money economy was still marginal at the outset, is very revealing of the complementary influences of political will and market forces. From the opening up of dirt roads, transport and input supply to crop loans and extension work on cotton ginning techniques, it was the state-owned development companies that handled all the organizational functions, including marketing, and made West Africa the world's foremost cotton exporter.

Again at the policy level, the liberalization of the grain trade in Mali and, more recently, the devaluation of the CFA franc, prompted rice farmers on the Office du Niger irrigation systems to rapidly intensify their production. Encouraged by the increase in paddy prices from CFAF70 to CFAF120 per kg between 1994 and 1996, they have greatly increased their use of fertilizer, and now broadcast sowing is being replaced by planting out, which gives significantly higher yields. The rapid development of market gardening and peri-urban farming, which has clearly been driven by the immediate proximity of markets, can also no doubt be considered a green revolution.

All these "revolutions" have been very limited geographically, however. The vast majority of rural areas have been left far behind. Yet in those areas, population growth destabilizes the traditional farming systems a little more each year. Fallow periods are shortened, soils are exposed to erosion by cultivation methods that constantly deplete the natural fertility of the land.

Farmers have absolutely no capacity to invest or carry out major improvements on their land and the big urban markets are far away. In short, there is no serious possibility of solving the problems of poverty and malnutrition among these population groups through a classic conversion to large-scale monocropping.

In the past few years, many researchers, leaders of rural organizations or NGOs and even politicians have expressed views in favor of more open-ended local development approaches. Participatory research and development schemes come under this heading; they recommend sustainable community-based natural resource management aiming for a more limited, but much less costly, yield increase, by gradually improving local farming practices. Large, land-hungry development projects that are ruinously expensive and inaccessible are thus giving way to methods that farmers can handle themselves, for combating erosion, for example, or for village-level irrigation. In the same way, diversifying production helps to maintain the balance and sustainability of a farm ecosystem by taking advantage of local biodiversity and environmental variations.

Agronomically speaking, a wide range of proven cropping techniques allow farmers to manage their land with very low input levels.

Some Sahelian societies had found their own short-term solutions to this fundamental problem by keeping stands of acacia albida. More recent and more widespread practices are compost-making, multiple cropping with a leguminous crop to fix atmospheric nitrogen, mulch or permanent ground cover to prevent evaporation and erosion, direct sowing and zero tillage, agroforestry, alley cropping; there are many such possibilities. Mixed crop and livestock farming systems, using the animals for draught power and manure, requires more investment and is technically more complicated.

Consistent with this type of diversified development, neighborhood agricultural research is already pursuing numerous local trials of new varieties and technical improvements that farmers can easily adopt.

On a larger scale, agronomic researchers are having to revise their priorities and extend their activities to more of the species that are actually grown in the regions concerned and are adaptable.

These green revolutions, in all their variety and with all their local particularities, are leading agricultural researchers to work directly with farmers and rely on their accumulated knowledge to improve husbandry on often over-exploited farm ecosystems.

Infinitely more complex than in the past, the challenge now is to deal simultaneously with two very different scales of times and space: meeting the immediate needs of local development, and preparing techniques for the future.

Box 4.11.
Nutritional status in Togo

Between 1984 and 1988 an increasing chronic malnutrition rate is observed within the child population. From 1984 to 1988, it is estimated that 29% to 33% of children are undernourished. During the same period, a 42% rate of anemia in women old enough to procreate is observed. Nutritional diseases include nutritional anemia as well as disorders and diseases related to micro-nutrient deficiencies. On the other hand, in some regions of the country the prevalence of night-blindness and of iodine and vitamin A deficiency is observed.

The 1987 Budget/Consumption survey revealed that the average food ration provided 1,900 cal/day, that is 83% of daily needs. Furthermore, in the rural areas, the poor and very poor households used about 70% of their resources to acquire these inadequate rations.

In terms of food security, it is certain that the coverage of needs is still uneven at regional level due to isolation and within households. It would seem that food security must be included in the concerns of Togo.

Source: National Poverty Eradication Strategy, Ministry of Planning of Togo/UNDP, 1995.

As to the policies required to help this process, there are big challenges facing elected officials and development experts:

– Changes are needed to the legal framework (land tenure law, company law, bank statutes) and taxation, in favor of private enterprise, especially for the development of small units to process and market farm produce and supply all the services farmers need.

– Finance requirements involve far smaller sums than the big irrigation schemes, but the small-scale decentralized rural credit systems that are indispensable for this type of development are in short supply, and the profitability of such systems is uncertain. The cost of road infrastructure for example, even for dirt roads, rises in proportion to the area to be served and constitutes a major financing challenge.

The scale and diversity of these green and sustainable local resource revolutions imply decentralization of certain State responsibilities. It is patently obvious, for example, that central government is not in a position to control access to or sustainable management of natural resources.

The irrational management that sometimes prevails in forestry, especially in charcoal production, is an eloquent example. All the indications are that local communities are better able to exercise the necessary control, especially if they can take a financial cut of the woodcutting taxes they levy on behalf of the State. Full-scale contractual local management practices have been tried out, for example for fuelwood in Niamey, capital of Niger.

Box 4.12.

The Gestion de Terroirs Approach to Environmental Degradation

The Gestion de Terroirs approach has developed in recent years in Sahelian West Africa as a locally based participatory means of addressing environmental degradation at the village level — terroir being defined as an area of a village or group of contiguous villages. Its success has led to its adoption in East Africa, as well as in South Asia and Australia, for programs as diverse as village land titling (Tanzania), land conservation for wildlife (Zimbabwe), forest management (India) and environmental education and action research (Australia).

Three main principles underlie the Gestion de Terroirs approach. First, projects strive to promote security of rights to resources, which is the basis for investment in the management and improvement of land and other natural resources. When, for example, customary systems of land tenure command little adherence — as in areas of in-migration, resettlement or conflicts — Gestion de Terroirs projects support the evolution of a local decisionmaking body capable of discussing the interests of different, possibly conflicting, groups. Popular participation is a second key element of the Gestion de Terroirs approach, because any hope of long-term success depends on working in the interests of local people, and because indigenous technical knowledge often provides the most useful basis for successful interventions. Finally, Gestion de Terroirs projects take a global, multidisciplinary approach encompassing pro-

duction, consumption, exchange and environmental and cultural systems in order to mirror the complex reality of a «terroir».

The Gestion de Terroirs approach usually involves a series of key steps : initiating discussions to diagnose environmental problems, electing a committee at the village level to oversee resource management, establishing boundries to the village's territory and mapping types of soils and forms of cultivation, and elaborating a management plan that clarifies the rules of access to different resources by each group in the village.

UNDP-UNSO's analysis of the progress made with the Gestion de Terroirs approach emphasises the need to scale up the approach and give it more of a regional scope. Changes in local resource management systems alone cannot foster sustainable development in Sahelian areas. Links need to be strengthened between local production units and regional economic networks. Moreover, the Gestion de Terroirs approach is more successful when it is adopted at the national level as part of a general rural development strategy. This highlights the need to ensure consistency between such micro projects and macro-level planning and budgeting. By the same taken, such micro projects can only be successful in conjunction with a decentralisation process that locates decisionmaking at the local level.

Source: UNDP, Progress against Poverty, New York, 1998.

Lastly, the success of these policies must be measured far more against the lasting reduction of malnutrition and improvements in rural living standards — which are indeed their objectives — than in conventional terms of return on investment or export volumes. But there is a big problem: how, and how far, should the logic of equity prevail over the economic rationale of national accounting?

3.2. Environment and poverty reduction

Growth policies that improve the situation of the poor can indirectly reduce pressure on natural resources by putting a brake on exploitation of ecologically vulnerable resources and by lowering fertility rates. They can also attenuate the distortions that cause energy wastage or are harmful to production. But a macroeconomic and sectoral growth policy can have a pernicious effect on the environment if other aspects of the government's actions lead to distortion or if the regulatory framework is inadequate.

Reform of the incentive system and institutional reorganization in the trade, energy and public sectors can help to protect the environment. In many countries, industrial firms have received subsidies and are protected from competition by restrictions on imports or other statutory measures. If the firms so protected are polluters, these practices are harmful to environmental quality and tend to perpetuate low-yield production methods. Subsidizing the price of oil, as Nigeria does, encourages overconsumption and waste, adding to atmospheric pollution.

Environmental damage is to be feared when the system of macroeconomic incentives changes while there are still distortions such as under-valuation of resource prices. For example, reducing macroeconomic distortions that hold back production of tradable commodities can have damaging ecological effects if the price of land from which these products are derived remains abnormally low. Thus State revenue from forestry rights is generally much less than it might be because forestry rights are cheap and payment rates too low.

For some types of activity and in some areas, repositioning macroeconomic policies sometimes leads to unacceptable environmental damage. When such damage is predictable, it is best to prevent it by directly tackling the specific environmental problems likely to arise. Macroeconomic and sectoral policies are too broad for countries to think they can be spared from taking specific environmental protection measures; but they must take care not to distort these policies on the pretext of protecting the environment.

It is also important, when rationalizing public expenditure, to determine which spending is essential for environmental protection, and take care to keep this sufficiently high. While its impact may be very hard to quantify, social spending—especially that designed to alleviate poverty and indirectly put a brake on population growth—may also have beneficial effects on the environment, perhaps even greater than those of spending specifically for that purpose. In this respect it would be a good idea to conduct further research into the ecological impact of the breakdown of public spending and the relative advantages of different budget allocations, and also determine how to rationalize public spending so as to protect the environment while at the same time alleviating poverty.

Box 4.13.

Strategies for natural resource management in Niger

As part of poverty control, strategic goals in terms of natural resource management consist on the one hand in limiting anthropogenic effects on the destruction of the natural elements of the productive capital and, on the other hand in developing and testing legal and socio-economic techniques for the settlement of selected local land tenure conflicts.

The conventional too sectorial and too technical approach to natural resource management which deprives the populations of effective responsibility has led to failure. In recent years, many experiments at both national and regional level have been conducted with a view to facilitating the full participation of the populations in the management of natural resources. It was on the basis of these experiments that the concept of land management was established as a basic approach to implementing the natural resource management strategy. Many scattered physical projects corresponding to various natural resource management problems were developed in Niger and in the sub-region. Many of them were largely accepted by the populations and were successful.

The concept of rural land refers to a group of families who have agreed to share the same territory on which they live permanently or seasonally and regularly carry out activities related to the utilization and exploitation of renewable natural resources available on these territories. This community may be a village, a village district or a group of villages, a pastoral community. The concept of rural land must be understood as a stretch of land and water from which a given community draws its means of subsistence. In the agro-pastoral zones, rural land is considered as a stretch of land on which communities of farmers and stockbreeders each enjoy traditionally recognized and often complementary rights of cropping and access.

The essential goal of the rural land approach is to try and develop an efficient and sustainable system enabling the communities to manage their natural resource capital on the basis of a plan that they will have designed for their rural land. This approach includes four major elements:

a) a significant involvement of the population in all phases of the planning and management process;

b) the development of incentives and capacities to allow the communities to manage their own development directly and efficiently;

c) the establishment of clear and freely negotiated relationships between the technical and administrative authorities and the local communities, and

d) the design of a concerted development plan resulting from demands freely expressed by the population.

This approach is essentially flexible and iterative (need to readapt the plan to new conditions), ascending and decentralized, multidisciplinary and multidimensional.

A consensus was reached on the steps to implement for each rural land (although the approach is still experimental to a large extent). These different steps can be schematically described as follows:

– institution of a climate of confidence and dialogue with the communities in order to facilitate a participatory approach;

– conduct of a diagnosis of the evolution of the rural land in physical terms (including the description of the specific production system of the area) and socio-economic terms making it possible to delimit the rural land and evaluate its resources, to know the structure and the socio-anthropological dynamics of the community, the potential and constraints in order to analyze the short, middle and long term objectives of the community;

– community organization favoring the emergence of real representativeness of their socio-anthropological specificity formally recognized within and beyond the limits of the rural land in order to deal on behalf of the community with issues related to land, natural resources and all aspects of rural land management and development;

– concerted design of a rural land management plan taking into account community objectives as well as the potential and limits of the resources in their environment;

– agreement between community and government in the form of contract whereby the Government plans to provide assistance while the community commits itself to respect the conditions of the management plan and especially those concerning development land protection and maintenance;

– implementation of the management plan with the involvement of the communities, decentralized government services, NGOs and private services.

Although the system appears to be extremely expensive, namely because of the need for close technical assistance, it will be the core of the strategy for the management and preservation of natural resources insofar as other expensive experiences were not successful.

Source: "National poverty eradication strategy in Niger", Government of Niger & UNDP, 1997.

---

4. Availability and accessibility of basic social services

It is widely agreed that satisfying basic needs in health, education and nutrition is not just an attractive goal in itself but also an important instrument for reducing poverty and increasing the well-being of the population. Giving all people access to basic social services helps to involve people more deeply in community life and decision making, hold back population growth, foster equity and equality between men and women, increase productivity and improve people's chances of achieving sustainable livelihoods.

Poverty can only be sustainably reduced if individuals have the means to take control of their lives through better investment in their basic capabilities. In this context it is of paramount importance to promote and foster access for all, and especially for poor or disadvantaged households, to basic social services, i.e. principally basic education, primary and reproductive health care, safe drinking water and nutrition. Thus the availability and accessibility of these basic social services have become top priority issues for many African countries.

Availability and accessibility of social services are thus among the strategic keys to poverty reduction. The benefits they bring are vitally important for improving poor people's living standards, increasing their social and human capital and fully including them in society. Higher incomes are not enough; the poor still need basic social services and a better capacity to help themselves and participate in community life, all of which can be achieved through better health and education. [1]

Table 4.1. –   Data on Education Expenditure related to Country Income

Individual GDP (in $ PPA)	Public expenditure as % of GDP	Public expenditure per student (in $)		
		Primary	Secondary	Higher
< 1.000 $	2.3 %	35	101	1.756
1.000-2.000 $	4.4 %	84	172	1.301
2.000-5.000 $	3.7 %	268	571	2.540
5.000-10.000 $	3.1 %	451	6.161	980
> 10.000 $	3.6 %	4.189	4.340	7.542

Sources: UNESCO, Statistical Yearbooks, 1993 & 1994; Report on Education in Africa, 1995.

---

1. UNDP, *World Human Development Report 1997* (New York: Oxford University Press, 1997); S. Larivière et F. Martin, *Cadre d'analyse économique de la pauvreté et des conditions de vie des ménages* (Université Laval, Québec, 1997); K. Subbarao, *Lessons of 30 Years of Fighting Poverty* (Québec, 1997); P. Bardhan, "Efficacité, équité et lutte contre la pauvreté", *Problèmes Economiques*, n°2520, 1997; UNICEF, *Suivi de l'Initiative 20/20: proposition et méthodologie* (New York, 1997).

The choice of basic social services stems from two observations. First, African governments' social policies in the 1960s to the 1980s paradoxically ended up improving access to social services for the better-off. In health care, for example, nearly 80% of overall spending, private and public, went to curative care, and in many cases about 80% of this was spent through hospitals. With no priority being placed on primary health care, the poor often did not have access to basic health services. Urban dwellers and the rich thus paradoxically profited most from free access to hospitals and health care. The overall expansion of the health care system has thus been to the detriment of preventive medicine and basic curative health care, the things that are of most benefit to the poorest. As a result, poverty and illness still go together, for children and adults alike. [1]

The situation in education is similar. Government policies have long favored secondary and higher education over basic education and literacy, which are of most benefit to the poor. In Sub-Saharan Africa, for example, in 1990, an average 22% of education budgets went to higher education, which benefits only 2% of the corresponding age group. As with health, supply is very much concentrated in the towns and so more easily accessible to the better-off. This has meant that most children attending primary school are the children of non-poor urban households. Thus while primary school enrolment rates have greatly increased, it is important to emphasize that those children who do not go to school are mainly children from poor homes.

Table 4.2. – Enrolment Rate related to Country Income

Individual GDP (in $ PPA)	Illiteracy rates	Gross enrolment rate		
		Primary	Secondary	Higher
< 1.000 $	58%	66%	13%	2%
1.000-2.000 $	46%	88%	33%	6%
2.000-5.000 $	25%	103%	61%	14%
5.000-10.000 $	15%	104%	64%	18%
> 1.000 $	5%	102%	92%	38%

Sources: idem.

---

1. UNDP, *Human Development Report 1993* (New York: Oxford University Press, 1993); World Bank, *World Development Report 1993: Investing in Health* (Washington: Oxford University Press, 1993); WHO, *World Health Report 1997* (Geneva: 1997); M. Gillis, D. H. Perkins, M. Roemer and D. R. Snodgrass, *Economics of Development*, 4th ed. (New York: Norton, 1996).

The second reason for introducing large-scale programs to give poor people access to basic social services is that this is one of the most effective and cost-effective ways of reducing poverty and broadening people's opportunities. For example, it has been shown that there is a close correlation between education and income, at both individual and country levels. Illiteracy is far more widespread in the least developed countries and gradually diminishes as national income increases.

Poor people's main resource is their labor; education increases people's productivity and so increases their income. This principle is unanimously acknowledged in the wage employment sector. But in Sub-Saharan Africa, wage employment accounts for only a tiny proportion of incomes. However, studies have shown a similarly beneficial effect on non-wage employment. A farmer who has been to school for four years has an output 8% higher than one who has never been to school. The same applies to work in the urban informal sector, where young people with a few years' schooling behind them move on to economic activities in which hourly earnings are higher. [1]

With regard to health, there is a strong correlation between income and individual or national life expectancy and mortality rates. The richer a household or nation, the better its overall health. The same applies to the relationship between an individual's health status and labor productivity. In Sierra Leone, for example, in the early 1990s, an increase in food energy intake improved farmers' health status and farm output greatly increased.

However, from the perspective of poverty reduction, access to basic social services does not just mean increased income or improved labor productivity. Data on African households confirm that the mother's educational level, for example, determines to a large extent the level of other social indicators such as infant mortality, child malnutrition, fertility rates, the children's school enrolment rates, and hence the household's standard of living in general. It has been estimated that for each year of schooling the mother has received, there is a 9% drop in mortality among the children under five years of age and a substantial increase in household health. [2] Similarly, proper and adequate nutrition has a favorable impact on a child's development and its social capital: a better nourished child is in better health and better able to learn.

Developing human capital is therefore a key to reducing poverty, and better health, nutrition and education reinforce each other. For these rea-

---

1. World Bank *World Development Report 1990: Poverty* (Washington, 1990); K. Subbarao, *Lessons of 30 Years of Fighting Poverty* (Quebec, 1997).

2. UNICEF, *Suivi de l'Initiative 20/20: restructuration des budgets nationaux et de l'aide extérieure* (New York, 1997).

sons, a poverty reduction program absolutely must favor poor people's access to these essential social services, based on:

– a quantitative increase in the services offered (primary schools, health centers);

– a qualitative improvement;

– the political will to make social services available and accessible, through increased and better distributed spending in these fields and a thoroughgoing reform of the institutions that deliver these services.

Box 4.14.

Strengthening social services for the poor in Lesotho

The objective above all is to improve the quality of primary health care and basic education in rural districts and urban centers identified as poor. The six districts selected have the greatest absolute number of poor and extremely poor people. At the same time, the Government wishes to extend its public assistance program to the poorest, mainly old, disabled or sick people.

It is important to emphasize that the Ministries of Health and Education have many difficulties in harmonizing their objectives and programs with those of the donors concerning certain activities or geographic regions. Despite the fact that the Ministries are making tremendous efforts to re-deploy their staff and resources in favor of poverty control in the targeted regions, there is a significant gap between the donors' resources and those of the Government.

For education, priority goes to basic education, to professional education and to the informal sector. These are the three sectors identified that are likely to have greater impact on the poor, be they children, young or adults people.

Source: Government of Lesotho, "Poverty Reduction in the Context of Good Governance", Geneva, 8th Round Table Conference, 1997.

4.1. Availability and accessibility of basic education

The principle of easier access for all to basic education was clearly asserted for the first time in 1990, at the World Conference on Education for All, which produced an agreement intended to intensify efforts to improve the quantitative and qualitative levels of schooling and adult education. The goal was to give everyone basic education and ensure that everyone could read in the first years of the 21st century.

Education policy has a fundamental part to play in poverty reduction programs and strategies. From this perspective, the main objectives are (i) to give political and financial priority to primary rather than secondary or higher education, (ii) to increase access to education, especially for girls and the most underprivileged, and (iii) to improve the quality and relevance of teaching, so as to genuinely strengthen the capacity of the poor and enable them to take control of their lives. In this context, one must obviously focus most on basic education, literacy and vocational education.

During the 1990s, the African countries generally sought to increase education supply by building schools and literacy teaching centers, so as to greatly increase literacy and school enrolment rates. The priorities seemed to be to quantitative: building schools and rapidly training more teachers. Indeed, the results have been fairly encouraging.

In Mauritania, the gross rate of primary school enrolment rose from 46% in 1990 to 87% in 1997; in Nigeria, it rose from 67% to 86% between 1990 and 1994. In Uganda, school enrolment as a whole rose from 25% to 41% between 1980 and 1990. Lastly, in Burkina Faso, between 1991 and 1994, the number of classes increased by 37% and over-all school enrolment rates from 30% to 37% in four years. [1]

The strategy of these countries in the 1990s was above all to strengthen basic education, mainly from a quantitative standpoint. The main objectives of these programs were to increase rates of primary school enrolment and reduce disparities in access, mainly by building classrooms, making better use of available resources and strengthening planning and management capacities. Similar programs were adopted in Mali and Senegal.

Thus in twenty years, school enrolment rates at all levels have greatly increased in Sub-Saharan Africa. Adult literacy rates have doubled, from 27% to 55%, while between 1961 and 1991 the net rate of school enrolment rose from 25% to 55% for primary school and 13% to 38% for secondary school.

However, apart from the acknowledged successes in increasing supply and the particular efforts made to give more poor children access to primary schooling, there are still many problems. Taking the countries mentioned above, for example, much effort needs to be made to improve school enrolment rates and integration into working life. In Mauritania, although gross primary school enrolment rates almost doubled in five years to 87%, the net rate is still only 54%. This 33% discrepancy seems essentially to indicate that the system is not very effective internally, with children starting their schooling late and big educational disparities between the sexes and between richer and poorer parts of the country. In Uganda, a thorough analysis of the situation reveals a very low quality education system, especially where the pupils are poor children, with overcrowded classrooms and lack of teaching materials. The knowledge acquired proves to be

---

1. UNDP, *Rapport sur le développement humain en Mauritanie 1996*; UNDP, *Rapport sur le développement humain durable au Burkina Faso, 1997*; UNDP, *Uganda Human Development Report 1996*; UNDP, *Human Development Report Nigeria 1996*.

ill suited to coping with life when the children leave school. In Nigeria, the declared political goal of achieving 100% primary school enrolment is invalidated by the poor quality of the lessons, the dilapidated state of class-rooms and material, the poor teacher motivation and the low level of resources deployed to achieve the stated goal. The results are mitigated in Burkina Faso too. The teaching system does not seem to be very effective; many children have to repeat a year, and it takes an average of twelve pupil-years to produce one primary school certificate. The teacher training is inappropriate. In this situation, it is more than difficult for a poor house-hold to make the necessary investment to get a child right through primary school, especially as the knowledge acquired is considered inappropriate.

Table 4.3. – Evolution of Primary Gross Enrolment Rates in Sub-Saharan Africa

Country	Primary GER (1988-92)				Growth		Reference years
	Boys		Girls				
Burkina Faso	40	46	24	29	+6	+5	87/91
Chad	73	89	29	41	+16	+12	87/91
Mauritania	60	70	42	55	+10	+13	88/92
Burundi	77	76	60	62	1	+2	87/92
Senegal	68	67	48	50	1	+2	87/91
Tanzania	64	69	64	67	+5	+3	88/92
Mali	29	32	17	19	+3	+2	87/91
Ethiopia	44	26	28	18	16	8	88/92
Guinea	42	57	19	27	+15	+8	88/92
Comoros	82	86	66	73	+4	+7	88/91
Côte d'Ivoire	87	81	61	58	6	3	88/91
Gambia	76	81	47	56	+5	+9	88/92
Ghana	78	80	62	67	+2	+5	87/91
Madagascar	94	81	90	77	13	13	89/93
Mozambique	76	69	59	51	7	8	87/92
Nigeria	77	85	59	67	+8	+8	87/91
Rwanda	73	78	70	76	+5	+6	88/91
Zaire	87	80	64	60	7	4	87/92
Botswana	108	114	114	118	+6	+4	88/92
Lesotho	100	98	123	113	2	10	88/92
Maurice	104	104	107	108	0	+1	88/91
Swaziland	104	116	103	114	+12	+11	88/92
Zimbabwe	128	123	124	114	5	10	88/92

Source: UNESCO, Report on Education in Africa, 1995.

Two sets of reasons combine to create this inefficiency:

(i) inappropriate teacher training (rushed recruitment and little further training for supervisors); scarcity of teaching aids and materials; inappropriate curricula; few days of actual teaching (inefficient staff management);

(ii) irregular attendance by the children, either because they must help with the family's workload or because the parents are not convinced that schooling is useful, and many children drop out during the year (lack of money during the "hungry gap").

On the other hand, school enrolment rates have actually fallen in many countries that have been through, or are experiencing, major crises or disastrous political and economic situations. In the Central African Republic, for example, primary school enrolment fell from 71% in 1980 to 48% in 1995. In Angola, the gross rate of school enrolment at all levels fell from 54% to 31% between 1980 and 1990. And in Burundi, the gross rate of primary school enrolment fell from 70% in 1992 to 43% in 1996. [1]

Thus in Sub-Saharan Africa over 80 million boys and girls have no access to primary schooling, only half the children who start school reach the fifth year of schooling, teaching is of lamentable quality and structures often ill adapted. And it is still mainly the children of poor households who do not attend school, which restricts their range of opportunities for future self-fulfilment. That is why it is important to target educational supply programs on particularly poor groups rather than limiting programs for strengthening basic education to aspects that make it more accessible for all.

Operational school facilities must therefore be made available in disadvantaged areas of town and country, the cost of sending children to school must be reduced, and a certain flexibility in school timetables and calendars must be allowed so that the young can combine work and education, helping out with farm work or having some income-generating activity. These are essential factors for making school available and accessible to the poorest children. As we shall see below, the problem of free basic education must also be examined. For the success of an education policy that targets the poor depends on poor households at least having access to free education.

Botswana has made access to primary school for all the core of its new education strategy, particularly targeting marginalized youth and the children of poor households. This strategy can be summed up in three points: policy reform, accessibility and equity and, lastly, the quality and relevance

---

1. *Rapport sur le développement humain en république centrafricaine,* avril 1996; V. Ngendakumana et E. Huybens, *Burundi: l'effet de la crise de sécurité et de l'embargo sur la situation de la pauvreté,* 1998; UNDP, *Human Development Report Angola,* 1998.

of the teaching. At policy level, it is essentially a matter of spelling out the curricula clearly and managing the education system better. As regards access and equity, the priority is to reach those 17% of children not enrolled. In this connection the government has decided to devote more resources to schools in the poor regions and remote villages, adapting curricula to these poor children and laying special stress on girls not enrolled in school, including bringing pregnant girls back to school. These measures also go hand in hand with a series of goals intended to improve the quality of basic teaching and making it more relevant to life outside school. The Botswana government's aims are:

– a population with better basic knowledge so they can take part in decisions,

– a more efficient informal sector thanks to appropriate skills and knowledge,

– more emphasis on technical education and vocational training,

– higher living standards and an overall improvement in health,

– a society with stronger capacities and so better able to seize opportunities. [1]

Poverty reduction was the goal of a program to provide schooling for the children of nomads in Nigeria, supported by UNESCO and UNICEF. Nigerian education policy recognizes that the nomads are a special group with a particular lifestyle and require specifically adapted teaching content and methods. The short term aim is to focus on basic functional literacy and basic arithmetical skills.

Three types of school are needed for the nomad children: conventional schools, field schools at certain points along the migration trails, and mobile classrooms. The teaching materials are portable and travel with the families. The curriculum is specially designed to contain enough references to the pastoralists' livelihood, cultural role, tasks, customs and concerns.

However, there are problems due to the limited resources allocated to training teachers and specialist supervisors for nomad education, supply of teaching materials and precise, applied research into education for the children of these nomadic herders and fisherfolk. [2]

Another factor in relation to basic education for all is the inequality of access between boys and girls. Strategies must be found to overcome the barriers to girls' enrolment and success at school. This is also a priority for poverty alleviation, as recent research has shown that basic education for

1. UNDP, UNICEF and Republic of Botswana, *Planning for People. A Strategy for Accelerated Human Development in Botswana,* 1993.

2. UNESCO, *Report on the state of education in Africa, 1995* (Dakar: UNESCO Regional Office for Education in Africa, 1995).

girls has a beneficial effect in this regard. The decline in infant mortality and fertility rates and the increased incomes and improved household living standards that result from educating girls represent major social benefits.

Girls' school enrolment rates have been rising steadily in most African countries since the late 1980s. In 1992, girls made up 45% of the total primary school population. But in countries such as Burkina Faso, Chad, Ethiopia, Guinea, Mali and Niger, no more than 40% of primary school children are girls, and this figure even be as low as 32%, in the case of Chad in 1992. [1] So much effort still needs to be made in this connection, and specific programs will be required.

A short-term plan of action in Mali (1995-98) aims for "the expansion of basic education for the benefit of girls". This was because, despite considerable efforts, the gross primary school attendance rate leveled out at 25.5% in 1992, with a minimum of 4.93% in one province.

The action plan is designed to increase school enrolment and success rates and the percentage of girls staying on through primary school, and to provide extra-curricular vocational training for girls and women.

Training is planned for national and regional teams. After evaluation of training needs will come a teacher training program. Extra tuition is organized for girls who are lagging behind, and there will be literacy classes for parents.

An operation research component will be included in the project, to study particular aspects of girls' school enrolment and the constraints on girls' education, and also to evaluate text books, the impact of the teaching given and girls' educational needs. The evaluation will also seek educational alternatives.

Awareness-raising programs will be run, using theatrical sketches, in areas where girls' enrolment rates are low. Parents will be targeted as much as other members of the community. One day of schooling for the girls will be instituted on a regular basis, and to reinforce the awareness scheme, healthy emulation will be generated with cookery and writing competitions, for example.

The project also provides for evaluation of documents and curricula and adaptation of text books, stripping out stereotypes that discredit women. To attract girls and prepare them for their future role, education for family life will be introduced into the curriculum for aptitude and career guidance classes.

---

1. UNESCO, *Report on the state of education in Africa, 1995* (Dakar: UNESCO Regional Office for Education in Africa, 1995).

In Chad, the program to get more girls attending school tried at first to gain a better understanding of the factors working against girls' schooling. Factors were identified both on the demand side (parents prefer to invest in education for their sons; girls have domestic tasks to fulfil and may marry very early; families' socioeconomic conditions may be an obstacle) and on the supply side (curricula irrelevant to the social and cultural realities of traditional communities; low-quality, poorly functioning school infrastructure; school timetables incompatible with girls' tasks at home and in the fields; dissuasive teacher perceptions of and attitudes to girls; scarcity of women teachers).

Given these constraints, an integrated regional mother-and-child program of action was set up, taking a community approach, with a view to improving girls' school enrolment rates.

The program is in three phases and one of its aims is to decentralize education decisions and give more training to all those who work in education. The existing teaching supervision structures will train the teachers, update the skills of future enablers, and train administrators, managers and assessors.

A focus on non-formal teaching is also needed, such as adult functional literacy classes, vocational training and satellite schools. If education is regarded as a way of reducing poverty, then programs must include capacity-building for poor adults by offering them literacy classes, a chance to learn a trade, or higher vocational training.

Simply increasing education supply is not enough; it must be of good quality and appropriate to poor people's needs, and more resources must be devoted to buying books and other teaching aids, and to teacher training and pay. Curriculum content must be reviewed to favor basic knowledge (arithmetic and language teaching) and applied knowledge (agriculture, hygiene, health, nutrition, home economics etc.).

In Togo, for example, the education component of the national poverty reduction strategy particularly stresses functional literacy and adult education. It aims to reduce illiteracy from 56% of the population to 28% in ten years, targeting the poorest regions and establishing equity of access for disadvantaged groups, especially women and girls. To achieve this, each socioeconomic group is asked to define its own strategies and objectives. In the countryside, for example, training for farmers will help them produce more using more appropriate technologies, and so shift from a subsistence economy to self-sufficiency. This logic should enable the government to gradually withdraw, giving way to state-owned companies, private enterprise and local communities who would garner the fruit of the learning process. [1]

---

1. UNDP et Ministère du Plan et de l'Aménagement du Territoire du Togo, *Stratégie nationale de lutte contre la pauvreté*, 1995.

The government of Burkina Faso, with UNDP support, has set up satellite schools and basic non-formal education centers (CEBNF, Centers d'Education de Base Non Formelle) in its drive to extend access to education and improve literacy rates. As conventional means do not guarantee education for all children between seven and fifteen years, the project takes account of the scale of poverty in the country, the gap between boys and girls and the country's practical needs to propose a new formula. Facilities, teacher training and teaching content have been adapted accordingly. As well as reading, writing and arithmetic, children can learn scientific, functional and civic skills. Learning to learn will take preference over knowledge as such.

Satellite schools are set up in villages with no primary school and CEB-NFs are open to young people who have dropped out. National languages are used and resource persons, chosen from the community for their skills or character, act as auxiliary teachers. The curricula have been adapted (they were designed in 1994-5) and will be used to produce appropriate teaching aids. [1]

Improving teaching quality is thus at the heart of the new basic education strategies. Teacher training and better teacher pay and social status, classroom equipment, supplying appropriate teaching material, avoiding overcrowding in the classroom, adapting curricula to the social realities of the country: all these are currently being debated and acted on in most African countries from Botswana, Burkina Faso, Cameroon, Ghana and Lesotho to Malawi, Mali, Niger, Nigeria, Namibia, Senegal, South Africa, Togo, Uganda and Zimbabwe.

Lastly, a complete reshaping of teaching content and broader access to basic education and literacy requires determination on the part of governments, which must provide the necessary resources to put these policies into effect. This raises a whole series of questions as to the possibility of additional finance for basic education. Can subsidies for higher education be frozen at current levels to release funds for primary education? Is it possible to give poor students exemptions or scholarships covering all the costs of higher education in engineering, management and medicine? Is it feasible to limit coverage of costs for higher education in the humanities and social sciences?

It may also be possible to reduce investment costs for school building schemes financed by donors. More should be done to shift some of the costs currently paid by governments to the community, by encouraging local people to contribute in kind or in labor to the building work. However, transferring too much of the load to local people may discourage

---

1. UNDP, *Rapport sur le développement humain durable au Burkina Faso, 1997.*

effort, especially if parents already have to pay a high proportion of educational operating costs. [1]

The new emphasis on girls' education, teaching quality, enhanced teacher status and better management of public spending on education is the core of the new education strategies incorporated into poverty reduction programs.

The problem of shifting public spending to education or from one education budget item to another, and of raising additional resources, will be examined at the end of this chapter.

4.2. Availability and accessibility of basic health care

Universal access to safe drinking water and health services is fundamental to household hygiene and health and a pre-condition for an improvement in living standards. Since 1980, the proportion of people in Sub-Saharan Africa with access to safe drinking water and health services has more than doubled in rural areas; it has also increased in urban areas, despite strong population growth.

In most countries, progress is accelerating, but it remains too slow. The two key problems are a lack of political commitment and a lack of emphasis on access to health services in health development plans. Some attention has been given to cities and towns, but rural areas continue to be neglected, and the utilization and maintenance of infrastructure have been practically ignored. [2]

Thus, while life expectancy in Sub-Saharan African rose from 40 to 51 years between 1960 and 1993, the region has only one doctor for every 18,000 people on average, compared with one doctor for every 7,000 people on average in other developing countries.

The two composite health indicators that best reflect the effectiveness of health care systems are the child mortality rate per 1,000 live births and the maternal mortality rate per 100,000 live births. [3]

On the scale of the continent, health indicators are correlated with levels of development as measured by per capita GDP, with some exceptions,

---

1. UNDP, *Human Development Report 1997* (New York: Oxford University Press, 1997).

2. For general information: World Bank, *World Development Report 1993: Investing in Health* (Washington: Oxford University Press, 1993); WHO, *World Health Report 1997* (Geneva: 1997); UNDP, *Human Development Report 1997* (New York: Oxford University Press: 1997); M. Gillis, D. H. Perkins, M. Roemer and D. R. Snodgrass, *Economics of Development*, 4ᵗʰ ed. (New York: Norton, 1996).

3. An estimated 90% of deaths from malaria and two-thirds of the world's HIV-positive people are in Sub-Saharan Africa.

negative for Côte-d'Ivoire, or positive for Tanzania and Burkina Faso, for example. The only specificity linked to the language zone is that cost recovery was implemented at the beginning of the decade in the CFA franc zone countries, while most of the East African countries, except South Africa, provide free health care.

Within countries, child and maternal mortality rates, reflecting the target groups of all health programs, point out the clear inequalities in access to health care, determined by income, geographical location and — in South Africa — race (in 1994, the infant mortality rate was 54 per 1,000 live births for the black population and 7 per 1,000 live births for the white population).

Access rates calculated on the basis of distance from health services measure a country's coverage in health infrastructure. They do not reflect the often extremely low utilization rates [1] of this infrastructure, which are due to a combination of factors: poor facilities, inadequate treatment and high total effective costs for users. This situation shows up in health indicators that are not commensurate with spending on the sector and results in extremely high unit costs for services, particularly because of the high proportion of fixed costs: wages, maintenance, equipment.

In this context, it is of paramount importance to promote and implement health care policies targeted towards the poor and aimed at enhancing access to health care — particularly primary health care, reproductive health and essential medicines — and improving the quality of care delivered.

The actions envisaged for health are similar to those recommended for education, i.e.:

– To increase the availability and accessibility of primary health care for the poorest people, particularly through the Bamako Initiative aimed at expanding health centers and their financing by local authorities. This should ensure better health coverage and more sustainable services.

– To enhance the quality of services and training of staff.

– To review public spending in the sector, to avoid wastage and to concentrate efforts on primary health care.

Until now efforts have concentrated on increasing the supply of health services, often to the detriment of quality. An increase in basic infrastructure has, however, made it possible to provide a minimum package of services (public health actions and essential clinical services) accessible to the whole population and to monitor the health status of the population.

---

1. In some countries, it is not uncommon to find health facilities with bed occupancy below 20% and even 10%, and nurse consultation rates of 2-3 per working day.

Table 4.4. – Health Indicators and Strong Trends of Basic Health Systems [a]

	Infant mortality rate [b]	Maternal mortality rate [b]	Issues specific to present situation (1998)
	1995	**1990**	
South Africa	66	230	Health care not free of charge except SMI, PF-SR... targeting financial and management efforts on poverty areas
Namibia	77	370	Regional disparities, acts free of charge or at very low rates
Zambia	202	940	Recent degradation, free health care, reflection about fixing a price scale and, exempting the poorest
Malawi	217	560	Free health care, degradation, lack of qualified staff, reflection about fixing a price scale
Tanzania	144	770	Problem of quality of health care, price fixing underway
Cameroon	102	550	Slow but steady improvement
Côte d'Ivoire	150	810	Indicators are of the same order as those of Tanzania and Benin that spend much less, despite a considerable improvement in the quality of training
Benin	169	990	Slow but steady improvement
Mali	241	1200	Poor coverage rate, problem of quality of health care
Burkina Faso	173	930	Increase in the financing, but problem of quality of services
Niger	320	1200	Strong recent degradation

a. It is not possible to get the trend because these indicators are not assessed annually. Furthermore, the increase in resources alone does not guarantee an increase in performance.
b. Infant mortality rate children age 0 to 4 years) and number of maternal deaths for 100 000 live births.

Source: World Development Report –, World Bank – 1997.

However, special efforts are still needed for the poorest households, particularly in rural areas, which are much more disadvantaged than urban areas in terms of health services.

In Lesotho, although there are numerous basic public facilities, poor people rarely make consultations, because of the excessive cost of these services. In response to this problem, special social security programs have been implemented to enhance poor people's access to health care. [1]

In Niger, where health infrastructure does not cover the whole country, plans to improve accessibility combine the decentralization of health services with the physical extension of geographical coverage. Priority is given to district health facilities, particularly in rural areas, to the detriment of hospitals and urban areas, so as to benefit the greatest number. [2]

Most of the programs for increasing the supply of district health centers under the Bamako Initiative include decentralization of the management of these services and a contribution to costs by the beneficiaries.

In addition to the availability of primary health centers, pro-poor health policies must also consider issues related to the cost of medicines. In most African countries, the cost of medicines is prohibitively high for poor and disadvantaged households. Since medicines are the second largest expense item after wages in health budgets, a major gain in efficiency could be achieved by drawing up a national list of essential medicines and setting up a central purchasing office. Many countries have such lists, but not all use them in the selection and purchase of medicines for the public sector.

In many African countries, setting up central purchasing offices to buy essential medicines and promoting generic medicines are the options chosen to favor access of the greatest number to medicines. This is the case in Burkina Faso, Mauritania and Senegal, for example.

However, increasing the supply and accessibility of medicines through a reduction in their cost is not the only way to improve people's health, particularly that of the poorest people. In Mauritania, a complete restructuring of the health system was undertaken from 1992 to 1997, based on:
– effective implementation of decentralization;
– generalization of primary health care and an essential medicines policy;
– enhancement of the operation of health facilities through community involvement and increased budget efforts from the State;
– improvement of health coverage, which reached 80% of the country in 1996, through the renovation and construction of facilities.

---

1. Government of Lesotho, "Poverty Reduction Within the Context of Good Governance", 8th Roundtable Conference, Geneva, 1997.
2. République du Niger, *Stratégies de lutte contre la pauvreté* (Niamey, 1996).

Despite advances in access to health care, Mauritanians' health status remains worrying, because of the poor quality of care, inadequate facilities, persistently high cost of treatment for poor households and shortages of staff. [1]

The situation is similar in Nigeria. National health policy emphasizes universal access to primary health care. To achieve this, responsibility for primary health centers and all primary health care has been given to local authorities. This has improved infrastructure coverage. However, still only 35% to 40% of the population makes use of the health care facilities, despite satisfactory geographical coverage. The main reason for this failure is the insufficient allocation of government funding to support this policy, which has affected the quality of facilities and treatment and the training and motivation of staff. [2]

Thus, in both Mauritania and Nigeria, policies based solely on a physical increase in primary health care have shown their limitations. Poor quality care and staff in one case and half-hearted commitment from the government in the other have compromised programs. It is clear that policies to promote universal access to primary health care must be accompanied by an improvement in the quality of care and an overall restructuring of the health sector, including cost rationalization, greater decentralization and better allocation of national resources to primary health care. These aspects of public health policy, when implemented within the framework of primary health care, should be supported by a strong contribution of grassroots communities to effectively raise the quality of care and favor accessibility.

In Uganda, national health policy also focuses on primary health care. Rather than physical, geographical accessibility, this policy emphasizes the involvement of grassroots communities in promoting disease control, health status and basic curative care. A specific system of social mobilization was set up to implement this policy. The involvement of communities in decision-making, fund-raising, implementation of local programs and supervision, in partnership with health professionals has produced encouraging results. The overall system of health management was restructured to decentralize decision-making to the level of districts, which have developed their own health plans. To improve the quality of care and training of staff, an information, education and communication (IEC) strategy was implemented to encourage patients and health staff to overcome "inadequate knowledge and negative attitudes and practices". These campaigns have also informed people's attitudes and choices in relation to HIV/AIDS and STDs, family planning, nutrition and disease prevention. [3]

---

1. UNDP, *Rapport National sur le Développement Humain en Mauritanie 1996.*
2. UNDP, *Human Development Report Nigeria 1996.*
3. UNDP, *Uganda Human Development Report 1996.*

In Botswana, health policy is also directed towards more efficient primary health care. Alongside specific actions aimed at promoting access to health care for the poorest people and achieving a more equitable supply of care, the strategy favors an improvement in the quality of care through:

– restructuring and improving training for health staff and implementing in-service training;

– priority on maternal and child health;

– intensifying social mobilization through grassroots management of health centers and vaccination and disease-prevention campaigns;

– strengthening intersectoral cooperation between health, education, environment, water and nutrition professionals. [1]

In Burkina Faso, the health strategy is also based on a qualitative increase in primary health care through three-fold action:

– decentralization of management and decision-making to district health centers;

– promotion of community involvement in management and contribution to costs of health services;

– improvement of human resource performance through a realistic integrated policy based on targeted, coordinated training. [2]

It would also appear important to ensure monitoring and evaluation of the health status of the population and the impact of health policies. A nation-wide community-based information system (CBIS) would make it possible to monitor children's growth and the prevalence of certain diseases. The active involvement of communities could considerably reduce costs and raise people's awareness of health and nutrition issues. The information gathered by such a system would be useful for targeting actions and budgets towards the most urgent needs, particularly the groups least served by existing public services.

These measures are not distinct from initiatives designed for the whole population, but simply take into consideration the budget constraints of the poor and include other important dimensions of poverty — access to productive resources, education, employment, income and a healthy environment. This last point is particularly important in urban areas. The improvement of poor people's health starts with the rehabilitation of disadvantaged urban districts, through the provision of rainwater and waste water drainage systems, garbage collection and recycling, a combination of coercive and incentive measures to collect and eliminate human and animal excrement and control of livestock farming in urban areas.

---

1. UNDP, UNICEF and Republic of Botswana, *Planning for People. A Strategy for Accelerated Human Development in Botswana*, 1993.

2. Gouvernement du Burkina Faso, *Rapport de Synthèse*, Table Ronde des Bailleurs de Fonds sur le Développement des Secteurs Sociaux, 1998.

Box 4.15.

Health development strategies in Niger: Decentralization and reorganization of the health system

The decentralization and reorganization of the health system will be achieved through the effective implementation of the "Three phase health development scenario", that is:

– the central level in charge of strategic support;

– the intermediate level (department in charge of technical support);

– the district level (district and village) corresponding to operational support.

This approach is focused on the effective development of the district the implementation of which will require the support of the two levels and the full community participation.

Decentralization will allow for the creation of budget management centers at district level and the establishment of health committees, bodies to monitor and coordinate health sector development actions in view of fully involving the populations in the management and control of resources.

The participation of the populations must be organized, regulated and targeted on the involvement of the populations in the management of health services and in decision-making concerning their health related problems in order to bring about self-reliance.

Source: Republic of Niger, "National poverty control strategy", 1997.

To be implemented effectively and to contribute to poverty reduction, all these measures require strong commitment from the State, restructuring and rationalization of the health care system based on decentralization and disbursement of adequate resources, particularly by the State.

The effectiveness of sectoral policy can be assessed by asking the following two questions. First, did the policy work to gradually eliminate the persistent favoritism towards urban areas in terms of the distribution of facilities and emphasis on curative care in health spending? If the health of the majority of the population is to be enhanced, policy makers should ensure that more funds are allocated to increasing and improving lower-level facilities offering basic preventive and curative care. Secondly, has the government sufficiently addressed the staffing imbalances that have persisted since independence between rural and urban health services and between the primary and tertiary levels of health care?

Through its management of the overall budget, the central government has a key role to play in securing equity by allocating more resources (or subsidies) to deprived areas. Budget restructuring is part of the sectoral reform that is altering the role of the State.

Can the State reduce or discontinue subsidies for specialized services? The government will need more effective policies for financing training of staff for primary health services, particularly nurses and midwives. The State should also find ways to ensure that doctors trained at great expense under the national budget effectively deliver the services that disadvantaged groups want. Contractualizing services between the State and doctors are a path to explore. Under a contract with the State, doctors would agree to provide services to disadvantaged groups in exchange for in-service training, the right to practice privately at the same time or to specialize at a later date.

Does decentralization of a large proportion of responsibilities to regional administrations and district offices of the health ministry increase efficiency? This depends on sufficient capacity and accountability at the lower levels of the national health system.

Many countries have already restructured their health systems, rationalized spending and allocated the necessary amounts to these reforms. Others are in the process of such reforms.

In Lesotho, the improvement of the basic health system, in addition to quantitative aspects, has mainly consisted in reform and decentralization of the health ministry and reallocation of the health budget in favor of primary health care. A sectoral investment plan has been implemented, with priority on the accessibility of health care for the greatest number.

In Togo, priority on the accessibility of services has led to a major reform of the health ministry aimed at greater deployment of staff in rural regions, better planning and maintenance of facilities, the systematic implementation of a staff training policy and the reallocation of resources towards primary health care.

The countries that have succeeded in considerably improving the health of their populations have emphasized the provision of a package of minimum services. In Zimbabwe, the decline in infant mortality and the increase in life expectancy can be partly explained by the fact that a whole range of public health services and clinical services have been financed by ordinary tax revenues.

It is only through health care close to people and a contribution from communities to the cost and management of health centers that universal access to health services can be achieved. However, this goal also requires an improvement in the quality of services and a restructuring of health policy to respond to Sub-Saharan Africa's health emergencies, through adequate vaccination, preventive and curative care and maternal and child health.

4.3. General policies favoring access to basic social services

First, the availability and accessibility of basic social services for the poor depend on clear political commitment. Empirical experience shows that increasing the physical supply of these services is useless unless quality is improved — problems such as waiting time, tips to public servants and transport costs need to be addressed. When the quality of service is low, the poor do not perceive the benefit of the availability of social services and do not try to have access to them.

The political will to improve the availability and the quality of services is as important as adequate targeting of the poor. A recent analysis of the incidence of spending in the social sectors in Africa shows that subsidies for education and health are rarely targeted to the poor and that the poor benefit only marginally from them, with the exception of primary education. [1] The main beneficiaries of the social services provided by the State are non-poor urban households. It is therefore important to target the delivery of services more effectively to the poor and to identify the most beneficial public spending for the poor.

The 20/20 Initiative is an ideal tool for demonstrating and measuring political commitment to promoting access to social services and for ensuring the necessary funds for more effective, better targeted basic education and health services.

Aware of these problems, the African countries participating in the 20/20 Initiative met in Ouagadougou in September 1998 to analyze the situation in preparation for the global meeting on the 20/20 Initiative in Hanoi in October 1998. This heightened awareness should encourage governments to begin making intra- and intersectoral reallocations of public spending, to pay more attention to the incidence and effectiveness of spending with regard to the poor and to familiarize themselves with new ways to raise additional resources for the basic social sectors.

Public spending programs that benefit the poor, particularly the provision of essential social services, should be protected and, if necessary, enhanced. These programs should be assessed to ensure that the real beneficiaries are the poor and that the distribution of investment will have a high rate of return for society. Finally, to ensure that public spending programs fulfil the needs they aim to meet, it is important to monitor actual spending and not only the distribution of budget credits.

The opportunity cost of allocating a share of the government's limited resources to funding actions targeted towards tiny fractions of the population must be considered, because there are strong arguments in favor of

---

1. K. Subbarao, *Lessons of 30 Years of Fighting Poverty* (Quebec, 1997).

another option, i.e. improving the provision of basic social services for the majority of the population. This choice may not only be more equitable, but also more efficient, because of economies of scale and externalities.

Table 4.5. – Public Education Expenditure of some African Countries (in percentage)

	Primary Education		Secondary Education		Higher Education	
	Poorest	**Richest**	**Poorest**	**Richest**	**Poorest**	**Richest**
Côte d'Ivoire (1995)	19	14	7	37	12	71
Ghana (1992	22	14	15	19	6	45
Guinea (1994)	11	21	4	39	1	65
Kenya (1992)	22	15	7	30	2	44
Malawi (1994)	20	16	9	40	1	59
Madagascar (1993)	17	14	2	41	0	89
South Africa (1994)	19	28	11	39	6	47
Tanzania (1993/94)	20	19	8	34	0	100
Uganda (1992)	19	18	4	49	6	47

Source: UNDP/UNICEF, "Report on Initiative 20/20 in Africa", 1998.

Table 4.6. – Incidence of Public Health Expenditure in some African Countries (in percentage)

	Primary Health Care		Clinics, Hospitals	
	Poorest	**Richest**	**Poorest**	**Richest**
Côte d'Ivoire (1995)	14	22	8	39
Ghana (1992	10	31	13	35
Guinea (1994)	10	36	1	55
Kenya (1992)	13	26	23	15
Malawi (1994)	–	–	–	–
Madagascar (1993)	14	30	10	29
South Africa (1994)	18	10	15	17
Tanzania (1993/94)	18	21	11	37
Uganda (1992)	–	–	–	–

Source: K. Subbarao, Lessons of 30 Years of Fighting Poverty, 1997.

Box 4.16.

Distribution of health expenditure in relation to geographic regions and racial groups in South Africa

Important disparities are observed in terms of health expenditure distribution between geographic zones and "racial groups". It 1987, health expenditure ratio between Africans and Whites was estimated at 1:4.3. That same year, the average per capita expenditure for each "racial group" was estimated as follows: Africans = 137.84Rand; Half-caste = 340.16 Rands; Indians = 356.24 Rands and Whites = 597.11Rands. But the poverty profile of South Africa identified the African population as the most affected by poverty.

Expenditure related disparities between the former "homelands" where the majority of Africans used to live as compared to South African provinces also make it possible to measure these disparities. In 1986/1987, the per capita public health expenditure ranged from 23 Rands in Lebowa and 91 Rands in Ciskei whereas it ranged from 150 to 200 Rands in the former South African provinces. The serious under-financing of health in the former homelands of the apartheid era partly explains the disparities in terms of health status between Whites and Africans. However, other factors influence this inequality. Inequalities in the distribution of revenue, differences in access to housing, differences in terms of education (particularly with respect to women) and many other factors have also contributed to the health related differences highlighted above.

Source: "20/20 Initiative for South Africa", UNICEF, 1997.

Another framework for the development of basic social sectors can be provided by general strategies and programs that include health and education. In Botswana, Burkina Faso, Lesotho, Mali, Niger and Togo, availability and accessibility of education and health services (as well as housing and safe drinking water) come under a combined program within the framework of the national poverty reduction strategy. From similar situations, i.e. a policy until now concentrated on geographical coverage that neglected qualitative aspects and institutional reforms, these countries are working to link the two sectors and develop them simultaneously. This approach is further strengthened by the implementation of the 20/20 Initiative which facilitates the design of comprehensive, coherent and coordinated policies on the development of the social sectors. In Burkina Faso in 1998, in preparation for a roundtable conference on the development of social sectors, the results of 20/20 studies were used as a basis for budget and financing the coordinated development of education and health. These studies can be an effective tool for governments to boost social services for all, particularly for the poor, within the framework of poverty reduction.

It would seem appropriate to end this part of the report with a focus on enhancing equity and the principle of free services for the poor. The utilization of social services is inequitable in all the countries. Secondary and higher education and referral hospitals are mainly used by the middle and high income groups. The emphasis on basic social services in the 20/20 Initiative aims to correct this imbalance.

The most disadvantaged groups are offered lower-quality social services, they use them less and, as a result, they consume less public spending than the middle and wealthy classes. In Burkina Faso, the poorest 40% of the population receive respectively 12% and 0.1% of the public spending allocated to secondary and higher education respectively. In basic education, inequalities in income are compounded by inequalities between urban and rural areas: in Burkina Faso, the poorest 40% of the population benefit from only 28% of public spending on education; in Benin, the poorest 38% of the population receive only 27% of this spending.

There are also disparities in South Africa: in 1996, the proportion of the population living in poverty, estimated at 53%, received 40% of public spending on education. In Mali, only 12% of the poorest third of children are enrolled in primary school, while 52% of the richest third are.

The utilization rates of health services by the poorest people are half those of the richest. The translation of this situation into public spending terms accentuates this inequality, because the non-poor population uses

Table 4.7. –   Incidence of Public Primary Education Expenditure based on the level of income per capita

	Burkina Faso – 1996			Benin – 1995-96		
	Popula-tion [a]	Gross enrolment rate	Public Expendi-ture	Popul. 5-14 years	Primary Enrolment	Public Expendi-ture
Poorest population	40	25	28	38	45	27
Vulnerable population	20	38	19	28	57	28
Population not poor	40	61	53	34	75	45
Total population	100	40	100	100	57	100

a. Grouping of quintiles.

Sources: Poverty profile, INSD Burkina Faso - ELAM Study 5 bis and 6, UNDP/INSAE Benin.

Table 4.8. –   Incidence of Public Health Expenditure based on the level
of income per capita

	Burkina Faso – 1996			Benin – 1995-96		
	Popula-tion [a] %	Numb. of visits per year	Public Expendi-ture %	Popula-tion %	Health service use rate	Public Expendi-ture %
Poorest population	40	0.48	16.9	33	24	22
Vulnerable population	20	0.96	15.0	24	35	23
Population not poor	40	1.77	67.6	43	41	54
Total population	100	1.09	100	100		100

a. Grouping of quintiles.
Sources: Poverty profile, INSD Burkina Faso – ELAM Study 5 bis and 6, UNDP/INSAE Benin.

more sophisticated services, which are either free or heavily subsidized (doctor consultations, pathology, x-rays, etc.).

Also, while poverty reduction programs emphasize poor people's access to essential social services, surprisingly these are always fee-paying services. Yet research has shown that one of the characteristics of poverty in Africa is extreme income poverty. As many studies have shown, free access to basic social services such as primary education or basic health care — like the subsidization of basic food products or certain public works programs — clearly favors poor people, given wealthy families' preference for private services in these two sectors, and the fact that poor families tend to be larger. In contrast, free access to universities and to more expensive care in urban hospitals is more likely to benefit wealthy families. [1]

The current practice in many countries of setting systematically low prices for social services regardless of their real cost, with rationing and a decline quality when there are budget restrictions, does not appear to have benefited poor people, in terms of either the quantity or the quality of the services provided. In some cases, the extremely costly services used by high-income groups are more heavily subsidized than less costly services. In this context, selective increases in user fees (with exemptions for people in situ-

---

1. P. Bardhan, "Efficacité, équité et lutte contre la pauvreté", *Problèmes économiques*, n°2520, 1997.

ations of extreme poverty and for access to certain basic services) are likely to enhance efficiency and equity.

Whatever the outcome of this debate, an improvement in the availability and accessibility of essential social services for poor households, based on the fundamental principles of equity and social justice and on efficiency, are an essential component of poverty reduction strategies sustainable in the long term.

5. Conclusions and recommendations

Basically, the activities and approaches devoted to poverty reduction at micro level should be based on upstream analysis and strategy and downstream operationalization.

Upstream, the government must be committed to effectively alleviating poverty and adopt the analytical and monitoring tools needed to identify appropriate actions and to assess their efficiency. The main aim is to reach a more comprehensive understanding of the phenomenon of poverty — both quantitative and qualitative — so as to optimize the design of a national poverty reduction strategy and to have a conceptual basis for projects designed and implemented to reduce poverty and promote access to basic social services.

The components of a poverty reduction program related to poor people's access to productive resources and social services should be organized under three cross-cutting dimensions that form an overall approach:

i) capacity-building (good governance);

ii) productive income-generating activities through access to productive resources and financial capital;

iii) access to basic social services.

Capacity-building is central to poverty reduction. Upstream, this involves strengthening the capacities of the national government to understand the phenomenon of poverty, to collect and analyze data, to implement monitoring tools and, finally, to design and execute a national poverty reduction strategy.

Downstream, this means strengthening the capacities of local authorities and grassroots organizations. Using tools designed on the basis of participatory development, this includes i) linking local organizations into networks to foster exchanges of experience and best practices; ii) expanding and supporting the involvement of the private sector and grassroots communities in the implementation of projects iii) strengthening the management capacities of grassroots communities.

Figure 4.1. – Typical scheme of 'micro' level intervention in poverty
reduction

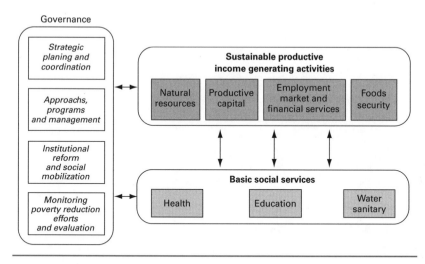

It is only through basic capacity-building, focusing on participatory development and good governance, that sustainable productive, income-generating activities can be implemented. Action needs to concentrate on access for the poor to available productive resources and to markets and financial capital and should be guided by the principles of sustainability and local ownership. Basic capacity-building is essential to poverty reduction projects involving income-generating activities. Setting up an agropastoral production activity, for example, requires commitment and capacity for implementation on the part of grassroots organizations in the area concerned and in other areas, such as management of water resources. The same applies to the development of any natural resource, which requires strong mobilization of village communities, a local vision of mid-term development and the implementation of management and productive activities.

Finally, basic capacity-building related to the development of income-generating activities will make it possible to operationalize the third dimension of this approach, access to basic social services. The commitment and initiative of grassroots communities, capitalizing on income generation, are the only way to enhance the sustainable, integrated accessibility of social services such as health, education and safe drinking water.

CHAPTER 5

Designing a poverty reduction strategy

1. Towards a participatory, national process

Identifying the main issues, understanding the phenomenon and determining the main causes of poverty form the basis for the design of national poverty reduction strategies.

Governments have prime responsibility for the design of these strategies and for their implementation through poverty alleviation programs and projects. However, while governments must take a leading role, they are by no means the only active and responsible stakeholders in this process. On the contrary, in an approach centered on human development, the design of a national poverty reduction strategy must be participatory and should include all the stakeholders who can contribute to this process or who are primarily affected by it, notably poor and disadvantaged groups.

The parties concerned by this approach include — apart from the government — members of parliament, academics, the private sector, trade unions, the media, NGOs and civil society organizations and, of course, grass-roots organizations, community groups and groups of poor people that have the necessary capacity to be represented or to make themselves heard.

UNDP can make a significant contribution by facilitating the consultative process, providing operational support for the design of the strategy based on the experience and comparative advantages acquired during the phases of defining, identifying and measuring poverty and by raising the financing needed to implement the program. However, it is important to stress the national content of this exercise: unless the process is appropriated by governments and by poor and disadvantaged target groups, it will not produce tangible operational results of benefit to the poor.

Box 5.1.

Letter of Intent of Sustainable Human Development Policy in Burkina Faso

In the perspective of focusing the country's development on human development and following the six commitments made by the Head of State, the Government formulated its Letter of Intent of Sustainable Human Development Policy (1996-2005) which was presented in October 1995 to the development partners of Burkina Faso, meeting at the Third Round Table Conference in Geneva. The sustainable human development strategy outlined in the letter is focused on a fundamental issue at stake, i.e., the guarantee of human security to each Burkinabè, enabling him/her to have access to:

– economic security related to paid employment;

– extended health security through access to cheaper medical care;

– food security defined as access to basic feeding including water;

– environmental security related to the preservation of a sound environment;

– individual and political security.

This willingness of the public authorities to restore the human dimension of development is a judicious choice. Conversely, no sustainable economic growth can be achieved without a minimum level of health, education, income, accessibility to basic goods and services, as well as the indiscriminate participation of all the components of society in the development process. That is why the governmental officers understood that economic growth and human development go hand in hand and mutually strengthen one another.

The urgent challenge that Burkina must absolutely take up is that of increasing the income level of its inhabitants and accelerating the development of its human resources and of its productive potential. The complexity of the situation requires a middle and long term global vision, distinguishing real opportunities and constraints, and giving greater importance to interdependence between partial visions. In the present context, what is required is to initiate an economic and social policy likely to reconcile the constraints of adjustment and the need for alternative choices in terms of sustainable development under a middle and long term strategy.

The strategic objectives by the year 2005 as defined in the Letter of Intent of Sustainable Human Development are focused on accelerating economic growth which must go hand in hand with optimal development of human resources, the reduction of social deficits and the improvement of the populations' income level. This calls for the implementation of a population growth control strategy, a dynamic policy of job and income creation, the promotion and valorization of women's role in the development process. The setting up of an efficient system of social protection and greater access to social services will also be encouraged. A special effort will be made to allocate sizeable resources to basic social sectors, in accordance with the 20/20 Initiative advocated by the United Nations and endorsed by the Government.

Source: "The national approach to sustainable human development: concept and major instruments", Luc-Joël Gregoire, UNDP, Working Paper Vol. 1, July 1998.

Some 20 Sub-Saharan African countries — including Benin, Botswana, Burkina Faso, Comoros, Guinea, Kenya, Lesotho, Madagascar, Malawi, Mali, Mauritania, Namibia, Niger, Senegal, South Africa, Togo, Uganda, Zambia and Zimbabwe — have drafted or are in the process of designing a national poverty reduction strategy.

In most countries, the processes of identifying and measuring poverty have been carried out with the support of the World Bank (see previous chapter). UNDP has also been actively involved in all the cases cited in this chapter, in facilitating the process, raising financing or providing technical support for the design of the strategy and programs. Roundtable conferences and poverty reduction frameworks are effective instruments for preparing these exercises.

Box 5. 2.

National Poverty Eradication Program for the 1998-2001 period
in Mauritania

Based on the results of the survey conducted in 1990, a strategy for poverty eradication in Mauritania was designed in 1993-1994 and presented to the Consultative Group of Mauritania that met in May 1994. Furthermore, a grass roots development coordination unit (UCDB) was established in 1996, within the Ministry of Planning. This unit, which results from merging the Social Dimension Project and the Adjustment of the Government-NGO Coordination Unit, is in charge of managing the whole of poverty control action and of coordinating the different programs. Its majors tasks consist in integrating the poverty control objectives into sectorial development programs, establishing dialogue structures involving the State, local communities and NGOs, assisting the Ministry of Planning in mobilizing financial resources to implement specific poverty control programs and, serving as interface between the Administration and program implementation agencies. Although the actions undertaken have helped to reduce poverty during the 1990-1996 period and to significantly improve the access of the populations, especially the poorest, to basic social services, the level of poverty still remains high.

The strategy was updated during a workshop held in October 1997. A new national poverty control program for the 1998-2001 period was designed. Although it fits into the overall development strategy, it is recorded in a separate document. This approach shows the willingness of the government to design policies that are focused on the poorest groups and to implement specific procedures of efficient poverty alleviation.

The end goal of the program is to get the maximum number of Mauritanians above the poverty threshold by improving their access to basic social services. This objective should be reached on the one hand through direct income generating activities mainly derived from entrepreneurial self-employment in rural areas: in the sector of agriculture, livestock and craft fisheries likely to strengthen food security as well as in the craft informal and manufacturing sector; on the other hand it can be achieved by expanding the coverage of health, drinking water, sanitation, education and training services. The program will be experimented in the three regions with highest poverty index.

The program estimated at 293 million dollars over 4 years will be financed by the Mauritanian State and by the donors (essentially donations).

National NGOs (69 in number) or international NGOs with a statute of development association and decentralized structures will implement the sub-programs. The beneficiaries will be individuals grouped into community type associations (cooperatives etc) and local communities.

The financed projects focus on three aspects: basic economic infrastructures (rural water supply and small hydro agricultural developments, schools, health centers, local markets, warehouses for storage, roads, sanitation etc); income generating micro-activities (collaborative production and service enterprises); micro-finance related systems

and institutions, namely the ones based on savings and co-responsibility of beneficiaries (savings and/or credit associations, mutual aid associations, security funds etc).

The approach selected is a participatory approach to grass roots development. The associations of beneficiaries must be involved in the projects and participate directly in their design and implementation. The issue at stake is to improve individual capacity to improve know-how, analyze and solve problems, make decisions and monitor plans of action. Only micro-finance related system creation projects will receive loans.

In order to provide efficient monitoring of operations by the various NGOs, the UCDB has developed a computerized data base. It centralizes several types of information (name and details of NGO, nature of projects implemented, sectors and areas of intervention, origin and amount of funding, beneficiary groups etc).

The access to the information is facilitated by the multiplicity of consultation criteria.

Source: Islamic Republic of Mauritania; National Poverty Eradication Program for the 1998-2001 period, February 1998.

Important new policy instruments (Poverty Reduction Strategy Paper – PRSP and Poverty Reduction and Growth Facility – PRGF) have been developed by the Bretton Woods institutions to serve as a common context for international interventions in low-income countries receiving concessional assistance and debt reduction programmes (HIPC).

The objective is to help the country authorities to produce a poverty reduction strategy in which policy actions to raise growth and reduce poverty are integrated into a coherent framework of macroeconomic, structural and social policies.

Five Principles Underlying the Poverty Reduction Strategy Paper (PRSP) approach are essentials:

– Country-ownership of a poverty reduction strategy is paramount. Broad-based participation of civil society in the adoption and monitoring of the poverty reduction strategy tailored to country circumstances will enhance its sustained implementation. In this context, Participatory process need to reflect the cultures, practices, and institutions of the countries concerned.

– The PRSP process confirms that poverty is multidimensional; specific actions are needed to enable the poor a share of the benefits from growth, increase their capabilities and well being, and reduce their vulnerabilities to risks. A poverty reduction strategy should integrate institutional, structural and sectoral interventions into a consistent macroeconomic framework.

– Medium-and long-term goals for poverty reduction, including key outcome and intermediate indicators, are needed to ensure that policies are well designed, effectively implemented and carefully monitored.A medium and long term perspective is needed, recognizing that poverty reduction will require institutional changes and capacity building-including efforts to strengthen governance and accountability.

– A medium and long term perspective is needed, recognizing that poverty reduction will require institutional changes and capacity building-including efforts to strengthen governance and accountability.

– National and international partners' willingness to make medium-term commitments will enhance the effectiveness of their support for a poverty reduction strategy.

2. Operational framework for the strategy

National poverty reduction strategies should cover and operate on the three essential levels of action: macro, meso and micro. The strategies must be comprehensive and take into account all the factors likely to facilitate or hamper their implementation. It is important not to neglect any of the levels of action and to ascertain the interactions and synergies between them to ensure an operational poverty reduction strategy.

The macro level is the country's overall policy framework and development objectives and priorities, including macroeconomic policies and governance. This is the general policy context, upstream from the design of strategies that will frame the programs and projects aimed at poor and disadvantaged social groups. It consists of macroeconomic policies, including tax and fiscal policy and policies on public spending, interest rates, prices, employment, social policies, trade, international development cooperation and governance issues. This general framework has a direct impact on poverty and should be designed or refocused according to poverty reduction objectives and issues.

The meso — or intermediate — level is concerned with translating development objectives and priorities into operational sectoral policies and programs. This level establishes communication and coordination between the overall development policy framework and the micro level of direct grass-roots development actions. Governments need adequate institutional capacities and tools to implement the objectives formulated at macro level. The meso level thus focuses on policy-making capacities and instruments capable of delivering services to the grass-roots level and meeting the needs of poor and disadvantaged groups. The concerns taken into account at this level are: the role of the State, the design of sectoral and thematic policies and the government's capacity to implement poverty reduction strategies that respond to the needs of the beneficiaries. It also involves strengthening the capacities of all the national stakeholders in the poverty alleviation process — including the private sector, NGOs, civil society and grass-roots organizations — and promoting the institutional reforms needed to ensure the effectiveness of poverty reduction programs — including the consolidation of legal and judicial systems and the implementation of decentralization processes.

Finally, the micro — or grassroots — level represents the materialization of policies into operational projects and tangible actions involving all stakeholders. This is usually the most developed level in a national poverty reduction strategy, if only because it is the only really operational and implemented level, the other two being more an expression of good intentions. The grassroots level covers all the activities affecting households directly, including poor people's access to productive resources (land, employment, credit, etc.) and basic social sectors.

When designing a poverty reduction strategy, it is important to ensure that all three levels are taken into account to facilitate information, communication and interaction between them and to produce a coherent operational strategy capable of achieving its poverty reduction objectives.

The overall development framework that forms the context for poverty reduction strategies has evolved over the past decade. Thirty-six countries in Sub-Saharan Africa were undergoing adjustment in 1990, but only one or two had designed a poverty reduction strategy. At 31 January 1998, 22 countries were undergoing adjustment and 22 have a poverty reduction strategy. This convergence of development approaches highlights the need to harmonize adjustment and poverty reduction policies and programs.

A new approach has emerged internationally — particularly in Africa from the early 1990s — concerning the assessment of poverty issues and the formulation of operational responses to them.

Table 5.1. – Summary of anti-poverty activities in African countries

Country	Diagnosis, profiles and evaluation of poverty at national level			Global and multidimensional strategy of poverty eradication		Sectoral and/ or regional strategies of poverty reduction	Strategies of economic and social support and reconstruction
	1985-1990	1991-1995	1996-1997	1985-1995	1996-1997	1990-1997	1995-1997
1 South Africa	–	+	+	–	–	+	+
2 Angola	–	–	+	–	–	+	+
3 Benin	+	+	+	–	+	+	–
4 Botswana	+	+	+	–	in progress 98	+	–
5 Burkina Faso	–	+	+	–	in progress 98	+	–
6 Burundi	–	+	–	–	–	–	+
7 Cameroon	–	+	+	–	in progress 98	+	–
8 Cap Verde	–	+	+	–	in progress 98	+	–
9 Comoros	–	+	+	–	–	+	–
10 Congo	–	–	–	–	–	–	+
11 Côte d'Ivoire	–	+	+	–	–	+	–
12 Djibouti	–	–	+	–	–	–	+
13 Eritrea	–	–	+	–	–	in progress 98	+
14 Ethiopia	–	+	+	–	–	+	–
15 Gabon	–	–	+	–	–	–	–
16 Gambia	–	+	+	–	–	+	–
17 Ghana	–	+	+	–	in progress 98	+	–
18 Guinea	–	+	+	–	+	+	–
19 Guinea Bissau	–	+	+	–	–	+	–
20 Equatorial Guinea	–	–	+	–	–	+	–
21 Kenya	–	+	+	–	–	+	–
22 Lesotho	–	+	+	–	+	+	–
23 Liberia	–	–	–	–	–	–	in progress 98
24 Madagascar	–	+	+	–	–	+	–
25 Malawi	+	+	+	–	+	+	–
26 Mali	+	+	+	–	+	+	–
27 Mauritius	–	–	–	–	–	–	–
28 Mauritania	–	+	+	–	+	+	–
29 Mozambique	–	–	+	–	+	+	+

Table 5.1. –   Summary of anti-poverty activities in African countries *(suite)*

Country		Diagnosis, profiles and evaluation of poverty at national level			Global and multidimensional strategy of poverty eradication		Sectoral and/ or regional strategies of poverty reduction	Strategies of economic and social support and reconstruction
		1985-1990	1991-1995	1996-1997	1985-1995	1996-1997	1990-1997	1995-1997
30	Namibia	−	+	+	−	in progress 98	+	−
31	Niger	−	+	+	−	+	+	−
32	Nigeria	−	+	+	−	−	+	−
33	Uganda	+	+	+	−	in progress 98	+	−
34	Rwanda	−	+	−	−	−	−	+
35	Central Afr. Rep.	−	−	−	−	−	−	in progress 98
36	Democratic Rep. of Congo	−	−	−	−	−	−	in progress 98
37	Sao Tome and Principe	−	−	+	−	−	+	−
38	Senegal	+	+	+	−	in progress 98	+	−
39	Seychelles	−	+	−	−	−	−	−
40	Sierra Leone	−	+	−	−	−	−	in progress 98/99
41	Somalia	−	−	−	−	−	−	in progress
42	Swaziland	−	−	+	−	−	+	−
43	Tanzania	−	+	+	−	−	+	−
44	Chad	−	−	+	−	−	−	+
45	Togo	−	+	+	−	+	+	−
46	Zambia	−	+	+	−	in progress 98	+	−
47	Zimbabwe	−	+	+	−	+	+	−
Total	**47 countries**	6/47	32/47	37/47	0/47	10 and 9 in progress out of 47	34/47	9 and 5 in progress

Sources: UNDP. "Studies of UNDP cooperation settings and national reports on human development", 1998.

Whereas between 1980 and 1990 only six countries had embarked on national analyses, profiles and assessments of poverty, 37 countries now have this research. And while no comprehensive, multidimensional poverty

Table 5.2. – Themes prevailing in the poverty reduction strategies and programs of 30 African countries South of the Sahara (1995-1997)

	Country	Rural Development and Food Security	Economic Management	Governance	Demarginalization of women and gender	Population	Job Security	Health + HIV	Education	Water and Sanitation	Private Sector	Environment	Infrastructures
1	South Africa			+				+				+	+
2	Angola	+	+	+				+				+	
3	Benin	+	+	+	+			+	+		+	+	+
4	Botswana	+	+		+			+	+			+	
5	Burkina Faso	+	+	+	+		+	+	+	+		+	
6	Cameroon		+	+	+		+	+	+	+	+	+	
7	Cap Verde	+		+	+	+	+	+	+		+	+	
8	Comoros	+	+	+		+		+	+		+	+	
9	Côte d'Ivoire		+	+	+		+	+	+	+	+	+	+
10	Ethiopia	+	+		+			+	+		+		
11	Gambia		+	+				+	+		+		
12	Ghana		+	+				+	+		+	+	
13	Guinea	+	+	+	+	+		+	+		+	+	
14	Guinea Bissau		+		+		+	+	+	+		+	
15	Kenya	+	+	+	+			+	+		+	+	+
16	Lesotho		+	+	+		+	+	+	+		+	+

Table 5.2. – Themes prevailing in the poverty reduction strategies and programs of 30 African countries South of the Sahara (1995-1997) (suite)

Country	Rural Development and Food Security	Economic Management	Governance	Demarginalization of women and gender	Population	Job Security	Health + HIV	Education	Water and Sanitation	Private Sector	Environment	Infrastructures
17 Malawi	+		+	+	+	+	+	+			+	
18 Mali	+	+	+	+		+	+	+	+	+	+	
19 Mauritania	+	+	+	+		+	+	+	+	+	+	+
20 Mozambique	+	+		+		+	+	+	+	+	+	+
21 Namibia	+	+	+	+				+	+	+	+	
22 Niger	+	+	+			+	+	+	+		+	
23 Uganda	+			+	+		+			+		
24 Sao Tome and Principe	+	+	+	+						+		
25 Senegal	+	+	+	+		+	+	+			+	
26 Swaziland	+		+			+	+				+	
27 Tanzania	+	+		+						+		
28 Togo	+	+	+				+	+			+	
29 Zambia	+	+	+	+		+	+	+		+	+	+
30 Zimbabwe	+	+		+		+	+	+		+	+	

Source: UNDP: "Review of poverty control strategies and programs in Africa", 1998.

reduction strategy had been designed — even less implemented — during that decade, since 1995 ten countries have designed such strategies and are working to implement them and nine others are in the process of designing strategies.

The policy directions and focus areas emphasized in the poverty reduction strategies and programs is interesting, because they shows the predominance of new themes — such as governance, economic management, employment promotion, development of the social sectors and advancement of women or gender issues — and the marginalization of other nevertheless important areas, such as infrastructure development.

A new partnership concerning the Poverty Reduction Strategy has been consolidated with the new initiative of IMF/IBRD: the Poverty Reduction Strategy Paper (PRSP). This initiative propose a close collaboration between Governments, international institutions, donors and civil society to support policy formulation and monitoring policy included in the PRSP exercise.

The contents of a Poverty Reduction Strategy Paper (PRSP) are likely to vary considerably between countries and will evolve over time.

The PRSP could begin by describing the nature and locus of poverty based on existing data. To the extent possible, this should go beyond consideration of the incomes and asset holdings of the poor to include regional, sectoral, environmental, demographic and gender dimensions of poverty, and highlight linkages between the institutional structure and poverty incidence.

The extent and nature of the country's vulnerability to exogenous shocks, and the impact of such shocks on the poor, could also be assessed in the PRSP to establish the risks to the poverty reduction strategy and provide a basis for considering policies to reduce these risks.

Building upon this description, the PRSP could provide an analysis of the macroeconomic, structural, social and institutional obstacles to faster growth and poverty reduction. The impediments to faster sustainable growth should be identified and policies to promote more rapid growth should be agreed upon i.e. structural reforms to create free and more open markets, including trade liberalization, privatization and tax reform and policies that create a stable and predictable environment for private sector activity. Obstacles to the poor contribution to, and sharing more fully in, the benefits of economic growth — for example, the slow growth of agriculture and the rural economy in general limited access to essentials services, and institutional obstacles that leave the poor with little voice and control over the kinds of services delivered to them — could be identified. This could include an analysis of the extent to which the poor benefit from existing public expenditures and the impact on the poor of the tax system. The PRSP could similarly, include an assessment of the constraints to private sector activity, as this is likely to be the engine of investment, job creation and growth.

The analysis of obstacles to poverty reduction should also seek to draw lessons from the country's recent experience including the role played by external assistance, and identifying the reasons for the success or otherwise of policies in reducing poverty.

3. Formulation and implementation of poverty reduction strategy

3.1. General strategy for Sub-Saharan African countries

Work-in-progress on the design and implementation of national poverty reduction strategies and the experience of UNDP in this area form the basis for an approach that integrates the objective of poverty reduction into the framework of a multidimensional development strategy, in line with the sustainable human development paradigm.

This approach comprises five interrelated phases:

• The first phase consists in assessing the poverty situation and the impact of existing direct poverty alleviation actions. This must be a comprehensive process, supported by coordinated instruments, such as living standard measurement surveys, poverty profiles, people's perceptions of poverty and human development indicators. The assessment should also include an analysis of macroeconomic and sectoral policies to ascertain the extent to which they take poverty reduction into account. This first stage must also make it possible to identify the structural causes and determinants of poverty and to evaluate the actions already undertaken in the country.

• The second phase involves the formulation of a strategic poverty reduction framework. This comprehensive and multidimensional framework must stress that poverty reduction is the central concern of the development strategy and that all policy directions and programs will be chosen and assessed in terms of their contribution to poverty reduction. These strategic poverty reduction frameworks generally break down into three levels of action:

– defining policy directions, priorities and strategic macroeconomic development options;

– setting overall and sectoral poverty-reduction objectives;

– designing institutional frameworks and participatory approaches that foster good governance through decentralized decision-making and institutional capacity-building so that development is managed by local authori-

Table 5.3. – Stages in the process of designing a national poverty reduction strategy

Process	Mechanisms and determinants
PHASE I Stage of identification, measurement and global appraisal of poverty.	1. Survey on household living conditions and poverty threshold. 2. Analysis of populations' perception about poverty and well-being and of the situation in terms of sustainable human development and social indicators. 3. Macro-economic diagnoses and sectoral and institutional studies related to poverty. 4. Identification structural causes and determinants of poverty. 5. Evaluation of on-going representative poverty reduction interventions.
PHASE II Stage of formulating a multidimensional global strategy	1. Definition of guidelines, priorities and macro-economic strategic main lines of development. 2. Determination of overall and sectoral objectives to reduce poverty. 3. Definition of institutional settings and participatory approaches.
PHASE III Central stage of defining national policies and programs and, implementing poverty reduction strategies.	1. Macro-economic policies and programs. 2. Policies and programs related to governance and population empowerment. 3. Sectoral policies and programs. 4. Social policies and programs (education, health, etc.). 5. Regional targeted programs and/or emergency programs.
PHASE IV Stage of presenting and discussing policies at international level with respect to major options and guidelines for human development and poverty reduction and mobilization of external resources [a]	1. Discussion of policies and guidelines in terms of poverty control within round table conferences and consultative groups. 2. Consolidation of devices for the implementing and monitoring of SAP and conditionality of assistance. 3. Joint committees, thematic/sectoral consultations among sponsors, debt restructuring committee.

a. Phase IV is, particularly for the Least Developed Countries, a crucial stage of discussing policies at international level and mobilizing resources. It can take place in parallel with or after phase III depending on national modalities and/or the degree of involvement of external partners.

ties with the participation of civil society in a democratic decision-making process.

• The third phase involves translating the policy directions that contribute to poverty reduction into specific policies and programs, through strategic planning and the implementation of development actions. This process includes: i) defining realistic strategic policy directions; ii) setting quantifiable objectives and sub-objectives, including the expected results, the target groups, the required resources and the timeframes for implementation; iii) raising financing and programming actions to achieve these objectives.

The third phase consists in formulating and implementing:

– macroeconomic and sectoral policies that support pro-poor economic growth;

– policies and programs in favor of governance and empowerment;

– social policies that contribute to efficient supply of social services, particularly basic services (health, education, water and sanitation);

– programs targeting specific regions and emergency programs for vulnerable groups or people living in poor or marginal areas with a view to facilitating direct access to the economic, social and infrastructural resources that can help them emerge from deprivation.

• The fourth phase is an opportunity for dialogue and exchange at international level on the major policy options and directions in human development and poverty reduction. It is also a favorable stage for raising the external financing needed to implement programs and projects. This stage can be supported by policy-dialogue and fund-raising instruments such as UNDP's general or thematic/sectoral Roundtable Conferences and the World Bank's country Consultative Group Meetings.

• The fifth phase consists in monitoring household living standards and evaluating the impact of the policies and programs implemented to reduce poverty, through efficient and inexpensive data collection and analysis that complement the work of national statistics institutes. This should include: i) regular monitoring of living standard indicators of poor households and a multiround survey on living standards repeated at regular intervals (every two years); ii) a participatory appraisal of representative poverty reduction actions; and iii) a more comprehensive evaluation of the mechanisms and systems that have an effect on poverty reduction.

An analysis of work-in-progress on poverty reduction strategies in Sub-Saharan Africa makes it possible to draw up a balance sheet and compare approaches taken in different countries. It also an opportunity to review the stages undertaken by various countries over almost a decade and to assess their commitment to and progress in achieving an integrated and multidimensional poverty reduction strategy.

Table 5.4. – Work-in-progress on poverty reduction strategies
in Sub-Saharan Africa (1990-1999)

Stages	Countries that have embarked on one or more stages	Number of stages completed
PHASE 1 1. Living standards measurement surveys and poverty line. 2. Analysis of the human development situation, social indicators and people's perceptions of poverty and well-being. 3. Assessment of macroeconomic and sectoral policies and institutional capacities from a poverty-reduction perspective. 4. Identifying the structural causes and determinants of poverty. 5. Evaluation of representative current actions to alleviate poverty.	Benin	$1 \Rightarrow 3$
	Botswana	$1 \Rightarrow 5$
	Burkina Faso	$1 \Rightarrow 5$
	Cameroon	$1 \Rightarrow 3$
	Cape Verde	$1 \Rightarrow 4$
	Chad	$1 \Rightarrow 3$
	Côte d'Ivoire	$1 \Rightarrow 4$
	Ghana	$1 \Rightarrow 4$
	Guinea	$1 \Rightarrow 4$
	Kenya	$1 \Rightarrow 4$
	Lesotho	$1 \Rightarrow 4$
	Malawi	$1 \Rightarrow 5$
	Mali	$1 \Rightarrow 4$
	Mauritania	$1 \Rightarrow 4$
	Mozambique	$1 \Rightarrow 2$
	Namibia	$1 \Rightarrow 4$
	Niger	$1 \Rightarrow 4$
	Nigeria	$1 \Rightarrow 3$
	Senegal	$1 \Rightarrow 4$
	South Africa	$1 \Rightarrow 3$
	Swaziland	$1 \Rightarrow 2$
	Tanzania	$1 \Rightarrow 2$
	Togo	$1 \Rightarrow 2$
	Uganda	$1 \Rightarrow 4$
	Zambia	$1 \Rightarrow 4$
	Zimbabwe	$1 \Rightarrow 5$
PHASE 2 1. Defining strategic macroeconomic policy directions for development. 2. Determining overall and sectoral poverty-reduction objectives. 3. Designing an institutional framework and participatory approaches.	Benin	$1 \Rightarrow 3$
	Botswana	$1 \Rightarrow 3$
	Burkina Faso	$1 \Rightarrow 2$
	Cameroon	$1 \Rightarrow 2$
	Cape Verde	$1 \Rightarrow 2$
	Chad	1
	Côte-d'Ivoire	1
	Ghana	$1 \Rightarrow 2$
	Guinea	$1 \Rightarrow 3$
	Kenya	1
	Lesotho	$1 \Rightarrow 3$
	Malawi	$1 \Rightarrow 3$
	Mali	$1 \Rightarrow 3$

Table 5.4. – Work-in-progress on poverty reduction strategies
in Sub-Saharan Africa (1990-1999) *(suite)*

Stages	Countries that have embarked on one or more stages	Number of stages completed
PHASE 2 *(...)*		
	Mauritania	$1 \Rightarrow 3$
	Mozambique	1
	Namibia	$1 \Rightarrow 3$
	Niger	$1 \Rightarrow 3$
	Nigeria	$1 \Rightarrow 2$
	Senegal	$1 \Rightarrow 3$
	South Africa	1
	Swaziland	$1 \Rightarrow 2$
	Tanzania	$1 \Rightarrow 3$
	Togo	1
	Uganda	$1 \Rightarrow 2$
	Zambia	$1 \Rightarrow 2$
	Zimbabwe	$1 \Rightarrow 3$
PHASE 3 1. Macroeconomic policies and programs. 2. Governance and empowerment policies and programs. 3. Sectoral policies and programs. 4. Social policies and programs (education, health, etc.). 5. Programs targeting specific regions and/or emergency programs.	Benin	$1 \Rightarrow 4$
	Botswana	$1 \Rightarrow 4$
	Burkina Faso	1/4
	Cameroon	1/3
	Cape Verde	1/2/3
	Chad	1/3
	Côte-d'Ivoire	1/3/4
	Ghana	$1 \Rightarrow 4$
	Guinea	1/4
	Kenya	1/2/4
	Lesotho	$1 \Rightarrow 4$
	Malawi	$1 \Rightarrow 5$
	Mali	$1 \Rightarrow 5$
	Mauritania	5
	Mozambique	1/3/4
	Namibia	$1 \Rightarrow 4$
	Niger	3
	Nigeria	1/3/4
	Senegal	$1 \Rightarrow 4$
	South Africa	1/3/5
	Swaziland	$1 \Rightarrow 4$
	Tanzania	3/4
	Togo	3/4
	Uganda	$1 \Rightarrow 4$
	Zambia	$1 \Rightarrow 4$
	Zimbabwe	$1 \Rightarrow 4$

Table 5.4. – Work-in-progress on poverty reduction strategies
in Sub-Saharan Africa (1990-1999) *(suite)*

Stages	Countries that have embarked on one or more stages	Number of stages completed
PHASE 4 1. Dialogue on poverty-reduction policies at roundtable conferences and Consultative Group meetings. 2. Consolidation of mechanisms for implementing and monitoring SAPs and aid conditionalities. 3. Joint committees, thematic/sectoral donor consultations, debt restructuring committees.	Benin Burkina Faso Cape Verde Lesotho Mali Namibia Niger Togo Zimbabwe	1 1 ⇒ 2 1 ⇒ 2 1 ⇒ 3 1 ⇒ 3 1 ⇒ 2 1 ⇒ 3 1 ⇒ 2 1 ⇒ 2
PHASE 5 1. Monitoring of living standards and evaluation of the impact of policies and programs on poverty reduction. 2. Participatory appraisals of representative poverty-reduction actions and mechanisms and systems with an effect on poverty reduction.	Benin Botswana Mali Niger Uganda Zimbabwe	1 1 1 1 1 1

1. Note: This analysis of work-in-progress on the design and implementation of national poverty reduction strategies is based on official documents provided by the countries under review and by the country offices of UNDP over the period 1990-1997.

Codes: A code of 1 ⇒ 4, for example, indicates that the phase has been undertaken through an integrated process consisting of four stages. A code of 1/3/5, for example, indicates that the phase has been fragmented and only stages 1, 3 and 5 have been undertaken.

2. Sources:

– Economic policy papers and national poverty reduction strategies from Sub-Saharan African countries, 1990-1998.

– Papers from general and sectoral/thematic Roundtable Conferences in Sub-Saharan African countries, 1995-1998.

– UNDP, *Review of Roundtable Processes* (New York, November 26, 1997).

Box 5.3.
Uganda: Poverty Reduction Strategy

Consultation Process

• In June 1997, Uganda launched the Poverty Eradication Action Plan (PEAP), following a national consultation process involving a cross-section of stakeholders (central and local government, civil society, and private sector). The PEAP provides national priorities for poverty reduction and guides sector policies

• A poverty status report (PSR) is produced on an semiannual basis to review the implementation of the PEAP. The 1999 PSR also incorporates data from the recent Uganda Participatory Poverty Assessment Project (UPPAP). The UPPAP directly consulted poor communities on their priorities, needs, and perceptions of the quality of service delivery and government policies.

• As a result of these extensive consultations, the level of government and civil society ownership of the PEAP is high.

Policy choices

The *Poverty Eradication Action Plan* presents a multidimensional analysis for poverty priorities. Examples of policy choices from the PEAP and UPPAP include the following:

• A larger weighting for the provision of domestic water in budgets at central and local levels as a result of the communities' identifying access to clean water as a priority;

• Inclusion of the constraints and priorities expressed by primary producers in the design of the National Plan for the Modernization of Agriculture; and

• A focus on security (individual, household, community, and regional) and governance as key components for reducing poverty.

Medium term budget framework (MTBF)

• In 1998/99, the government adopted a MTBF, under which medium-term budget priorities are formulated consistent with the PEAP and medium-term financial stability. Under the MTBF, line ministries are provided global budgetary ceilings on which base their sectoral allocations. New sectoral working groups comprising the Ministry of Finance, line ministries, and technical advisors were established to help develop sectoral priorities within the expenditure limits.

• For the first time, civil society is involved in the dialogue on priorities and spending commitments.

• To better reflect district poverty priorities and to bring local governments into the medium-term expenditure process, local government officials also prepare medium-term expenditure plans.

• This process feeds into the budget framework paper and annual budgets.

Poverty Action Fund

• The government established a Poverty Action Fund (PAF) to enhance transparency and monitoring of HIPC Initiative and other donor resources of expenditure programs focused on poverty.

• The PAF has four critical features: it involves civil society in the selection of programs and projects; it is fully integrated in the budget: it allocates 5 percent of fund to monitoring; and it involves both civil society and government in monitoring the impact of PAF outlays.

Institutional changes

• Institutional changes include the increased role of districts in the development, selection, and implementation of the PEAP; strengthening of the partnership between government and civil society; and the creation of more open political environment where previously sensitive issues (e.g., land ownership, women's empowerment, security, corruption, and governance) are now part of the policy dialogue.

Policy implementation and Decentralization

• Recent UPPAP findings demonstrate major differences in the poverty profile among districts. As a result, policymakers recognize the need for flexibility in determining priorities and budgets of different districts.

• Decentralization helped expedite the implementation of equalization grants to enable districts to meet locally identified poverty priorities, and the need for greater flexibility in the design of conditional grants was recognized.

District participatory planning

• Initially, the UPPAP will work directly with ten districts to strengthen their capacity to consult poor communities in the areas of district planning and budgeting

Monitoring Intermediate and Targets Policy Outcomes

• A transparent budget process with multiple channels for accountability (local constituencies, such as local authorities, press, community groups, NGOs and donors) is being developed. To increase the transparency in decentralized expenditure management of the PAF, advertisements are placed in the press indicating amounts disbursed to each district. In the education sector, budget allocations for schools are posted on some notice boards. Civil society (NGOs, district official, parliamentarians, and media) meets quarterly with central government officials to discuss delivery against budget allocations.

In addition, the Poverty Monitoring Unit Integrates annual household surveys, conducted by the Uganda Bureau of Statistics, with other data sources (e.g., participatory analysis, sector surveys, and line ministry data sources) to ensure that policy is continually influenced by poverty data and perceptions of the poor.

Source: Government of Uganda. Poverty Eradication Action Plan. Kampala, 1999

Box 5.4.

Poverty Eradication Strategy and Programs in Mali

Mali, following the example of a number of Sub-Saharan African countries and the recommendations of the UNDP Board of Administrators, undertook since 1994 to promote the concept of sustainable human development. To that effect and with UNDP assistance the country initiated and implemented a project to materialize this new concept focused on poverty eradication. The project was designed with four phases.

1°) The first phase of the process was the diagnostic phase. It aimed at taking stock of the situation of human development in Mali. This phase consisted in conducting studies geared towards a better knowledge of the features and determinants of poverty and the analysis of the impact of economic and social policies on human development.

The studies are the following: i) Diagnostic stock taking of SHD in Mali; ii) impact of economic and social policies on SHD in Mali; iii) Qualitative study of poverty (study of the mechanisms of poverty and exclusion); Poverty profile (quantitative study) in Mali; v) Study on street children in Mali; vi) Study on social capital in Mali.

2°) The second phase consisted in establishing the institutional setting and a device for the promotion of Sustainable Human Development /Poverty Eradication, including the SHD / PC observatory which is a structure of analysis, warning and advice.

3°) The third phase consisted in designing a national poverty eradication strategy based on a participatory approach which helped identify a number of strategic guidelines and priority actions. This phase was the logical follow-up of the study phase. It draws inspiration from the studies and surveys conducted on the results of typical interventions in the area of poverty alleviation. Its validation is performed in a participatory manner at both regional and national level before it is submitted to the Council of Ministers and to the donors for approval.

4°) The fourth phase of the process consists in presenting the poverty eradication strategy to the partners of Mali at a Donor Round Table Conference. This conference aims at mobilizing the development partners of Mali on the strategy in view of implementing the action plan of this strategy.

5°) The fifth phase consists in implementing the action plan of the strategy over the 1998-2002 period.

The national poverty eradication strategy includes 8 main lines and 41 actions. Its fundamental options are: i) targeting actions that come within the scope of the socio-economic sphere of the poor; ii) strengthening capacities and iii) harmonizing actions accepted at the macro, meso and micro levels to ensure greater synergy of daily poverty alleviation actions.

Two important intervention areas related to poverty, eradication, i.e., promotion of women and preservation of the environment, were not selected as separate main lines. This is due to two major concerns: on the one hand their transverse nature allows for their integration into the other accepted main lines and actions; and on the other hand, it was deemed preferable to avoid a "ghetto" approach for themes that are so important in poverty reduction.

Eight strategic main lines were accepted:

1. To improve the economic, political, legal, social and cultural environment in favor of the poor.

2. To promote income generating activities and self-employment for the poor.

3. To improve access to financial services and other production factors for the poor.

4. To promote the development and improve the performance of the agro-food businesses in which the poor are concentrated.

5. To improve access to education and training for the poor.

6. To promote access to basic health, nutrition, drinking water and sanitation for the poor.

7. To improve the housing conditions of the poor.

8. To ensure efficient coordination of the poverty eradication strategy.

Source: Government of Mali and United Nations Development Program in Bamako, 1997.

Box 5.5.
Ghana: Poverty Reduction Strategy

In the light of the analysis above, the PRSP could define medium and long-term outcome-oriented targets for the country's poverty reduction strategy, and set out the macroeconomic, structural, and social policies that together comprise a comprehensive strategy for achievement of these outcomes.

The priorities for policy action would be clearly stated and incorporated in an action plan, taking into account what is known of the linkages between different policies, their appropriate sequencing and the expected contribution of policy actions to the attainment of intermediate indicators. This the heart of the PRSP — an action plan focusing on priorities to raise sustainable growth and reduce poverty.

It would specify key actions and policies consistent with this overall framework covering a horizon of at least three years. Similarly, a timetable of key policy actions over this three-year period, including institutional reforms and technical assistance, could be included in a policy matrix.

The PRSP would describe the framework and mechanisms for monitoring implementation, including the extent and planned development of participatory processes designed to strengthen accountability, the indicators to be monitored and the planned frequency of reporting and monitoring.

The PRSP could also outline the principles of the country's external borrowing strategy and the appropriate degree of concessionality of this borrowing given current and prospective external debt levels.

This analysis is based on a qualitative assessment of the stages completed or under way from the perspective of UNDP's approach in five phases. It highlights — all other things being equal — clear differences in the approach to achieving a poverty reduction strategy. Strategies such as those designed and currently implemented in Benin, Botswana, Namibia, Mali, Niger and Zimbabwe appear credible. In contrast, some countries that have already embarked on these processes do not seem to have a comprehensive approach to the problem and are experiencing difficulties in sequencing the different stages. The governments of these countries need to be made aware of the importance of an integrated, multidimensional process and its appropriation by national stakeholders.

3.2. Specific strategies for countries in crisis

In countries in a situation of conflict or crisis, there are enormous obstacles to implementing equitable, sustainable poverty reduction processes, even though this is exactly the type of approach these countries need to tackle the multidimensional difficulties they are experiencing. The decline of the State and the withdrawal of the international community except for humanitarian actions, which are by nature temporary, increase the complexity of designing, appropriating and implementing national poverty reduction strategies. The five-phase framework proposed here therefore needs to be adapted and specific support measures implemented to assist these countries to emerge from crisis.

In these situations, it is important to design integrated programs aimed at establishing links between emergency humanitarian assistance, peace-making efforts and economic and social rehabilitation and reconstruction. National reconciliation and poverty reduction initiatives are the cement that will strengthen these links. Several programs have been implemented to date, with varying success, given the complexity of such exercises. After the severe crises in Burundi and Rwanda, UNDP and the United Nations system deployed innovative actions there, such as the Continuum Project. This project aims to ensure an effective transition phase between humanitarian relief and a return to development.

In Burundi, while the civil war and subregional tensions continue to pose a serious threat to social and economic reconstruction, UNDP is focusing its assistance on a three-year program, 1998-2000, aimed at mitigating the impact of the crisis on vulnerable sections of the population and at fostering self-help for the victims of conflict and the rehabilitation of grassroots communities. These activities will also support reconciliation between the communities and the peace process embarked on by the government.

As an innovative response to the crisis and a way to progress towards rehabilitation and peace, UNDP has chosen to focus on one strategic area

— poverty reduction — for its first development cooperation framework in Burundi.

UNDP's action is determined by the major causes and manifestations of poverty and the types of groups worst affected and breaks down into three aspects:

– assisting the government in managing the main challenges it faces, particularly peace and national reconciliation;

– contributing to meeting the needs of grass-roots communities, including war-torn communities, while assisting the reconstruction of the country's weakened social fabric and strengthening people's capacities for self-help through specific actions, such as income-generating activities and community health;

– supporting the farm sector as a source of income for the rural population and environmental regeneration with a view to achieving sustainable food security.

Through its first development cooperation framework with Burundi, UNDP plans to invest fully in the resettlement and reintegration of the victims of conflict through strategic, institutional and operational support. With a concern for sustainability, reintegration actions will be accompanied by support for current attempts at coexistence, as a way of bridging the gap between humanitarian relief and development.

Community-based capacity-building initiatives undertaken under the Continuum Project are being pursued and consolidated, alongside action to strengthen the capacities of local structures. This includes the promotion of income-generating activities in the form of micro-projects in favor of the poorest people, aimed at self-employment and self-help for disadvantaged groups, particularly women, who make up the vast majority of the population affected by the crisis. Sufficient resources will be allocated to awareness-raising and advocating gender equality.

In a situation of widespread food insecurity and malnutrition, UNDP intends to give special support to food security. This will contribute to eliminating poverty among the most disadvantaged and vulnerable groups. Action will be directed at two areas: integrating agriculture and livestock farming to promote integrated management of basic production units with the aim of increasing the productivity of family farms, with special attention for women; and assisting efforts to boost production and distribute quality seed, which had virtually disappeared since the crisis.

At the operational level, through the work of non-governmental organizations and by strengthening local structures, UNDP contributes to poverty alleviation by promoting a participatory approach to the development and management of natural resources based on community income-generating initiatives. The same applies to the development of watersheds and reclamation of swampland, for which a guiding framework is needed to ensure people's access to this land in a context of scarce farmland, while protecting the environmental balance to which these fragile ecosystems contribute.

Finally, UNDP encourages the participation of grass-roots communities and the inclusion of their social and economic concerns in the peace process.

In response to the governance situation, UNDP also needs to provide effective support for the United Nations peace and political mediation efforts and for the consolidation of the legal system and the sound management of public affairs. [1]

In Ethiopia, a rehabilitation and poverty reduction program is being implemented with varying success, even as renewed conflict with Eritrea may jeopardize this approach. Ethiopia was devastated by 30 years of war, with thousands of returning refugees, some 400,000 demobilized soldiers and major rehabilitation and reconstruction needs. In 1992, the Ethiopian Social Rehabilitation and Development Fund began a community-based approach to rehabilitation and development. In its initial phase, 1,220,000 people benefited from more than 200 projects: clinics, schools, sewerage systems, public latrines, small dams and income-generating businesses such as mills, quarries and electrical and mechanical workshops. At the same time, community organizations, local government staff and NGOs worked together to improve the planning of projects and build capacities. The fund is expanding so that it can implement small-scale community projects throughout rural Ethiopia. UNDP is assisting in raising the $243 million needed for this phase and for the introduction of mechanisms to manage these funds efficiently. The World Bank, Canada, Italy, Norway and Sweden have joined UNDP and the Ethiopian government in this effort. [2]

At this stage, it is too early to measure the medium and long-term impact and effectiveness of the programs undertaken in Burundi, Rwanda and Ethiopia, although they are urgently needed in the short term.

---

1. Rosine Coulibaly, *Note sur le sixième programme de coopération du PNUD au Burundi 1998-2000*, mai 1998.
2. UNDP, *Eliminer la pauvreté: année internationale de l'éradication de la pauvreté*, 1996.

PART THREE

External mobilization for poverty reduction in Africa

CHAPTER 6

Role of donors
in poverty reduction action

1. Introduction: international awareness
of the poverty problem

An understanding of the importance of poverty reduction began to develop in the late 1980s and early 1990s. There were two reasons for this. First, the development strategies of the previous 30 years — focused on large-scale infrastructure and efforts to promote exports and trade — had clearly reached their limits. Second, it was felt that the 1980s were lost years for poor people, given the negative social effects of structural adjustment programs (SAPs), particularly on disadvantaged groups. Responding to these failures, the international community began to reconsider traditional development paradigms and to take the theme of poverty into account.

Since the late 1980s, non-governmental organizations (NGOs) and civil society organizations have made poverty alleviation a central component of their approach to development. Also, the World Bank's *World Development Report 1990* focused entirely on poverty. However, it was not until the Copenhagen Summit for Social Development in 1995, at which civil society organizations played a leading role, that the international community publicly acknowledged the importance of the poverty problem.

At the World Summit for Social Development, held in Copenhagen in March 1995, the heads of State and leaders of more than 180 countries recognized the growing problem of global poverty, and agreed to take steps to alleviate the problem. The Copenhagen Declaration on Social Development states:

> "We gather here to commit ourselves, our governments and our nations to enhancing social development throughout the world so that all men and

women, especially those living in poverty, may exercise the rights, utilise the resources and share the responsibilities that enable them to lead satisfying lives and to contribute to the well-being of their families, their communities and humankind. To support and promote these efforts must be the overriding goals of the international community, especially with respect to people suffering from poverty, unemployment and social exclusion". [1]

For this reason, the Copenhagen Summit and the resultant Declaration and Programme of Action are major milestones in the international community's growing awareness of the phenomenon of poverty. The participating governments agreed to work towards eradicating poverty by formulating and implementing national poverty eradication plans to address the structural causes of poverty, encompassing action on the local, national and international levels. The specificity and magnitude of poverty in Sub-Saharan Africa were given particular mention:

"While these problems are global in character and affect all countries, we clearly acknowledge that the situation of most developing countries, and particularly of Africa and the least developed countries, is critical and requires special attention and action. [...] these countries [...] require the support of the international community". [2]

Although the main responsibility for eradicating poverty lies with the national governments — this is clearly specified in the second commitment of the Copenhagen Summit — the support of the international community is nevertheless needed if the poorest countries are to develop and implement poverty reduction strategies and programs.

"We commit ourselves to the goal of eradicating poverty in the world, through decisive national actions and international cooperation, as an ethical, social, political and economic imperative of humankind".

Explicit reference is made to the undertakings of the international community, which agrees to provide technical and financial assistance with the aim of reducing poverty.

"At the international level, we will:

Strive to ensure that the international community and international organisations, particularly the multilateral financial institutions, assist developing countries and all countries in need in their efforts to achieve our overall goal of eradicating poverty and ensuring basic social protection;

Encourage all international donors and multilateral development banks to support policies and programs for the attainment, in a sustained manner,

---

1. *Copenhagen Declaration on Social Development*, World Summit for Social Development, Copenhagen, 1995.

2. *Copenhagen Declaration on Social Development*, World Summit for Social Development, Copenhagen, 1995.

of the specific efforts of the developing countries and all countries in need relating to people-centred sustainable development and to meeting basic needs for all; to assess their existing programs in consultation with the concerned developing countries to ensure the achievement of the agreed program objectives; and to seek to ensure that their own policies and programs will advance the attainment of agreed development goals that focus on meeting basic needs for all and eradicating absolute poverty. Efforts should be made to ensure that participation by the people concerned is an integral part of such programs;

Focus attention on and support the special needs of countries and regions in which there are substantial concentrations of people living in poverty, in particular in South Asia, and which therefore face serious difficulties in achieving social and economic development". [1]

A wide range of poverty reduction measures are recommended within this framework. While national governments are required to take prime responsibility for implementing these measures, the Conference nevertheless recommended that the international community should provide support, especially to African countries, least developed countries and countries in crisis.

In particular, the support of the international community is sought in the following actions:
— formulating integrated strategies for poverty eradication;
— improving access for poor people to productive resources and infrastructure;
— meeting the basic human needs of all;
— enhancing social protection and reducing vulnerability.

In addition to the specific support provided by external partners to achieve these priority objectives, specific recommendations are included for donors. These indicate that donors should seek to:
— foster an enabling environment for poverty eradication;
— coordinate policies and programs to support the measures being taken in developing countries, particularly in Africa, to eradicate poverty;
— promote international cooperation to assist developing countries in their efforts towards achieving gender equality and the empowerment of women;
— strengthen the capacities of developing countries to monitor the progress of national poverty eradication plans;
— address the special needs of small island countries, landlocked countries and war-torn countries in order to eradicate poverty.

---

1. "Poverty Eradication", *Copenhagen Declaration on Social Development*, World Summit for Social Development, Copenhagen, 1995.

More than 180 States accepted the declarations and commitments of the Copenhagen Summit. In addition, hundreds of NGOs and civil society organizations were involved in drafting the resolutions and took part in the summit proceedings. As a result, the World Summit for Social Development considerably increased awareness of the need to alleviate poverty. It also had a major influence on new development strategies and policies, as well as on the donors' areas of focus.

The Copenhagen Summit represents the broadest consensus ever achieved both in terms of building awareness and of developing an agenda for the eradication of poverty. [1] The importance of alleviating poverty as part of efforts to promote sustainable human development was also recognized by the General Assembly of the United Nations, which declared 1996 International Year for the Eradication of Poverty. This was followed by the first United Nations Decade for the Eradication of Poverty (1997-2006).

The main objective of this initiative is to further raise awareness among States, opinion-makers and international public opinion with regard to the structural causes and complex and multidimensional nature of poverty. The aim is for everybody to understand that eradicating poverty is vital to consolidating peace and achieving sustainable human development.

Thus, while the governments of developing countries must play a leading role in implementing poverty reduction strategies and programs, the international community is firmly committed to providing support, particularly to African countries and LDCs. The agencies of the United Nations system and bilateral and multilateral donors have all agreed to support the governments as they introduce poverty reduction strategies and programs.

The agencies of the United Nations system — through preparations for the Copenhagen Summit and implementation of the 20/20 Initiative — have already appropriated the need to address the problem of poverty and are working to meet their commitments. Through a series of actions, such as declaring 1996 as International Year for the Eradication of Poverty and implementing the 1996 Special Initiative for Africa, they have put poverty at the heart of sustainable human development.

Bilateral donors are sending out the same message in their declarations of intent. Poverty alleviation has been explicitly defined as a development priority since the Copenhagen Summit. In 1996, at the 34th high-level meeting of the OECD's Development Assistance Committee (DAC), the chairman's report, *Shaping the 21st Century: The Contribution of Development Cooperation*, stressed the importance of poverty issues. [2]

---

1. UNDP, *Eliminer la pauvreté: année internationale de l'éradication de la pauvreté*, 1996.

2. "Shaping the 21st Century: The Contribution of Development Co-operation", *Development Co-operation, 1996 Report* (Paris: DAC-OECD, 1997).

The report identified poverty reduction as the main objective of development: the proportion of people living in extreme poverty must be halved by 2015.

This commitment was renewed in 1997 at another high-level OECD meeting. At this meeting, a document discussing the outlook for development for 2020 identified the links between globalization and poverty. Once again, attention was focused firmly on alleviating poverty, at the level of poor people and households. [1]

Thus, in terms of political commitment, the international community and all the development partners are expressing support for the objectives of poverty eradication formulated at the Copenhagen Summit. Looking beyond these declarations of intent, however, it is essential to analyze the aid flows for poverty reduction, as well as donors' policies and actions, in order to better identify the manner in which these political commitments are being translated into action.

2. Official development assistance for poverty reduction in Sub-Saharan Africa

In recent years, official development assistance (ODA) has continued to fall, as a result of the budgetary pressures on the total amounts allocated to aid. Total ODA, i.e. comprising bilateral and multilateral assistance, fell from $66 billion in 1994 to $59 billion in 1995 and just $55 billion in 1996. [2] In real terms, aid declined by 4% in 1996 compared with the previous year, by 16% compared with 1992 and by 8% in comparison with 1990-1995. In 1996, total aid came to a mere 0.25% of the combined GNP of DAC members, i.e. the lowest in 30 years.

Looking more specifically at assistance for Africa, $20 billion was earmarked in 1996 compared with over $21 billion in 1993. Similarly, Sub-Saharan Africa received $16.7 billion in 1996 compared with $17.3 billion in 1993. These figures show a gradual deterioration in aid flows to Africa. [3]

The same trend emerges for least developed countries. Total funds allocated to LDCs account for a quarter of all aid, even though this group of countries accounts for only one-eighth of the population in the developing world. Nevertheless, aid flows to LDCs are in constant decline. The share of ODA allocated to LDCs in the GNP of the members countries of the

---

1. DAC-OECD, *Globalisation and Linkages to 2020: Can Poor Countries and Poor People Prosper in the New Global Age?* (Paris, 1997).

2. DAC-OECD, *Development Co-operation, 1996 & 1997 Reports* (Paris, 1997 & 1998).

3. See Chapter One for a detailed analysis of aid flows to Sub-Saharan Africa.

Table 6.1. – Official Development Assistance for African countries, 1993-1996

Net total ODA from DAC countries to Africa					
in millions of dollars	1993	1996	in millions of dollars	1993	1996
Algeria	349	309	Madagascar	363	364
Egypt	2401	2212	Malawi	498	501
Libya	6	10	Mali	366	505
Morocco	713	651	Mauritania	328	274
Tunisia	228	126	Mauritius	26	20
North Sahara not broken down	42	54	Mayotte	83	130
TOTAL North Sahara	*3737*	*3362*	Mozambique	1183	923
Angola	294	544	Namibia	155	189
Benin	289	293	Niger	347	259
Botswana	133	81	Nigeria	279	192
Burkina	470	418	Rwanda	358	674
Burundi	218	204	Saint-Helena	15	16
Cameroon	545	413	Sao Tome	47	47
Cap Verde	118	120	Senegal	504	582
Central African Republic	173	167	Sierra Leone	19	19
Chad	228	305	Somalia	209	195
Comoros	50	40	Sudan	890	91
Congo	123	430	Swaziland	458	230
Dem. Rep. Congo	178	167	Tanzania	53	31
Côte d'Ivoire	765	968	Togo	953	894
Djibouti	134	97	Uganda	98	166
Equatorial Guinea	53	31	Zambia	612	684
Eritrea	68	157	Zimbabwe	872	614
Ethiopia	1094	849	South Africa	500	374
Gabon	102	127	South Sahara not broken down	275	361
Gambia	87	38	Africa not specified	414	915
Ghana	618	654	*Total South-Sahara*	*17330*	*16746*
Guinea	410	295			
Guinea-Bissau	96	180	*Total Africa*	*21477*	*20678*
Kenya	911	606	*Total DC*	*57061*	*58480*
Lesotho	143	107	*% Africa/DC*	*37.6*	*35.3*
Liberia	123	207			

Source: DAC, OECD, Report 1997.

OECD's Development Assistance Committee (DAC) fell from 0.09% in 1990 to 0.07% in 1995. This is less than half the aid targets and commitments agreed at the Paris Conference in 1990.

The initial picture emerging from this analysis of global aid flows to LDCs and the countries of Sub-Saharan Africa does not appear to corroborate the political declarations and commitments made to reducing poverty. On the contrary, the trend is towards a reduction in aid flows to the poorest countries.

Box 6.1.

Africa and low-income Asia: Financing comparisons and contrasts

In 1995, the countries in Sub-Saharan Africa, comprising many of the world's poorest countries, collectively received $22 billion in net external capital flows. The low-income countries in Asia (excluding the giants of China and India) also attracted $24 billion in external capital in 1995. But there, the similarity ends:

* External flows to Sub-Saharan Africa are almost exclusively in the form of official development aid (ODA), mostly as grants. Finance from private sources (foreign direct investment, international bank lending and portfolio debt and equity finance) is a relatively minor element. Over the last decade, this overall composition has changed little, unlike the level of external finance for development which has dropped by about 25 per cent in constant terms (adjusted for prices and exchange rates).

* In sharp contrast, net external flows to the Asian LICs (excluding China and India) have doubled in real terms over the last decade. The dominance of official flows to this area in the mid-1980s has gradually given way to a more balanced structure of external flows. Private flows now account for about half of net external financing.

Source: DAC-OECD, *Development Co-operation, 1996 Report* (Paris, 1997).

However, there are no statistics directly available on the sums allocated specifically to poverty alleviation. For this reason, there are many outstanding questions regarding the mobilization of aid against poverty and the effective impact of this assistance on poor population groups. Apart from general statistics on national income, current statistical tools cannot be used to ascertain precisely the share of aid allocated to population groups that have been identified as poor. Similarly, in the breakdown of aid sectors, there is no "poverty reduction" sector. It is therefore necessary to establish the types and volumes of aid that are most likely to have a positive impact on the poverty and marginalization of poor people. DAC member countries are currently studying ways of obtaining improved statistical data on the degree of targeting for their poverty reduction aid.

In addition to the indicators specific to LDCs and the Sub-Saharan African countries, and which are used to target those countries that are considered to be poorest, data concerning aid allocated to the social sectors in general or to basic social services, as part of the 20/20 Initiative, should make it possible to better assess the level, volume and quality of part of the aid allocated to poverty reduction.

Our analysis of the assistance received by LDCs showed that this aid is decreasing constantly. It is important to conduct a similar analysis of aid earmarked for the social sectors.

In the 1990s, it appears that donors have focused particularly on assistance for education, access to safe drinking water and health care. Education accounted for 16% to 18% of total bilateral assistance; water for around 8%, compared with 2% in the 1970s; and health for between 5% and 7%. [1] However, an examination of social spending in 66 developing countries revealed that, between 1986 and 1996, growth in spending as a percentage of GDP came to barely 0.1% for education and 0.3% for health. Moreover, in the Sub-Saharan African countries, per capita spending on education fell by around 0.5%. [2] It would therefore seem that considerable efforts still have to be made vis-à-vis the poorest countries.

Spending on the basic social sectors as defined by the 20/20 Initiative — i.e. flows of aid allocated to basic education, primary health care, reproductive health, safe drinking water and sanitation — amounted to just 10%-11% of the total ODA of donors. Moreover, governments allocated 13% of their budget on average to this type of expenditure. [3] Considerable progress remains to be made if the target of 20% is to be reached.

The proportion of ODA allocated to essential social services varies from country to country. Cameroon and Côte d'Ivoire earmark less than 10%, compared with nearly 20% in the other countries that are implementing the 20/20 Initiative, and 30% in Namibia.

It appears therefore that data on aid flows are not entirely consistent with the commitments made to eradicating poverty, and the political will displayed to this end. This is true of the targeted countries (i.e. the poorest countries) and of the sectors that have the greatest impact on poverty (i.e. the basic social sectors of the 20/20 Initiative).

It is essential to introduce statistical indicators that specifically target poverty because the figures available at present cannot accurately measure the total amount of funds allocated to this field. Therefore, after this brief

---

1. DAC-OECD, *Development Co-operation, 1996 Report* (Paris, 1997).
2. "Sample of 66 Economies: Social Spending Rises and Indicators Improve With IMF-Supported Programs", *IMF Survey* 23 February 1998.
3. UNICEF, *Suivi de l'Initiative 20/20* (New York, 1997).

Table 6.2. – Proportion Official Development Assistance allocate to ESS

As % of total ODA	Year	Basic Education	Basic Health and nutrition	Water and sanitation	Total ODA ESS
South Africa					n.a.
Namibia	1995	9.0	8.2	13.2	30.3
Zambia	1997				< 20.0
Malawi	1997				> 20.0
Tanzania	1997				< 20.0
Cameroon	1996/97	2.5	3.2	2.4	8.1
Côte d'Ivoire	1994				9.3
Benin	1996	7.4	6.9	4.1	18.4
Mali	1996				22.6
Burkina Faso	1997	4.5	8.1	4.4	17.0
Niger	1995	5.4	7.3	5.4	18.1

Source: national documents on Initiative 20/20, 1997-1998.

statistical overview, it may be useful to examine the policies of bilateral and multilateral donors in the field of poverty reduction. This will give greater insight into the will of the different parties and help to identify more clearly the efforts they have made.

3. Donor policies with regard to poverty

An analysis of aid flow statistics does not clearly show donors to be supporting national poverty reduction policies and programs. Nevertheless, the donors seem to be genuinely committed to supporting poverty reduction actions.

For this reason, it is important to analyze in greater detail the different policies and options adopted by donors in their efforts to alleviate poverty. By doing this, it is possible to identify the donors that have included the objective of reducing poverty in their mandates, objectives or development cooperation programs. [1]

---

1. See Table 1, which lists the mandates and objectives of the main donors, as well as sectors and themes of operation.

Box 6.2.

OECD: Development partnerships in the new global context

"We endorse the following strategic orientations, and commend them for active support in our own countries and throughout the international community:

– Combating poverty at its roots is a central challenge.

Support for development reflects our enduring concern for the human dignity and well being of others. Despite the promising trends in many developing countries, more than one billion people still live in extreme poverty. Yet, building on lessons learned, there are good prospects for significantly reducing poverty in the coming years.

We will focus our support on strategies and programmes that will work to enable the poorest to expand their opportunities and improve their lives."

Source: DAC-OECD, "Shaping the 21st Century: The Contribution of Development Cooperation" (Paris, 1996).

Several donors have made poverty reduction a priority objective, including Belgium, Canada, Denmark, Finland, Sweden, IFAD, UNDP and the World Bank. [1]

If a donor identifies poverty reduction as a central focus of strategy, this should constitute a firm and unequivocal commitment reflecting the donor's determination to reduce poverty. It follows from this that all the donor's activities must be directed towards, and justified by, this key objective. However, there is a risk that all the donor's actions could be interpreted as being part of a poverty reduction strategy, without any detailed objectives being set or justification being given in terms of poverty reduction. As we have seen throughout this study, poverty reduction is not a synonym for development as a whole.

Some donors, including Australia, Germany, Italy, Switzerland, the United States, the ADB, the European Union, UNFPA and UNICEF, have established poverty reduction as one of a range of specific objectives.

Other donors have not identified poverty reduction as a priority or as a specific objective in their development work. These include the IMF, France, Austria, Spain and Japan. Although these donors do not make explicit reference to poverty reduction in their core policies, however, they are nevertheless conducting a range of actions that can be interpreted as

---

1. See DAC-OECD, *Development Co-operation, 1996 Report* (Paris, 1997); UNDP, *Donors' Aid Policies and Priorities* (New York, 1994); A. Cox and J. Healey, *Poverty reduction: A Review of Donor Strategies and Practices* (Paris: OECD, 1997).

Table 6.3. – Aid and poverty reduction profiles of the main bilateral donors [a]

Country	Aid policies	Aid to Africa	Sectors	Themes
Australia	Capacity building of partner countries in education, health and governance – Strengthening of international and regional trade and investment systems	Aid is concentrated on the Pacific region. Little support is given to African countries, with the exceptions of Ethiopia, Mozambique, Zimbabwe and Tanzania.	– Education – Health – Economic management – Regional cooperation	– Private sector – Governance – Capacity building
Austria	Three priority objectives: – Sustained economic growth – Access to social services – Environmental protection	Africa is one of the most strongly assisted regions, with aid going to: Burkina Faso, Burundi, Cape Verde, Kenya, Mozambique, Namibia, Rwanda, Senegal, Tanzania, Uganda and Zimbabwe.	– Economic management – Management and protection of natural resources – Education and training – Agriculture and rural development – Industry	– Private sector – Gender issues – Environment – Training
Belgium	Three key components of development cooperation: – Governance – Participation – Poverty reduction	24 focus countries, 14 in Sub-Saharan Africa: Burkina Faso, Côte d'Ivoire, Mali, Niger, Benin, Burundi, Congo, Rwanda, Kenya, Uganda, Ethiopia, Tanzania, South Africa and Angola.	– Health – Education and training – Agriculture and food security – Basic infrastructure – Governance	– Gender issues – Environment – Social economy and poverty reduction – Private sector
Canada	Six priorities: – Fulfilment of basic needs – Infrastructure – Human rights – Private sector – Women's participation – Environmental protection	40% of assistance goes to Sub-Saharan Africa, principally: Ghana, Mali, Burkina Faso, Guinea, Cameroon, Ethiopia, Côte d'Ivoire and all the countries of southern Africa.	– Agriculture – Education – Food aid – Economic management – Natural resources – Infrastructure	– Gender issues – Poverty reduction – Private sector – Environment

Table 6.3. – Aid and poverty reduction profiles of the main bilateral donors [a] (suite)

Country	Aid policies	Aid to Africa	Sectors	Themes
Denmark	Basic objective of poverty reduction through economic and social development founded on: – Improvement of living standards – Human rights – Women's participation in development – Environmental protection	20 focus countries, 13 of which are in Africa and receive almost 60% of total aid. They include Burkina Faso, Benin, Ghana, Kenya, Mozambique, Tanzania, Uganda, Zambia and Zimbabwe.	– Social and administrative infrastructure – Emergency assistance – Agriculture – Industry – Transport and communications – Water and sanitation	– Environment – Gender issues – Democracy and human rights
Finland	Objective of poverty reduction through: – Promotion of sustainable development and well-being in developing countries – Democracy and human rights – North-South partnership	Sub-Saharan Africa receives 35%-40% of total ODA. The main recipients are Ethiopia, Eritrea, Kenya, Mozambique, Namibia, Tanzania and Zambia.	– Agriculture and forestry – Industry and trade – Health and population – Emergency assistance – Transport and communications	– Poverty eradication – Environment – Democracy and human rights – Grassroots participation – Gender issues
France	Three fundamental lines: – Human development – Productive development – Cultural development on the basis of three priorities: + Environment + Institutional development + Poverty reduction	Significant involvement in intermediate countries. Within Africa, this includes Côte d'Ivoire, Cameroon, Gabon and Senegal. For the LDCs: Guinea, Madagascar, Burkina Faso, Mali, Niger, Chad, Mozambique and Congo.	– Rural development – Debt and economic management – Industry and trade – Education – Health – Town planning – Support for administration	– Private sector – Environment – Decentralized development cooperation – Governance and rule of law
Germany	Three areas of operation: i) poverty reduction through structural reforms and support for private enterprise; ii) protection of natural resources; and iii) education and training	Main recipients include: Kenya, Zambia, Burkina Faso, Ghana, Senegal, Madagascar, Zaire, Tanzania and Zimbabwe	– Infrastructure – Humanitarian aid – Education	– Poverty reduction – Private sector – Environment

Table 6.3. – Aid and poverty reduction profiles of the main bilateral donors [a] *(suite)*

Country	Aid policies	Aid to Africa	Sectors	Themes
Italy	The objective of development cooperation is to promote autonomous economic, social and cultural development through: – Fulfilment of basic needs – Self-sufficiency in food – Development of human resources – Environmental protection	Focus countries in Africa: Angola, Ethiopia, Mozambique, Somalia et Tanzania	– Food and humanitarian aid – Health – Agriculture – Education – Science and technology – Transport and communications	– Environment – Gender issues – Anti-drug measures – Poverty reduction
Japan	Charter of Japanese assistance in 1992. Aims to take into account the suffering resulting from famine and poverty, through the following: – Democracy and human rights – Environmental protection – Promotion of peace and limitation of military expenditure – Prosperity	12% of total assistance is designated for African countries, principally in southern Africa, Kenya and Ghana.	– Energy – Transport and communications – Water and sanitation – Education – Agriculture	Environment and population – HIV/AIDS – Raising financing – Aid coordination
Netherlands	Sustainable poverty reduction, primarily in disadvantaged countries, through: – Participatory process – Promotion of partnerships – Policy dialogue in the following areas: environment, urban poverty, research and gender issues	58% of assistance to LDCs, above all the countries of East, Southern and Sahelian Africa.	– Education – Economic management – Agriculture – Industry and mines – Transport and communications	– Environment – Poverty reduction – Gender issues – Partnerships and participatory development

Table 6.3. – Aid and poverty reduction profiles of the main bilateral donors [a] (suite)

Country	Aid policies	Aid to Africa	Sectors	Themes
New Zealand	Promote economic and social development of partner countries via: – Training and education – Political reforms and sound management – Private sector development	Assistance primarily to the Pacific countries and to nine African countries: Botswana, Kenya, Malawi, Zimbabwe, Lesotho, Tanzania, Zambia, Uganda and the Seychelles.	– Social infrastructure – Education – Agricultural development – Health	– Gender issues – Environment – NGOs – Human rights
Norway	Objective of poverty reduction through: – Participatory and grassroots development – Conservation of natural resources – Democracy and human rights – Promotion of education and the 20/20 Initiative	72% of assistance is dedicated to those countries that are considered the poorest, including, in Africa: Botswana, Mozambique, Namibia, Tanzania, Zambia and Zimbabwe.	– Transport and communications – Emergency assistance – Social and administrative infrastructure – Education – Agriculture – Energy	– Poverty reduction – NGOs – Private sector – Environment – Gender issues
Portugal	Guarantee the economic development and security of partner countries via: – Consolidation of democracy – Education and training – Economic growth – Promotion of private enterprise	95% of Portuguese cooperation is directed to Mozambique, Angola, Cape Verde, Guinea-Bissau and Sao Tome and Principe.	– Economic and development management – Industry and trade – Education – Health	– Environment – Private sector – Democracy – National capacity building
Spain	The basic objectives of development cooperation are: – Sustainable development – Human resources development – Extending the influence of Spanish language and culture with the ultimate goal of eradicating poverty	Little involvement in Africa and variable from year to year. Active in Equatorial Guinea, Angola and Mozambique.	– Education – Health – Emergency assistance – Economic management – Industry and energy	– Poverty eradication – Private sector – NGOs and decentralized development cooperation

Table 6.3. – Aid and poverty reduction profiles of the main bilateral donors [a] *(suite)*

Country	Aid policies	Aid to Africa	Sectors	Themes
Sweden	Raise living standards for the poorest populations, through: – an increase in resources – economic and social equality – economic and political autonomy – institution of a democratic society – natural resources and the environment – equality between the sexes	Recipient countries in Africa are Angola, Botswana, Eritrea, Ethiopia, Guinea-Bissau, Cape Verde, Kenya, Lesotho, Mozambique, Namibia, South Africa, Tanzania, Uganda, Zambia and Zimbabwe.	– Emergency assistance – Health and population – Agriculture – Transport and communications – Industry – Education	– Promotion of democracy – Gender issues – NGOs – Environment
Switzerland	Development is based on the work of those communities called upon to participate in development activities, including: – Poverty reduction – Promotion of social equity – Sound management of public affairs – Environmental protection	37% of total ODA goes to Sub-Saharan Africa, primarily Benin, Madagascar, Rwanda, Mozambique, Tanzania, Mali and Burkina Faso.	– Agriculture – Emergency assistance – Education and training – Social and urban infrastructure – Industry	– Environment – Poverty reduction – NGOs – Gender issues – Participation and development
United States	Six main lines of development policy: – Sustainable development – democracy and human rights – Promotion of peace – Humanitarian aid – Promotion of prosperity – Diplomatic actions	Africa accounts for 20% of total aid, which is directed primarily towards South Africa, Botswana, Kenya, Zimbabwe, Zambia, Uganda, Tanzania, Malawi, Mozambique, Cameroon, Ethiopia, Eritrea, Côte d'Ivoire, Senegal and Ghana.	– Debt and economic management – Humanitarian and food aid – Health and population – Agriculture – Education – Trade and industry	– Private sector – Support for democracy – Environment – HIV/AIDS

a. Compiled using the following documents: DAC-OECD, *Development Co-operation, 1996 Report* (Paris, 1997); UNDP, *Donors' Aid Policies and Priorities* (New York, 1994); A. Cox and J. Healey, *Poverty reduction: A Review of Donor Strategies and Practices* (Paris: OECD, 1997); *Socio-Economic, Monetary and Resource Tables 1995*.

poverty alleviation measures (see Table 1 on core policies and priorities of the main bilateral donors in terms of poverty alleviation). [1]

Identifying poverty reduction as a specific objective avoids any confusion between the poverty problem and the development paradigm as a whole. However, this separation can make it difficult to ascertain the exact priority given to poverty, which in turn makes it harder to evaluate performance against targets.

However, to assess the effective involvement of donors and gain an understanding of their strategies and activities in the field of poverty reduction, it is not enough to simply establish whether or not they have included the topic of poverty reduction in their mandates and objectives. It is more pertinent to analyze the aims and strategies of donors in their efforts to explicitly or implicitly reduce poverty.

An examination of the development policies of the principal donors and multilateral development agencies reveals three main approaches to poverty reduction. The first involves promoting economic growth. Here, the main focus of the poverty reduction drive consists in achieving strong, sustainable growth. The World Bank, the IMF, and several bilateral donors, including Australia, France and the United States, as well as the ADB and the European Union, have all adopted this approach. The second consists mainly in providing for people's basic needs in terms of education, health, access to drinking water and food. Belgium, Germany, the Nordic countries and UNICEF, have opted for this approach. A third group, comprising mainly IFAD, UNDP, and the Netherlands, is attempting to develop a comprehensive and specific approach to poverty based on the concept of sustainable human development: the main three components of this approach are growth, fulfilment of basic needs and implementation of a participatory process.

3.1. Poverty reduction and economic growth

The position of the World Bank is considered as a reference in efforts to reduce poverty. Many donors hold similar views and have adopted policies in a similar vein. [2]

The World Bank views steady growth as a fundamental prerequisite for reducing poverty, a prerequisite that may even suffice in itself providing

1. See *Comparative Study on EU Aid for Poverty Reduction* (Paris: Dial, 1997) and L. de Boisdeffre, *Etude comparative sur l'aide à la réduction de la pauvreté* (Paris: Dial, 1996).

2. World Bank, *World Development Report 1990: Poverty* (Washington: Oxford University Press, 1990); K. Subbarao, *Lessons of 30 Years of Fighting Poverty* (Quebec, 1997); United Nations, *The Work of the United Nations System in Poverty Alleviation* (Geneva, 1995).

that the distribution of growth benefits the poor, notably through new employment opportunities. The Bank's strategy is therefore based on three areas of focus: i) identify a mode of growth that will include poor people and offer them opportunities for greater well-being. This will involve putting in place long-term macroeconomic and institutional reforms designed to increase demand for unskilled labor on the job market and to eliminate the factors that discriminate against small-scale entrepreneurs; ii) develop human capital by giving poor people better access to basic social services, mainly basic education, primary health care and family planning; and iii) provide a social safety net for those who cannot benefit from the advantages brought by economic reform (the extremely poor).

The central development paradigm of the World Bank can thus be seen to focus on economic growth and the development of the private market. Anti-poverty actions are simply measures to attenuate the negative effects of socially-excluding economic growth.

In this approach to poverty alleviation, economic growth is the fundamental consideration. Poverty reduction is seen as the result of a process based primarily on economic development and overall growth, rather than on a strategy implemented with the specific aim of helping poor people. Donors who have opted for a strategy of this type, in which targeted actions are implemented only as part of emergency operations (social safety nets, social protection for vulnerable groups, aid for the poorest) include France, the UK, the United States, the ADB and the European Union.

Strategies to promote steady, sustainable economic growth generally focus on structural economic reform: growth, particularly in agriculture; the promotion of productive infrastructure (transport, energy, communication); and access to technology, credit and employment. The second aspect to be considered, alongside economic development, is the building of human capital. This depends primarily on initiatives to develop basic education and heath. Last, specific aid programs are put in place for the poorest and most vulnerable groups. These may take the form of social safety nets, in the case of the World Bank, or support for vulnerable groups through social development funds, in the case of France or the ADB, for example. These social safety nets or social funds are international income support programs designed to protect individuals and households who are unable to provide for their own needs in the short or long term. These initiatives are measures designed to alleviate the negative effects of market conditions rather than a genuine poverty reduction strategy.

The World Bank, the IMF and the ADB have adopted an essentially quantitative approach to poverty. In operational terms, this approach takes the form of specific actions that seek to reduce poverty by improving productivity and increasing income and employment in poor regions.

Box 6.3.
Strategy of the World Bank in poverty reduction

The Country Assistance Strategy (CAS) set up by the Bank originally focused on five areas in its description of measures to be taken: labor-intensive growth, development of the private sector, improved management of the public sector, development of human resources and environmental protection. However, these strategies had no clearly defined objectives, nor did they initiate an in-depth discussion on the best way to help poor people. Focusing heavily on long-term growth, they did not take concrete measures to reduce poverty.

Today, efforts to alleviate poverty are part of a general Country Assistance Strategy, involving a close partnership between the authorities and civil society, commitment from the government and pro-poor social services programs.

Moreover, an examination of the Bank's 406 projects shows that the main objective of the Bank's operations in Africa is to establish favorable conditions for long-term growth. A number of projects include components favorable to poor people and rapid progress is possible provided that public expenditure is reallocated.

The Bank recognizes that many adjustment programs have no impact on the distribution of additional growth, even though a number of programs include components favoring poor people. Investments in infrastructure (electricity, telecommunications, roads, ports) have little direct impact on poor people in the short term and tend to bring benefits for the cities rather than for rural areas.

In order to have a direct impact on poor people, projects seeking to build capacity must focus on the development of small or micro companies. But out of 41 projects, only one had a component of this type. Clearly, much remains to be done!

The Bank spent $2,339.3 million between 1992 and 1994 and $1,732.1 million between 1995 and 1997 on non-targeted services projects in the areas of education, health and water in urban areas. The objective of these programs in 1992-94 was to raise poor people's incomes, to improve employment opportunities and to increase the availability of social services. However, little is known about their real impact.

Over the same periods, the Bank spent $1,549.6 million and $1,450.3 million respectively on the provision of services targeting basic education, primary health care, food security and social funds, for modest unit costs. For the most part, beneficiaries were involved in the formulation of projects, most of which sought to deliver social services to poor people (Madagascar and Mauritania).

An examination of the rural development portfolio shows a sharp drop in loans for rural roads since 1995, viewed against loans for the road sector as a whole.

Similarly, the program for loans in the water sector gives priority to urban systems and does not meet the priorities of rural communities, even though some progress has been seen recently, in Benin for example.

With respect to education and health, the situation is not as mediocre.

The 1996-1998 action plan for Africa made provision for loans of between $0.9 billion and $1.3 billion for education, and between $0.6 billion and $1.3 billion for health. As a result, the volume of direct loans favoring the development of human resources and poverty reduction has risen to 38% of total planned loans.

Efforts focus on primary education and on a range of independent actions in the short, medium and long to promote health care, the accent being on basic services.

Last, agriculture accounts for just 13% of total loans and less than 20% of projects. Around a third of agricultural loans are classed as targeting poor people.

The World Bank has taken a critical look at its own actions. It realizes that the country assistance strategies have minimal impact on poor people and appears to regret that it did not work with the beneficiaries to set up small-scale decentralized programs in favor of rural communities in low-potential regions. The Bank recognizes that it under-estimated the time required to make substantial progress against poverty in Africa and that it did not take sufficient account of the differences between countries and changing national situations. The Bank acknowledges that it does not have a sufficient understanding of what causes poverty and how to remedy it.

In the table below, the Bank lists its current projects seeking to promote growth: (US$ millions)

	Financial years 1992-94	*Number of projects*	*Financial years 1995-97*	*Number of projects*
Structural adjustment	2,848.1	29	2,222.0	32
Infrastructure	1,094.7	19	1,363.3	29
Capacity building	736.8	41	978.2	38
Miscellaneous	226.4	7	87.0	4
Total	4,906.0	96	4,549.5	103

Source: World Bank, Poverty Reducation: Progress and challenges in the 1990s, Washington, 1997.

Other donors also believe that poverty reduction is linked to economic growth, but they have adopted a multidimensional approach to the problem. Their actions seek to improve the well-being of the poor and give them greater access to productive resources. Increasingly, this approach is focusing on the need for the participation and empowerment of poor people.

3.2. Poverty reduction and fulfilment of basic needs

Other donors prefer to support actions aimed at meeting the main needs of poor people, such as basic education, primary health care and nutrition.

Table 6.4. – Policies and strategies implemented by multilateral donors to reduce poverty [a]

Organization	Aid policies	Sectors	Themes
African Development Bank	Promote the economic development and social progress of members through social and economic growth, promote public and private investment and support development plans and policies. Promote regional integration.	– Agriculture – Infrastructure – Transport and communications – Industry – Health – Education	– Environment – Poverty reduction – Gender – Health/Population – NGOs
European Union	Four objectives: – Economic development – Regional and international integration – Poverty reduction – Consolidation of the rule of law	– Agriculture – Economic management – Education – Health – Infrastructure – Transport and communications – Trade	– Poverty reduction – Human rights – Environment – Gender issues
International Monetary Fund	– Facilitate increased world trade with a view to increasing employment, income and productive capacity – Promote stability in trade and public finances – Put in place a system of international payment and transfer and limit restrictions on foreign trade – Encourage macro-economic reform.	– Economic management and debt – Development management	– Alleviate poverty by minimizing the harmful effects of reforms on poor people
World Bank	The main objective is to raise living standards in developing countries by providing loans, credit and advice, and also by encouraging other investors to participate. Against this backdrop, one of the main objectives is to reduce poverty and promote sustainable development through: – efficient use of the labor force – access to basic social services – protection of vulnerable groups.	– Economic management and debt – Agriculture and rural development – Education – Health – Infrastructure – Food aid	– Environment – HIV/AIDS – Gender – Poverty reduction

a. United Nations, *The Work of the United Nations System in Poverty Alleviation* (Geneva, 1995); DAC-OECD, *Development Co-operation, 1996 Report* (Paris, 1997); African Development Bank, *Annual Report 1996*.

To this end, a number of donors have opted for specific actions based on a policy dialogue or direct financial aid, the objective being to channel public spending towards basic social services. The 20/20 Initiative, set up by UNICEF and UNDP, adopted by the international community at the Copenhagen Summit and supported by a number of donors (Belgium, Germany and the Nordic countries) is considered to provide donors with a relevant and useful indicator on poverty reduction and human and social development. Pursuing efforts to meet basic needs more effectively, Spain, the UK, the United States, the World Bank and other donors have decided to significantly increase the proportion of aid intended for the social sectors. Nevertheless, this area is not the main focus of donors' efforts in poverty reduction and the total amount remains modest with respect to the objectives of the 20/20 Initiative.

In general, the donors above do not focus exclusively on efforts to satisfy basic needs, even though they believe that this is an essential condition for reducing poverty. Their actions take place within a broader strategy whose areas of focus include economic development, particularly with respect to the living standards of poor people and, more specifically, poor people in rural areas. Reflecting this, the donors are providing substantial support for small farmers and encouraging intensified agricultural research, aimed at fostering job creation, and the development of activities linked to access to microcredit. Particular attention is being given to the management of natural resources, environmental protection and participatory grassroots development.

Increasingly, donors are according greater importance to two topics: reducing the exclusion of poor people and increasing their empowerment. These objectives — often expressed implicitly — are shared by all donors, regardless of whether their main concern is to boost economic growth or to fulfil basic needs. This has important implications for efforts to identify and target poor people in their communities. It means that issues related to institutions, participation and capacity-building are recognized as being of fundamental importance in efforts to alleviate poverty. Lastly, it is important to stress the particular efforts made to reduce discrimination against women. All donors acknowledge that progress in this area will play an essential role in reducing poverty.

Looking beyond the varying options adopted in poverty reduction, we can therefore see that the policies implemented by donors are gradually converging, moving towards a multidimensional standpoint based on the principles of human development advocated by UNDP.

Box 6.4.
Poverty reduction strategy under Belgian cooperation

Economic growth brings about prosperity, but this prosperity must be equitably distributed. That is why social development must contribute to significant improvement of indicators used by the UNDP to calculate the human development index of a country.

Keen on contributing to this social development, the Belgian cooperation focuses particularly on:

(1) Negotiating the introduction of social standards in general bilateral cooperation agreements so as to guarantee minimal rights to the populations. This means that special reference will be made to abiding by the five basic principles adopted by ILO (International Labor Organization): (i) freedom of property owners' syndicate; (ii) banning of slavery; (iii) no discrimination against sex, race or ideology; (iv) banning of all forms of forced labor; (v) banning of child labor.

The same respect for the human being must be part of international trade relations. The latter must take into account the ecological, social and ethnic clauses and identify products manufactured with dignity. The objective of our international cooperation rests indeed on dignity and on the emancipation of the human being.

(2) Negotiating the integration of the 20/20 clause, adopted during the Copenhagen Social Summit, into general bilateral cooperation agreements urging the beneficiaries to devote at least 20% of their public budget to social projects (if these countries have not reached this percentage yet) and donors to invest at least 20% of their assistance into social domains.

(3) To assist in developing (bottom-up) social security systems required for protection against poverty.

(4) Focusing its assistance on the sectors focusing on social development: public health, agriculture and food security, education, basic infrastructures, consolidation of society).

(5) Supporting initiatives related to social economy because they guarantee the participation of the local population, ensure local ownership through joint management and, offer immediate response to social needs locally felt.

(6) To fight any form of discrimination based on gender and assist the most vulnerable groups of the population such as (ethnic) minorities, local populations, etc. Given that in these population groups women are often doubly discriminated against, additional attention must be paid to their involvement in development initiatives.

Source: "Policy Plan for International Cooperation" Secretariat of State in charge of Development Cooperation, Belgium, 1998.

3.3. *Poverty reduction from the standpoint of sustainable human development*

Efforts to address the poverty problem from the perspective of human poverty generally cover a number of issues: economic growth, access to

Table 6.5. – Agencies of the United Nations system and poverty reduction

Organization	Poverty reduction policy	Main poverty reduction actions
ECA (Economic Commission for Africa)	Poverty cannot be eradicated without steady economic growth bringing benefits for the greatest number. The main aim of the Commission in this respect is to strengthen the capacity of each country to take into account the needs of beneficiaries and to promote their full participation.	– Building governments' capacity to meet the basic needs of poor people – Building capacity for population issues, HIV/AIDS, family planning and health – Building capacity for environmental protection and the management of natural resources – Improving housing – Agriculture and rural development
FAO	Reduce poverty in rural areas by bringing about substantial improvements in agriculture and rural development, particularly in Asia and Africa, where most poor people live.	– Analysis and support for policies aimed at reducing the negative impact of structural adjustment on poor people – Food and nutritional security – Greater access for poor people to productive resources, including land – Support for grassroots organizations – Advancement of rural women – Promoting the inclusion of poor people in local-level decision-making in rural areas
IFAD	The sole mandate of this organization is to eradicate rural poverty.	Activities targeting poor people in rural areas: – Agricultural development through irrigation schemes and enhanced productivity – Development of fisheries and livestock farming – Credit for agricultural activities – Conservation of soil and water resources

Table 6.5. – Agencies of the United Nations system and poverty reduction *(suite)*

Organization	Poverty reduction policy	Main poverty reduction actions
ILO	Three main fundamental objectives: – Reduce poverty – Promote democracy – Protect workers As part of the above objectives, the ILO focuses on poor workers and on the aspects of economic growth linked to labor-intensive activities and appropriate technologies. The objective is to stimulate strong economic growth in order to develop productive employment.	– Studies and analyses on the structure and trends of links between employment and poverty – Support for self-employment and small businesses in rural and urban areas – Greater access for poor people to credit, production resources and markets – Support for women producers in the informal sector and in rural areas – Building the capacity of producers in the informal sector and rural areas. – Social safety nets
UNDP	UNDP's overarching goal is to eradicate poverty. All its activities are directed towards and assessed in terms of this objective. Poverty eradication is considered to be the most effective way to strengthen a country's capacity and thus to promote sustainable people-centered development and safeguard the planet for future generations.	– Sustainable employment and livelihoods – Advancement of women – Environmental protection and regeneration – Governance and empowerment In this respect, building national capacities to alleviate poverty and encouraging grassroots participation are considered to be two of the main topics.
UNESCO	Education does not guarantee economic well-being, but it strengthens individuals. Basic education creates or consolidates the necessary conditions for poverty reduction through its dynamic effects on the population and its impact on social, cultural, economic and political life.	– Basic education – Literacy
UNFPA	A strategy focused on the poorest countries, providing support for the social sectors necessary to sustainable development. The strategy focuses on those suffering from inadequate reproductive health. As a result, activities are concentrated on the very poorest.	– Reproductive health – Population and development strategies – Gender issues

Table 6.5. – Agencies of the United Nations system and poverty reduction *(suite)*

Organization	Poverty reduction policy	Main poverty reduction actions
UNHCR	The HCR acts as a catalyst in the management of problems linked to refugees. It seeks to ensure that activities in favor of refugees and displaced persons are integrated in development activities. In this respect, the HCR helps to eradicate poverty.	– Food and emergency aid – Support for refugees and displaced persons – Support for development activities related to refugees and displaced persons
UNICEF	UNICEF considers access to basic social services as the best and most effective way to combat the various manifestations of poverty. The organization seeks to deliver the basic social services necessary for the survival, protection and development of women and children. As stated in the 20/20 Initiative, basic social services comprise drinking water and sanitation, primary health care and family planning services, basic education and nutrition programs.	– Implementing the 20/20 Initiative. – Basic education – Primary health care and family planning – Safe drinking water and sanitation – Nutrition programs – Assessment of poverty among women and children
WFP	The WFP focuses on food for poor people as part of food for work programs.	– Promoting the productive use of poor people's greatest resource, i.e. their labor, through food for work programs – Supporting and expanding social services for poor people – Providing safety nets for the poorest people: refugees, displaced persons, victims of natural disasters and the chronically poor
WHO	The ultimate objective of the WHO is for all individuals to enjoy as good a level of health as possible. To this end, a particular focus is placed on people in the poorest countries of the world.	– Intensifying cooperation with the 26 poorest countries – Building the capacity of the health sector in the poorest countries – Targeting the poorest populations and setting up specific health programs

resources for poor people, fulfilment of basic needs, and topics linked to capacity-building and the participation of poor people in the decision-making that will affect their lives and in the implementation of poverty reduction programs. This view is shared by most of the agencies of the United Nations system (with the exception of the IMF and the World Bank) and by the Netherlands. Moreover, many donors whose strategies are focused on efforts to meet basic needs are gradually converging towards this comprehensive, human and multidimensional approach.

Against this background, the objective is to support the implementation of a comprehensive and multidimensional poverty reduction process, taking into account the different factors inherent to human poverty. The idea is to reverse the development paradigm and to place poverty reduction at the heart of the development process. UNDP appears to be playing a leading role in disseminating and establishing this concept of human poverty.

In general, efforts to reduce human poverty cover most of the concepts listed above, with a particular focus on the factors below:
– a process of efficient, equitable economic development that includes poor people and that has a positive impact on their lives;
– the definition of specific national poverty reduction programs and strategies, centered on human poverty;
– access to basic social services for poor people (basic education and literacy, primary health care, drinking water and sanitation, maternal and child health, nutrition);
– a policy to develop productive employment through the development of agriculture, SME/SMIs and microenterprises;
– the improvement of the long-term framework for identifying, assessing and understanding poor people and poverty, with a view to conducting long-term monitoring and evaluation;
– efforts to build capacity at macro, meso and micro level, and to empower poor people with a view to making them active stakeholders in the decision-making process and in the implementation of programs that concern them.

4. Thematic and sectoral approaches to poverty reduction

It is not the intention of this report to make an exhaustive analysis or list of the development actions, programs and projects of donors in the field of poverty reduction, but rather to broadly outline the main sectors and themes addressed by donors and international development agencies as part of their efforts to support national approaches to poverty reduction.

This overview will give a brief summary of the themes addressed by the donors in terms of resources or activities in the field of poverty reduction.

4.1. Research on poverty

The main studies on poverty in each country — whether profiles of poverty or public spending reviews — were conducted in the first instance by the World Bank, and subsequently continued by UNDP from a broader perspective based on a comprehensive and multidimensional analysis of poverty.

Studies on poverty in Sub-Saharan Africa suffer from variable quality. The conceptual framework necessary for an analysis of poverty appears to be inadequate. As a result, poverty tends to be studied through quantitative assessments based on income, which do not take sufficient account of the characteristics of poor people and communities. As a result, the picture painted by the analysis is flawed. Moreover, the results of studies on poverty are rarely incorporated into policy recommendations, and there is no systematic approach to establishing the necessary links between macro, meso and micro levels.

Nevertheless, a number of agencies of the United Nations system have sought — in different ways — to overcome these shortcomings. Some are focusing on their own areas of expertise or specific mandates — as in the case of FAO, IFAD, the ILO, UNICEF and the WHO — to conduct thematic or sectoral studies on poverty and health, agriculture, women and children. Others are adopting a comprehensive and innovative approach to assessing poverty and identifying its causes. This is the approach currently implemented by UNDP, as seen in earlier chapters.

Overall, donors have not invested to any great extent in systems to observe, monitor and evaluate programs set up to identify and reduce poverty. This situation reflects a general lack of interest in such systems, which are difficult to implement because of their prohibitive cost. As a result, most evaluations focus on the different activities, on the results obtained, and also on budget control. Results are rarely viewed against the objectives of poverty reduction. Some donors adopt a "project" approach to evaluating the efficiency of their programs, but the conclusions of such assessments are very general. They give no clear and detailed indication of the results achieved in terms of poverty reduction.

4.2. Social dimensions of structural adjustment and debt relief

At macroeconomic level, there have been few activities and projects focusing specifically on poverty reduction. In general, development partners tend to limit their efforts in this area to the social dimensions of structural adjustment and the debt problem.

4.2.1. Social dimensions of structural adjustment

The constraints and limitations of structural adjustment — as seen through its impact on poor communities — have highlighted the need for programs designed to attenuate the negative social impact of adjustment measures. [1] With reference to this point, it is important to stress the influence of UNICEF and the initiative commonly referred to as "adjustment with a human face". For UNICEF, the problem is not to establish whether adjustment makes poverty worse, but to see how adjustment programs can be refocused in order to increase the participation of poor people in the process of economic and social development and to ensure that vulnerable groups are well protected during periods of economic stagnation and austerity. The efforts of UNICEF in this area have greatly influenced the implementation of new adjustment programs, as illustrated by the Social Dimensions of Adjustment project.

The Social Dimensions of Adjustment (SDA) project supported by the ADB, UNDP and the World Bank, reflects the standpoint set out above. The aim is to encourage short-term action on the part of governments to attenuate the negative impact of adjustment on poor people.

More specifically, the objective is to give adjustment policies a social component through measures to provide safety nets for poor people. The social funds set up by France and the ILO are part of the same approach. The idea is to define specific instruments for the protection of groups identified as being particularly vulnerable to the impact of adjustment programs.

4.2.2. Debt relief initiatives

In earlier chapters, it was shown that the Sub-Saharan African countries are shackled by debt. The debt burden is an obstacle to economic growth and to the implementation of the — often costly — programs set up to alleviate poverty. At bilateral level, most donors have granted substantial debt relief over the past few years. Debt problems are now widely recognized as having significant impact on national growth and aid policies and, as a result, many bilateral donors — notably Australia, Canada, Denmark, Ireland, Luxembourg, the Netherlands, New Zealand, Sweden and Switzerland — no longer provide ODA in the form of loans. Other donors, notably Finland, are cutting back on this type of operation or, as in the case of Germany, no longer apply it to the poorest countries. Increasingly, bilateral aid is donated.

---

1. See G. Aho, S. Larivière et F. Martin, *Manuel d'analyse de la pauvreté: applications au Bénin* (Université Laval, PNUD, 1997); K. Subbarao, *Lessons of 30 Years of Fighting Poverty* (Quebec, 1997).

Box 6.5.

Scope for debt relief from HIPC creditors

The aggregate debt of HIPC creditors is divided — in roughly equal proportions — among Paris Club, multilateral institutions and non-OECD countries. The relative weight of these creditors, however, is very different when disaggregated at the country level. While debt concessionality plays an important role in determining relative servicing burdens, percentage shares of debt held by different creditors suggest where action needs to be taken. Multilateral debt figures importantly in this regard, accounting for more than 50 per cent of outstanding debt in 17 HIPCs: non-OECD and OECD bilateral creditors account for similarly high shares in five HIPCs respectively.

While potentially 41 HIPCs could ultimately benefit from the proposed HIPC debt initiative, eleven countries have been identified as likely near-term candidates given their debt profile, economic prospects and repayment schedules. There are questions as to whether the Paris Club debt relief will meet the specific needs of these countries, given the scope of previous Paris Club debt relief and restrictions on the range of eligible debt (e.g. ODA, short-term debt and post-cut-off-date debt are not eligible). On the other hand, reduced multilateral debt servicing obligations will provide welcome relief to this group.

Source: DAC-OECD, *Development Co-operation, 1996 Report* (Paris, 1997).

Moreover, bilateral donors have made significant efforts to forgive debt, both at unilateral level ($18 billion forgiven between 1990 and 1995), and within the framework of the Paris Club, through which $4.5 billion was converted into local-currency financing for programs on the environment, poverty reduction, health and education. A number of countries, including Canada, France, Switzerland and the United States, have set up debt relief initiatives, involving the cancellation, conversion or buyback of debt. Measures of this nature, which forgive or reduce debt, should have a highly favorable impact on development, but only if steps are taken to ensure the efficiency of this aid and to incorporate the issue of poverty reduction into initiatives set up to reduce debt. It is difficult to say to what extent these different initiatives have been beneficial for Sub-Saharan Africa to date.

Until recently, no solution had been found to the question of multilateral debt. Initiatives focused solely on bilateral debt. Nevertheless, the heavily indebted poor countries (HIPC) debt initiative should provide a basis on which to work out a coherent response to the problem.

An agreement has now been made through the Development Committee and the Interim Committee on the HIPC debt initiative. Financed by multilateral and bilateral creditors, the agreement is expected to cost between $5.6 billion and $7.7 billion, depending on such factors as the export performance of debtor countries. Under the terms of the agreement, the gradual debt relief granted by bilateral donors and the private sector will be backed up by multilateral debt relief totaling an amount that is sufficiently high for the countries concerned to return to a sustainable level of debt. It is important to note that this initiative seeks primarily to integrate countries into the globalization process rather than help them to reduce poverty.

Burkina Faso, Côte d'Ivoire and Uganda — three countries in which external debt is estimated at over 200% of export earnings — joined the group of countries eligible for the multilateral debt relief initiative in 1997. The objective is to lower the net present value of debt-to-exports ratio to 200% or below. Nevertheless, it is important to stress the slow pace and the stringent demands of the process, as well as the small number of African countries likely to benefit.

The G7 meeting on HIPC II and PRSP (Poverty Reduction Strategy Papers) held in Paris in December 10, 1999 announced that four countries (Uganda, Bolivia, Mozambique and Mauritania) are on track for receiving debt relief in January 2000 under the Enhanced HIPC Initiative.

In addition to these four, Mali (April), Senegal (February), Benin (February), Burkina (March), and Tanzania (March) could begin receiving debt relief depending on decisions to be taken by the IMF/WB Spring Meetings. The decision points (in brackets) are based on Bank and Fund staff assessments about when the necessary documents would be ready.

On the issue of implementation of the PRSP's, there was a consensus among the G7 that, retroactively, some countries should move quickly to decision points, where they would begin to receive interim debt service relief and exit from the programme (i.e. receive unconditional debt stock reduction) when they have a PRSP approved by the Boards of the Bank/ Fund. There was also a consensus among the G7 that new non-retroactive cases should have a PRSP in place by the decision point and reach the completion point when they have met targets outlined in the PRSP. The debt reduction efforts will be very important for the annual debt service, national budget and basic social services, which must benefit from this initiative.

Box 6.6.

Questions for Country Authorities to Consider When Designing a PRSP

A. Obstacles to poverty reduction
- What are the key patterns of poverty in its various dimensions?
- How are these influenced by the level and pattern of growth; public policy; public service provision; social and institutional functioning; and by exogenous shocks?
- What are the main obstacles to more rapid growth and to spreading the benefits of growth to the poor?

B. Objectives and targets
- What targets for the various dimensions of poverty reduction have been established?
- What are the targets for selected intermediate indicators?

C. Strategy/Action Plan
- What are the priority public policies to increase growth and reduce poverty?
- What institutional changes are needed to implement the strategy?
- How can public spending and institutions be made more efficient and responsive to the needs of the poor?

D. Monitoring and Evaluation Systems
- What is the framework for monitoring progress of the strategy and what

is the involvement of civil society in the process of evaluation?
- What safeguards ensure the transparency and accountability of public budgeting and expenditure?

E. External Assistance and the External Environment
- What level of external assistance is expected to be available to support the country's efforts?
- Could more assistance be effectively absorbed, and if so, what would be the likely impact on poverty reduction goals?
- How does technical assistance, from all sources, support implementation of the strategy?
- What would be the effect of greater access to partner country markets on growth and poverty reduction?

F. The participatory Process
- What was the nature of the participatory process and how were the views and interests of the poor incorporated?
- What impact did the process have on the formulation and content of the strategy?

Source: IMF and IDA Poverty Reduction Strategy, Papers-operational issues. Discussion Paper, December 1999.

4.3. Institutional support, good governance and the participatory approach

One innovative and essential focus of donors' efforts to reduce poverty lies in institutional support and the promotion of good governance at macro, meso and micro levels.

Box 6.7.

Guiding Principles for Dialogue for Democratic Development

I. Democratic principles are universal

The values of democracy are by and large universally shared and find their origin and inspiration in diverse cultures.

II. Democratic systems may vary

The democratic political system is the institutional and procedural expression of these values. It varies from country to country, depending on social, cultural, demographic and historical factors. Democratic systems are unique. Differences in systems, procedures and institutions, however, do not mean that any one system is qualitatively better or worse than any other system.

III. Democratization is a process

The time factor, however, does introduce a valid classification in stages of democratic development, along a democratic continuum. This can rage from non-democratic, via systems in transition to democracy and newly-established democracies, to consolidated democracies. With this classification — which basically indicates the development of democratic systems of governance — a qualitative evolution can be assessed and distinguished from a more static framework. A more dynamic framework reflecting a democratic political culture may thus be developed. This would allow for the identification of a differentiated approach tailored to the specific stage of democratization.

IV. Democracy is never completed

It is not a finished product, even in consolidated democracies. Democracy and democratization are two sides of the same coin. Democracy must continually reinvent and adapt itself, hence the possi-

bility of reciprocity in the dialogue about sustainable democratic development. Futhermore, the complexities of the democratic governance system and the interations among the systems internationally, make it advantageous to share experiences and knowledge in these fields.

V. Democracy must be sustainable

To be sustainable, democracy cannot be imported. It must be « home-grown ». Locally-owned and locally-driven democratic reform agendas stand the best chance of being sustainable. The « ownership » of the democratization process is key to its sustainability. The policy needs to develop its political systems, based on universal democratic values, according to the unique needs of their societies and at a pace that can be managed by available skills and resources.

VI. Democracy is inclusive

Democracy encompasses the state, civil society and the private sector, all share joint and complementary responsibilities for its advancement. Inclusion and participation are two key dimensions of democratization. This inclusive and participatory approach constitutes the basis for a pluralistic partnership.

VII. Democracy assistance must be based on partnership

External support to the democratization process must be based on dialogue and mutual obligation found in a common commitment to democracy and a shared understanding of the challenges of democratization. This should be founded on the notion of joint responsibility and shared commitments.

Source:European Commission. The challenge of the partnership beetween the European Union and the ACP states. 1998.

Box 6.8.

French Development Fund (Agence Française de Développement):
Participatory development and poverty eradication

The objective consists of making investments or conducting new activities as close as possible to the populations concerned, so as to facilitate "insertion", "ownership" and "durability" beyond the support phase. These grant consuming approaches are fully justified for countries where there are no institutional settings likely to help organize, structure and meet the expectations of the populations. Very often, they are implemented by non-governmental organizations that can get involved over a long period in activities requiring the mobilization of the "civil society".

Three intervention domains were given greater importance: rural area, urban area and support to decentralized systems. Proximity projects, therefore, target the poor populations and, in that respect, they fit in line with the poverty alleviation action advocated by the major bilateral assistance bodies (World Bank and UNDP).

In the urban area, operations funded by the FDF are based on the mobilization of the population. For instance, for district development in Porto-Novo and Cotonou (Benin), the solution was to resort to "labor intensive" actions making it possible to distribute income and to install equipment. In Bamako (Mali), the constitution of groups of qualified youth made it possible to promote the collection of household waste and user groups facilitated district level drinking water provision and management.

In the rural area, local development operations consist in facilitating the funding of small projects defined by the populations towards sustainable land development and, hence the preservation of natural resources. Again, the approach gives greater importance to population mobilization and grouping like in Burkina Faso, Ganzourgou, where an increasing portion of project funding tends to be paid by local communities.

Decentralized financial systems address populations who have no access to conventional banking system due to lack of security, illiteracy or distance. Cumulated commitments of the FDF for the 1987-1996 period amount to about FF 400 billion for assistance to some thirty programmes. These supports are meant to meet the populations' strong demand for (savings and credit) financial services, in view of establishing financially and institutionally self-sufficient networks.

Finally, since 1995, the FDF has been trying to promote viable organizations targeting very small enterprises. The objective consists in increasing the technicality, productivity and managerial quality of these (trade and craft) enterprises.

Source: FDF Activity Report, 1996, Paris, 1997.

Most donors agree — albeit with slightly differing standpoints — on the need to stress the principles of good governance and adapt the overall institutional framework. To this end, they are supporting decentralization and devolution initiatives that will improve the availability of services meeting the needs of poor people. Moreover, donors feel that it is essential to build the institutional capacities of poor people and increase their participation in the development actions that concern them.

As a general rule, the main priorities are to define an institutional framework favorable to poor people, encourage the participation of poor people and reduce discrimination. Canada, for example, is striving to build the capacities of organizations working with poor people, while Germany is highlighting self-advancement and the organization of groups of poor people in the long term. Sweden is seeking to promote local authorities and develop electoral processes that will increase the participation of poor people and women, and the UK sets particular store by a participatory approach.

Further, one of the main characteristics of poverty reduction programs, notably at meso and micro level, is that implementation tends to make substantial — and sometimes virtually exclusive — use of NGOs. Many bilateral and multilateral donors are working increasingly with NGOs, which are considered to play a vital role in providing a direct interface with poor people. Nevertheless, it should be borne in mind that NGOs — despite their growing importance — still play only a limited role in the definition and implementation of donor strategies for poverty reduction

4.4. Access to productive resources and factors of production

For many donors, giving poor people greater access to productive resources is a fundamental condition for reducing poverty. Access to natural resources, especially in rural areas, is considered to be one of the most effective ways of improving the living standards of poor households. For this reason, many donors have defined development strategies incorporating a specific component focusing on agricultural development and natural resource management, aimed at poor people in rural areas.

Austria, Belgium, Canada, Denmark, France, Ireland, Italy, Japan, Norway, the Netherlands, Sweden, the UK, the United States, the European Union, FAO and IFAD consider that the best way to reduce poverty in rural areas is to increase agricultural productivity and provide substantial support for rural development. Key instruments of this policy are natural resources (land, wood and water) accessible to poor people, appropriate technology (irrigation, traction, etc.) and the principles of participatory management of the environment.

However, since land-access policies often require land reforms, they are rarely backed by development partners. The same applies to appropriate technologies, an area not widely supported by donors, exceptions being the Belgium, the UK, UNDP and the World Bank.

The other main focus of efforts to improve access to productive resources in urban and rural areas is the introduction of microfinancing instruments. Most donors, whether bilateral or multilateral, have set up microcredit programs or projects for poor people. These initiatives target either the urban poor, to promote self-employment and SMEs/SMIs, or the rural poor, to promote income-generating activities. Access to credit for poor people — through specific projects promoting employment in urban areas or a microcredit module in an integrated rural development program — is considered by donors to play an essential role in poverty reduction.

4.5. Availability and accessibility of social services and the 20/20 Initiative

Access to basic social services is viewed as having a vital role in the poverty reduction strategies adopted by donors, alongside economic growth, employment and capacity-building.

The World Bank's Social Dimensions of Adjustment projects have always focused on access to education and health care. Working through public spending reviews or through the implementation of projects in education and health, the projects have sought primarily to increase the services available in these two areas. France, the ADB, the European Union, the IMF and the World Bank have highlighted the importance of government spending on education and health. However, a recent IMF study showed mixed results in these areas. Although 66 developing countries studied by the IMF increased spending on education by 0.1% of GDP between 1986 and 1996, a closer analysis of the data relating to Africa shows a decrease in real spending per capita of around 0.5%. In terms of health, although spending in these 66 countries grew by 0.32% of GDP between 1986 and 1996, real spending per capita shows a contrasting situation. The increase was around 4.1% in Asia, compared with just 2% in Africa.

Several donors, including the Netherlands, the Nordic countries and several agencies of the United Nations system including UNDP and UNICEF, have stressed the need to refocus these projects on key social services, notably basic education, primary health care, reproductive health, nutrition and access to drinking water and sanitation. This is because programs highlighting social services in general do not necessarily target the poorest population groups, since they often focus on urban areas and large-scale infrastructure, such as universities, central hospitals or urban water supply.

In response to this situation, Belgium, the Netherlands and the Nordic countries are supporting the joint efforts of UNDP, UNFPA, UNICEF, UNESCO and the WHO with respect to the 20/20 Initiative. If essential services are targeted by efforts to increase access to social services, it should be possible to reach poor population groups more effectively and meet their fundamental needs.

Box 6.9.

The Objectives of the 20-20 Initiative

Proposed for the first time in the 1992 World Human Development Report, the 20/20 Initiative was picked up again in 1995 by the World Social Development Summit. It lays down guiding principles for mobilizing the necessary resources that will give access to basic social services to everybody. The general idea is that the countries should allocate about 20% of their budget to these services — and the donors should allocate 20% of their financial assistance — which would be enough to ensure universal coverage by these services.

In April 1996, at the invitation of Norway and Netherlands, representatives of 40 countries met in Oslo with NGOs, United Nations Organizations and the Bretton Woods institutions in order to discuss the implementation of the 20/20 Initiative. They explored solutions for designing agreements between public authorities and donors in view of improving the funding of basic social services. The Oslo Consensus that resulted stimulated support action and provided a common definition of these services to encompass "basic education, primary health care including gynecology and obstetrics and population oriented programs, nutrition programs, access to drinking water and to sanitation structures as well as institutional means to provide these services".

How has the situation developed since? Based on available incomplete data, it is assumed that 13% of national budgets and 10% of financial assistance provided by donors are presently allocated to basic services. For some years now, however, some progress is being observed. Under the OECD Development Committee, the donor countries are presently discussing means to improve the control of bilateral assistance related to basic services.

In Oslo, some developing countries expressed their interest in the continuation of 20/20 type development agreements signed with the donor community. UNICEF is assisting those countries in examining budgeted expenditure and opportunities for reorganizing public expenditure in favor of basic social services. As for the UNDP, it is assisting the countries in integrating their social services into larger scale endeavors to reduce poverty.

The Oslo Consensus led to convening consultative groups and round table conferences to take stock of the money allocated to basic social services in the light of the guiding principles of the 20/20 Initiative. Ethiopia considers the reform and funding of education as one of its first agenda items of the forthcoming meeting of its consultative group. All these developments suggest that the developing countries and the donor community are paying more attention — and financial means — to guarantee access to basic social services for everybody.

Source: World Human Development Report, 1997, UNDP, 1997.

4.6. Food security and the environment

Food security and environmental protection are another major focus of donor policies in poverty reduction. Looking beyond efforts to raise incomes, strong support for agriculture and rural development is considered to be essential for food security. Many donors have made this requirement a central component of their development strategies, providing either emergency aid or long-term support. Nevertheless, it is important to note that this area was already a focus of particular attention for donors even before the theme of poverty reduction became in itself one of the objectives of development. Overall, no thinking or strategies appear to be in preparation at present to show the links between food security and poverty reduction.

The same is true of the environment. All the donors have adopted this fundamental topic and associated it with poverty reduction. However, the close, interactive links between the environment and poverty are rarely highlighted. With the notable exception of Canada, the Netherlands, the Nordic countries and the agencies of the United Nations system, few partners make any real attempt to establish conceptual and operational links between the environment and poverty in their development cooperation programs.

5. Conclusions

The World Summit for Social Development organized in Copenhagen in 1995 gave the international community an opportunity to make a firm commitment to eradicating poverty. This determination to address the causes of poverty has since been reiterated on many occasions, as part of the United Nations Year and Decade for the Eradication of Poverty, through the Special Initiative for Africa, and at meetings of donors organized by the OECD's Development Aid Committee (DAC). There appears to be genuine political will and commitment to supporting developing countries in their efforts to alleviate poverty.

However, a contrasting situation emerges after examination of the policies implemented and the aid flowing to poor countries and to the sectors particularly relevant to poverty reduction. The situation is characterized by i) a constant decrease in aid for Africa and LDCs and ii) a lack of clarity in the support provided for poverty reduction efforts by the international community.

The concept of poverty has no unanimously accepted definition, and the objective of eradicating poverty is not always clearly expressed in the mandates, strategies and development cooperation policies of donors, with the exception of certain multilateral donors in the United Nations system and Belgium, the Netherlands and Nordic donors. A number of significant shortcomings can be highlighted concerning the integration of poverty reduction in donors' policies and their support for the design of national poverty reduction strategies:

    – the very perception of the problem of poverty is recent and there is no operational consensus;

    – the mandates and objectives of donors with respect to poverty reduction are generally defined by their head office; the broad principles of international commitments are not necessarily taken into account and issues are not discussed with other donors, developing countries, or organizations associated with development, such as civil society and NGOs;

    – the priority of poverty reduction with respect to other development objectives is not always clearly expressed;

    – the relation between the poverty reduction objectives set out in donor documents on general development policy and the work conducted by donors in the field is not always clearly identified or put into practice;

    – donors rarely discuss poverty reduction policies and actions; the dialogue is often limited to an exchange of information;

    – little discussion takes place with recipient countries on sectoral policies and local policies to reduce poverty;

    – efforts to raise financing do not appear to be bearing fruit, insofar as it is possible to tell without reliable statistical indicators.

Looking at the main sectors and topics addressed by donors with respect to poverty reduction, it can be seen that efforts and activities tend to be concentrated in two or three sectors. Despite the commitment made by the international community at Copenhagen, only the World Bank and UNDP appear to be truly active in promoting a better understanding of the situation and encouraging the formulation of strategies, the other donors being very much on the fringe. The same applies to the monitoring and evaluation of poverty, for which little support is provided.

Donors appear to be concentrating almost exclusively on topics relating to the fulfilment of basic needs, food security and rural development, with a strong focus on topics relating to gender, the environment and the involvement of NGOs. However, we are also seeing an — as yet — timid increase in support for capacity-building at macro, meso and micro level. Despite this, there is little effort at present to establish relations between macroeconomics and poverty, the environment and poverty, and fair access to certain factors of production such as land or appropriate technologies. The policies and programs implemented by donors in the field of poverty reduction tend to have the following characteristics:

    – a limited interest in the importance of fiscal policy as the possible instrument of a redistribution policy, and in the links between macroeconomics and poverty.

– certain deficiencies in the conceptualization of poverty and in the capacity of initiatives to reach poor people: in project documents, the beneficiaries are rarely identified as specific groups. Even when the beneficiaries are more clearly defined, the distinction between the different layers of poverty is unclear. For example, "urban youth" includes the extremely poor, the poor and the non-poor;

– a growing interest in the situation of women. Donors are currently opting for an integrated approach to the situation of women;

– a relative lack of participation by poor beneficiaries in project design. Projects are identified by the central government or by the donors themselves, so they do not necessarily meet the needs of beneficiaries;

– innovative actions to increase institutional capacity and the sustainability (institutional, financial, technological and environmental) of projects: the sharing of costs and the adoption of a program-based approach rather than a project-based approach.

It can be seen that although poverty reduction is becoming an increasingly important component of donors' development policies, considerable efforts are still necessary to increase dialogue on policies and on financing, to harmonize concepts and operational approaches and to identify the most relevant activities in the area of poverty reduction. Nevertheless, due recognition should be given to the efforts made by the majority of donors to include this new paradigm in their development policies.

CHAPTER 7

UNDP support for national poverty reduction strategies

1. Role and characteristics of UNDP assistance for poverty reduction

1.1. Mandate from the World Summit for Social Development

At the World Summit for Social Development in Copenhagen in 1995, the heads of State and leaders of more than 180 countries recognized the worsening problem of poverty across the world and committed themselves to take action to reduce it.

The Copenhagen Declaration and Programme of Action that they ratified recognizes *"the urgent need for national strategies to substantially reduce generalized poverty, including measures to eliminate the structural barriers that prevent people from escaping poverty, with specific timetabled commitments to eliminating extreme poverty by a target date to be chosen by each country in the framework of its national context."*

In particular, governments promised to pursue the poverty eradication objective *"as an ethical, social, political and economic imperative for humanity"* by ensuring that *"people living in poverty have access to productive resources, including credit, land, education and training, technology, knowledge, information, and public services."* They committed themselves to:

"formulating or strengthening, as early as possible, and implementing national poverty reduction plans to address the structural causes of poverty, encompassing action on the local, national, subregional, regional and international levels. These plans should establish, within each national context, strategies and affordable time-bound goals and targets for the substantial reduction of overall poverty and the eradication of absolute poverty. In the context of national plans, particular attention should be given to employment creation as a means of eradicating poverty, giving appropriate consid-

eration to health and education, assigning a higher priority to basic social services, generating household income, and promoting access to productive assets and economic opportunities".

While recognizing that governments, in partnership with civil society, have prime responsibility for eradicating poverty in their own countries, the papers of the Summit for Social Development acknowledge the critical role the United Nations system should play in assisting developing countries. The point is made that cooperation between the specialized UN agencies, and international programs and associated funds should be improved at country level, in particular by strengthening the role of the Resident Coordinator on Operational Activities for the United Nations system. The Resident Representatives heading UNDP's 132 offices in developing countries act in this respect as coordinators of all the UN's operational development assistance. The Copenhagen Summit consequently gave UNDP a special mandate to *"organize United Nations system efforts towards capacity-building at the local, national and regional levels, and [...] support the coordinated implementation of social development programs through its network of field offices".*

The eradication of poverty is the development goal for the new millenium and a priority initiative for the United Nations Development Group (UNDGO) and of course UNDP. The Common Country Assessment (CCA) and the United Nations Development Assistance Framework (UNDAF), new instruments of cooperation, could provide a plateform to support the Government's process of integration of Poverty Reduction Strategy Paper (PRSP), the new conditionality Reform of the European Union, the Debt reduction initiative (HIPC I and II) and the 20/20 initiative.

1.2. UNDP's comparative advantages

The quality and extent of cooperation between African countries and the United Nations Development Programme depend on its proven comparative advantages in poverty reduction. UNDP has provided effective, appreciated support for producing governmental plans of action and national programs. It has the advantage of being an impartial and neutral development partner, and is therefore able to bring a special perspective on such matters as policy dialogue, formulation of strategies and operational programs, and raising financing. Its comparative advantages include:

i) **The universal scope of the action of UNDP and the United Nations system**, and their ability to identify, analyze and disseminate experience and development approaches that have been used in particular countries or regions, and support the exchange or transfer of technology and experience appropriate for the conditions of the recipient country or region;

ii) **Neutral cooperation**, without conditionalities and often adapted to the specific circumstances of the beneficiaries;

iii) **A multisectoral and cross-sectoral conception of development**, in harmony with the principles and priorities of sustainable human development;

iv) **A program approach** that seeks to take into consideration national development priorities and strategies, and use both consultation and coordination methods and the participatory procedures belonging to development operators and beneficiary communities;

v) **Sociogeographical targeting** of the most vulnerable social groups and the most disadvantaged areas;

vi) **Potential for coordinating the various funds and agencies of the United Nations system**, so as to harmonize the action of institutions and agencies with specific mandates;

vii) **Potential for advocacy** with the international community, particularly at roundtables and world summits held under the auspices of the United Nations.

Given the general characteristics of the United Nations system, and its major priorities, African governments and their development partners are pursuing the efforts and actions that have already begun so that the objectives of sustainable human development and the principles that guide it are increasingly translated into the day-to-day practice of development cooperation. The experience and know-how acquired by UNDP in the world and Sub-Saharan Africa are particularly relevant in the following fields:

i) National capacity-building

In international development cooperation, UNDP's major concern remains the provision of high-quality technical assistance to help developing countries acquire the national skills and capacities to implement their policies for growth and development. This involves building a capacity for macroeconomic, sectoral and regional analysis for the management of economic growth and social development. The United Nations system possesses, within its specialized agencies, recognized experience in perspective studies, strategic planning, programming, management, evaluation and monitoring of development programs and projects. The design, implementation and monitoring activities supported by the United Nations system generally involve considering regional development, decentralization, participation and good governance, and increasing use of national expertise and consultation in the framework of the implementation of the program approach.

The United Nations system provides beneficiary countries with useful experience and know-how in access to diversified sources of expertise and training throughout the world for economic and social development: (i) help in implementing innovative types of aid and cooperation such as Technical Cooperation among Developing Countries (TCDC), regional cooperation, Transfer of Knowledge Through Expatriate Nationals (TOK-TEN), (ii) the National Technical Cooperation Assessment and Programmes exercise (NATCAP), (iii) the United Nations Volunteers (UNV), and the use of support from NGOs and civil society organizations to implement programs and projects, and (v) accurate targeting of eligible groups, particularly the most disadvantaged, such as women, children, and other more specific social categories.

ii) Social development for poverty reduction

With its annual world human development report, which first appeared in 1990 and continues to reveal its universal application, and with the adoption by its Executive Board in 1994 of a plan of action called "Initiative for Change", redefining priorities to promote a new development culture, UNDP has decided to focus its action on the promotion and implementation of the concept of "sustainable human development" (SHD). This concept aims mainly at poverty reduction and improvement in the status of women, the development of employment and environmental protection. Efforts are concentrated on enabling communities to adopt the SHD approach and translate it into strategies for individuals, families, communities, villages, local authorities, peri-urban areas, towns, regions and countries, so as to contribute to both the emergence and fair redistribution of opportunities of growth for sustainable development.

The funds and agencies of the United Nations system, each under its own mandate, develop mechanisms and tools for making this concept operational. In particular the Special Initiative for Africa and the 20/20 Initiative jointly seek to make these recommendations operational and work to intensify poverty reduction operations.

• United Nations Special Initiative for Africa

This 1996 initiative by the UN Secretary-General, based on the findings of all the world summits and research done in Africa, refocused current priorities on four general themes: providing a chance for development in Africa by creating conditions of peace and cooperation favorable to progress; giving hope to the next generation by guaranteeing access to education, health care and permanent employment; strengthening institutional capacities to meet criteria of good governance; and responding significantly to the urgent survival needs of Africa's people.

To ensure the conditions for achieving the objectives involved in these general themes, the initiative recommends a strategy comprising five essential elements in order to meet in a concerted fashion the major challenges that threaten Africa: i) meeting people's needs for water resources to guarantee their food security and economic and social activities; ii) food security to be understood as the ability to have access to suitable nutritional standards while safeguarding natural resources and the environment and meeting the needs of women, who are to be seen as agents of development; iii) strengthening institutional capacities with the aim of consolidating peace and progress, with a major role accorded to civil society; iv) social progress through access to, and meeting basic human needs for, indeed rights to, education, health care and employment; v) raising internal and external financing, and debt relief.

- 20/20 Initiative

This initiative launched in 1994 jointly by five UN funds and agencies and endorsed by the Copenhagen Summit recommends a reallocation of national budgets and official development assistance in favor of basic social services, which would receive 20% of the total amounts raised by the internal and external sources of financing for development. This would be a way of putting into practice the objectives of the world summits to ensure that essential social sectors receive substantial resources to eradicate extreme poverty.

The initiative focuses particularly on the proper definition of the sectors eligible when criteria for allocating resources are being considered. They are the basic social services: primary health care, i.e. basic preventive and curative care, reproductive health care, including family planning, basic education, comprising pre-school education, primary schooling, literacy and skill training; nutrition, public hygiene and drinking water supply for rural, peri-urban and urban areas.

iii) Raising financing and coordination of aid

- At government level

UNDP is an active advocate of national capacity-building for raising financing, managing and coordinating aid, and the impact this has on development. The roundtable conferences, either general or thematic/sectoral, devised by UNDP are a useful tool for this. They set up, with UNDP support, a permanent policy dialogue and monitoring/evaluation of the implementation of development programs. UNDP's role is mainly to act as an interface between governments and their development partners. A large number of African least developed countries have opted for the donor roundtable process in order to achieve policy dialogue and optimize fundraising, and manage and coordinate aid effectively. Some general and thematic roundtables have addressed national poverty reduction policies and strategies in Africa.

• At UN system level

UNDP plays a key role in supporting the coordination of the UN system. For example, the roundtable process has been made easier by promoting the concept of UN System Resident Coordinator, the aim of which is precisely to improve complementarity between agencies. Particular stress is laid on mechanisms for consultation and coordination between the various relevant agencies operating within the UN system. This approach is intended to achieve greater harmonization and synergy in policies, strategies and programs, and greater effectiveness and impact of UN System operations in the field, so as to provide a coordinated, coherent response to requests from governments.

Box 7.1.

The UNDP and the Bretton Woods institution:
close collaboration in the PRSP exercise

Further to the high-level meeting the UNDP Administrator, Mr. Mark Malloch Brown, had in Washington DC, on 21 January 2000, with M. James Wolfensohn, President of the World Bank, and to a meeting Mr Zéphirin Diabre had with the IMF on 13 January 2000, UNDP, World Bank and IMF confirmed that there was an added value in having a strong partnership between the three organizations (i) to leverage upon existing good practices and (ii) to help the governments of programme countries in closing, optimally, the institutional and policy gaps in the design and implementation of sound and efficient poverty reduction strategies.

This partnership should be guided by the following principles:

i.   ensure that the Government keep the leadership role throughout the exercise;

ii. help countries conduct an effective participatory process in the PRSP exercise;

iii. build on existing work and hence avoid duplication and redundancy;

iv. maintain a regular channel of communication and information amongst the three institutions and reinforce close and transparent working relationships and whenever and wherever feasible, organize joint missions in support of the preparation of the PRSPs;

v.   support capacity development of Government and Civil Society, in the process of the PRSP exercise, especially for poverty monitoring.

Source: UNDP, February 2000.

In December 1999, the Executive Boards of the IMF/IBRD endorsed a new policy instrument, the Poverty Reduction Strategy Paper (PRSP) to serve as a common context for Bank and Fund interventions in low-income countries receiving concessional assistance. Beginning with the 41 countries classified as heavily indebted poor countries (HIPC), the PRSP will, over the next couple of years, be applied to an additional 30 countries receiving financing from IDA or ESAF.

Box 7.2.

Burkina Faso – Pilot Case on Conditionality Reform

In 1997-1998, a two-year pilot was launched under the coordination of the EC with the objectives of:
• Improving and strengthening government ownership in program implementation;
• Smoothing aid flows and reducing disruptive suspensions;
• Enhancing aid effectiveness through program monitoring on the basis of performance indicators;
• Improving donor coordination.

The principal interim conclusions of this pilot case based on three joint donor missions are:
• Ownership has to be taken into account in the design stage, not just in the implementation of the reforms program; ownership is not simply the adoption of donor-favored policies;
• The results expected of adjustment programs should be made explicit; the establishment of clear government objectives and their publication aids ownership and the assumption of responsibility;
• The focus on outcome indicators — which measure results — helps ownership, informing the government of the effectiveness of its policies, and making it accountable for them. It also helps donors to improve donor coordination;

• More work is required to establish outcome indicators of budgetary management;
• While it is essential that donor support be linked to outcome indicators, this shift needs to be both gradual (given the large change involved from policy-based aid), and graduated (with more or less according to results achieved rather than a cut-off of aid), given the objective of smoothing aid flows;
• The broadened dialogue between donors and government as a result of the focus on performance was the most important innovation which requires a fundamental change from both donors and government.

The keys issues for future work are seen as:
• The need to identify appropriate indicators in certain sectors (such as agriculture, health and education), to improve data quality and interpret outcomes with care.
• The most effective way to link aid levels to performance.

11 donors participated to this initiative: Austria, Belgium, Canada, Denmark, France, Germany, Japan, the Netherlands, Switzerland, UNDP and World Bank.

Sources: SPA Working Group on Economic Management; Conditionality Reform: the Burkina Faso Pilot Case, November, 1999 and Conclusions de la 4ᵉ Mission Conjointe des Bailleurs de Fonds portant sur le test de la nouvelle approche de la conditionalité, 8-12 novembre 1999.

The central objective of a country's PRSP is to ensure that policy actions to increase growth and reduce poverty are integrated into a coherent macroeconomic framework after extensive consultations with national stakeholders. Additionally, this country-owned document seeks to identify policy targets and interventions that would allow a country to make progress toward the agreed International Development Goals.

In particular, the recent shift from the "Washington" to the "post-Washington Consensus" (defined by the holistic and coordinated approach to development for sustainable growth and poverty alleviation) was stressed as having serious policy and institutional implications for assistance provided by international development agencies, including UNDP.

The participation of key donors and multilateral institutions in the formulation of the Poverty Reduction Strategies is encouraged and the integration and synergies between new initiatives as PRSP, HIPC, 20/20 initiative and conditionality reform of the European Community are promoted.

United Nations Development Group (UNDGO) agreed with Africa UNDP's assessment that there is now a convergence among the broader international community as to the priority focus of development cooperation.

The eradication of poverty is the development goal for the new millenium and a priority initiative for UNDGO. The Common Country Assessment (CCA) and United Nations Development Assistance Framework (UNDAF) could provide a platform for CO's to engage with the PRSP when they are prepared by the government with the World Bank and the International Monetary Fund in consultation with other partners.

1.3. Sustainable human development and priority themes for poverty reduction

Following the decisions of the Copenhagen Summit, UNDP's Executive Board agreed in June 1995 to make the eradication of poverty its essential priority for action. All UNDP activities now focus on, and are evaluated with respect to, the ultimate aim of eradicating poverty. UNDP's overall efforts are to develop and consolidate countries' capacities for sustainable human development, development focused on people's well-being and subordinating other parameters to this objective. UNDP activities in its other fields — promotion of sustainable employment and livelihoods, greater responsibility for women, environmental conservation and regeneration, good governance and stronger institutions — are thus closely linked to the eradication of poverty.

1.3.1. Sustainable employment and livelihoods

The lack of sufficient income to afford food, shelter, adequate clothing and other necessities for a decent standard of living for oneself and one's family is certainly the most obvious symptom of poverty. Although UNDP sees poverty as a complex, multidimensional problem requiring action on a number of fronts, it is currently accepted that most people in poverty put their need for regular income very high on their list of priorities.

Roughly 30% of the world's total workforce, some 2.8 billion people, are not engaged in productive work according to the International Labor Organization. This includes over 120 million unemployed and roughly 700 million underemployed. They account for most of the poor in absolute terms throughout the world.

In helping countries develop their own strategies for eradicating poverty, UNDP stresses the entrepreneurship and self-advancement of people in poverty. Employment growth in the formal sector is encouraged, and the expansion of informal livelihoods such as self-employment on small farms and in microenterprises.

In rural areas, creating jobs to reduce poverty means focusing on agricultural diversification, access to productive land, price policy and the expansion of produce markets. It also requires improvements in basic infrastructure, the transfer and adaptation of appropriate environmentally-friendly technologies, and the assurance that loans, extension services and other resources are available.

In urban areas, support for self-employment and the development of microenterprises requires the availability of credit, training and an appropriate, affordable technology, and the removal of regulatory and administrative obstacles to businesses in the informal sector and the reduction of market-entry barriers.

1.3.2. Advancement of women

The World Conference on Women in Beijing in 1995 drew the world's attention to the fact that a disproportionate percentage of women live in poverty. Women have long been refused access to the same opportunities as men in education, training and land tenure, and are overburdened with work involved in family responsibilities, water transport and fuel gathering. They are also largely excluded from decision-making processes. They are often left alone as heads of household when their husbands leave home to find work, or are faced with disaster when they are confronted with armed conflict or crisis. UNDP's *Human Development Report 1995* themed on women made some general observations on persistent or increasing inequalities between men and women:

– two out of three illiterates are women,

– women are 70% of the billion people round the world living in absolute poverty,

– women's salaries are on average only two-thirds of men's,
– the distribution of income, land, credit and social services remains more favorable to men.

UNDP's policy on gender equality in development sees women not as a separate group requiring special attention but as full members of society, alongside men, disadvantaged by inequalities of all sorts. UNDP consequently helps governments focus on the social, economic, political and cultural forces that restrict the opportunities available to women, especially poor women; these forces determine what activities men and women may engage in, what responsibilities they have, how they behave towards one another, what attitudes form the perception of each sex, and how women and men control resources and take part in decision-making.

To help women escape from poverty, UNDP supports the development of national policies that broaden women's opportunities in education, training and health care. It seeks to provide them with access to income, markets and resources, especially land, credit and information. It recommends the abolition of all the legal and cultural barriers to women's full participation in society, in order to give them the right to own land and productive resources, borrow money and inherit in a fair and non-discriminatory fashion.

This approach is based on the established fact that the welfare of a community as a whole improves when the opportunities for women increase. For example, it is now recognized that the education and training of women help reduce fertility rates, improve family health and nutrition, and contribute to raising household income. Women's participation in national decision-making attracts better focused and more sustainable attention to actions in favor of social development.

1.3.3. Environmental conservation and regeneration

The deterioration of a country's basic natural resources as a result of over-consumption and poor management of environmental capital is one of the prime causes of poverty, and vice versa. For example, the depletion of soil and water resources can dramatically reduce farmers' incomes, lower the nutrition status of the community and accentuate economic imbalances. At the same time, those who live in absolute poverty in rural areas are victims of a situation they cannot control. Their very survival forces them to overgraze their livestock and cut down what trees are left for fuel, even if this means more rapid degradation of the environment.

Because of the inextricable links between poverty and the environment, UNDP assists governments and grassroots development stakeholders to design and implement policies and operational programs in these fields. It encourages environmentally-friendly farming practices, fisheries and forestry techniques that ensure food security and provide livelihoods, while maintaining long-term sustainability of resources. It recommends improved access to land for small farmers, the protection of traditional knowledge and the practices of nomadic and sedentary peoples, the promotion of the traditional rights of farmer-herders of access to resources, etc. All these actions can significantly contribute to more sustainable crop and livestock farming methods that will ensure a decent standard of living for present generations while conserving and regenerating the environment for future generations.

The urban population of developing countries has tripled in the last 30 years, and it has been estimated that at the end of this century half of all urban dwellers are living in poverty. UNDP's priority here is to unite governments and urban dwellers in efforts to ensure drinking-water supply and adequate sanitation systems, develop waste treatment and chemical pollutant control, rehabilitate districts and prevent deterioration in the living standards of the poor.

In disaster-prone areas, groups living in poverty are always the hardest hit by drought, floods and earthquakes. UNDP focuses on disaster prevention and the management of early warning systems to reduce the vulnerability of these areas.

UNDP supports a number of networks that strengthen local institutions, share relevant reproducible experience and provide local solutions in the fields of the environment and poverty alleviation. Farmers, NGOs, community organizations and many other stakeholders in investigation and action are invited to contribute actively to the design and implementation of innovative programs for poverty reduction.

1.3.4. Governance and capacity-building

Poverty often goes with inequality. It is the result of deep-seated differences in the distribution of a society's power and resources that prevent some groups from participating fully in the economic, political, social, cultural and even spiritual life of their communities.

An important step towards eradicating poverty is the establishment of a enabling political environment in which resources and opportunities are fairly distributed and all individuals have the chance to take part in the decisions that affect their lives. As a "nonpolitical" partner in development, UNDP is ideally placed, and recognized as such, to help countries tackle this sensitive and complex task. By promoting transparent and efficient systems of government and public administration, it helps a number of countries address the deep causes of poverty and inequality and remove the structural barriers that restrict the choices and opportunities available to individuals and families.

The main features of this support comprise the promotion of an efficient public sector accessible to the greatest number, gender equality, human rights, a non-discriminatory and stable legal framework providing people with access to a judicial system that is independent, fair and efficient; a budget process for managing public resources that is transparent and rational; decentralization and the promotion of local initiatives.

2. Approaches, programs and achievements

The analysis of approaches and operational programs, internationally, regionally and nationally, demonstrates how UNDP works to help governments and citizens to eradicate poverty. Some operations illustrate the way UNDP is playing the part assigned it in Copenhagen for capacity-building and coordination, and others, which began before the Copenhagen Summit and have intensified since, reveal the tangible effects of these activities on people's lives.

2.1. Regional cooperation with Africa

2.1.1. Regional Cooperation Framework for Africa (1997-2001)

The first UNDP Regional Cooperation Framework for Africa covers 1997-2001, and is the general frame of reference for approaches and activities initiated by UNDP in the countries of Sub-Saharan Africa. It was produced on the basis of evaluations of previous regional programs, consultations with local UNDP offices, and the results already identified of the new approaches developed by UNDP.

As a result of the conclusions and recommendations of these studies, the cooperation framework is highly focused, with clearly defined objectives and an effective strategy for implementation. It improves the planning and coordination of UNDP aid, its management and follow-up, and its evaluation, including the establishment of reference data and performance indicators. It pays greater attention to UNDP's comparative advantages and the effects of its operations. It also aims to improve quality control, exchange of information, and the acquisition of knowledge about organization and management.

i) Some new principles and criteria are defined more closely in UNDP's new approaches to poverty reduction and the achievement of sustainable human development objectives. The emphasis is on the need to target UNDP operations, the more so since aid resources are diminishing.

ii) The new approaches aim to strengthen interactions with national programs by involving beneficiaries at design and implementation phases, and stressing the regional nature of the operations. African stakeholders and their development partners are invited to take part in the main programs and initiatives. The regional programs are planned and implemented in close collaboration with world programs.

iii) The principle of the program approach is systematically applied and has already increased the thematic interactions between programs and projects. For example, the half-way evaluation of the fourth regional program revealed that most of the projects contributed directly or indirectly to poverty reduction; encouraged the development of the private sector; improved relations between enterprises and governments, and encouraged job-creating activities of particular relevance to the poor. The program also involved more men and women in a wide range of activities. The HIV/AIDS program innovated by raising awareness, setting up networks and support groups, examining ethnic and legal aspects, and achieving the capacity-building required to devise appropriate ways of resisting the epidemic.

iv) In terms of local appropriation, important lessons have been learned from these programs, which have aroused a greater sense of ownership and a clearer commitment from the participating countries. Issues of appropriation, especially of poverty reduction programs, are therefore taken into account from design phase to implementation and evaluation phases.

v) Cooperation with the Economic Commission for Africa and UN specialist bodies, and the economists at UNDP's Regional Bureau for Africa, who almost all work in local offices, have improved the quality of upstream dialogue concerning measures to be taken. Together with input from other development partners, this contributes to a more effective implementation of economic reform programs in the countries.

2.1.2. Strategy and means of execution of UNDP regional programs

UNDP's general strategy is to use the comparative advantage of regional operations as a means of capacity-building in Sub-Saharan countries in the fight against poverty with a view to sustainable human development. The regional approach has three main features: i) it addresses problems common to more than one country that require the simultaneous action of all the countries involved; ii) it enhances the sense of ownership and improves coordination between partners; iii) it encourages the sharing of knowledge, information and experience within the region and with other regions.

The regional framework is implemented by a variety of operations at national and regional level to i) initiate policy dialogue and support the formulation of strategies; ii) extend the concept of development, particularly the sustainable human development paradigm; iii) implement programs and projects; and iv) raise financing and create alliances. These operations cover the scope of the objectives UNDP has adopted for poverty reduction.

They imply three major themes that can be identified in poverty reduction activities: capacity-building in development management, income generation and environmental conservation, and improved governance.

i) *Capacity-building in development management for poverty reduction*

The main objective of UNDP regional program is to help African countries acquire and build the capacity for managing development with a view to eradicating poverty. To achieve this, UNDP and its associated funds aim to i) strengthen program beneficiary countries' long-term strategic planning potential using national long-term perspective studies and developing knowledge- and experience-sharing networks; ii) form networks and alliances for poverty reduction; and iii) build national and regional capacity to determine options compatible with food security, natural resource management and HIV/AIDS control.

National long-term perspective studies make an important contribution to steering development strategies towards the long term, by placing short-term macroeconomic situations within a longer-term perspective and a strategic plan. In the new phase that began in mid-1997, UNDP African Futures project continues to give priority to the creation of national capacities for strategic planning by providing technical support, training and methodological instruments for the national teams working on studies in each country. This sub-program is implemented in collaboration with the main government institutions and regional and national organizations. It encourages participation at all levels in identifying a national vision, design of strategic studies, construction of scenarios including various options for the future, formulation of a national development strategy and the design and implementation of programs and plans of action.

Under the sub-program for helping countries and beneficiaries in Sub-Saharan Africa to implement recommendations for the eradication of poverty formulated by the main UN world conferences, such as the Copenhagen Summit in 1995, certain critical areas for action are targeted, particularly the following:

– *The food security program.* This will set up and build the capacities essential for sustainable food security. The project collaborates with subregional organizations on four interdependent operations: improving sectoral information; analyzing policy; improving farming systems, and improving research systems. UNDP aims to provide advice and support in this field to build capacities in joint partnership with the action of the Food and Agriculture Organization (FAO), ECA, the Southern African Development Community (SADC), the Permanent Inter-State Committee for Drought Control in the Sahel (CILSS), the Liptako Gourma Integrated Development Authority, the Economic Community of West African States (ECO-

WAS), and the Consultative Group on International Agricultural Research (CGIAR).

– *The program on HIV/AIDS and development.* This increases the means available to the public sector, civil society organizations, private enterprises and national and regional awareness networks for developing effective reactions to the epidemic. To that end, data from experience are identified, used and exchanged so that the communities affected can express their needs, experience and reactions to the epidemic. UNDP works in close collaboration with UNAIDS, the German agency for technical cooperation and the regional and subregional organizations combating AIDS and sexually transmitted diseases.

– *The program for natural resource management.* The program aims mainly at improving partnerships in natural resource management and the strategies linking regional and national operations, encouraging dialogue between countries, and coordinating initiatives under the Global Water Partnership (GWP).

ii) Poverty reduction through income-generation and environmental conservation

The close relationship identified between poverty reduction, income-generating activities and the fight against the degradation of the environment has been given careful attention by UNDP, through regional programs such as the Africa 2000 Network and Microstart, and the transformation of UNCDF into a fund for community and local development.

• Africa 2000 Network

The Africa 2000 Network is a UNDP support program for grassroots initiatives that aims to promote sustainable development by considering both the protection of the environment and the improvement of communities' living standards. Specifically, the program combats poverty by mobilizing and supporting grassroots communities and NGOs working to protect the environment and promote ecologically sustainable development by implementing self-advancement activities.

Long-term development objectives include the prevention or reduction of desertification and environmental degradation, the achievement of ecologically sustainable development in rural areas, and increased food and fuelwood production by efficient natural resource management.

In general, the network's strategy is to encourage communities to work for sustainable development through:

– a participatory approach — bottom-up — motivating communities to manage natural resources themselves in a sustainable manner;

– flexibility of response to villagers' requests and needs, so as to enable them to achieve the objectives they have set themselves;

– financial support to enable them to undertake action on the ground;
– priority use of local expertise;
– development of partnership with civil society and grassroots communities.

This general strategy is translated into action in the twelve African countries concerned — Burkina Faso, Burundi, Cameroon, Ghana, Kenya, Lesotho, Mauritania, Senegal, Tanzania, Uganda and Zimbabwe — in the light of the specific realities in each country and government policies and strategies for environmental protection and sustainable development.

The Africa 2000 Network at present supports over 700 projects in the twelve countries. The assistance is provided directly to grassroots community organizations, training and research institutions, and the NGOs working with these groups. The cumulative total contributed by the main donors (Canada, Denmark, European Union, France, Japan, Netherlands, Norway) to finance the Network's programs was $22,822,719 at 31 December 1997.

In terms of impact, the environment is admittedly an essential element in sustainable development. However, it should be realized that the effects of environmental protection operations take a long time to be perceptible. Even so, the approach of working at the grassroots level, using the participatory method, encouraging the reproduction of the most successful community projects, makes it possible to assess the impact of the action taken.

The Africa 2000 Network supports projects in a range of fields combining natural resource management and socioeconomic activities. Some operations in the social field (erosion control, collective plant nurseries, etc.) cannot pay for themselves and consequently require subsidies, whereas others of a more economic nature (fish farming, market gardening, etc.) can be financed by loans. In either case the innovative feature of the network is that it links the improvement of methods of production and reproduction of natural resources (agro-forestry, erosion control, land improvements, etc.) with "marketable" socioeconomic activities that will generate income or provide self-sufficiency. This has consequences for the choice of financing: basically, activities that help conserve and protect natural resources should be subsidized. And socioeconomic activities should receive loans (where they are mainly market-based) or a mixture of subsidies and loans (where they are partly market-based and partly subsistence).

Local financial institutions have often developed lending policies that are out of tune with the socioeconomic realities of low-income groups, especially women. The rules and red tape do not encourage those who may want to set up a business but are not conversant with sophisticated management methods to seek loans. Furthermore, these institutions are located in urban areas, serving a specific set of customers, and occasionally finance short- and medium-term operations, such as crop loans, house-building loans, etc.

Women and low-income groups are effectively excluded from the traditional financial channels because they have little or no income, and are thus insolvent. Their ignorance of the rules and procedures, a result of widespread illiteracy, is a further obstacle.

NGOs have started credit programs to stimulate income-generating activities. But the approach used still does not encourage private initiative: some occupational categories whose success depends on their individual qualities (craftspeople, fisherfolk, etc.) do not have access to these credit programs, which are aimed first at larger groups.

Credit thus wrongly becomes a subsidy, since the recipients cannot repay it and so the credit stops. Because of generalized poverty, loans are often used to meet basic needs (health, children's education, housing), which ought in theory to be subsidized. It is time to distinguish between financing basic needs and economic activities, so as to form a bridge between rehabilitation and the support of economic activities.

Funds to support initiatives from low-income groups are set up in order to give these groups the financial resources to create income-generating activities, and become in the medium term individual or collective microenterprises.

The support fund aims to finance wholly or in part income-generating or job-creating development projects on behalf of the groups most disadvantaged in financing, by helping them with loan guarantees and access to credit. The fund's resources come initially from internal and external donors. Later it will receive the income from credit and guarantee operations. Evaluation of these groups' financing needs is due to be made by a study to determine the initial endowment of the fund.

The fund's operations cover credit and guarantee; but credit is its main purpose. An individual may have access to credit on condition that his or her activities:

– use raw materials produced by disadvantaged or marginalized groups;
– sell processed products, manufactured by these groups or associations from marginalized communities, especially women.

The credit is subject to a rate of interest at least equal to the opportunity cost of the money (market rate), whatever the source of the finance: grants, subsidies, etc.

The rule is that "any activity producing goods or services" must be financed by loans. Actual subsidies go to basic services: training, support, institutional costs, initial creation of the conditions for production. The fund may give its guarantee to credits allocated by local financial institutions on the same conditions as credit itself. Operations financed by the fund must be profitable in financial and economic terms, and equitable in social terms.

Box 7.3.

The regional Microstart program

Credit and savings mobilization services in favor of the populations are a poverty control instrument. Despite the present day importance of micro-financing activities, the UNDP remains limited in its actions. Indeed, due to its financial regulations, it cannot use its resources to grant loans or establish security funds except those of the UNCDF and UNIFEM. Nevertheless, its financial regulations stipulate that "micro-capital" grants may be given to support credit projects or other loan activities of non-governmental organizations. It is in that context that the Microstart program is being implemented.

Microstart is a pilot program conducted in 25 selected countries. The funds are granted to local organizations at the maximum of $ 150 000 per organization to cover loans and overheads. In that context, the utilization of UNDP resources for credit activities is limited to one million dollars per country. Besides this micro-financing of capital granted to local organizations in charge of generating and granting credits to the poorest, the project also aims at strengthening the managerial capacities of the selected NGOs. In that context, a selected contracting party provides a range of technical services to local organizations.

The objectives of Microstart are the following:

– to reach a very low income clientele,
– to mobilize other funding sources,
– to achieve operational sustainability within 3 years and financial sustainability within 5 years for the supported local organization.

Grant recipients are private or public organizations considered as able to become reliable providers of micro-financing services. These may be financial sector institutions willing to initiate micro-financing services or already existing micro-financing institutions. Existing local organizations are given greater importance, even if they have not had any micro-financing experience. Indeed, they have basic infrastructure and are known by the populations, which facilitates access to the target group.

The micro-financing model is based on group solidarity. While the loan remains individual, a group nevertheless serves as loan security. Indeed in the absence of material guarantee, a social guaranty can operate. No new loans are granted until all members of a group have paid back. In that case, if a member defaults, the other members can exert pressure on him/her to pay back, or they will have to pay back for him/her. The idea of a group also solves the problems of controlling and utilizing funds. Indeed, members can control themselves on fund utilization in productive activities. As members know one another, this system excludes bad debtors (high risk persons) at the time of setting up the group.

By granting loans to existing organizations, the model introduces micro-financing projects into other types of programs. This is an optimal means to mobilize the other productive assets already made available to the population under the program (water supply, irrigation program, etc.)

Source: "UNDP Policy on Credit and Micro-Capital Grants", New York, 1997.

Examples of areas of action are:
- agriculture: crops, fisheries, livestock, fish farming, bee-keeping, etc;
- processing of agricultural produce;
- trade between groups and regions, etc.

• UNCDF: a fund for community and local development

The concept and program of the United Nations Capital Development Fund (UNCDF) are closely linked to UNDP's general operations. Now that UNDP is focusing on sustainable human development, UNCDF's stress on poverty reduction, local governance and participation is likely to intensify and extend its impact. UNCDF works downstream, mainly in rural areas, to implement and develop the ideas, strategies and policies designed upstream by governments and supported by UNDP.

UNCDF is now redefining its role, in order to become a local and community development fund, the term "local" to be understood both geographically and institutionally. In general, assistance from UNCDF takes one or more of the forms described below, with investments of between $500,000 and $5 million per project:
- Microcredit and guarantee fund projects. These services, provided either in direct cooperation with an NGO or via banks, are intended to help individuals and households create capital for productive farm or non-farm activities, by improving their access to credit (and other financial services).
- "Model" infrastructure projects. Major investment, either strategic or technically complex, for promoting regional development (main roads, irrigation systems, power plants) is easier to decide if a "model" approach is used whereby results and activities are precisely determined in advance. Responsibilities for planning and management, however, will, as far as possible, be delegated to local institutions.
- Local development funds. These financing mechanisms are set up according to demand, and must be accessible to and managed by communities or local authorities, to make investments defined locally, in order to improve small-scale rural infrastructure or natural resource management, when decision-making is decentralized to the lowest level possible.

As part of its shift towards local development, UNCDF is gradually giving priority to programming investments made and managed by rural communities and decentralized administrations, where the key component is a version, adapted to local conditions, of what is generally known as a "local development fund". In ecologically fragile and overpopulated areas, local development programs are associated with a long-term strategy of restoring the environment in eco-development terms.

At the same time, UNCDF is establishing innovative mechanisms for facilitating the access of small businesses to microcredit, more directly supporting the livelihoods of families in rural areas and small towns, so as to increase the support for infrastructure.

Box 7.4.
Local development planning in Zambia

Since the elections of October 1991, Zambia adopted a structural adjustment program including a Public Sector Reform Program, providing for resource decentralization and power devolution to local administrations. In that context, a five year project of district level planning, implementation and development in the eastern Province was recently approved (1994), with a joint UNDP (US $ 1 million) and UNCDF (2.6 millions) financing. The project includes UNCDF assistance in financing, planning and decentralized management of infrastructures.

The overall objective of the project is to establish a district development fund (DDF) in order to provide the extra-budget resources needed to implement local development plans designed by recently elected district authorities, in order to develop basic social and economic infrastructure in the poorest areas, to initiate decentralized procedures of participatory planning and to strengthen managerial capacities.

The project will aim at:

– strengthening the capacities of the district level planning and counseling provincial Unit to design and implement local development plans using participatory methods and hence strengthening the role, flexibility and responsibility of the public sector in order to promote sustainable human development;

– establishing a district level local development fund in order to provide the district counselors and the communities with the financial resources required for a development planning worthy of the name. The development fund will finance:

– grass roots micro-projects initiated by the communities (for instance, water supply and sanitation systems, dispensaries, primary schools, community or local access roads for marketing and storage.

– to integrate district and community micro-projects into the normal procedure of planning and financial year of the decentralized administration.

Provincial authorities in charge of planning will coordinate district level activities and distribute funds to districts. District counselors will be responsible for managing the development fund (by equitably distributing the requests of individual communities) assisted by technical advisers and community supervision. The recipient communities will contribute in cash or kind to micro-project cost by at least 25%. In general, the communities will implement infrastructure micro-projects unless those are district level projects, in which case it will be entrusted to private enterprises.

Source: UNCDF, "Poverty Reduction", New York, 1995.

Among UNCDF's innovative initiatives in poverty reduction, eco-development and eco-swaps occupy a preponderant position. Eco-development has been designed and tested by UNCDF as a way of helping communities to meet the challenges of development in regions that are both over-populated and ecologically fragile. The aim of the new approach is to set up a participatory development process aiming to restore an ecological equilibrium threatened by degradation of natural resources, improve food security, and fulfil people's basic needs more effectively.

The long-term development strategies and annual programs devised by communities, and ranked in an order of priority they have chosen, contain two aspects: i) investment and planning in natural resources, and ii) investment linked to the development of productive activities or the creation of social services. By making investments that meet immediate needs, UNCDF provides an incentive for local authorities to take part in environmental restoration activities that will only give results in the long term: this is the principle of the exchange between development and ecology, known as eco-swap. Within eco-development this goes with setting up economic and social infrastructure in order to develop, with local authorities, intermediate urban centers that will become sources for the creation of viable jobs for the unemployed in rural areas and sources of services for the surrounding farming areas.

Another important UNCDF activity for poverty reduction concerns microcredit and the setting up of guarantee funds. Over one-quarter of the projects financed by UNCDF in the last four years have provided revolving microcredits or guarantees to financial intermediaries granting microcredits. UNCDF has considerable and varied experience in this field so essential for the success of poverty reduction programs. However, since the percentage of loan approvals in recent years has been low, UNCDF has decided to extend its microcredit and guarantee programs in order to increase its support for infrastructure.

Despite the proven capacity of microenterprises and small businesses in the least developed countries to meet their obligations, there is a real need to develop financially viable microcredit mechanisms. For that it is necessary to i) cut the transaction costs of credit operations, ii) attract savings, iii) encourage loans to borrowers marginalized by the formal banking sector, and iv) ultimately develop the links between rural areas and national capital markets.

To encourage the development of decentralized microcredit programs in rural areas, UNCDF helps local financial intermediaries (local branches of official banks, NGOs providing financial services, village banks and cooperatives, etc.) to procure the necessary liquidity to refinance the loans they have granted to microentrepreneurs (credit projects). To ensure local ownership of these mechanisms and programs, UNCDF recommends a participatory approach:

– Working plans are produced together with local intermediaries in order to define i) what categories of microenterprise or individual will be eligible for the project, and ii) what measures will need to be taken to give the intermediaries the means to manage the microcredit effectively. To increase the viability of the operation, the intermediaries promise to match the external resources provided by UNCDF with resources raised locally.

– Credit projects are not restricted to the supply of external liquidity, but have two other aims: i) introduce the intermediaries to the special needs of microentrepreneurs by the experience they gain, and continue the process; ii) get potential borrowers into the habit of applying for credit and dealing with financial intermediaries.

iii) Improving governance

Most of the problems that arise in the management of public affairs are national matters, although some, like the restoration of peace and aid to refugees, require a regional approach. The regional program is thus also directed towards the problems of governance common to a number of countries, so as to encourage firm initiatives to increase public accountability and transparency in decision-making, promoting the political transition towards democratic practices, protecting human rights, empowering civil society organizations, and preventing conflicts.

Here UNDP has developed the Special Initiative for Governance in Africa (SIGA), which supports African countries in improving their programs of governance. There are five main aspects:
– training for government teams and policy-makers;
– transparency and accountability in the management of public resources;
– emancipation of civil society;
– consolidation of political transition and democratization programs;
– formulation of a policy for peace and stability in Africa, and application of methods for conflict prevention, mediation and settlement. [1]

UNDP and the UN Economic Commission for Africa (ECA) have also initiated a series of Africa Governance Forums (AGFs). These high-level meetings aim to put together regional and national partnerships to meet these challenges, give impetus to operational programs of good governance, and ensure a consensus long-term vision of development in Africa. [2]

---

1. UNDP, *Compendium of Africa Governance Programmes, Vol. 1-2* (New York, June 1997).
2. UNDP, *The Africa Governance forum: Conceptual Framework* (New York, June 1997).

- Empowerment of civil society organizations in poverty reduction and political participation

The objective of this program is to build the capacities of selected NGOs and partners in civil society so as to enable them to take an active part in policy dialogue and thus strengthen the consensus for formulating approaches to poverty reduction and the proper management of public affairs. UNDP supports training and network consolidation to that end.

Action relating to the restoration of peace, and conflict prevention and management, is intended to support the efforts of African countries to i) set up mechanisms for anticipating conflict and devising ways of avoiding it; ii) manage conflicts when they occur; iii) address the deep-seated causes of conflict; and iv) develop peace consolidation measures in the post-conflict phase.

The results expected from this program are the establishment of an early warning system at the OAU and capacity-building for OAU agents in decision-making, preventive diplomacy, and raising financing.

The regional program for gender equality aims to consolidate current efforts with a view to abolishing inequalities between the sexes in Africa. The program supports and develops networks and institutions that encourage regional cooperation and information exchange in this field. The regional network of female parliamentarians and councilors is strengthened so as to support women holding posts of responsibility in politics and decision-making posts. The regional training institutes, such as the African Institute for Economic Development and Planning, the Council for the Development of Economic and Social Research in Africa (CODESRIA), and the Panafrican Institute for Development (IPD) are supported in establishing training modules on the analysis of policies and the management of public affairs. This program is implemented in close cooperation with the United Nations Development Fund for Women (UNIFEM) and the Economic Commission for Africa (ECA), and also the regional organizations that are more particularly concerned with women's issues, such as the Women's Development Foundation and the Forum of Women in Development (FOWODE).

- Development of the private sector

The main objective is to encourage poverty reduction and economic growth by fostering the development of the private sector and job opportunities. Here UNDP helps the countries in the program establish an appropriate legislative, regulatory and financial framework so as to attract foreign investment and enable those countries to compete more effectively in the world economy. The financial sub-program encourages the development of entrepreneurship, improved access to microfinance, especially for women, and capacity-building targeted on the economic advancement of women.

The objective is to take advantage of economic reform to attract more capital to African markets and expand the productive sector. The main activities are: a) supporting business associations, investment promotion organizations, capital market authorities and other groups in the private sector; b) supporting countries' efforts to design programs in favor of the private sector, particularly those whose objective are to integrate SMEs into the formal economy; c) forming networks of talented African entrepreneurs to act as a catalyst in attracting foreign and domestic investors; and d) developing regional marketing strategies. The program aims to ensure diversified and effective technical cooperation and training. UNDP seeks to use existing national capacities in these areas and to increase them. Its operations complete those of the International Financial Corporation (IFC), the African Development Bank (ADB), commercial associations, investment promotion bodies, capital market authorities, and groups in the private sector.

The objective of the Enterprise Africa program and related initiatives is to provide a regional institutional framework for the coordination of SMEs in Africa and the promotion of African entrepreneurship. To that end, technical cooperation is provided for formulating programs on entrepreneurship and enterprise development. This initiative facilitates small businesses' access to credit and encourages the formation of networks of enterprises in the region and the study of the possibility of an inter-regional network. The basic services provided include entrepreneurship training, consultancy services for management, the identification of sources of credit for businesses, subcontracting opportunities and other forms of interaction between enterprises, and consultancies for African governments.

The results expected from the Enterprise Africa initiative are the introduction of new programs for entrepreneurship in 20 African countries; the training of 5,000 entrepreneurs, at least 40% women; 150 links are being established between African SMEs and foreign firms; 200 workshops on entrepreneurship will have been held in Africa by the end of 1999.

Furthermore, together with the ILO, UNDP has launched the "Jobs for Africa" initiative. Complementing or supporting the 20/20 Initiative, this new instrument should encourage dialogue on public spending policy and improve the allocation of that spending. The instrument is intended to provide a critical analysis of Public Investment Programs (PIP) with a view to evaluating the impact of public investment on job creation and poverty reduction. The attempt will be made to concentrate a large proportion of public investment on those sectors that have the greatest impact for poverty reduction.

This initiative attempts to link overall macroeconomic policy on public investment more effectively with local investment, such as rural dirt-roads and irrigation, so as to concentrate it more on the most disadvantaged groups. It is an example of the new approach of providing clearer links between macro and micro levels for work on the ground with the poorest people. The backbone of the project is obviously linked to strategies to promote jobs for poverty reduction. At present, the regional project covers a number of countries including Burkina Faso, Cameroon, Côte d'Ivoire, Ethiopia, Mali, Nigeria, Senegal, Uganda, Zambia and Zimbabwe.

Within these objectives, the project has two main aspects: i) concentrating public investment on labor-intensive infrastructure projects that employ poor people and are located in the most disadvantaged regions; ii) reforming the capital market to provide the poor with access to credit to finance self-employment and microenterprises in the urban and rural informal sector.

To ensure that this project reaches the regions and households who are actually the poorest, the targets chosen will be the most disadvantaged in the countries concerned. Local communities will be fully involved in the process so as to identify their investment needs. As with the new local social funds, communities will be associated with the management, implementation and monitoring and evaluation of projects so as to increase the impact of these anti-poverty activities.

It is instructive to note that a genuine link has finally been achieved between the macro level, relating to the public spending reviews and the public investment policy dialogue, and the grassroots level, relating to genuine participation by communities in the implementation of investment projects for reducing poverty.

- Promoting trade and increasing intra-regional
  and inter-regional cooperation

The objective of this sub-program is to build essential capacities in the private sector and establish conditions more favorable to promoting trade between African countries and between Africa and the rest of the world.

The program brings together a wide range of partners: it is implemented by national governments and regional institutions with the support of the United Nations Conference on Trade and Development (UNCTAD), the International Trade Centre (ITC) and the World Intellectual Property Organization (WIPO). UNDP is responsible for overall coordination of the initiative. The beneficiaries are mainly African entrepreneurs, who will thus be able to meet the new challenges raised by the extension of the world market.

The program supports regional arrangements for formulating policy and developing cooperation. It supports activities such as the development of the African economic community, the local initiative fund, the Tokyo

International Conference on African Development (TICAD), etc. This assistance enables African countries to undertake more effectively operations to cope with common problems, develop pilot projects, hold regional meetings, engage in technical cooperation and training, and strengthen South-South cooperation. The main partners are governments, intergovernmental organizations, NGOs and civil society organizations, national and regional institutions and UNDP offices in each country.

Box 7.5.

UNDP strategy to support poverty reduction strategies at country level

Important new policy instruments (Poverty Reduction Strategy Paper — PRSP and Poverty Reduction and Growth Facility — PRGF) which integrate poverty reduction strategies with the HIPC 2 initiative have been developed by the IMF and World Bank. These have been endorsed by the major donors and by the IMF/WB Executive Board meeting in December 1999, to serve as the guiding framework for the Bretton Woods Institution's assistance in future.

This presents a major opportunity to carry forward the ideas UNDP, and the UN system, have been advocating for the past 15 years. In particular, the emphasis on national ownership and the use of participatory processes, which are approaches that UNDP has traditionally promoted and supported, is very welcome.

It has now been agreed that UNDP, together with the other UN system agencies, will be a partner in the PRSP process, building on UNDP's experience in supporting the development of Poverty Reduction Strategies through participatory processes.

A growing number of partner governments are also requesting UNDP's support in the PRSP process, in recognition of our experience in this area

(e.g. Benin, Burkina Faso, Mali, Uganda, Tanzania, Honduras, Bolivia, Nicaragua, Niger, Chad, Cameroon, Zambia, etc).

Over the past 10 years, UNDP has built up considerable capacity working in this area, including the Global Human Development Report, the Global and Regional Poverty Reports; National HDR's, Vision 20/20, Poverty Assessments, Poverty Monitoring Systems, use of participatory processes for strategy development, etc... These assets provide us with a solid foundation to play a critical role in the PRSP process.

In addition, UNDP, as the host of the Resident Coordinator System, is ideally placed to ensure that the strengths of the UN system in each country are brought in to support this process.

The management of linkages so as to maximize impact of development will present a challenge to all partners including the UN System. The Common Country Assessment (CCA) should feed into the Poverty Analysis and the United Nations Development Assistance Framework (UNDAF) should be derived from it, closely related to the PRSP.

UNDP'S role in Poverty Reduction Strategy Paper (PRSP)

(i)   Support the process elements with strong emphasis on national ownership and participation of civil society, and all national stakeholders. Building capacity for the long-term ownership and management of these processes will be UNDP's most important contribution.

(ii)   Build national capacity for as many of the processes as possible with special emphasis on Poverty Monitoring. Key tools will include the National HDR, National long-term perspectives, NLTPS, poverty Assessments, 20/20 initiative.

(iii) Bring the UN System into the key processes using CCA-UNDAF as National coordination Framework.

(iv)   Assist Government to develop an Advocacy/Partnership Strategy and build capacity to ensure that all national partners (including CSO and private sector) play their full role in defining poverty, developing the strategy, implementing programmes and monitoring results.

(v)   Bring into process the products of UNDP's and UN agencies work in Poverty Reduction.

Source: Report on the UNDP Seminar on Support Strategies to Country Offices on Poverty Reduction Strategies and Issues related to PRSP and HIPC II.
Nouakchott, Mauritania, 11-13 January 2000.

2.2. Country operations and achievements in the 1990s

At national level, UNDP's operations in the countries of Sub-Saharan Africa come under four complementary headings:

i) policy dialogue and formulation of strategies for development and poverty reduction;

ii) examination of development paradigms, including sustainable human development, through the global *Human Development Report*, and the production of national human development reports;

iii) operational activities to implement programs and projects;

iv) raising financing and formation of alliances.

In almost all countries in Sub-Saharan Africa, UNDP's support is mainly or entirely concerned with poverty reduction, which is an integral part of its mandate. In general, this assistance is based on analyses of poverty, formulation of strategic frameworks for poverty reduction, raising financing for poverty reduction, and the implementation and impact of operational programs and projects in this field.

The poverty analysis phase has led to the production of national human development reports in 33 African countries and poverty profiles for nearly 40 countries. Over 20 African countries have designed national poverty reduction policies with UNDP support, leading in many cases to general roundtable conferences on the topic, as in Botswana, Lesotho, Mali, Namibia and Niger.

UNDP's offices in Africa generally carry out operational poverty reduction programs and projects. These address issues of management of the economy and development, income generation, environmental protection, good governance and access to essential social services. To give a clearer idea of UNDP's national strategies and assistance, it may be useful to review and analyze the poverty reduction operations undertaken in selected countries in Sub-Saharan Africa.

• *Angola. The challenges of reconstruction and economic and social recovery for poverty reduction*

UNDP operations focus on three main fields: a) post-conflict aid; b) poverty reduction; and c) governance. They support the peace process and economic and social reconstruction. Following the end of the conflict, the government considers that there is a crucial link between humanitarian aid and economic revival. Over 100,000 soldiers have to be demobilized and reintegrated into civil society. Their smooth and efficient entry into productive activities should reduce the risk that they will take up arms again and threaten the country's peace and development. Most soldiers are expected to find it hard to return to civilian life in the absence of insufficient educational attainment for the labor market, and also because of their traumatic experiences during the war.

To promote reintegration, the plan is to strengthen the capacities of the national institute for the socio-occupational reintegration of veterans by providing financial aid for the community advisory and career service for demobilized soldiers. Funds will be set up in the Institute for support to veterans and their family members for projects with a quick return. The quick-return project fund in the institute's community advisory service will act as a catalyst, helping overcome the obstacles that may hinder the effective integration of veterans and their families.

The government is aware that the best way of reducing poverty is to have a coherent strategy of economic recovery and growth. The private sector, seen as an engine of growth, will continue to benefit from appropriate incentives to play a role as catalyst in poverty reduction. The government has taken measures to remove the obstacles the private sector faces and to strengthen that sector's role in the economy.

Box 7.6.

National Reports on Human Development: a real impact

To date, 40 African countries have drafted National Reports on human development. These national reports on human development are an efficient tool for public authorities, institutions of the civil societies, representatives of the political class and universities in their concerted human development efforts. They contribute indeed to bring various groups together and to cement consensus on a middle and long term vision. Finally, well independently written as they are, they pave the way to new prospects of thought and action, an essential feature in facing the challenges of human development and poverty eradication.

Reviewing their utilization revealed the following four major trends:

• **Promoting human development.** The national reports consider the human development issue as the most important and require that public action be refocused on people. They play an important role in the dialogue between development partners and supplement the planning efforts of the authorities as well as initiatives from the civil society and donor financed reports and studies.

• **Highlighting essential concerns.** In most countries, the first national report provides a human development profile,

whereas subsequent reports are thematic. Benin, Burkina Faso, Cameroon, Madagascar, Namibia, Nigeria and Sierra Leone have all published reports focused on the theme of poverty.

• **Emphasizing equity in development planning.** Because they provide many indicators and indices, these reports make it possible to monitor the progress and decline of human development and poverty. One of the most interesting features in many national reports is related to the breaking down of human development indicators (HDI, SHDI, HPI) according to regions, provinces, rural or urban areas or ethnic groups, which make it possible to better tackle equity issues. This break down is an invaluable planning tool for public powers and makes it possible to target development programs and public expenditure in favor of areas underprivileged in terms of human development.

• **Articulating people's expectations and priorities.** Some reports provide an interesting insight into the perception that the populations have about human development as well as about their concerns and priorities which are integrated into the analysis of measures to be taken.

Sub-Saharan African countries that have published a human development report

Angola, 1997, 1998, 1999	Ghana, 1997	Niger, 1998
Benin, 1997, 1998	Guinea, 1997	Nigeria, 1996, 1997
Botswana, 1997	Guinea-Bissau, 1997	Uganda, 1996, 1997
Burkina Faso, 1997, 1998, 1999	Equatorial Guinea, 1997	Central African Republic, 1996
	Kenya, 1998	Sierra Leone, 1996
Burundi, 1997	Lesotho, 1998	South Africa, 1998
Cameroon, 1992, 1993, 1996, 1998	Liberia, 1998	Swaziland, 1998
	Madagascar, 1997	United Republic of Tanzania, 1997
Cap-Verde, 1997	Malawi, 1997, 1998	Chad, 1997
Comoros, 1997, 1998	Mali, 1995, 1997	Togo, 1995, 1997
Côte d'Ivoire, 1998	Mauritania, 1996, 1997	Zambia, 1997
Ethiopia, 1997, 1998	Mozambique, 1996, 1997	Zimbabwé, 1998
Gambia, 1997	Namibie, 1996, 1997	

Source: UNDP, World Human Development Report, 1999, New York, 1999.

However, the government considers that the cornerstone of its national strategy for poverty reduction is the community recovery program presented at the Brussels conference. The program's prime objective is to increase people's involvement in improving their living standards and fulfilling basic needs, and their access to income-generating activities.

Poverty has a major impact at all levels of society. Those most affected are the war-wounded and disabled, refugees and displaced persons. Women have been hit particularly hard by being forced to act as heads of household without the necessary resources. The incidence of poverty in Angola causes grave concern at the highest policy-making levels. The Programa Nova Vida is evidence of the concerns aroused by the reduction of social protection, while the Programa de Politica Econômica e Social do Governo, adopted in 1997, also addresses poverty. As a result of differences between provinces, community programs are probably most effective and sustainable way of reducing poverty.

These programs focus on the following priority fields:
– raising productive capacity in crop and livestock farming, forestry, fisheries and the private sector.
– improving social sectors, particularly basic education, primary health care, and aid for vulnerable groups.
– improving basic infrastructure, particularly roads and bridges, water and power, housing and small-town infrastructure.
– management capacity-building at national, provincial and local level.

The "demarginalization" of women is also a central feature of UNDP support program for Angola. Women were particularly vulnerable to the effects of war. Most households are headed by women, who have limited access to economic resources. Efforts need to be made to counter the effects of the war and the traditional attitudes and practices that hinder women's effective participation in the economy. In all of these programs, UNDP pays particular attention to the gender-specific dimensions, and targets female-headed households as priority beneficiaries. The program focuses on women's employment and working conditions, especially in rural areas, and it helps them create or take part in small enterprises with credit and new technologies.

UNDP's cooperation with national institutions is based on capacity-building in the collection and analysis of data to design strategies and measures to reduce poverty. UNDP works with other UN bodies, NGOs and community organizations to consolidate a consensus on poverty reduction initiatives and facilitate synergy between them. The program's success will be judged by quantifiable practical criteria such as a lower incidence of poverty, active and increasing participation by women, higher incomes in the areas chosen for projects, and the sustainability of programs.

- *Benin. Institutional capacity-building, good governance*
  and community development for poverty reduction

UNDP cooperation with Benin as part of the fifth program cycle (1993-97) focuses on two fields: capacity-building for financial and economic management, and improving people's living standards. The activities undertaken have comprised: a) development of analytical and measurement tools for the various dimensions of poverty; b) monitoring and evaluation of the employment situation; c) support for grassroots communities in improving their living standards; d) support for good governance through administrative reform, strengthening of the judicial system, and the implementation of the national program for revitalizing the private sector.

At operational level, projects have contributed to an increase in the capacity for self-advancement in rural communities by helping them increase their incomes and improve access to social services. Meanwhile, the credit section introduced into these regions in cooperation with UNCDF has facilitated villagers' access to credit, increased local savings, raised household incomes and strengthened entrepreneurial spirit.

Following the development partners roundtable held in Geneva in 1992, the government adopted poverty reduction as the main objective of its development policies and strategies and UNDP is helping by consolidating the general framework, the guidelines for the national poverty reduction strategy, building institutional capacities for development management and raising the resources necessary for carrying out poverty reduction programs of action.

Through the framework program for institutional management capacity-building adopted in December 1995, UNDP aims to redefine the role of the government and the State, and contribute to management capacity-building and the consolidation of the democratization and decentralization processes. This last objective is where this program coincides with the objectives of good local governance contained in the community development program.

UNDP support program covers the following fields: a) rationalization of administrative structures through the introduction of a system for evaluating the performance of services; b) improvement of the system for programming investment and building the capacity to analyze the impact of economic policies and examine prospects; c) strengthening social change monitoring units and the managing bodies of future decentralized authorities.

- *Burkina Faso. Priority for poverty reduction*
  and the development of essential social services

By adopting a "letter of intent" on sustainable human development policy in 1995, the Burkinabè government displayed its determination to meet the persistent challenge of the most visible manifestations of poverty, such as illiteracy, malnutrition, low incomes, and in general, difficulties of access to remunerative employment and basic social services. The program's resources help the government address the cross-cutting concerns of sustainable human development. UNDP's country cooperation framework for 1997-2001 in Burkina Faso concentrates on: i) management of the economy and governance; ii) environmental protection and food security; and iii) poverty reduction and the development of social sectors that represent half of available resources.

The program for poverty reduction and the development of social sectors has the following priority objectives: i) achieve better understanding of the phenomenon of poverty; ii) increase the involvement of grassroots communities and develop income-generating activities; iii) improve the supply, accessibility and appropriateness of basic social services.

The priorities of the poverty reduction program comprise three main components which cover coherent sets of activities by nature and impact.

1. Strategic poverty reduction initiative

An effective poverty reduction policy requires first an accurate quantitative and qualitative understanding of the phenomenon. Consequently, the program will i) study the availability and accessibility of basic social services as defined in the 20/20 Initiative; ii) analyze the level of expenditure at present allocated by the government and its external partners for the access of all to basic social services; iii) introduce a formal system for annually producing the national report on sustainable human development; iv) support the formulation of a national poverty reduction strategy.

These operations involve both strengthening operational synergies between the structures responsible at national level for statistics and designing development strategies and policies, Ouagadougou University and the national SHD working group, and mobilizing the ADB and the UN agencies for this project.

2. Grassroots community initiatives and income-generating activities

One of the most urgent challenges facing Burkina Faso is to raise people's incomes and accelerate the development of human resources and productive potential through an integrated multidisciplinary anti-poverty approach. This involves a policy of promoting the self-advancement of civil society structures within village and peri-urban communities relating to the development of productive income-generating activities, with particular attention to women's advancement and gender issues. The actions of this program are targeted as a priority at the poorest provinces and are integrated with the support arrangements of the various development partners active in rural and peri-urban areas (European Union, the Austrian, Canadian, Danish, Dutch, French, and German development cooperation agencies, and NGOs).

There are two sub-programs:

– Support for community initiatives to strengthen local grassroots organizations through a self-advancement approach focusing on their own development initiatives. It contributes to building capacities for managing micro-projects through training; initiating and implementing micro-projects for agro-pastoral production, rural water supply, and non-industrial mining activities; and establishing networks among local development organizations with a view to experience-sharing.

– Improving women's access to credit by aiding the support fund for women's remunerative activities (FAARF), which aims to make credit available to women, individually or organized in associations, for starting small-scale income-generating activities.

3. Program for the development of social sectors

This involves meeting the challenges of accessibility and availability of basic social services. Operations address the improvement of the quality, availability and appropriateness of primary health care and basic education, and increasing people's participation; the program also supports AIDS control. In helping poverty reduction, this program targets primarily the most vulnerable groups, particularly women and children.

- *Cape Verde. A specific poverty reduction program*

In Cape Verde a program of this sort is justified by the need to implement adequate, targeted resources to remove the structural obstacles that perpetuate poverty.

Activities are based on the priorities decided by the government within the framework of the national poverty reduction program, and focus on issues related to the formulation of anti-poverty policies and strategies at national level, and support for practical measures of self-advancement and capacity-building for the poor. They will comprise action at two levels. At central level, UNDP, in partnership with the World Bank, will provide the government with assistance in producing the national poverty reduction program document, defining policies and the strategic framework. It provides a substantial methodological support for formulating strategies, and the basic studies required for identifying the program's priority actions. Training sessions are held for specialists in social communication so as to intensify the campaign against poverty with properly targeted messages. At local level, assistance is provided to implement the priority actions of capacity-building in the municipalities most affected by poverty.

UNDP provides support, within the national poverty reduction program, for the formulation and implementation of professional training and job creation programs, together with specialist national institutions. In its support for the development of the private sector, it concentrates on income-generating microenterprises and activities. These have great potential for development with the liberalization of the economy and guarantee the creation of stable jobs and high levels of income for the poor.

This support takes the form of: a) technical assistance in devising a regulatory framework in municipalities for decentralizing funds to support private sector development, and setting up a system of credit for microenterprises; b) support for professional training centers and the organization of a professional training system; c) technical and financial support for holding capacity-building workshops to promote microenterprises and income-generating activities; and d) local capacity-building (NGOs and community organizations) in finding innovative activities likely to create jobs and act as incubators for small projects to reduce poverty at local level. Assistance is provided for groups of female heads of households identified as the poorest, young people, families, and certain village groups for training in and acquisition of technologies and resources through microcredits, in crop and livestock farming, fisheries, and other processing activities.

Within the national environmental conservation program and the national desertification control plan, UNDP provides support at institutional level for a) regional planning, b) management of coastal zones, c) protection of biodiversity and genetic resources, d) monitoring of climatic change and prevention of natural disasters, e) information and training, and f) follow-up to the various international conventions and treaties ratified by Cape Verde. These actions will use the resources raised by the Capacity 21 program, the Global Environment Facility (GEF) and other bodies. At operational level, support for capacity-building in water supply and management in certain rural areas and the implementation of the UN Convention to Combat Desertification will be financed by UNCDF and UNSO funds already approved. With a view to raising resources, UNDP will pay particular attention to the use of wind and solar power in rural areas, management of urban space, sanitation in urban and rural centers, and the education, awareness and training in environmental issues.

- *Ghana. A program of capacity-building and poverty reduction*

UNDP's main strategic objective is to help the country encourage sustainable human development, with a particular stress on poverty reduction. Two priority themes have been identified: poverty reduction and capacity-building, with gender equality applying to both.

Based on the national poverty reduction framework designed with the help of UNDP, a support document for the poverty reduction program has already been produced in association with UN organizations and various bodies concerned. The document was approved by the government in January 1997.

Upstream, implementation of the program has begun in management capacity-building for the national development planning commission, the ministry of local authorities and rural development, district assemblies, etc., in terms of policy analysis and development of participatory methodologies. The capacities of the statistical service and the institute for statistical, social and economic research are being strengthened in order to provide annual monitoring and evaluation of the poverty reduction programs and the publication of a national human development report.

Downstream, where most of the program's resources are used, it supports the evaluation of participatory methodologies. The availability of basic services is being improved and the opportunity for the poor to access, use, manage and maintain these services is being increased. The resources granted for activities and resources of NGOs, community and private sector organizations are also being strengthened to enable them to participate fully in the creation of jobs and income.

Women's access to infrastructure and skills (management, enterprises, occupations, etc.) is given high priority. Women's awareness of civic and legal matters is encouraged and incentive programs are organized to promote girls' education.

UNDP works with other partners, such as the African Development Bank, World Bank and other bodies, to support the government's efforts to establish a social investment fund and contribute to community sustainable development projects and private-sector initiatives. Two feasibility studies are already underway in association with FAO, ILO, UNIDO, World Bank and UNDP. The intention is that the pillars of the fund should be stress on grassroots communities and access for the poor to credit.

At the same time, UNDP is helping the government establish a national program for capacity building and development to develop and rationalize the country's capacities, accelerate economic growth and ensure sustainable human development in five priority fields: a) formulating general guidelines; b) promoting the private sector; c) managing the public sector; d) decentralization; and e) human resources management.

- *Malawi. Poverty reduction and sustainable livelihoods*

There is a clear convergence between the objectives and priorities defined by the government and UNDP's mandate in Malawi, which is to promote sustainable human development through capacity-building. In these two fields the government and UNDP cooperate in:

a) *Reducing poverty by creating sustainable livelihoods,* mainly by target-ing action on groups living in absolute poverty and other disadvantaged groups in both rural and urban areas. UNDP supports the efforts made to increase the means for analyzing and monitoring poverty reduction policy and promoting participatory management of development.

b) *Capacity-building to empower local authorities:* UNDP supports the formulation, implementation and monitoring of community development initiatives, and helps the central government to improve its service to rural areas by providing training and support services in such fields as planning, financial management, participatory rural development, promotion of women's involvement in development, and the strengthening of local administrations.

c) *Ensuring the advancement of women and equality between the sexes,* by arguing for the allocation of at least 20% of available resources in the pro-gram to women's empowerment. The government has proposed that UNIFEM should support the implementation in Mali of the Beijing Action Plan and the policies formulated for that purpose by UN bodies.

d) *Promoting sustainable management of the environment and natural resources:* the government recognizes that it is important to formulate devel-opment strategies that respect the environment and to integrate environ-mental issues into development management systems at national level and at the level of districts, municipalities and communities. It is determined to integrate environmental issues into all activities supported by UNDP and increase the means available for applying international conventions on the environment.

- *Mauritania. Management and protection of the environment for poverty reduction*

On the basis of the prospects for development of the national economy and analyses of the state of sustainable human development, three priorities have been adopted in the country cooperation framework for 1997-2001: a) poverty reduction; b) environmental management and conservation; c) governance.

Under poverty reduction, there are three components:

– *Support for capacity-building and policy implementation.* This is intended to refine the national poverty reduction strategy by implementing monitoring and evaluation mechanisms. To that end, basic social data will be updated, and indicators of success improved so as to redirect policies and programs and form the basis for the new sustainable human develop-ment observatory. This component also cover the implementation of employment policy, stressing monitoring and evaluation.

– *Support for the private sector.* This is intended to promote and support the private sector, particularly by introducing a framework of incentives and regulations (investment code, customs system, commercial law) and a capacity-building program (training for private entrepreneurs, commercial information, management support, support for the informal sector). This component complements the support from donors such as the World Bank.

– Both components are flanked by *direct support for poverty reduction actions* such as: i) creation of labor-intensive socio-productive infrastructure in rural and peri-urban areas; ii) introduction of income-generating activities through microfinance intended to provide start-up capital for 80 peri-urban and rural women's cooperatives; iii) consolidation of the institutional framework for coordinating and executing poverty reduction programs; iv) enhancing food security by increasing the output and farm productivity of rural people, rehabilitating urban farming, mainly in Nouakchott, and provide access to clean water in rural areas. Seven *wilayas* (administrative districts) will be involved, covering 100 villages and grassroots communities.

Under environmental management and conservation, national objectives cover: desertification control, rational use of natural resources, and management of the environment.

UNDP assists the government to pursue its sustainable development strategy by helping devise a program of action (national Agenda 21) and integrate it into the national planning process. The salient features of this program of action are the following:

– *Desertification control.* In Mauritania, desertification control remains an integral part of poverty reduction activities, since desertification poses a constant threat to water points, housing, and factors of production such as dams and arable land, socio-productive infrastructure, and consequently human survival. This sub-program is intended to support the implementation of the UN Convention to Combat Desertification, which Mauritania has recently ratified.

– *Rational use of natural resources.* UNDP support here is used for: i) protection of forests and reduction of pressure on woodland resources through the development and support of alternative sources of renewable energy; ii) reducing the problems related to the overuse of aquifers; and iii) identifying and implementing the actions necessary to reduce the ecological consequences of the entry into service of the Diama and Mannantali dams.

– *Environmental management.* UNDP resources are used in order to help prepare and implement: i) an urban environmental management plan comprising factors related to sanitation and waste treatment; ii) a coastal development plan.

• *Mozambique. Investment in human capital and poverty reduction*

The government has invested in human capital by improving education, health services and social services, essential elements of its poverty reduction strategy. It is gradually extending the coverage of the school system, while improving its quality. This requires the reconstruction of destroyed infrastructure, teacher training, and raising incomes to cover current expenses. These initiatives are part of the strategic education plan introduced by the government to follow on from the World Conference on Education for All. The plan was formulated with help from UNDP in cooperation with UNESCO, the World Bank, the Swedish development cooperation agency and other donors. With this program, the government intends to increase by 86% the school enrolment ratio by 2002. In implementing the education plan, the government will be supported by UNDP, which will continue its support for primary teacher training throughout the country so as to increase the number of teachers and improve the quality of teaching.

The government has maintained its objective of ensuring access to health services, and considerable resources have been allocated to this sector in order to strengthen preventive care services, develop health care infrastructure and modernize the whole primary health system. UNDP is also participating in the development of programs designed to improve health care delivery at local level, particularly in the North of the country. In its efforts to remedy the serious problem of unemployment among marginalized young people, the ministry for social action has devised a national plan of action for the young. UNDP, UNFPA and other associated bodies are cooperating in formulating a social program of action to promote professional training, access to education and the creation of jobs for young people and other vulnerable groups.

- *Namibia. Integrated poverty reduction at community level in rural and urban areas*

Local poverty reduction programs in rural areas are aimed at the most marginalized groups. They have adopted a concerted, cross-sectoral approach, including grassroots agricultural operations and complementary activities for health, education, water supply and small businesses. In urban and peri-urban areas it is necessary to improve skills to create jobs and sustainable livelihoods.

Poverty reduction is one of the four objectives of the first national development plan. The government has produced a national poverty reduction plan, and will examine this issue with its partners at the next donor roundtable.

UNDP is determined to act as a catalyst in the cooperation between government, donors, the private sector and NGOs to arrive at integrated, targeted and effective programs for poverty reduction in Namibia. To that end, support is provided to the government to link more specifically the national poverty reduction plan, strategy and program, and to promote synergy between all the players. To set the ball rolling, UNDP is providing support in the context of the thematic group on poverty alleviation, which is already working to develop an integrated community program for poverty reduction, starting with a pilot program in the Ohangwena region. UNDP mobilizes grassroots and other resources in cooperation with other UN bodies and donors, to support the poverty reduction program, targeting women and vulnerable and marginalized groups.

Unemployment, estimated to be 19% in urban areas, mainly affects the young. UNDP assistance to reduce poverty in urban areas targets street children.

In the subsistence economy, women make an essential contribution to poverty reduction and improved living standards. The government is using legislative initiatives, programs and actions in its continued effort to "demarginalize" Namibian women. More effort is needed to combat traditional attitudes which hinder women's involvement in economic life and ban them from decision-making positions.

UNDP is also supporting the government's efforts to extend the coverage of basic social services to more poor groups.

- *Zimbabwe. An integrated strategy for managing development and poverty reduction*

In February 1995, the Zimbabwean government launched a national plan of action to alleviate poverty. With technical assistance from UNDP, NGOs, community organizations, the private sector and other components of civil society worked to improved the living standards of the poorest segments of the population. To support the plan of action, UNDP and other donors financed a national poverty evaluation study, which provided a complete picture of poverty in Zimbabwe from the answers to a questionnaire circulated in 16,000 homes and among the homeless. UNDP and the government also held six workshops to discuss poverty reduction in the context of sustainable human development. UNDP encourages dialogue about poverty between the government and civil society through a poverty forum and a national committee. The result of this dialogue is reflected in the national human development report which the Forum prepared with the University of Zimbabwe. UNDP also envisages translating the Plan of action into local languages to achieve greater community involvement in poverty reduction. UNDP and the government have begun discussions about integrating the Plan of action in Zimbabwe's national development plans and the second phase of its economic reform program. The World Bank is jointly financing some of these activities.

Four major areas for action are envisaged in poverty reduction; they take the form of four specific programs related both to the formulation of a national policy and to local initiatives: capacity-building for implementing the plan of action; job creation (including aid to the unstructured sector, framework-organizations, women working in mines, cultural tourism, training for entrepreneurs and help for enterprise creators, other activities generating local employment); support for decentralization; national policy and program of drought management.

The operations planned in this sector will improve the principles for action and monitoring of poverty reduction; they are intended to directly benefit the most disadvantaged groups through the creation of jobs and sustainable livelihoods.

Poverty reduction involves achieving sustained economic growth that generates investment and jobs. The current priority is to reduce the budget deficit and create an environment favorable to economic activity through improved management of the public sector, strategic planning, and new partnerships between the State and the private sector. The Zimbabwean government considers that because UNDP has already taken part in the country's past major reforms, it is better placed than anyone to help it acquire the capacities to control and target its development, and manage its economic transformation more effectively.

UNDP's assistance is part of a varied program of support for development. One of the major objectives of the program is to help the government build its capacities to harmonize and coordinate the various reforms it has undertaken. The program also aims at giving the government the technical capacities to manage its action and strategic planning on the basis of a comprehensive vision of development focusing on the general objective of poverty reduction.

3. Management, monitoring and evaluation procedures

The strategies encouraged by UNDP aim at a more flexible participatory approach to implementing the various regional and national programs. The general principle for action is to attract and retain the most reliable and efficient experts (i.e. both traditional development partners and new partners, including African NGOs and civil society organizations, private consultancies, universities and other research institutes) while ensuring the continuous supply of services and a strict obligation to render accounts. The regional program also identifies and develops a core of national and regional institutions and improves their ability to implement effective programs by forming networks and developing active partnerships.

The regional and national programs focus on UNDP's basic principles for monitoring and evaluating results. The monitoring and evaluation system is an important instrument of management used for decision-making. It enables all the stakeholders to ensure that their programs and activities remain relevant over time as conditions change. For each sub-program, a working plan is drawn up at design stage, containing precise objectives and appropriate timeframes and performance indicators for evaluating progress achieved. These indicators concern both quantitative and qualitative changes. They are based on reference data established before the programs are introduced and agreed in consultation with the various development partners. By monitoring performance, the evaluation system guides decisions about allocating resources so that the overall objectives of the program and its associated funds are achieved. It will also be a major instrument for measuring progress made in capacity-building and the long-term viability of activities.

The programs and projects are the subject of annual examination meetings during attended by all partners. Furthermore, the implementing bodies produce annual interim reports on future working plans and the likely volume of resources available. The main findings of the annual examination meetings and reports are notified to the program management supervision committee. Under the rules and procedures of UNDP, the regional program will be subject to a three-yearly examination in 1999 in consultation with the supervision committee and the evaluation bureau. Programs financed by grassroots resources will be evaluated independently and the findings reviewed with all partners.

4. Financing poverty reduction

UNDP support for anti-poverty programs comes mainly from: i) national and regional allocations from UNDP's core resources, roughly $1 billion a year, from the voluntary contributions of Member States, and ii) "shared-cost" contributions or cofinancing of specific poverty reduction activities from the governments of recipient countries and other donor countries.

In March 1996, UNDP launched a new "poverty reduction strategic initiative" clearly targeted and explicitly designed to support the monitoring and implementation by countries of the commitments they made at the Copenhagen Summit. The aim of this initiative is to help countries formulate or strengthen national strategies and plans for the reduction of poverty and inequality. UNDP, Denmark and the Netherlands are the donors behind this initiative.

Box 7.7.

The United Nations System-wide Special Initiative on Africa
and the United Nations Development Assistance Framework

The Special Initiative, among other objectives, aims at promoting and coordinating cooperation between the various United Nations specialized institutions and, at increased harmonization in order to support national priorities, reduce transactions costs, improve assistance efficiency and ensuring that the resources of the United Nations bodies are utilized more profitably. The new system wide programming instrument, the United Nations Development Assistance Framework (UNDAF), which was designed to facilitate the reform of the United Nations Organization, although at it initial stage, it contributes to strengthen coordination and collaboration at national level. The synergy between the objectives of the special Initiative and the strategy underlying the United Nations Development Assistance Framework should be fully used.

The substantive issues adressed by the UNDAF include:

– National needs and priorities.

– Coordinated follow-up to UN conferences and support for the implementation of conventions and declarations.

– Crosscutting issues such as human rights, food security, environmental sustainability, population, gender equality, poverty eradication, governance, HIV/AIDS and the promotion and protection of children's rights.

– Regional and sub-regional issues, including specific UN initiatives, of pressing concern to a country.

The initiatives taken in ten African countries (South Africa, Ghana, Kenya, Madagascar, Malawi, Mali, Mozambique, Namibia, Senegal and Zimbabwe) concretely illustrate the manner in which the United Nations' country teams harmonize the efforts they are making under the collegial leadership of the resident coordinator. Some activities jointly taken under the Special Initiative and the UNDAF such as concerted programming are taking shape but they need to be tested and implemented, namely in the priority sectors defined after the refocusing of the special initiative, taking into account the objectives aimed at by the UN major conferences.

UNDP participation and support are essential for the viability of the special Initiative and the chairperson of the United Nations Development Group, who is the UNDP Administrator guides policy coordination, supervises implementation and ensures that the system of resident coordinators runs smoothly and facilitates coherent grouping of the many facets of activities conducted at national level by the United Nations bodies. In that respect, the UNDP plays a leading role in coordinating the activities conducted in the priority sectors of the special Initiative related to the management of public affairs and to sustainable modes of subsistence in the zones considered as marginal in environmental terms.

Source: UNO, *United Nations System-wide Special Initiative on Africa,* New York, 1998.

The initiative supports actions to evaluate poverty at national and regional levels, to determine its profile, causes, extent and distribution within a country or region. It helps governments set up national targets and objectives for poverty reduction and contributes to implementing the 20/20 Initiative at national and regional level and giving an impetus to the development of appropriate poverty reduction strategies. The initiative also finances activities such as national public awareness campaigns and advocacy campaigns to mobilize civil society organizations, the private sector and other groups to join the government in coordinated action to reduce poverty.

In more general terms, UNDP would like to benefit from the potential support expected from the United Nations System-wide Special Initiative on Africa.

5. Conclusion and prospects

In Africa, the magnitude of the challenge to be met in poverty reduction remains vast and requires the mobilization of all partners involved in the development process. In 1997, income poverty affected some 220 million people in Africa, roughly 45% of the population. Poverty is extending its grip on the continent and particularly the least developed countries. Furthermore, Sub-Saharan Africa has the highest incidence and fastest increase in poverty: it is estimated that income poverty will affect half the population of the region by 2000. Within Africa, women, children and old people are the most affected by human poverty.

In overall human development terms, the challenges of Sub-Saharan Africa are considerable. The health and education indicators show severe deficiencies. The morbidity and mortality rates are now higher in Africa than in the rest of the world. Health and nutrition standards have deteriorated, and Africa is the continent hardest hit by AIDS. Furthermore, recent armed conflicts have caused terrible damage and destruction.

Some striking successes have, however, been recorded. Between 1960 and 1995, life expectancy at birth in Sub-Saharan Africa rose from 40 to 51 years. Between 1970 and 1995, the adult literacy rate more than doubled. From 1960 to 1995, net enrolment ratios increased from 25% to 50% for primary school and from 13% to 38% for secondary school. The proportion of the population with access to safe drinking water rose from 25% in 1980 to 43% in 1995. There has also been significant progress in the advancement of African women: for example, female literacy as a percentage of male literacy is over 60, a higher proportion than in the Arab States and South Asia.

Despite the extent of human poverty, the long-term negative trends can be reversed if the international community and African governments decide to put poverty reduction at the center of their concerns and their development strategies and policies. Important steps have been taken in this direction since 1995-96. To that end, the international community, following the Copenhagen Summit, has set itself ambitious objectives in poverty reduction.

By 2000, universal access to basic education should be achieved, and at least 80% of children of primary school age should complete their primary education. Life expectancy should be no lower than 60 in any country, and the health status of all the peoples in the world should enable them to lead socially and economically productive lives, by guaranteeing a secure and nutritionally adequate supply of food at national and international level.

Poverty reduction has been explicitly stated as a development priority, following the Copenhagen Summit. In 1996, at the 34th high-level meeting of the OECD's Development Assistance Committee (DAC), poverty reduction was considered to be the main objective of development: the proportion of people living in extreme poverty was to be halved by 2015.

These ambitious objectives can only be achieved by a firm commitment and determined action by the whole international community in favor of poverty reduction. A first important stage will be the production of national policies and plans of action for poverty reduction. This is a way of formulating or strengthening the implementation of national poverty reduction plans that focus on the structural causes of poverty, including action at local, national and subregional level. The plans should establish for each country's circumstances strategies, objectives and targets to be achieved within a reasonable period for the substantial reduction of general poverty and the eradication of absolute poverty. National plans should pay particular attention to job creation, access to basic social services, income generation and promotion of access to productive resources and economic opportunities.

The comparative advantages of UNDP will enable it to act as catalyst for poverty reduction initiatives. UNDP has provided effective and recognized support for the formulation of government plans of action and national programs. It has the advantage of being an impartial and neutral development partner, providing therefore a particular point of view on issues of policy dialogue, formulation of strategies and operational programs and financing. These specific actions can only be effective and achieve their objectives with the support of the entire international community and the full involvement of donors in poverty reduction activities.

As can be seen from the analyses made internationally and nationally and the analysis of country cooperation frameworks in 1998, over 30 countries have designed poverty reduction strategies with the support of UNDP/Africa, and 23 African countries have focused their human development report on poverty, compared with 10 in 1996. Benin, Burkina Faso, the Comoros, Guinea, Madagascar, Namibia, Nigeria and Uganda have for the first time produced a national report on this theme. When national reports are used in internal consultation within societies, they reveal the differences between a quantitative and a qualitative vision of poverty, in particular, when possible, between poverty defined by the level of income and poverty in human living standards.

In 1997 and 1998, UNDP made use of the descriptions of poverty and public spending reviews produced jointly with the World Bank. The information thus provided about the nature and extent of poverty showed the measures to be taken to reduce it.

Whereas between 1980 and 1990 only six countries had undertaken analyses, profiles and evaluations of poverty at national level, thirty-seven have now made such analyses. Similarly, whereas in the same period no overall multidimensional poverty reduction strategy had been defined, let alone implemented, now ten countries have formulated strategies and are beginning to implement them, and nine other governments are currently designing such processes.

Poverty reduction cannot depend simply on an international commitment to these objectives. Initiatives must be introduced for the region as a whole and within each African country. Regional operations must be envisaged to build the capacities available in Sub-Saharan African countries to reduce poverty as part of sustainable human development. The regional approach should exhibit three features: i) address problems common to more than one country whose solution requires simultaneous concerted action by all the countries involved; ii) strengthen the sense of ownership and ensure better coordination and interaction between partners; iii) encourage the exchange of knowledge and sharing of information and experience within the region and with other regions.

At national level, the prime responsibility for poverty reduction lies with national governments. Actions and operations in Sub-Saharan Africa should use four complementary methods: i) policy dialogue and support for the formulation of strategies; ii) more extensive examination of development ideas, particularly the sustainable human development paradigm; iii) operational activities to implement programs and projects; and iv) raising financing and creating alliances.

When a poverty reduction strategy is being designed, it is important to ensure that the macro, meso and micro levels are considered in order to construct a coherent whole likely to facilitate the flow of information, communication and interaction between the levels, and also arrive at an operational strategy that perfectly meets its poverty reduction objectives, including the objectives of raising incomes, meeting essential needs, and capacity-building for the poorest groups.

Analysis of the guidelines and methods selected for poverty reduction strategies and programs is highly instructive, because it reveals the predominance of new themes such as governance, economic management, employment promotion, development of social sectors, and the advancement of women and gender issues.

An important element in the action UNDP has taken in States to reduce poverty is its action against HIV/AIDS. UNDP remains in the vanguard of HIV/AIDS awareness campaigns in African countries. In Uganda, for example, UNDP support is helping to slow infection rates. In December 1997, UNDP funded a seminar of African mayors, held in Abidjan, Côte d'Ivoire, leading to the creation of an alliance of African mayors against HIV/AIDS.

After 20 years' sustained efforts, UNDP has practically succeeded, together with the World Bank and bilateral donors, in eradicating river-blindness in the river basins of the Niger and Volta, recovering land for more than one million people in 10 West African countries. The disadvantaged in Africa do not generally have access to clean water and sanitation. In 12 countries, UNDP, together with the World Bank and bilateral donors, has brought clean water to millions of people in rural communities and assisted the creation of waste treatment companies.

In 1995, following the decisions of the Copenhagen Summit, UNDP made poverty reduction the essential priority of its action. This involves developing or consolidating capacities for human development in regions and countries. UNDP support for African countries in poverty reduction has translated into operations at global, regional and national levels.

UNDP's main objectives and plans of action for the years ahead concern:

– strengthening policy dialogue and sustainable human development strategies through a more effective implementation of the UN Special Initiative for Africa;

– Supporting the formulation of strategies and operational programs of economic and social development and poverty reduction so that they are more people-centered;

– Providing better access for people to basic services and the fulfilment of minimum requirements;

– Intensifying national advocacy and capacity-building actions to raise financing, manage and coordinate aid, and their impact on development;

– Creating partnerships with civil society and the mobilization of donors in favor of poverty reduction programs. In countries in crisis, this involves supporting early warning mechanisms and national programs for reconciliation, rehabilitation and reconstruction;

   – Supporting national programs for managing the economy and the implementation of the Highly Indebted Poor Countries (HIPC) debt initiative;

   – Supporting initiatives that enhance African countries' integration into the world and regional economies.

Only by implementing and reinforcing action at the global, regional and national levels, by attacking poverty in all its dimensions — monetary and human — with an approach that integrates the macro, meso and micro levels, will it be possible to meet the challenges of poverty reduction and reverse the poverty trend in Africa.

By supporting these various activities, UNDP determines its focuses for support and operations in Africa, recommends improvement and innovative practices to ensure observable progress in poverty reduction, and, above all, assists governments, and development partners in the broadest sense, to design and implement sound operational poverty reduction strategies. This approach can only be successful if all stakeholders accept genuine responsibility: governments, civil society, development partners. This whole-hearted involvement will also require the formation of strategic alliances between the players to meet the challenges posed by poverty in Sub-Saharan Africa.

Annexes

Annexes

Poverty profiles

1. Absolute and relative poverty

Apart from utilitarian and non-utilitarian considerations, poverty is generally defined as "a state of deprivation of well-being judged inadequate to live decently". [1] Since poverty is related to well-being, discussions about defining and measuring poverty naturally resemble discussions about well-being. Using this reference concept, the distinction is made between absolute and relative poverty.

1.1. Absolute poverty

The term "absolute poverty" is used when an individual, household or family does not possess the attributes considered to be those of well-being. [2] Absolute poverty is thus related to a poverty line expressed in absolute values and corresponding to the ability to meet minimum needs. The poverty line calculated from data on individual and household consumption, where a cut-off threshold is laid down below which individuals and households are considered to be poor, use this absolute approach.

Similarly, with the absolute income approach, a person is in absolute poverty if their income falls below a poverty threshold defined in terms of people's income. For example, the World Bank standard for identifying poverty, less than $1 per person per day, is an absolute definition of poverty based on income.

---

1. S. Larivière & F. Martin, *Le cadre d'analyse économique de la pauvreté et des conditions de vie des ménages* (Québec, 1997).

2. See also Renata Lok Dessallien, *Poverty, Module 1 - Poverty Indicators*, Technical Support Document (UNDP, SEDEP/BPPS, 1995).

The advantage of this approach is that it sets a predefined, fixed poverty line, so that it is possible to count the number of individuals or households below the line and thus clearly identify a group of people considered to be poor. In general, the people below the poverty line are divided into two groups: the poor and the extremely poor, for whom income or consumption are not even sufficient to meet minimum food requirements. In Sub-Saharan Africa, the absolute approach, with the calculation of an absolute poverty line, has been adopted by nearly 25 countries. In general, these thresholds have been calculated on the basis of calorie consumption or from a threshold combining food and non-food expenditure, or again by the World Bank standard of $1 per person per day.

1.2. Relative poverty

The relative poverty approach is closer to the concept of inequality, since it is concerned with the relative differences between people in a given community. Relative poverty varies and takes different forms even within the community or social group being examined. Relative poverty can thus be found in any social stratum of a society, within both the groups called "poor" and those with higher living standards.

The term "relative poverty" is used, for example, for people who are less well off than other members of the same community. In terms of income, a person is relatively poor if they belong to a bottom income group (such as the poorest 10%).

Relative poverty thresholds are less frequently used for measuring poverty. The reason is that the poor groups identified by this method are ultimately one end of the income distribution curve. In general, when this method is adopted, the measurement used corresponds to a predetermined percentage of the population (from 25% to 50%) whose income is lower than the national average.

2. Different types of absolute poverty line

Poverty lines for international comparison. For international comparison, the World Bank uses a poverty line set at $1 (1985 PPP$) per person per day. This poverty line is based on consumption.

It is recommended to use a poverty line of $2 (PPP) for Latin America and the Caribbean, and a poverty line of $4 (1990 PPP$) for Eastern Europe and the Newly Independent States. For comparison among industrialized countries, the poverty line is $14.40 (1985 PPP$) per person per day.

• *National poverty lines.* Developing countries that have set national poverty lines generally use the food poverty method. These lines indicate the insufficiency of economic resources to meet minimum food require-ments. There are three main methods for measuring food poverty.

• *Cost-of-basic-needs method*. Here the poverty line relates to the cost of a basic diet for the main age, gender and activity groups, plus a few essen-tial non-food items. A survey then establishes the proportion of people liv-ing in households whose consumption (or sometimes whose income) falls below this line. The basic diet may be defined as the least expensive foods needed to meet basic nutritional requirements, the typical adult diet in the lowest consumption quintile (20%) or the investigator's notion of a mini-mal but decent diet. The choice of the food and non-food items is necessar-ily arbitrary.

• *Food energy method*. This is based on the consumption expenditure that just enables a person to acquire a sufficient quantity of food to meet predetermined food energy requirements. Dietary energy intake, as the dependent variable, is regressed against household consumption per adult equivalent. The poverty line is set at the level of total consumption per per-son at which the statistical expectation of dietary energy intake exactly meets average dietary energy requirements.

• *Food share method*. This consists in calculating the food budget that covers the cost of acquiring just sufficient nutrients. If the cost of basic nutrients is a third of a household's total consumption, the poverty line is set at three times that cost.

All three methods to setting the food poverty line are sensitive to the price levels used to determine the cost of all the food items. Each of them focuses on the quantity of calories or dietary energy, because food defi-ciency due to insufficient economic resources is considered in most societ-ies as evidence of poverty. However, at the suggestion of UNDP, poverty lines increasingly include the non-food share of consumption, from the viewpoint of access to basic goods and human poverty.

3. Poverty indicators

3.1. Poverty rate or incidence of poverty

The poverty rate, or incidence of poverty, is simply an estimate of the percentage of people living below the poverty line. This indicator gives no information about the depth of poverty and cannot therefore take account of any deterioration in living standards among people who are already poor.

Figure A1.1. Measurement of poverty

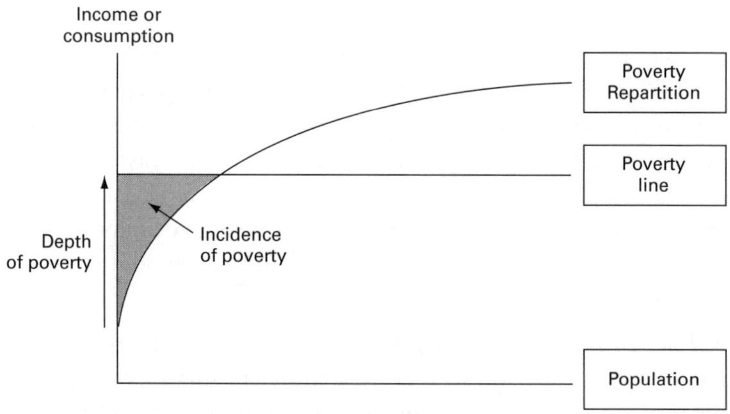

3.2. Depth of poverty

The depth of poverty can be measured as the average distance below the poverty line, expressed as a percentage of that line. This average is calculated from the whole population, poor and non-poor. Since this measurement — also called the poverty gap — shows the average distance of the poor from the poverty line, it gives a better picture of any deterioration in living standards.

3.3. Severity of poverty

The severity of poverty can be measured as a weighted average of the squared distance below the poverty line, expressed as a percentage of that line. The weights are given by each individual gap. Again the average is calculated from the whole population. Since the weights increase with poverty, this measure is sensitive to inequalities among the poor.

3.4. Transient or temporary poverty, and chronic poverty

As its name suggests, transient poverty refers to short-term, temporary or seasonal poverty, and chronic poverty to long-term or structural poverty. The poverty line refers to the group of people who, according to the season, are above or below the poverty line.

3.5. Vulnerability

Vulnerability has two sides: external exposure to shocks, stress and risk, and internal defencelessness, a lack of means to cope with crises without devastating effects.

4. Surveys used to construct poverty profiles

4.1. Quantitative surveys

The most comprehensive of the main household surveys that have been used to define poverty thresholds in Sub-Saharan Africa are the Living Standards Measurement Studies (LSMS) initiated and implemented by the World Bank. [1] This survey collects information and data under the following modules: household consumption and expenditure; education; health; employment and income-generating activities; housing; etc. It is subdivided into three types of questionnaires concerning: i) households; ii) the community; and iii) prices. The household questionnaire, for example, comprises 17 sections and over 50 identifiable items within these sections.

This "household" module takes longest and requires most tact. It is intended to give an overall appreciation of quality of life, consumption and incomes in households. The community module covers the community's access to basic infrastructure and social services. It also includes farming practices, the seasonal employment market, and wage variations. The price module measures household purchasing power, concentrating on the cost of the purchases and sales made by low-income households.

In general, apart from its exhaustive nature, the implementation of this survey raises a number of problems noted by the World Bank itself. First, it is a long and expensive survey. It lasts 18-20 months and costs on average $500,000-$700,000. Second, it occupies many state services for months in collecting the data and analyzing the results. Third, since most of the analysis is done in Washington, there is little or no national capacity-building, poor appropriation of the findings in the country concerned, and poor accessibility of the findings for national experts. This is why very few African countries have been able to conduct more than one survey of this type, which makes it impossible to achieve any useful evaluation of changes in poverty and incomes.

However, most of the poverty lines set in the Sub-Saharan African countries have been calculated from the data from these surveys. Botswana, the Comoros, Cape Verde, Guinea Bissau, Kenya, Lesotho, Malawi, Mali, Namibia, Togo, Uganda and Zimbabwe have established their poverty lines on the basis of LSMS surveys or budget/consumption surveys.

---

1. See also G. Aho, S. Larivière et F. Martin, *Manuel d'analyse de la pauvreté: applications au Bénin* (Université Laval, PNUD, 1997); M. Grosh and P. Glewwe, *A Guide to Living Standards Measurement Study Surveys and Their Data Sets* (Washington: World Bank, 1995); Renata Lok Dessallien, *Poverty, Module 2 - From Data Collection to Poverty Assessments*, Technical Support Document (UNDP, BPPS, 1996).

Budget/Consumption Surveys adopt the same approach. [1] These are surveys similar to the first module of the LSMS survey concerning household income and expenditure, including data on the structure and composition of households and their income and consumption, mainly of food. They exhibit the same qualities and defects as the LSMS surveys. Their cost is estimated at $500,000-$700,000 over 16-18 months, and they can also be used to calculate a poverty line. In general, in developing countries, these surveys have only been carried out in urban areas with the quite precise objective of establishing a consumer price index. This is the case, for example, in Guinea, where the exercise was used to calculate an urban poverty line. [2]

The World Bank is aware of the limitations of these methodologies, basically cost, staff time for surveys and analysis, and poor appropriation of exercises and findings. It has decided to use a more manageable methodology for evaluating household consumption and income with the more explicit aim of defining poverty thresholds. These are the **Household Priority Surveys** which mainly cover household income and consumption. Like the LSMS surveys, they aim to produce socioeconomic indicators and identify poor or vulnerable groups, mainly by analyzing household consumption. In general, these priority surveys concentrate on identifying, analyzing and monitoring the population groups most affected by structural adjustment policies. The standard questionnaire, applicable in all countries, comprises 13 sections that are fairly similar to the "household" module of an LSMS survey.

This method tends to be more manageable and less expensive than a complete budget/consumption survey: the questionnaire is shorter, the sample is smaller, and the analysis less exhaustive. It generally takes 7-8 months to collect and analyze the data, at an average cost of $300,000. The World Bank recommends, however, that for effective monitoring of household consumption and vulnerable groups, a survey of this sort should be repeated every two or three years, which naturally increases its cost and use of human resources. Among Sub-Saharan African countries, Burkina Faso, Guinea, Mauritania, Niger, Senegal, Zambia and others have carried out this sort of study and used the findings to define poverty lines. [3]

---

1. See also United Nations Department of Technical Cooperation for Development, *Household Income and Expenditure Surveys: A Technical Study* (New York, 1989).

2. Y. Diabate et M. Kessaba, *Pauvreté en Guinée: analyse micro-économique* (Conakry: PNUD, 1995).

3. INSD, *Analyse des résultats de l'enquête prioritaire sur les conditions de vie des ménages,* (Burkina Faso, 1996).

The ILO has set up relatively similar instruments to evaluate the structure of poverty. These are the **Rapid Assessment Surveys of Poverty (RASPs)**. The main items assessed are the following:

- identification and structure of households,
- health,
- education,
- income-generating activities,
- employment status,
- household income and expenditure,
- characteristics of housing,
- food consumption.

Relatively rare in Sub-Saharan Africa, these surveys have been applied in urban areas to extend analyses of employment and poverty. However, in Cameroon, Côte d'Ivoire, Madagascar, and Mali they have been used to establish urban poverty lines. [1]

4.2. Qualitative surveys [2]

• *Intensive sociological and anthropological methods*

Intensive sociological and anthropological surveys are based on participatory observation, the methodological foundation of both sociology and anthropology. They therefore require an extended stay by the researchers within the community, with the prime aim of participating in community life and observing the behavior and reactions of individuals and the group. The type of data collected includes information about individual and particularly collective values, ideas, culture and behavior.

In general, these methods are not very practical for producing a poverty profile, because they are too general and not specifically addressed to the aim of the research, namely poverty. Furthermore, the methodology is complicated and the surveys long and expensive. No poverty profile for a country in Sub-Saharan Africa has therefore used this sort of method for assessing perceived and qualitative aspects.

---

1. M. Hopkins, *A Short Review of Contemporary Thinking about Anti-Poverty Strategies* (Geneva, 1997).

2. On participatory methodologies, see G. Aho, S. Larivière et F. Martin, *Manuel d'analyse de la pauvreté: applications au Bénin* (Université Laval, PNUD, 1997); J.M. Cohen and N. Uphoff, "Participation's Place in Rural Development: Seeking Clarity through Specificity", *World Development*, vol.8, 1980; S. Paugam, "Représentation et perception de la pauvreté", *Problèmes économiques*, n°2508, 1997; World Bank, *Methods and Tools for Social Assessment and Participation* (Washington, 1995); Renata Lok Dessallien, *Poverty, Module 2 - From Data Collection to Poverty Assessments*, Technical Support Document (UNDP, BPPS, 1996).

• *Beneficiary assessment*

This sort of method is generally used to evaluate the effectiveness of a particular program or project. It involves systematic consultation of all those who took part in a project in order to identify their reactions, points of view and perceptions of the work in progress.

A survey of this type carried out in the Comoro Islands with population groups considered to be poor was used to define a subjective poverty threshold for urban and rural areas. The survey sought to define poverty more accurately, identify the poor, and also identify perceptions of the causes of poverty and the solutions to be applied in poverty reduction.

Based on individual interviews or focus groups, this method involves choosing a representative sample, rigorously selecting the investigators, and properly clarifying the objectives. It is useful to note that this method can be attached, for its sample and investigation type, to an LSMS survey. In that case it complements and assesses more accurately people's concerns under the themes addressed in the LSMS survey.

The pattern for the individual interview or focus group is generally to cover the following theme:
  – health: perception, accessibility, etc.,
  – education: perception, accessibility, problems encountered, etc.,
  – food and nutrition,
  – use of natural resources,
  – sources and use of income,
  – definition of poverty and well-being.

Although this type of survey collects data considered as reliable as the quality of the sample, it raises major concerns. Because it depends on a survey of living standards, this lengthens the analysis phase, and it is restricted to essentially quantitative themes. It is an accompaniment to the quantitative survey rather than a complementary approach.

• *Rapid participatory appraisal (RPA)*

Chambers began this approach in the 1970s. It attempts to put communities at the core of the development process by sharing the viewpoint of ordinary people about problems and their solutions. In general, these methods involve local participation at every stage of the approach, using a multidisciplinary team and simple, informal techniques — mainly questionnaires, interviews, participatory observation, case studies, etc. Their main objective is to complement quantitative approaches to achieve a better knowledge of the needs and responses of grassroots communities. [1]

---

1. R. Chambers, "The Origins and Practice of Participatory Rural Appraisal", *World Development*, vol. 22, n° 7, 1994.

An essential characteristic of these methods is the use of diversified, complementary tools. The main techniques used in RPA surveys are:
- group interviews and semi-structured interviews,
- listening to the most disadvantaged population groups,
- participatory analysis and modeling,
- oral history and life stories,
- seasonal and historical diagrams,
- analysis of daily activities,
- ranking preferences for well-being and wealth,
- institutional Venn diagrams; triangulation and verification of results.

Despite the amount of relevant information this sort of survey can produce, the method suffers from a number of serious constraints. First, the sample size is generally small and unrepresentative. Second, as with LSMS surveys on the quantitative side, the method is cumbersome, time-consuming and requires intensive know-how and human resources. Third, given the number of tools used, the method is not standardized and makes it hard to establish comparisons and synergies with the findings of quantitative surveys.

- *Participatory poverty assessments in rural and urban areas*

The methodology used to assess people's perceptions of well-being and poverty have two components, interviews with focus groups and the use of "weighted individual voting" to rank the dimensions of poverty and the recommended solutions. The aim of the focus groups is to reveal the main dimensions of well-being and poverty as perceived by local people. Each focus group is chosen to be homogenous on three criteria: age (young, adult, elderly), sex, and location of village or district in each region/town surveyed.

The "weighted individual voting" method aims to establish for each individual a ranking of priorities in the determining factors for improving well-being, by socioeconomic category. A series of pictures representing important factors for well-being as identified by people in focus groups are prepared by a specialized team. This type of survey is carried out in the form of a vote in which each participant is asked individually and in private to rank the pictures of well-being likely to increase their degree of well-being and reduce their degree of poverty. Altogether, dozens of dimensions of well-being are identified and each one is represented by more than one picture, to avoid rationing.

4.3. Hybrid methods

Sentinel Surveillance Sites (SSSs) were developed by UNICEF in the 1980s. This type of survey aims primarily to evaluate the impact of policies and projects on target groups, by means of diversified tools: interviews, discussion groups, and the production of relevant databases.

SSS surveys have the advantage of being fast, relatively inexpensive (roughly $40,000 to $50,000) and requiring not much time (about 3 months). Although they are based on limited samples, they can provide policy-makers with useful information on precise topics. These studies raise a number of problems, however, to do with insufficient data control; excessive similarity in the site selected, and changes in household behavior caused by the frequent survey visits. However, these surveys are an important source of information for constructing the socioeconomic indicators of a poverty profile.

5. Socioeconomic indicators

5.1. Household income and consumption

From the various surveys of household living standards (LSMS, budget/consumption surveys, priority surveys of ILO RASP surveys) and the demographic surveys or censuses carried out in a country, it is possible to acquire a comprehensive view of households, their structure, consumption, income and output. The following topics arise in the study of households:

* *Demographic information on the structure, size and demographic behavior of poor households*
  – size of household,
  – age and sex structure,
  – dependency ratio: number of non-active members (children and old people) over active members,
  – sex of head of household,
  – total fertility rate: average number of births per woman in her lifetime.

Census results, demographic studies, and demography and health surveys provide useful data that can be used, to determine these categories.

* *Information on the incomes of poor households*

The level and distribution of incomes are important determining factors for the analysis of poverty. Apart from indicators of the sources and types of income, a number of indicators are used to assess more accurately the level and distribution of incomes and ensuing inequalities. Examples are the Lorenz curve and the Gini and Theil coefficients, which cover various aspects of income distribution.

- *Information on consumption expenditure of poor households*

The structure of consumption expenditure can be used to characterize households by describing the breakdown of food and non-food expenditure. The value of studying the structure of expenditure is to measure the relative importance of goods and services consumed by households according to their level of poverty, which gives some indication of the likely impact of price variations on household purchasing power. One may expect basic products, especially food, to make up a significant share of total expenditure by the poor.

Apart from household consumption structure, examination must be made of price policies and their impact on the consumption of the poor in general, and their consumption of public services in particular. Then, it is important to identify the main risks encountered by the poor in consumption: type of risk, possible occurrence and recommended solutions. This section should also consider information on household behavior in the face of changes in incomes and prices.

In general, this information has already been used to devise those poverty lines that are based on household consumption. As mentioned in the section on poverty thresholds, poor and extremely poor households devote over half, or even two-thirds, of their expenditure to food. This is a fundamental fact about poverty in Sub-Saharan Africa. For example, in Benin, Burkina Faso and Mali, poor rural households spend at least 75% of their income on food.

- *Information on the property and assets of poor households*

The property and assets of a household comprise basically of its tangible goods and financial assets, if any. This indicator is useful because it represents the household's wealth reserve and thus affects income flow. Furthermore, some households, particularly in rural areas, may be income poor, but rich when their assets are taken into account. In general, particularly in rural areas, the possession of means of production, such as plows, carts and cattle are important elements for characterizing poverty. In examining the assets of the poor it is important to focus on assets relating to their productive technology. A better assessment of financial assets requires answers to questions about credit and savings: how do the poor manage to save and how much?

- *Information on employment*

Employment is a major criterion to examine, because it often determines the earning of income and contributes to self-respect. There is wage employment and self-employment (as in the case of the farmer or urban microentrepreneur). It is important to examine employment as a whole, both formal and informal, rural and urban, even if in most cases analyses of employment are restricted to urban areas.

The ILO RASP surveys on poverty and the urban labor market in Sub-Saharan Africa are major reference bases in addressing the problem of employment and poverty. The following factors and indicators are crucial in analyzing the relationship between employment and poverty: total activity rate (working population over total population); actual unemployment rate; underemployment rate (number of individuals having worked for a monthly wage below a certain amount, compared to the total working population); stratification of the labor market; offers of employment; and finally, problems related to access to employment, mobility and segmentation of employment and work.

This section on employment is often considered to be fundamental. In analyses of income, consumption and access to social services, employment plays a predominant role. There is a high correlation between under- or unemployment and poverty.

5.2. Availability and accessibility of essential social services

Following on from the themes of the income and consumption of poor households, and studies and analyses of social well-being; the accessibility and availability of social services are crucial features for identifying the poor, achieving a clearer picture of poverty, isolating the main characteristics and determining the causes. From the point of view of sustainable human development, the fulfilment of basic needs and access to basic social services are at the heart of human poverty.

A number of existing surveys and studies can be used as a basis for research and sources in constructing indicators. One example is the demographic and health surveys (DHSs) which cover health aspects. These are comprehensive, in-depth surveys that examine the main characteristics of the demography and health of a given country. Other surveys on education, consumption, nutrition and farming are useful supports for this theme. [1] The questions to be answered are the following:

1. What social indicators give a clearer picture of the living standards of the poor, in terms of mortality, life expectancy, school enrolment, literacy, and nutrition status? How have they moved over time? What are the main factors determining these changes?

2. To what extent do the poor have access to public and private social services, and what reasons explain any lack of availability or accessibility?

---

1. For an extensive analysis of these different types of survey, their strengths and weaknesses, see Renata Lok Dessallien, *Poverty, Module 2 - From Data Collection to Poverty Assessments*, Technical Support Document (UNDP, BPPS, 1996).

Box A1.1

Developing Social Accounting Matrices (SAMs)
and environmental accounting matrices to assess poverty

Demo-economic accounts are intended to construct a vision of the economy based on the main social groups that contribute to it, rather than on economic sectors. These accounts are presented in a Social Accounting Matrix (SAM), where rows and columns represents the resources and uses of the various accounts considered. The starting point in constructing an SAM is the final expenditure of various categories of household and administration. Each category of urban and rural household identified in the population matrix is allocated a (provisional) total expenditure, broken down by item and origin, domestic or imported. The analyst then works back to determine the incomes that lie behind this expenditure, the good and services used by agents and activities, the transfers that balance the current and capital accounts, etc. Since the matrix balances, the incomes of the various agents (households and administration) arising from the production process and transfers are equal to their expenditure.

The main exogenous data are the structural data relating to final and intermediate expenditure, and the flow of goods and services and financial flows between the country and the rest of the world, provided by the balance of payments, all of which form the limits to the system.

The image of the real economy provided by the SAM is less accurate than in the national accounts for areas such as public-sector accounts, but more comprehensive for the relations between domestic supply and demand, the identification of the contributions of urban and rural areas to the economy, the production and consumption of nontraded goods and services, and the informal sector's contribution to the economy.

The inclusion of household activities, particularly women's work, in the assessment of well-being and total activity is a positive feature for analysis and action.

A similar effort should be made at national or subregional level to find and classify elements that could be used to produce environmental accounts.

- *Information on the nutrition status of the poor*

Nutrition indicators provide key information on the well-being of the members of poor households, children's opportunities to enjoy adequate physical and mental development, and adults' capacity to lead a productive and pleasant life.

For the direct assessment of children's nutrition status, the WHO recommends using three indicators: weight-for-age (underweight), height-for-age (wasting), and weight-for-height (stunting). For adults, food needs are evaluated by estimating requirements in energy and protein. Given the age, weight and height of the person, the Body Mass Index (BMI), also referred to as Quetelet's Index, is calculated (BMI is defined as weight (in kg) divided by the square of one's height (in m): kg/m2). This gives the degree of energy deficiency or obesity. In the particular case of pregnant and nursing mothers, it is better to use clinical data, or better still pathology to identify cases of nutritional anemia, say, or other micronutrient deficiencies.

- *Information on the health status and educational attainment of poor households*

To characterize the health status of households, indicators often used are infant mortality (in first year), child mortality (one to five years), mortality, vaccination rate, morbidity from diseases such as malaria, respiratory infections, diarrhea and sometimes poliomyelitis. Given the generally unfavorable social and health environment in which the poor live, they may be expected to be more vulnerable to disease and have a worse health status than the non-poor.

With respect to education, the main indicator used for children is the school enrolment ratio by age group and sex. For adults, it is the literacy rate. The members of poor households may be expected to have lower average levels of education than members of non-poor households.

- *Indicators of availability of health care and education services*

The availability of health care is measured by the following indicators:
− health infrastructure available for the household within a reasonable distance: primary health center, maternity clinic, hospital, pharmacy;
− medical staff available: basic health agent, nurse, midwife, doctor, traditional healer;
− type of health service available: vaccination, access to medicine, operations, assisted child-birth, health information;
− quality of care offered: health framework and medical practices.

However, even if health care is available, households may not use it, either because it costs too much, or because they prefer other forms of health treatment. It is essential to measure by group of poor and non-poor households: 1) frequency of use of health services and other forms of treatment (self-medication, prayer, etc.); 2) reasons for the choice of health services used; and 3) average expenditure on each type of health service.

The availability of education services is measured by the following indicators:
− school infrastructure available for the household within a reasonable distance: primary school, secondary school, vocational training center;
− type of educational program offered;
− quality of services offered.

As for health, educational services may be offered, but households may not use them for various reasons: 1) they may be considered too expensive; 2) parents may not see the value of sending their children to school, either out of ignorance or because they believe that the school curriculum does not properly prepare their children for working life; 3) parents may need their children to work to contribute to family income.

The measurement is made by group of poor and non-poor households of: 1) school enrolment ratio by age and sex; 2) school drop-out rate by age and sex and reasons; 3) percentage of children older than the normal age for their educational level; and 4) average education expenditure per child enrolled.

- *Information on housing*

The point of these indicators is to characterize household accommodation and establish the links between their housing and their living standards. Poor households may be expected to live in less permanent and salubrious accommodation, which contributes to their poor health status and low productivity. Both urban and rural accommodation should be covered.

5.3. Environment and natural resources

In general, poverty profiles pay little attention to information and indicators concerning the environment and access to natural resources such as land and water. However, under the sustainable development approach, these are clearly essential factors in poverty and its causes. At the very least, they are aggravating factors. The following themes appear to be of prime importance in any comprehensive human poverty profile:

• What access do the poor have to natural resources, particularly water, wood and land? What quantitative and qualitative changes have there been in the availability and accessibility of natural resources? Here, indicators of accessibility of clean water, types of water supply, types of energy used, and land statutes are of prime importance.

• What are the main trends of environmental degradation in poor regions, in terms of soil, desertification, biodiversity, water points, forests, wild animals, marine habitat, etc? The conclusions and follow-up to the United Nations Conference on Environment and Development held in Rio in 1992, and the conventions that resulted, have demonstrated the close links between environmental degradation and poverty. Close attention should be paid to these issues.

• What is the impact of the environment on the health of the poor? Whether pollution in urban areas or sanitation, these issues provide a more complete vision of the relationship between poverty and environment.

• Analysis and measurement should be made of the availability of clean water and sanitation services for the poor, and their accessibility.

5.4. Gender indicators

Any analysis of indicators should take gender into account. This involves disaggregating the indicators for gender where possible and constructing gender-related analyses. It is also useful to construct specific gender indicators such as the:

- gender-related development index (GDI),
- gender empowerment measure (GEM).

5.5. Measuring and analyzing human development

- *Human development index (HDI).*

The Human development index measures the overall achievments in a country in three basic dimensions of human development — longevity, knowledge and a decent standard of living. This composite index is measured by life expectancy, educational attainment (adult literacy and combined primary, secondary and tertiary enrolment) and real per capita GDP (purchasing power parity adjusted).

- *Human poverty index (HPI).*

The HPI concentrates on the deprivation in three essential dimensions of human life already included in the HDI. The variables are the percentage of people likely to die before age 40, the percentage of adults who are illiterate, and deprivation in overall economic provisioning, reflected by the percentage of people without access to health services and safe water and the percentage of malnourished children under five.

Poverty and the human development indices

1. Human Development Dimensions

The Human Development Report has developed and constructed several composite indices to measure different aspects of human development.

The human development index (HDI) has been constructed every year since 1990 to measure average achievements in basic human development in one simple composite index and to produce a ranking of countries. The gender-related development index (GDI) and the gender empowerment measure (GEM), introduced in Human Development Report 1995, are composite measures reflecting gender inequalities in human development. While the GDI captures achievements in basic human development adjusted for gender inequality, the GEM measures gender inequality in economic and political opportunities. Human Development Report 1997 introduced the concept of human poverty and formulated a composite measure of it – the human poverty index (HPI). While the HDI measures average achievements in basic dimensions of human development, the HPI measures deprivations in those dimensions. Table 1 presents the basic dimensions of human development reflected in the human development indices, and the indicators used to measure them.

2. What Does the HPI-1 reveal?

Calculated for 92 developing countries, the HPI-1 reveals the following:

– Human poverty ranges from a low 2.6% in Barbados to a high 65.5% in Niger. Several countries have an HPI-1 of less than 10%: Bahrain, Barbados, Chile, Costa Rica, Cuba, Fiji, Jordan, Panama, Trinidad and

Table 1. –   HDI, GDI, HPI-1, HPI-2 –same dimensions,
               different measurements

Index	Longevity	Knowledge	Decent standard of living	Participation or exclusion
HDI (Human Development Index)	Life expectancy at birth	1. Adult literacy rate 2. Combined enrolment ratio	Adjusted per capita income in PPP$	–
GDI (Gender-related Development Index)	Female and male life expectancy at birth	1. Female and male adult literacy rate 2. Female and male combined enrolment ratio	Adjusted per capita income in PPP$, based on female and male earned income chares	–
HPI-1 (Human Poverty Index) for developing countries	Percentage of people not expected to survive to age 40	Adult illiteracy rate	1. Percentage of people without acess to safe water 2. Percentage of people without access to health services 3. Percentage of underweight children under five	
HPI-2 (Human Poverty Index) for industrialize countries	Percentage of people not expected to survive to age 60	Adult functional illiteracy rate	Percentage of people living below the income poverty line (50% of median personal disposable income)	Long-term unemployment rate (12 months or more)

Source: Human Development Report Office, 1999.

Tobago and Uruguay. These developing countries have overcome severe levels of poverty.

– The HPI-1 exceeds 33% in 37 of the 92 countries, implying that human poverty affects at least a third of the people in these countries. Others have still further to go in reducing human poverty. The HPI-1 exceeds 50% in Benin, Burkina Faso, the Central African Republic, Chad, Ethiopia, Guinea, Guinea-Bissau, Mali, Nepal, Niger and Sierra Leone, suggesting that poverty affects at least half the population.

Differences in human development exist not only between countries and between North and South. National human development data, disaggregated by region, gender, ethnic group or rural and urban areas, reveal significant disparities within countries. And disparities of all kinds are interrelated and overlapping.

When the HDI and the HPI are disaggregated along the rural-urban divide, they document higher progress in human development and less deprivation for people in urban areas than for those in rural areas. The rural-urban divide in Botswana provides a good example.

According to Botswana's national human development report, the country's HPI-1 dropped from 32.2% to 22% between 1991 and 1996. Yet poverty persists even today, though at very different levels in urban and rural areas. People in Botswana's urban areas are better off, with an HPI-1 of 11.7%. In rural areas the HPI is more than twice as high – 27%.

3. The human poverty index

The human poverty index is a multidimensional measure of poverty.

3.1. Computing the human poverty index for developing countries

The human poverty index for developing countries (HPI-1) concentrates on deprivations in three essential dimensions of human life already reflected in the HDI – longevity, knowledge and a decent standard of living. The first deprivation relates to survival – vulnerability to death at a relatively early age. The second relates to knowledge – being excluded from the world of reading and communication. The third relates to a decent living standard in terms of overall economic provisioning.

In constructing the HPI-1, the deprivation in longevity is represented by the percentage of people not expected to survive to age 40 (P_1), and the deprivation in knowledge by the percentage of adults who are illiterate (P_2). The deprivation in living standard is represented by a composite (P_3) of three variables – the percentage of people without acess to safe water (P_{31}), the percentage of people without acess to health services (P_{32}) and the percentage of moderately and severely underweight children under five (P_{33}).

The composite variable P_3 is constructed by taking a simple average of the three variables P_{31}, P_{32} and P_{33}. Thus

$$P_3 = \frac{P_{31} + P_{32} + P_{33}}{3}$$

Following technical note 1 in Human Development Report 1997, the formula for the HPI-1 is given by:

$$HPI - 1 = [1/3(P_1^3 + P_2^3 + P_3^3)]^{1/3}$$

3.2. Computing the human poverty index for industrialized countries

The human poverty index for industrialized countries (HPI-2) concentrates on deprivations in four dimensions of human life, quite similar to those reflected in the HDI – longevity, knowledge, a decent standard of living and social exclusion. The first deprivation relates to survival – vulnerability to death at a relatively early age. The second relates to knowledge – being deprived of the world of reading and communication. The third relates to a decent standard of living in terms of overall economic provisioning. And the fourth relates to non-participation or exclusion.

In constructing the HPI-2, the deprivation in longevity is represented by the percentage of people not expected to survive to age 60 (P1), and the deprivation in knowledge by the percentage of people who are functionally illiterate as defined by the OECD (P2). The deprivation in standard of living is represented by the percentage of people living below the income poverty line, set at 50% of the median disposable personal income (P3). And the fourth deprivation, in non-participation or exclusion, is measured by the rate of long-term (12 months or more) unemployment (P4) of the labour force.

Following technical note 1 in Human Development Report 1997, the formula for the HPI-2 is given by:

$$HPI - 2 = [1/4(P_1^3 + P_2^3 + P_3^3 + P_4^3)]^{1/3}$$

Source: UNDP. Human Development Report, 1999. New York: Oxford University Press, 1999.

ANNEXE 3

Bibliography

Published books and articles

Abdelmalki, L., & Mundler, P., *Economie du développement. Les théories, les expériences, les perspectives*, Paris, Hachette, 1995.

Adedeji, A. Green, R. & Janha, A., *Rémunération, productivité et fonction publique : priorités pour le relèvement de l'Afrique subsaharienne*, PNUD & UNICEF, New York, 1995.

Adepoju, A., *Population, Pauvreté, Programme d'Ajustement Structurel et Qualité de la Vie en Afrique subSaharienne*, PHRDA Research Paper n°1, Dakar, 1996.

Aho, G., Larivière, S. & Martin F., *Manuel d'analyse de la pauvreté. Applications au Bénin*, PNUD, Université Nationale du Bénin & Université Laval, Québec, 1997.

Ainsworth, M., *The Côte-d'Ivoire Living Standards Survey. Design and Implementation*, LSMS Working Paper 26, Banque Mondiale, Washington D.C., 1986.

"Analyse des dépenses locales de 23 pays ayant appliqué un programme FASR", *Bulletin du FMI*, 28, juillet 1997.

Appleton, S., "Problems of Measuring Changes in Poverty over Time: The Case of Uganda 1989-92", *Poverty, Policy and Aid*, IDS Bulletin, Vol 27, n° 1, 1996.

Ashe, J. & Cosslett, C.E., *Credit for the Poor, Past Activites and Future Directions for the United Nations Development Programme*, UNDP Policy Discussion Paper, New York, 1989.

Azam, J.- P., Chamba, G., & Guillaumont P. & S., *The Impact of Macroeconomic Policies on the Rural Poor, Analytical Framework and Indicators*, UNDP Policy Discussion Paper, New York, 1994.

Banque Mondiale, *La pauvreté, Rapport sur le Développement dans le monde 1990*, Washington D.C., 1990.

Banque Mondiale, *Structural Adjustment and Poverty: A Conceptual, Empirical and Policy Framework,* Report N°8393-AFR, Document of the World Bank, Washington, DC, 1990.

Banque Mondiale, *Poverty Reduction Handbook*, Washington D.C., 1993.

Banque Mondiale; *Investir dans la santé. Rapport sur le développement dans le monde 1993*, Washington D.C., 1993.

Banque Mondiale; *Une infrastructure pour le développement. Rapport sur le développement dans le monde 1994*, Washington D.C., 1994.

Banque Mondiale, *Ajustement en Afrique : réformes, résultats et chemin à parcourir*, New York & Washington, 1994.

Banque Mondiale, *The Social Impact of Adjustment Operations: an Overview*, Washington, 1995.

Banque Mondiale, *Un continent en transition : l'Afrique subsaharienne au milieu des années 1990*, Washington, 1995.

Banque Mondiale, *Methods and Tools for Social Assessment and Participation*, Washington, 1995.

Banque Mondiale, *Poverty Reduction and the World Bank: Progress and Challenges in the 1990s*, Washington D.C., 1996.

Banque Mondiale, *Faire reculer la pauvreté en Afrique Subsaharienne. Résumé Analytique*, Washington D.C., 1996.

Banque Mondiale, *Confronting AIDS. Public Priorities in a Global Epidemic*, New York & Washington, 1997.

Banque Mondiale, *World Debt Tables*, Washington, 1997.

Bardhan, P., "Efficacité, équité et lutte contre la pauvreté", *Problèmes économiques*, n°2.520, 1997, pp. 8-16.

Baulch, B., "Neglected Trade-Offs in Poverty Measurement", *Poverty, Policy and Aid*, IDS Bulletin, Vol 27, n° 1, 1996.

Bener, L & Pisnath, S., *Gender and Poverty: An Analysis for Action,* Gender in Development Monograph Series, 2, UNDP, New York, 1996.

Bjorkman, H., "La pauvreté dans la perspective du Développement Humain", *Conférence Internationale sur les Approches Economiques de Lutte contre la Pauvreté*, PNUD & Université Laval, Québec, 1997.

Boateng, E.O., Ewusi, K., Kanbur, R. & McKay, A., *Un profil de pauvreté au Ghana :1987-1988*, Banque Mondiale, Document de travail N°5, Les dimensions sociales de l'ajustement en Afrique Subsaharienne, Washington D.C., 1992.

Boltvinik, J., "Poverty Measurement and Indicators of Development", *Poverty Monitoring: And International Concern*, chap. 4, edited by Rolph Van der Hoeven and Richard Anker, UNICEF, New York, 1994.

Booker, W., Singh, P. & Savane, L., *Household Survey Experience in Africa*, LSMS Working Paper N°6, Banque Mondiale, Washington D.C., 1980.

Burkina Faso, *Analyse des Résultats de l'Enquête prioritaire sur les Conditions de Vie des Ménages*, Ministère de l'Economie et des Finances & Projet d'Appui Institutionnel aux Dimensions Sociales de l'Ajustement, Ouagadougou, 1996.

Burkina Faso, *Le Profil de la Pauvreté au Burkina Faso*, Ministère de l'Economie et des Finances & Projet d'Appui Institutionnel aux Dimensions Sociales de l'Ajustement, Ouagadougou, 1996.

Bureau International du Travail, *Employment, Growth and Basic Needs: A One-World Problem*, New York, 1977.

Bureau International du Travail, *Estimates and Projections of the economically Active Population*, Genève, 1996.

Carruthers, I. & Chambers, P., "Rapid Appraisal for Rural Development", *Agricultural Administration* 8, 6, 1981, pp. 407-422.

Carvalho, S. A., *Indicators for Monitoring Poverty*, Excerpt from presentation entitled at DAC seminar on Evaluation of Aid Interventions for Poverty Reduction, Copenhagen, 1995.

Chambers, R., *Rural Appraisal: Rapid, Relaxed and Participatory*, Institute of Development Studies, University of Sussex, Sussex, 1992.

Chambers, R. "The Origins and Practice of Participatory Rural Appraisal" in *World Development*, Great Britain, Vol. 22, n° 7, 1994.

Chambers, R. & Guijt, I., "Participatory Rural Appraisal - Five Years Later: Where are We Now?", *Forests, Trees and People Newsletter*, n° 26/27, 1985.

Chander, R., Grootaert, C., & Pyatt, G., *Living Standards Surveys in Developing Countries*, LSMS Working Paper 1, Banque Mondiale, Washington D.C., 1985.

Chapelier, G. & Tabatabai, H., *Development and Adjustment*, UNDP Policy Paper Discussion, New York, 1989.

Cohen, J. & Uphoff, N., "Participation's Place in Rural Development: Seeking Clarity through Specificity", *World Development*, Vol. 8, 1980.

Cornia, G. A., Jolly, R. & Stewart, F., *Adjustment with a Human Face*, 2 vol., Londres, UNICEF, 1987.

CNUCED, *Les Pays les moins avancé, Rapport 1996*, New York & Genève, 1996.

Dawson, J. & Oyeyinkin, B., *Structural Adjustment and the Urban Informal Sector*, Genève, OIT, 1993.

Deaton, A., *Analysis of Household Expenditures*, LSMS Working Paper N°28, Banque Mondiale, Washington D.C., 1988.

"Dépenses et indicateurs sociaux. Etude d'un échantillon de 66 pays", *Bulletin du FMI*, mars 1998.

Desai, M., Sen, A. & Boltvinik, J., *Social Progress Index: A Proposal*, UNDP, New York, 1992.

Dubois, J.-L., "Mise en place d'un Système de Suivi de la Pauvreté urbaine au Bangladesh", *Conférence Internationale sur les Approches Economiques de Lutte contre la Pauvreté*,

Université Laval, Québec, 1997.

Dubois, J.-L., "Quels systèmes d'information pour les politiques de lutte contre la pauvreté", *Cahiers de Sciences Humaines*, 32 (4), 1996, pp. 869-91.

"L'expérience du Programme Micro-Réalisations au Burkina Faso", Conférence Internationale sur les Approches Economiques de lutte contre la Pauvreté, Université Laval, Québec, 1997.

FAO, *State of World's Forests*, Rome, 1997.

FAO, *La situation mondiale de l'alimentation et de l'agriculture 1997*, Rome, 1997.

Fonds d'Equipement des Nations Unies, *Réduction de la pauvreté, participation et meilleure gouvernance locale le rôle du FENU*, New York, 1995.

Fonds International de Développement Agricole, *The World of the Rural Poor, State of World Poor*, FIDA, Rome, 1992.

Fields, G.S., "Changes in Poverty and Inequality in Developing Countries" *The World Bank Research Observer*, 4, n°2, 1989, pp.167-185.

Fonds Monétaire International, *Statistiques Financières Internationales*, FMI, Washington, 1989-1996.

Fonds des Nations Unies pour les Activités en matière de Population, *Etat de la population mondiale 1996*, FNUAP, New York, 1996.

Fonds des Nations Unies pour les Activités en matière de Population, *Etat de la population mondiale 1997*, FNUAP, New York, 1997.

Garson, J., *Microfinance and Anti-Poverty Strategies. A Donor Perspective*, UNCDF Policy Series, New York, 1996.

Ghai, D., *Economic growth, Structural Change and labour Absorption in Africa*, Document de travail UNRISD, Genève, 1987.

Gillis, M., Perkins, M.R., Roemer, M. & Snodgrass, D.R., *Economie du développement*, trad. B. Baron-Renault, Paris, Bruxelles, De Boeck Université, 1998.

Graeme, D., *Agriculture and Economic reform in sub-saharan Africa*, Banque Mondiale, Working Paper 18, Washington, 1996.

Grégoire, L. J., "L'évolution de la zone franc et l'opportunité d'une dévaluation du franc CFA", *L'Année Africaine 1987-1988*, Bordeaux, éd. Pedone, 1989.

Grégoire, L. J., *Le Zimbabwe. Evolution économique et perspectives*, Paris, éd. L'Harmattan, 1989.

Grégoire, L. J., *L'Afrique et les perspectives nouvelles de résolution du problème de la dette*, Bordeaux, Institut d'Etudes politiques - CEAN, Travaux et Documents, n°24, 1989.

Grégoire, L. J., "L'insertion économique internationale de l'Afrique", *Afrique : la déconnexion par défaut. Etudes Internationales*, vol. XXII, n°2, 1991.

Grégoire, L. J., Kankwenda *et alii. La lutte contre la pauvreté en Afrique Subsaharienne*, Paris, éditions Economica, 1999.

Grootaert, C. & Kanbur, R., *Policy-Oriented Analysis of Poverty and the Social Dimensions of Structural Adjustment: A Methodology and Proposed Application to Cote d'Ivoire, 1985-88*, World Bank, Washington D.C., 1990.

Grosh, M. E. & Glewwe, P., *A Guide to Living Standards-Measurements Surveys and their Data Sets*, World Bank, Washington, D.C., 1995.

Haut Commissariat des Nations Unies pour les Réfugiés, *Rapport annuel 1996*, HCR, Genève, 1996.

Inter-American Development Bank, "Characteristics of Poverty", *Social Tensions and Social Reform, Toward Balanced Economic, Financial and Social Policies in Latin America, A Progress Report*, Chap. 2, Washington D.C., 1995

Human Needs. A Contribution to the Current Debate, Katrin Lederer éd., Cambridge & Königstein, 1980.

Kanbur, R., *La pauvreté et les dimensions sociales de l'ajustement structurel en Côte d'Ivoire*, DSA, document 2, Banque Mondiale, Washington D.C., 1990.

Kankwenda, M., "Le FMI dans la crise économique du Zaïre", *Analyses Sociales,* vol.1, n°1, 1984.

Kankwenda, M., "Crise économique, ajustement et démocratie en Afrique", CODESRIA, *Processus de démocratisation en Afrique*, Dakar, 1995.

Kankwenda, M., "Démocratisation de l'ajustement ou socialisation du développement au Zaïre", *Africa Development*, vol. XXI, n° 2 & 3, 1996.

Kondé, M. & al., *Enquêtes participatives sur la pauvreté en milieu semi-urbain et en milieu urbain : cas des villes de Dédougou et de Ouagadougou*. Banque Mondiale, Ouagadougou, 1994.

Lachaud, J.-P., *Pauvreté et Marché du travail urbain en Afrique subsaharienne*, Analyse comparative, Institut International d'Etudes Sociales, Genève, 1994.

Lachaud, J.-P., *Croissance économique, Pauvreté et Inégalité des revenus en Afrique Subsaharienne : Analyse comparative*, Centre d'Economie du Développement - Université Montesquieu, Bordeaux, 1996.

Lachaud, J.-P., *Pauvreté - Vulnérabilité et Marché du Travail au Burkina Faso*, Ministère de l'Economie et des Finances & Centre d'Economie du Développement, Université Montesquieu-Bordeaux IV, Ouagadougou, 1997.

Lachaud, J-.P., *Salaire d'efficience, vulnérabilité du travail et chômage urbain au Burkina Faso*, Bordeaux, Université Montesquieu-Bordeaux IV, 1997.

Laliberté-Beringar, D., "Un Programme Tanzanien de Développement des Micro-Entreprises (SEDA)", *Conférence Internationale sur les Approches Economiques de Lutte contre la Pauvreté*, Université Laval, Québec, 1997.

Larivière, S. & Martin, F., "Cadre d'Analyse Economique de la Pauvreté et des Conditions de Vie des Ménages", *Conférence internationale sur les Approches Economiques de Lutte contre la Pauvreté,* Université Laval, Québec, 1997.

Larocque, P., Nteziyaremye, A., Larivière, S. & Martin, F., *Les pratiques de microcrédit dans les pays en développement*, Ottawa, DID, 1996.

Legros, H., "La pauvreté dans la perspective du développement humain durable", *Initiative Stratégique de Lutte contre la pauvreté*, vol.1, Ouagadougou, 1998.

Legros, H. & Guillet, I., "Perception des aménagements de la moyenne vallée du fleuve Sénégal. Un exemple : le village de Mbolo Birane", *Revue belge de géographie*, 52, 1994.

Legros, H., & Thoveron, G., *Méthodologie et politique africaines*, Civilisations; Bruxelles, ULB, 1993.

Lessard, P., "Point de vue d'un Praticien sur les Interventions à Caractère Economique visant la Réduction de la Pauvreté", *Conférence Internationale sur les Approches Economiques de Lutte contre la Pauvreté*, CECI & Université Laval, Québec, 1997.

Lindauer, D., Meesook, O. & Suebsaeng, P., "Government Wages policies in Africa: some Findings and Policies Issues", *Research Observer*, vol.3 - 1, 1988.

Mehrotra, S. & Jolly, R., *Development with a Human Face. Experiences in Social Achievement and Economic Growth*, Oxford, Clarendon Press, 1997.

Momar-Coumba, Diop, *La Lutte contre la Pauvreté à Dakar. Vers la définition d'une politique municipale*, Dakar, 1996.

Nations Unies, *Handbook of Household Surveys* (Revised Edition), Studies in Method series F, n° 31, UN, New York, 1984.

Nations Unies, *Développement du secteur informel en Afrique*, New York, 1992.

Nations Unies, *Household Income and Expenditure Surveys: A Technical Study*, National Household Survey Capability Programme, UN, New York, 1989.

Nations Unies, *Women in a Changing Global Economy: 1994 Survey on the Role of Women in Development*, Department for Policy Coordination and Substainable Development, New York, 1995.

Nations Unies, *Sommet mondial pour le développement social : Déclaration de Copenhague sur le développement social*, Copenhague, 1995.

Nations Unies, *Annuaires Statistiques 1980-1995*, Département des Affaires Economiques et Sociales, New York, 1980-1996.

Nations Unies, *United Nations Concern for Peace and Security in Central Africa*, New York, 1997.

OCDE, *Coopération pour le Développement*, Comité d'Aide au Développement, Rapports 1991 à 1997, Paris, 1991-1998.

OMS, *Rapport sur la santé dans le monde 1997 : Vaincre la souffrance, enrichir l'humanité*, Genève, 1997.

Paugam, S., "Représentation et perception de la pauvreté", *Problèmes économiques*, n°2.508, 1997, pp. 8 - 12.

"Pauvreté dans le monde : Evolution contrastée", *Problèmes économiques*, n°2535, 1997, pp. 24 -29.

PNUD, *Guide du secteur privé : pour un programme d'action*, New York, 1996.

PNUD, *Forum sur la gouvernance en Afrique : cadre conceptuel*, New York, 1997.

PNUD, *Some Lessons Learned in Supporting the Transition from Poverty to Prosperity in Vietnam*, UNDP Staff Paper, Hanoi, 1997.

PNUD, *Microstart. A Guide for Planning, Starting and Managing a Microfinance Programme*, New York, 1997.

PNUD, *La Gouvernance en faveur du développement humain durable*, Document de politique générale du PNUD, New York, 1997.

PNUD, *Futurs Africains, quelques repères. Cinq années d'études nationales de perspectives à long terme en Afrique*, PNUD/Futurs Africains, Abidjan, 1997.

PNUD, *Governance for sustainable Growth and Equity, Conference Paper1*, New York, 1997.

PNUD, *Répertoire des programmes de gouvernance en Afrique : responsabilité et transparence*, 2 vol., Accra, 1998.

PNUD, *Rapport Mondial sur le Développement Humain 1992*, New York, Paris, Economica, 1992.

PNUD, *Rapport Mondial sur le Développement Humain 1993*, New York, Paris, Economica, 1993.

PNUD, *Rapport Mondial sur le Développement Humain 1994*, New York, Paris, Economica, 1994.

PNUD, *Rapport Mondial sur le Développement Humain 1995*, New York, Paris, Economica, 1995.

PNUD, *Rapport Mondial sur le Développement Humain 1996*, New York, Paris, Economica, 1996.

PNUD, *Rapport Mondial sur le Développement Humain 1997*, New York, Paris, Economica, 1997.

PNUD, *Rapport Mondial sur le Développement Humain 1998*, New York, Paris, Economica, 1998.

Programme des Nations Unies pour l'Environnement, *Rapport annuel 1996*, PNUE, Nairobi, 1997.

Ravallion, M., *Poverty Comparisons: A Guide to Concepts and Methods*, LSMS Working Paper 88, Banque Mondiale, Washington D.C., 1992.

Ravallion, M., *Comparaisons de la pauvreté, concepts et méthodes, Etude sur la mesure de la pauvreté*, Document de travail 122, Banque Mondiale, Washington D.C., 1996.

Ravallion, M., *How Well Can Method Substitute for Data? Five Experiments in Poverty Analysis*, Policy Paper from the Policy Research Department, World Bank, Washington D.C., 1995.

Richards, P. & Leonor, M., *Target Setting for Basic Needs*, BIT, Genève, 1982.

Rist, G., *Le développement. Histoire d'une croyance occidentale*, Paris, Editions de Science-Po, 1996.

Rodgers, G., Gore, Ch. & Figueiredo, J. B., *Social Exclusion: Rhetoric, Reality, Responses. A Contribution to the World Summit for Social Development*, IILS & PNUD, Genève, 1995.

Saint-Hilaire, J. & Ouédraogo, A., *Etude de cas : les caisses villageoises au Burkina Faso*, Ottawa, DID, 1996.

Sanou, M. & Lachaud, J.P., *Pauvreté et Marché du Travail à Ouagadougou (Burkina Faso)*, Institut International d'Etudes Sociales, Genève, 1993.

Sen, A. *Poverty and Famines: An Essay on Entitlement and Deprivation*, Oxford, Oxford University Press, 1981.

Sen, A., *The Standard of Living*, Cambridge, Cambridge University Press, 1987.

Shaffer, P. "Beneath the Poverty Debate: Some Issues", *Poverty, Policy and Aid*, Sussex, IDS Bulletin, Vol 27, n° 1, 1996.

Snrech, S., *Pour préparer l'avenir de l'Afrique de l'Ouest : une vision à l'horizon 2020. Synthèse de l'étude des perspectives à long terme en Afrique de l'Ouest*, OCDE/BAD/CILSS, Paris, 1994.

Steward, F., *Adjustment and Poverty: Options and Choices*, Londres, 1995.

Streeten, P., "Poverty Concepts and Measurement" in *Poverty Monitoring: And International Concern*, Chap. 2, edited by Rolph Van der Hoeven and Richard Anker, UNICEF, New York, 1994.

Subbarao, K., "Lessons of 30 Years of Fighting Poverty" *International Conference on Developing Economic Approaches to Fight Poverty*, World Bank & Université Laval, Québec, 1997

Todaro, M., *Economic Development in the Third World*, New York, Londres, Longman, 1989.

Toye, J. & Carl, J., "Public Expenditure Policy and Poverty Reduction: Has the World Bank Got it Right?", *Poverty, Policy and Aid*, IDS Bulletin, Vol 27, n° 1, 1996.

UNESCO, *Rapport sur l'état de l'éducation en Afrique,* Paris, 1996.

UNICEF, *Pauvreté en Afrique de l'Ouest et du Centre : Points de repère pour la programmation,* New York, 1995.

UNICEF, *Monitoring Progress Toward the Goals of the World Summit for Children: A Practical Handbook for Multiple-indicator Surveys,* New York, 1995.

UNICEF, *Equipping Country offices to better Forecast Emergencies in West and Central Africa Region,* Abidjan, 1996.

UNICEF, *La situation des enfants dans le monde 1996,* New York, 1996.

UNSO, *Aridity Zone and Drylands Populations,* New York, 1997.

USAID, "A Study for the SPA Working Group on Poverty and Social Developement", *Alternative Survey Methodologies for Monitoring and Analysing Poverty in sub-Saharan Africa,* Chap. 4, Washington D.C., 1995.

Vandemoortele, J., "Labour Market Informalisation in sub-Saharan Africa", *Toward social Adjustement,* ed. Standing. G & Tockman, V., Genève, OIT, 1991.

Van der Hoeven, R., "Structural Adjustment, Poverty and Macro-economic Policy", *The Poverty Agenda: Trends and Policy Options, New Approaches to Poverty Analysis and Policy - III,* IILS-ILO, Genève, 1995.

Watkin, K., *The Oxfam Poverty Report,* Oxfam Policy Department, Oxford, 1995.

Webster, L. & Fidler, P., *Le secteur informel et les institutions de micro-financement en Afrique de l'Ouest,* Banque Mondiale, 1995.

Women's World Banking, *Les chaînons manquants : des sytèmes financier au service du plus grand nombre,* New York, 1995.

Women's World Banking, *Rapport de l'atelier des praticiens africains de la micro-finance,* New York, 1996.

Unpublished documents

Adei, S., "Poverty in Namibia: Structure, Causes and Reduction Strategies", A Discussion paper (Notes) prepared for the UNDP Regional Bureau for Africa Economists' Cluster Meeting in Lomé, 1997.

Afrique du Sud, *Public Expenditure on Basic Social Services in South Africa,* Financial and Fiscal Commission, UNICEF & PNUD, Johannesburg, 1998.

Amoako, K.Y., "Les défis du développement en Afrique au Vingt et Unième siècle", Commission Economique pour l'Afrique, Conférence des Ministres africains chargés de la planification, Ouagadougou, 1995.

Angola, *Human Development Report Angola 1997*, PNUD, Luanda, 1997.

Banque Africaine de Développement, *Annual report 1996*, BAD, Abidjan, 1996.

Banque Mondiale, *Un peuple résistant dans un milieu hostile : évaluation de la pauvreté au Niger*, Document de la Banque Mondiale, Washington D.C., 1996.

Banque Mondiale, "Methods and Tools for Social Assessment and Participation", Draft Paper from the Social Policy and Resettlement Division, Environment Department, World Bank, Washington, D.C., 1995.

Banque Mondiale, *Zambia Poverty Assessment*, Volume 1, World Bank, Washington D.C., 1994.

Banque Mondiale, *Burkina Faso : Revue des dépenses publiques*, rapport 11901 BUR, Région Afrique, Washington D.C., 1993.

Bénin, *Rapport sur le Développement Humain au Bénin, 1997*, Gouvernement du Bénin & PNUD, Cotonou, 1997.

Bénin, *Perception des dimensions de la pauvreté, du bien - être et de la richesse en milieu rural au Bénin*, Ministère du Développement Rural & PNUD, Cotonou, 1996.

Bénin, *Profil de pauvreté et caractéristiques socio-économiques des ménages ruraux*, "Etudes sur les conditions de vie des ménages ruraux au Bénin", 5 vol., Ministère du Développement Rural & PNUD, Cotonou, 1996.

Bénin, *Perception des dimensions de la pauvreté, du bien - être et de la richesse dans les quartiers pauvres en milieu urbain au Bénin*, Institut National de la Statistique et de l'Analyse Economique & PNUD, Cotonou, 1996.

Bénin, *Profil de pauvreté et caractéristiques socio-économiques des ménages urbains*, "Etudes sur les conditions de vie en milieu urbain au Bénin", 3 vol., Institut National de la Statistique et de l'Analyse Economique & PNUD, Cotonou, 1996.

BIT, *Social exclusion and Anti-Poverty Strategies, Research project on the Patterns and causes of Social Exclusion and the Design of Policies to Promote Integration: A Synthesis of Findings*, Genève, 1995.

Boisdeffre, L. de, "Etude comparative sur l'aide à la réduction de la pauvreté", DIAL, Paris, 1996.

Botswana, *Planning for people. A Strategy for Accelerated Human Development in Botswana*, Ministry of Finance and Development Planning, PNUD & UNICEF, Gaborone, 1993.

Burkina Faso, *Rapport sur le développement Humain Durable, Burkina Faso 1997*, PNUD, Ouagadougou, 1997.

Burkina Faso, "Les dépenses publiques et leurs impacts. Le cas de l'éducation et de la santé au Burkina Faso", Ministère de l'Economie et des Finances, Ouagadougou, 1997.

Burkina Faso, "Analyse d'incidence des dépenses publiques en éducation et en santé", Ministère de l'Economie et des Finances, Ouagadougou, 1997.

Burkina Faso, *L'Initiative 20/20 au Burkina Faso : l'allocation des ressources budgétaires et extérieures aux services sociaux de base*, Ministère de l'Economie et des Finances & PNUD, Ouagadougou, 1998.

Burkina Faso, *Enquêtes participatives en milieu urbain et en milieu rural sur les perceptions des dimensions du Bien-être, de la Pauvreté et sur les problèmes d'accès aux services sociaux de base au Burkina Faso*, Initiative Stratégique de Lutte contre la Pauvreté, Ministère de l'Economie et des Finances & PNUD, Ouagadougou, 1998

Cameroun, *Rapport sur Développement Humain au Cameroun 1996 : Secteur privé et développement humain*, PNUD, 1996.

Cameroun, *Restructuration du budget national du Cameroun*, République du cameroun & UNICEF, 1997.

Carvalho, S., "Excerpt from presentation entitled *Indicators for Monitoring poverty*, at DAC seminar on Evaluation of Aid Interventions for Poverty Reduction", Copenhagen, 1995.

Centrafrique, *Rapport sur le développement humain en République Centrafricaine 1996*, PNUD, Bangui, 1996.

Caisse Française de Développement, *Rapport Annuel 1996*, Caisse Française de Développement, Paris, 1997.

Coalition Mondiale pour l'Afrique, "Etude sur le passage à la démocratie en Afrique", note analytique, Maastricht, 1997.

"Comparative Study on European Aid for Poverty Reduction", Record of the Seminar on the Second Phase of the Collaborative Research Project, DIAL, Paris, 1997.

Côte-d'Ivoire, *Financement des secteurs sociaux de base : suivi de l'Initiave 20/20 en Côte d'Ivoire*, Institut national de la Statistique & UNICEF, Abidjan, 1997.

"Critical capacities for the mobilisation and efficient allocation of domestic and external financial ressources", Commission Economique pour l'Afrique, Nations Unies, Adis Abeba, 1995.

"Documents de travail de la Convention sur la désertification", Paris, 1994.

Grahmel, F., *La pauvreté à travers les études nationales de perspectives à long terme*, PNUD/Futurs Africains, Abidjan, 1998.

Grégoire, L.J., "La démarche nationale en faveur du Développement Humain Durable: concept et principaux instruments", Atelier d'information, de formation et de concertation sur le DHD, PNUD, Bobo-Dioulasso, 1998.

Grégoire, L.J., Le Burkina Faso et l'Initiative des pays pauvres lourdement endettés: défis de l'allègement de la dette au profit du développement humain durable. PNUD, Working Paper Vol III, août 1999.

Grégoire, L.J., Mondialisation et pauvreté: défis et stratégies au plan international, régional et national. Symposium International sur les sources de croissance dans le contexte de la mondialisation et de la régionalisation. Ouagadougou 1-4 décembre 1999.

Griffin, K., "Macroeconomic Reform and Employment: an Investment-led Strategy of Structural Adjustment in sub-Saharan Africa", *Poverty Reduction Module 4. Macroeconomic Policies and Poverty Reduction*, UNDP, New York, 1997.

Griffin, K., "The Structure of Incentives", *Poverty Reduction Module 4. Macroeconomic Policies and Poverty Reduction*, UNDP, New York, 1997.

Guinée, "Finances publiques et développement humain", Rapport de l'Atelier national sur le développement humain durable, PNUD, Conakry, 1995.

Guinée, "Pauvreté et participation populaire en Guinée : analyse sociologique", Rapport de l'Atelier national sur le développement humain durable, PNUD, Conakry, 1995.

Guinée, "Pauvreté en Guinée : analyse micro-économique", Rapport de l'Atelier national sur le développement humain durable, PNUD, Conakry, 1995.

Guinée, "Secteurs sociaux et restructuration budgétaire", Rapport de l'Atelier national sur le développement humain durable, PNUD, Conakry, 1995.

Hopkins, M., "A Short Review of Contemporary Thinking about Anti-Poverty Strategies for sub-Saharan Africa", MHConsulting, PNUD, Genève, 1997.

Kankwenda, M., "L'endettement de l'Afrique lui permet-il de lutter efficacement contre la pauvreté et pour la croissance économique?", *Communication aux journées de réflexion sur la croissance et la lutte contre la pauvreté*, Kinshasa, 1988.

Kankwenda, M., "Le concept de Développement Humain Durable", Conférence à l'Université de Ouagadougou, Ougadougou, 1998.

Lachaud, J.P., *Pauvreté - Vulnérabilité et Marché du Travail au Burkina Faso*, Ministère de l'Economie et des Finances & Université Montesquieu-Bordeaux IV, Ouagadougou, 1997.

Legros, H., "La problématique de la pauvreté au Burkina Faso", Atelier d'information, de formation et de concertation sur le DHD, PNUD, Bobo Dioulasso, 1998.

Lesotho, *Action Plan in Support of the Poverty Reduction Programme Within the Context of Good Governance*, Government of Lesotho, 8th Round Table Conference, Genève, 1997

Lesotho,_Poverty Reduction within the Context of Good Governance*, Government of Lesotho, 8th Round Table Conference, Genève, 1997.

Mckinley, T., "The Macroeconomic Implications of Focusing on Poverty Reduction", *Poverty Reduction Module 4. Macroeconomic Policies and Poverty Reduction*, UNDP, New York, 1997.

Malawi, *Situation Analysis of Poverty*, Gouvernement du Malawi & PNUD, Lilongwe, 1993.

Malawi, *20/20 Initiative for Malawi*, University of Malawi & UNICEF, Lilongwe, 1997.

Mali, *Stratégie Nationale de lutte contre la pauvreté*, 3 vol., Ministère de l'Economie, du Plan et de l'Intégration & PNUD, Bamako, 1998.

Mauritanie, *Rapport sur le Développement Humain Durable 1996 en Mauritanie*, Ministère du Plan & PNUD, Nouakchott, 1996.

Mbelle, A. V. Y. & Kilindo, A.A.L., *Prospects Implementation of the 20/20 Initiative on Budget and Aid Restructuring in Favour of Basic Social Services in Tanzania*, Dar es Salaam, 1997.

Miyata, H., "Japan's Cooperation with Developing Countries and Economies in Transition", Briefing Note, Tokyo, 1996.

Mumina, F. J., "Economic and Social Aspects of Poverty and Its Eradication in Kenya", A Discussion paper (Notes) prepared for the UNDP Regional Bureau for Africa Economists' Cluster Meeting in Lomé, Nairobi, 1997.

Museruka, F., "Rapport sur la pauvreté : l'expérience du réseau Afrique 2000", Memorandum, Ouagadougou, 1998.

Namibie, *Namibia: Monitoring the 20/20 Compact*, UNICEF, Windhoek, 1998.

Nations Unies, *Poverty Elimination in Viet Nam*, UNDP/UNFPA/ UNICEF, Hanoi, 1995.

Nations Unies, "The Work of the United Nations System in Poverty Alleviation", Report of the CCPOQ Working Group on Poverty, Genève, 1995.

Ngendakuma, V. & Huybens, E., *L'effet de la sécurité et de l'embargo sur la situation de la pauvreté*, PNUD & UNICEF, Bujumbura, 1998.

Niger, *Premier Rapport National sur le Développement Humain*, République du Niger & PNUD, Nyamey, 1997.

Niger, *Programme Cadre national de Lutte contre la Pauvreté*, 3 vol., Ministère des Finances et du Plan, Niamey, 1996.

Niger, *L'Initiative 20/20 : Examen des possibilités de mobilisation de ressources additionnelles en faveur des secteurs sociaux essentiels,* Ministère des Finances et du Plan & UNICEF, Niamey, 1997.

Nigeria, *Human Development Report, Nigeria 1996*, PNUD, Lagos, 1997.

OCDE, "Poverty Reduction: a Review of Donor Strategies and Practices", Forum on Key Elements for Reduction Strategies, Londres, 1997.

OCDE, "Atelier de lancement de la revue de l'aide au Mali, Note de discussion", OCDE, Direction de la coopération pour le développement, Paris, 1997.

Ouédraogo, H., "Base de données du Développement Humain Durable du PNUD", Atelier d'information, de formation et de concertation sur le DHD, PNUD, Bobo Dioulasso, 1998.

Ouganda, *Ugandan Human Development Report 1996*, PNUD, Kampala, 1996.

Patnaik, P., "A Note on the Redistributive Implications of Macroeconomic", *Policy Poverty Reduction Module 4. Macroeconomic Policies and Poverty Reduction*, UNDP, New York, 1997.

"Pauvreté au Sénégal : Manifestations et stratégie de lutte", Réunion des Economistes du Bureau Régional pour l'Afrique, Lomé, 1997.

Plan de politique pour une coopération internationale, Royaume de Belgique, Bruxelles, 1998.

PNUD, "L'action du PNUD contre la pauvreté : 1996, Année Internationale pour l'élimination de la pauvreté", Dossier de presse, New York, 1996.

PNUD, *Calling Attention to Poverty in Africa*, Press Clippings commemorating the International Day for the Eradication of Poverty, New York, 1996.

PNUD, "Donor's Aid Policies and Priorities", Memorandun, PNUD, New York, 1994.

PNUD, "From Poverty to Equity: An Empowering and Enabling Strategy. A Framework for planning UNDP's Response to Copenhagen", Draft UNDP Framework for Copenhagen Implementation, New York, 1995.

PNUD, "Microstart. Description du programme pour les bureaux extérieurs et les bureaux régionaux du PNUD", Private Sector Development Programme, BPPS, New York, 1997.

PNUD, "Lauching of UNDP Poverty Strategies Initiative", Memorandum, New York, 1996.

PNUD, "Le PNUD et la lutte contre la pauvreté dans le monde", Dossier de presse, New York, 1997.

PNUD, "Poverty Eradication: A Policy Framework for Country Strategies", New York, 1995.

PNUD, "Poverty Strategies Initiative, Terms of Reference", United Nations Development Programme, New York, 1996.

PNUD, "Poverty, Module 1. Poverty Indicators", UNDP Technical Support Document, New York, 1995.

PNUD, "Poverty, Module 2. From Data Collection to Poverty Assessments", UNDP Technical Support Document, New York, 1996.

PNUD, "Poverty, Module 3. Poverty measurement: Behind and Beyond the poverty Line", UNDP Technical Support Document, New York, 1997.

PNUD, "Poverty Reduction Module 4. Macroeconomic Policies and Poverty Reduction", UNDP Technical Support Document, New York, 1997.

PNUD, "Rôle du PNUD dans la lutte contre le VIH et le SIDA : Plan Directeur", PNUD, Policy Framework, New York, 1997.

PNUD, *Socio-Economic Monetary and Resource Tables 1995*, UNDP, New York, 1996.

PNUD, "Specific Actions Requested of All Resident Representatives in Poverty Eradication and Copenhagen Follow-up", Direct Line n° 6, New York, 1995.

PNUD, "Strategic Entry Points for UNDP Support to the Formulation of National poverty Eradication Strategies", Attachment 4, UNDP, New York, 1997.

PNUD, "Strengthening of Support to UNDP Poverty Elimination", Attachment 2, UNDP, New York, 1997.

PNUD, "Synthesis of Responses from Country Offices to Direct Line N°1 on Poverty", SEPED/BPPS/UNDP, New York, 1995.

PNUD, "UNDP Policy on Credit on Credit and Micro-Capital Grants", Memorandum, New York, 1997.

PNUD, *Implementation Strategy for the First Regional Cooperation Framework for Africa, 1997 - 2001*, Executive Doard of the UNDP and of the UNFPA, New York, 1997.

PNUD, *Cadres de coopération de pays et questions connexes*, "Premier cadre de coopération avec le Bénin, 1997 - 2001", Conseil d'Administration du PNUD et du FNUAP, New York, 1997.

PNUD, *Cadres de coopération de pays et questions connexes*, "Premier cadre de coopération avec le Botswana, 1997 - 2002", Conseil d'Administration du PNUD et du FNUAP, New York, 1997.

PNUD, *Cadres de coopération de pays et questions connexes*, "Premier cadre de coopération avec le Burkina Faso, 1997 - 2001", Conseil d'Administration du PNUD et du FNUAP, New York, 1997.

PNUD, *Cadres de coopération de pays et questions connexes*, "Premier cadre de coopération avec le Cameroun, 1997 - 2001", Conseil d'Administration du PNUD et du FNUAP, New York, 1997.

PNUD, *Cadres de coopération de pays et questions connexes*, "Premier cadre de coopération avec les Comores, 1997 - 2000", Conseil d'Administration du PNUD et du FNUAP, New York, 1997.

PNUD, *Cadres de coopération de pays et questions connexes*, "Premier cadre de coopération avec la Côte d'Ivoire, 1998 - 2000", Conseil d'Administration du PNUD et du FNUAP, New York, 1997.

PNUD, *Cadres de coopération de pays et questions connexes*, "Premier cadre de coopération avec Djibouti, 1997 - 2001", Conseil d'Administration du PNUD et du FNUAP, New York, 1997.

PNUD, *Cadres de coopération de pays et questions connexes*, "Premier cadre de coopération avec l'Ethiopie", Conseil d'Administration du PNUD et du FNUAP, New York, 1996.

PNUD, *Cadres de coopération de pays et questions connexes*, "Premier cadre de coopération avec l'Erythrée, 1997-1999", Conseil d'Administration du PNUD et du FNUAP, New York, 1996.

PNUD, *Cadres de coopération de pays et questions connexes*, "Premier cadre de coopération avec le Gabon, 1997 - 2001", Conseil d'Administration du PNUD et du FNUAP, New York, 1997.

PNUD, *Cadres de coopération de pays et questions connexes*, "Premier cadre de coopération avec la Gambie, 1998 - 2001", Conseil d'Administration du PNUD et du FNUAP, New York, 1998.

PNUD, *Cadres de coopération de pays et questions connexes*, "Premier cadre de coopération avec le Ghana, 1998 - 2000", Conseil d'Administration du PNUD et du FNUAP, New York, 1997.

PNUD, *Cadres de coopération de pays et questions connexes*, "Premier cadre de coopération avec la Guinée, 1998 - 2001", Conseil d'Administration du PNUD et du FNUAP, New York, 1998.

PNUD, *Cadres de coopération de pays et questions connexes*, "Extension du sixième programme de pays pour le Kenya", Conseil d'Administration du PNUD et du FNUAP, New York, 1997.

PNUD, *Cadres de coopération de pays et questions connexes*, "Premier cadre de coopération avec le Lesotho, 1997 - 2000", Conseil d'Administration du PNUD et du FNUAP, New York, 1997.

PNUD, *Cadres de coopération de pays et questions connexes*, "Premier cadre de coopération avec le Mali, 1998 - 2002", Conseil d'Administration du PNUD et du FNUAP, New York, 1998.

PNUD, *Cadres de coopération de pays et questions connexes*, "Premier cadre de coopération avec Maurice, 1997-1999", Conseil d'Administration du PNUD et du FNUAP, New York, 1997.

PNUD, *Cadres de coopération de pays et questions connexes*, "Premier cadre de coopération avec la Mauritanie, 1997-2001", Conseil d'Administration du PNUD et du FNUAP, New York, 1996.

PNUD, *Cadres de coopération de pays et questions connexes*, "Premier cadre de coopération avec le Mozambique, 1998 - 2001", Conseil d'Administration du PNUD et du FNUAP, New York, 1997.

PNUD, *Cadres de coopération de pays et questions connexes*, "Premier cadre de coopération avec le Nigeria, 1997 - 2001", Conseil d'Administration du PNUD et du FNUAP, New York, 1997.

PNUD, *Cadres de coopération de pays et questions connexes*, "Premier cadre de coopération avec l'Ouganda, 1997 - 200", Conseil d'Administration du PNUD et du FNUAP, New York, 1996.

PNUD, *Cadres de coopération de pays et questions connexes*, "Premier cadre de coopération avec la République du Congo, 1997 - 2000", Conseil d'Administration du PNUD et du FNUAP, New York, 1997.

PNUD, *Cadres de coopération de pays et questions connexes*, "Premier cadre de coopération avec le Rwanda, 1998 - 2000", Conseil d'Administration du PNUD et du FNUAP, New York, 1998.

PNUD, *Cadres de coopération de pays et questions connexes*, "Premier cadre de coopération avec Sao Tome et Principe, 1997 - 2001", Conseil d'Administration du PNUD et du FNUAP, New York, 1997.

PNUD, *Cadres de coopération de pays et questions connexes*, "Premier cadre de coopération avec les Seychelles, 1997-1999", Conseil d'Administration du PNUD et du FNUAP, New York, 1997.

PNUD, *Cadres de coopération de pays et questions connexes*, "Premier cadre de coopération avec le Soudan, 1997 - 2001", Conseil d'Administration du PNUD et du FNUAP, New York, 1997.

PNUD, *Cadres de coopération de pays et questions connexes*, "Premier cadre de coopération avec le Swaziland, 1997-1999", Conseil d'Administration du PNUD et du FNUAP, New York, 1997.

PNUD, *Cadres de coopération de pays et questions connexes*, "Premier cadre de coopération avec le Tchad, 1997 - 2000", Conseil d'Administration du PNUD et du FNUAP, New York, 1997.

PNUD, *Cadres de coopération de pays et questions connexes*, "Premier cadre de coopération avec le Togo, 1998 - 2001", Conseil d'Administration du PNUD et du FNUAP, New York, 1998.

PNUD, "Initiative Stratégique de Lutte contre la Pauvreté, Document de projet", Ouagadougou, Janvier 1997

Raffinot, M., "Stratégies Nationales de Réduction de la Pauvreté. Etude de cas du Burkina Faso", PNUD, New York, 1997.

Rahman Khan, A., "Macroeconomic Policies and Poverty: An analysis of the Experience in Ten Asian Countries", *Poverty Reduction Module 4. Macroeconomic Policies and Poverty Reduction*, UNDP, New York, 1997.

Reed, D. & Sheng, F., "Macroeconomic Policies, Poverty and the Environment", *Poverty Reduction Module 4. Macroeconomic Policies and Poverty Reduction*, UNDP, New York, 1997.

Sanou, M. & Lachaud, J.P., *Pauvreté et Marché du Travail à Ouagadougou (Burkina Faso)*, Institut International d'Etudes Sociales, Genève, 1993.

Sanou, M. & Ouédraogo, E., *Profil de pauvreté urbaine au Burkina Faso et accès aux services sociaux de base*, Initiative Stratégique de Lutte contre la Pauvreté, Ministère de l'Economie et des Finances & PNUD, Ouagadougou, 1997

Sinane, A. M., "Pauvreté et Croissance - Le cas d'une petite Economie insulaire : les Comores", A Discussion paper (Notes) prepared for the UNDP Regional Bureau for Africa Economists' Cluster Meeting in Lomé, 1997.

Sénégal, *Plan d'Orientation pour le Développement économique et social 1996-2001*, Ministère de l'Economie, des Finances et du Plan, Dakar, 1997.

Singh, A., "Openness and the Market Friendly Approach to Development: Learning the Right Lessons from Development Experience", *Poverty Reduction Module 4. Macroeconomic Policies and Poverty Reduction*, UNDP, New York, 1997.

TICAD, *Déclaration de Tokyo sur le développement de l'Afrique*, TICAD, Tokyo, 1993.

Togo, *Développement Humain Durable: Rapport annuel Togo 1995*, Ministère du Plan et de l'Aménagement du Territoire & PNUD, Lomé, 1995.

Togo, *Programme national de lutte contre la pauvreté*, 2 vol., Ministère du Plan et de l'Aménagement du Territoire & PNUD, Lomé, 1995.

Tore Rose, "Stratégie et programmes de lutte contre la pauvreté au Mali.", PNUD, Bamako, 1998.

UNESCO, "La Pauvreté au Burkina Faso: Revue de Littérature et Extensions (Provisoire)", Faculté des Sciences Economiques et de Gestion, Université de Ouagadougou & UNESCO, Ouagadougou, 1997

UNICEF, "Analyser la priorité, l'efficacité et l'équité du financement public de la santé et de l'éducation en Afrique francophone", Document de travail interne, Abidjan, 1997.

UNICEF, "Suivi de l'Initiative 20/20 : restructuration des budgets nationaux et de l'aide extérieure, proposition de méthodologie", New York, 1997.

UNICEF & PNUD, "Rapport de l'atelier technique régional francophone sur l'Initiative 20/20", Cotonou, 1997.

UNICEF, *Sentinel Site Surveys*, Informal Note, New York, 1996.

UNICEF & PNUD, "Mise en oeuvre de l'Initiative 20/20 : définitions, modalité et suivi", document prépratoire à la réunion internationale d'Oslo sur l'Initiative 20/20, New York, 1996.

"L'Initiative 20/20 : atteindre l'objectif d'un accès universel aux services sociaux essentiels en vue d'un développement humain durable", note conjointe FNUAP, OMS, PNUD, UNESCO & UNICEF, 1995.

Definitions of statistical terms

Budget deficit or surplus Central government current and capital revenue and official grants received, less total expenditure and lending minus repayments.

Commercial energy use The domestic primary commercial energy supply. It is calculated as local production plus imports and stock changes, minus exports and international marine bunkers.

Contraceptive prevalence rate The percentage of married women of child-bearing age (15-49) who are using, or whose husbands are using, any form of contraception, whether modern or traditional.

Current account balance The difference between (a) exports of goods and services as well as inflows of unrequited transfers but exclusive of foreign aid and (b) imports of goods and services as well as all unrequited transfers to the rest of the world.

Daily per capita calorie supply The calorie equivalent of the net food supply (local production plus imports minus exports) in a country, divided by the population, per day.

Dependency ratio The ratio of the population defined as dependent – those under 15 and over 65 – to the working-age population, aged 15-64.

Discouraged workers Individuals who would like to work and are available for work, but are not actively seeking it because of a stated belief that no suitable job is available or because they do not know where to get jobs.

Education expenditure Expenditure on the provision, management, inspection and support of pre-primary, primary and secondary schools; universities and colleges; vocational, technical and other training institutions; and general administration and subsidiary services.

Enrolment The *gross enrolment ratio* is the number of students enrolled in a level of education, regardless of age, as a percentage of the population of official school age for that level. The *net enrolment ratio* is the number of children of official school age (as defined by the education system) enrolled in school as a percentage of the number of children of official school age in the population.

Exports of goods and services The value of all goods and non-factors services provided to the rest of the world, including merchandise freight, insurance, travel and other non-factor services.

External debts Debt owed by a country to non-residents repayable in foreign currency, goods or services.

Food aid in cereals The quantity of cereals provided by donor countries and international organizations, including the World Food Programme and the International Wheat Council, as reported for a crop year.

Foreign direct investment An investment in a country involving a long-term relationship and control of an enterprise by non-residents. It is the sum of equity capital, reinvestment of earnings, other long-term capital and short-term capital as shown in the balance of payments.

Gini coefficient Measures the extent to which the distribution of income (or, in some cases, consumption expenditures) among individuals or households within an economy deviates from a perfectly equal distribution. The coefficient ranges from 0 – meaning perfect equality – to 1 – complete inequality.

Gross domestic investment Outlays on additions to the fixed assets of the economy plus net changes in the level of inventories.

Gross domestic product (GDP) The total output of goods and services for final use produced by an economy by both residents and non-residents, regardless to the allocation to domestic and foreign claims. It does not include deductions for depreciation of physical capital or depletion and degradation of natural resources.

Gross national product (GNP) Comprises GDP plus net factor income from abroad, which is the income residents receive from abroad for factor services (labour and capital), less similar payments made to non-residents who contribute to the domestic economy.

Infant mortality rate The probability of dying between birth and exactly one year of age times 1,000.

Infants with low birth-weight The percentage of babies born weighing less than 2,500 grams.

Inflation A fall in the purchasing power of money reflected in a persistent increase in the general level of prices as generally measured by the retail price index.

Life expectancy at birth The number of years a newborn infant would live if prevailing patterns of mortality at the time of birth were to stay the same throughout the child's life.

Literacy rate (adult) The percentage of people aged 15 and above who can, with understanding, both read and write a short, simple statement on their everyday life.

Maternal mortality rate The annual number of deaths of women from pregnancy-related causes per 100,000 live births.

National poverty line The poverty line deemed appropriate for a country by its authorities.

Officials development assistance (ODA) Grants or loans to countries or territories that are undertaken by the official sector, with promotion of economic development and welfare as the main objective, at concessional financial terms.

Portfolio investment flows (net) Non-debt-creating portfolio equity flows (the sun of country funds, depository receipts and direct purchases of shares by foreign investors) and portfolio debt flows (bond issues purchased by foreign investors).

Primary education Education at the first level (level 1), the main function of which is to provide the basic elements of education.

Private consumption The market value of all goods and services, including durable products, purchased or received as income in kind by households and non-profit institutions.

Public expenditure on education Public spending on public education plus subsidies to private education at the primary, secondary and tertiary levels.

Public expenditure on health Recurrent and capital spending from central and local government budgets, external borrowings and grants (including donations from international agencies and non-governmental organizations) and social health insurance funds.

Purchasing power parity (PPP) At the PPP rate, one dollar has the same purchasing power over domestic GDP that the US dollar has over US GDP. PPP could also be expressed in other national currencies or in special drawing rights (SDRs). PPP rates allow a standard comparison of real price levels between countries, just as conventional price indexes allow comparison of real values over time; otherwise, normal exchange rates may over – or undervalue purchasing power.

Real GDP per capita (PPPs) The GDP per capita of a country converted into US dollars on the basis of the purchasing power parity exchange rate.

Sovereign long-term debt rating As determined by Standard and Poor's, an assessment of a country's capacity and willingness to repay debt according to its terms. The ratings range from AAA to CC (investment grade AAA to BBB -, and speculative grade BB+ and lower).

Tax revenue Compulsory, unrequited, non-repayable receipts collected by central governments for public purposes.

Total debt service The sum of principal repayments and interest actually paid in foreign currency, goods, or services on long-term debt, interest paid on short-term debt, and repayments to the IMF. Total debt service is an important indicator to measure a country's relative burden to service external debt.

Total fertility rate The average number of children that would be born alive to a woman during her lifetime if she were to bear children at each age in accord with prevailing age-specific fertility rates.

Under-five mortality rate The probability of dying between birth and exactly five years of age times 1,000.

Underweight (moderate and severe child malnutrition) Moderate refers to the percentage of children under age five who below minus two standard deviations from the median weight for age of the reference population. *Severe* refers to the percentage of children under age five who are below minus three standard deviations from the median weight for age of the reference population.

Unemployment All people above a specified age who are not in paid employment or self-employed, but are available and have taken specific steps to seek paid employment or self-employment.

Unpaid family workers Household members involved in unremunerated subsistence and non-market activities, such as agricultural production for household consumption, and in household enterprises producing for the market for which more than one household member provides unpaid labor.

Waste recycling The reuse of material that diverts it from the waste stream, except for recycling within industrial plants and the reuse of material as fuel. The recycling rate is the ratio of the quantity recycling to the apparent consumption.

Box tables

Tables

ANNEX 7

Figures

Abreviations

ADB	African Development Bank
AIDS	Acquired immunodeficiency syndrome
AGDSD	Agence pour la Gestion de la Dimension Sociale du Développement (Agency for the Management of the Social Dimensions of Development
AGEPIB	Agence de Gestion et de Promotion des Initiatives à la Base (Agency for the Management and Promotion of Grassroots Initiatives)
AGETUR	Agence de Gestion des Travaux Urbains (Agency for the Management of Urban Works)
AHSP	African Household Survey Program
CAS	Country Assistance Strategy (world bank)
CBS	Consumption-Budget Survey
CCA	Country Common Assessment
CGIAR	Consultative Group on International Agricultural Research
CIS	Commonwealth of Independent States
ECOMAC	Modèle Macroéconomique de Prévision (Macroeconomic Forecasting Model)
ECOSOC	Economic and Social Council (of the United Nations)
ECVR	Enquête sur les Conditions de Vie des ménages Ruraux (Survey on the Living Standards of Rural Households)
ELAM	Enquête Légère Auprès des Ménages en milieu urbain (Small scale survey of Urban Households)

EPP	Etudes des Perceptions de la Pauvreté par la Population (Study of the Population Perceptions of Poverty)
EPPR	Etude sur les Perceptions des dimensions du bien-être, de la pauvreté et de la richesse en milieu urbain (Study of Perceptions of Dimensions of Well-Being and Wealth in Poor Urban Setting)
EU	European Union
FAO	Food and Agriculture Organization
FDI	Foreign direct investment
GATT	General Agreement on Tariffs and Trade
GDI	Gender-related development index
GDP	Gross domestic product
GEM	Gender empowerment measure
GNP	Gross national product
HCR	United Nations High Commissionner for Refugees
HDI	Human development index
HPI	Human poverty index
HIPCs	Heavily indebted poor countries
HIV	Human immunodeficiency virus
IFAD	International Fund of Agricultural Development
IEC	Information Education and Communication (Campaign)
ILO	International Labour Organization
IMF	International Monetary Fund
NER	Nominal Exchange Rate
IOM	International Organization for Migration
IPU	Inter-Parlimentary Union
ITU	International Telecommunication Union
NGO	Non governmental organization
NPL	National Poverty Line
ODA	Official development assistance
OECD	Organization for Economic Co-operation and Development
PADEM	Programme Africain d'Enquêtes auprès des Ménages (African Household Survey Program)
PEESI	Programme d'Etudes et d'Enquêtes sur le Secteur Informel (Study and Survey Program for the Informal Sector)

PISAP	Permanent Information System for the Analysis of Poverty
PPP	Purchasing power parity
PRA	Participatory Rural Appraisal
PRGF	Poverty Reduction and Growth Facility
PRSP	Poverty Reduction Strategy Paper
RPAM	Rapid Participatory Appraisal Methods
SAM	Social Accounting Matrix
SAP	Structural Adjustment Program
SDD	Social Dimensions of Development
SHD	Sustainable Human Development
TRIPS	Trade-Related Aspects of Intellectual Property Rights
UEMOA	Union Economique et Monétaire Ouest Africaine (West African Economic and Monetary Union)
UNCTAD	United Nations conference on Trade and Development
UNDAF	United Nations Development Assistance Framework
UNDGO	United Nations Development Group
UNDP	United Nations Development Programme
UNESCO	United Nations Educational, Scientific and Cultural Organization
UNICEF	United Nations Children's Fund
UNOPS	United Nations Office for Projects and Services
USAID	United States Agency for International Development
WHO	World Health Organization
WTO	World Trade Organization

Contents

PART THREE
External mobilization for poverty reduction in Africa

ANNEXES

Impression : EUROPE MEDIA DUPLICATION S.A.
53110 Lassay-les-Châteaux
N° 8028 - Dépôt légal : Décembre 2000